'WE IN SCOTLAND'

Thatcherism in a Cold Climate

'WE IN SCOTLAND'

Thatcherism in a Cold Climate

David Torrance

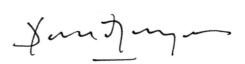

BIRLINN

The Author and Publishers acknowledge the generous support of
John Clark, Peter de Vink and Malcolm Scott without whom
this publication would not have been possible.

First published in 2009 by
Birlinn Limited
West Newington House
10 Newington Road
Edinburgh
EH9 1QS

www.birlinn.co.uk

ISBN: 978 1 84158 816 2

British Library Cataloguing-in-Publication Data
A catalogue record for this book is available from the British Library

Typeset by Iolaire Typesetting, Newtonmore
Printed and bound by the MPG Books Group

CONTENTS

ACKNOWLEDGEMENTS

LIKE MANY BOOKS, *'We in Scotland' – Thatcherism in a Cold Climate* reflects something of the author's own past. Although I was born under the ill-fated government of James Callaghan in the summer of 1977, I was still very much a child of the Thatcher era. My father worked as an engineer for one of the UK's biggest state-owned utilities, British Telecom (BT, although still part of the General Post Office when I was born), while my mother worked part-time as a cleaner for the NHS. I was educated at state schools in Edinburgh and joined my father on anti-Poll Tax demonstrations. I was, therefore, a witness to many of the events described in this book and fascinated by the Thatcher–Scotland dynamic even as a child.

My father was also a member of the Scottish National Party and was, in the nicest possible way, what Labour often derided as a 'Tartan Tory'. He owned his own home, accepted his shares when BT was privatised and believed resolutely in low tax. Nevertheless, he could not identify with the Conservatives and certainly not with Margaret Thatcher. My mother, meanwhile, was apolitical. While my father defaulted on his Community Charge payments, hers were always paid on time.

While I was researching this book I asked my father if, on balance, he felt he had done well out of Thatcherism. His unequivocal response was 'yes', so he is not a bad proxy for many of the issues addressed in this book. The idea for the project, however, came not from my parents but from my publisher, Hugh Andrew, and happily overlapped with something I had been thinking about doing for some time. My first two books, *The Scottish Secretaries* and a biography of the late George Younger, inevitably touched on the 1980s, so researching those whetted my appetite for a more in-depth study.

As ever, the finished product would not have been possible without incurring several debts. I would like to record my thanks to the following, all of whom spoke to me either in person, by telephone or by email: Bill Aitken, Keith Aitken, Neal Ascherson, Lord Bell of Belgravia, John Campbell, Graeme Carter, Campbell Christie, Alistair Cooke, Gavin Corbett, Cairns Craig, Tam Dalyell, Andrew Dunlop, Lord Forsyth of Drumlean, Lord Foulkes of Cumnock MSP, Sir Charles Fraser, Lord Fraser of Carmyllie, Murdo Fraser MSP, Sir William Kerr Fraser, Michael Fry, Michael Gove MP, Lord Griffiths of Fforestfach, Lord Hamilton of Epsom, Professor Ross Harper, David Heald, Lord Heseltine, Sir Michael Hirst, Bill Hughes, Sir Bernard Ingham, Bill Jamieson, Quintin Jardine, James Kelman, Bob Kernohan, Lord Lang of Monkton, Lord Lawson of Blaby, Isobel Lindsay, Magnus Linklater, Kenny MacAskill MSP, Lord Macdonald of Tradeston, Peter Mackay, Kenneth Mackenzie, Anne Mackintosh, Peter MacMahon, Sir John Major, Sir George Mathewson, Stephen Maxwell, Jack McConnell MSP, Gavin McCrone, David McLetchie MSP, Sir Albert McQuarrie, Arthur Midwinter, Councillor Eric Milligan, Nanette Milne MSP, Ferdinand Mount, John Mullin, Alex Neil MSP, John O'Sullivan, John Redwood MP, Harry Reid, Sir Malcolm Rifkind MP, Alex Salmond MSP, Lord Sanderson of Bowden, Lord Sewel of Gilcomstoun, Sir Stephen Sherbourne, Tommy Sheridan, Jim Sillars, Lord Steel of Aikwood, Allan Stewart, Rae Stewart, Stuart Trotter, Lord Turnbull of Enfield, Peter de Vink, Betty Waddell, Bill Walker, Gordon Wilson and Pete Wishart MP.

Many of them commented on sections of the manuscript, while individual chapters were read by Keith Aitken, Graeme Carter, Murdo Fraser, Gerry Hassan, Neil Mackinnon, Gavin McCrone, Arthur Midwinter, David Scott and Sir Stephen Sherbourne. My special gratitude goes to those who took the time to read, and comment on, the whole text: Dr Peter Caterall, Chris Collins, Colin Faulkner, Andrew Kerr, Professor James Mitchell at Strathclyde University, Alex Neil MSP, Douglas Pattullo, Andrew Riley and my brother, Michael Torrance, who also kept me right on legal terminology. Although they all saved me from several howlers and instigated many improvements, any remaining errors of fact or interpretation are entirely my responsibility.

In terms of sources, I was saved from hours of labour by the diligent scholarship of Chris Collins, who not only edited the CD-ROM, *Margaret Thatcher: Complete Public Statements 1945–1990*, but maintains the excellent Margaret Thatcher Foundation website, www.margaretthatcher.org, an invaluable resource which deserves to be imitated by other such archives. Similarly Andrew Riley, Archivist of the Thatcher Papers at the Churchill Archives Centre, never tired of digging out pre-1979 papers, tracking down photographs and offering guidance. Thanks must also go to Lord Forsyth and Mark Worthington for facilitating access to Baroness Thatcher. As ever, the British Library in London and the National Library of Scotland in Edinburgh were ideal facilities in which to doze, people-watch, check secondary sources and bash out various drafts. I also had the benefit of a week at Hugh and Claire Vance's home 'La Primaudaie' in Brittany, where, courtesy of their daughter Andrea, I was able to write much of the book's first, hopelessly unsuitable, draft.

Hugh Andrew at Birlinn was as indulgent a publisher as ever, tolerating two deadline extensions and my usual habit of writing 20,000 words too many. His production team, particularly Jim Hutcheson, Kenny Redpath and Andrew Simmons, also did their usual professional job. Philip Hillyer, meanwhile, was a diligent and sympathetic copy-editor. For help with the pictures, I must thank – among others – the *Scotsman* picture library and the *Herald*'s photograph archive at the Mitchell Library in Glasgow. Rob Gibson MSP also leant me his original copy of the SNP's 'She's got Scotland's oil' poster, while Jonathan Scott at STV sorted out a screen grab of Kirsty Wark interviewing Mrs Thatcher. Finally, Steve Richmond kindly let me reproduce one of his photographs in the plates section, as did David Rees his flattering portrait of the author.

I shall end with some words of wisdom from the Lady herself. 'I have never read a book about myself and I do not intend to start now!' Mrs Thatcher told the *Glasgow Herald* in 1989 when asked about Hugo Young's biography, *One of Us*. 'I have got much more important things to do and more interesting things to do!'[1] And quite right too.

David Torrance
January 2009
Edinburgh

---

[1] Interview for *Glasgow Herald*, 31/5/1989, MTF.

LIST OF CARTOONS

LIST OF PLATES

Mrs Thatcher in Edinburgh on her first visit to Scotland as leader of the Conservative Party (© *The Scotsman Publications Ltd*).

Michael Forsyth presents Mrs Thatcher with roses on her 51st birthday (© *Press Association*).

Mrs Thatcher campaigning in Leith during the 1979 general election campaign (© *The Scotsman Publications Ltd*).

Mrs Thatcher watching pipers at the Argyll Conservative ceilidh (*Courtesy of the Churchill Archives Centre*).

Mrs Thatcher delivering a speech in Scotland (*Courtesy of The Herald & Evening Times picture archive*).

A regal visit to the *Glasgow Herald* on the occasion of its bi-centenary (*Courtesy of The Herald & Evening Times picture archive*).

With Lord Home at a Chequers luncheon (*Courtesy of Viscountess Younger of Leckie*).

George Younger talking to Lord Margadale (*Courtesy of Viscountess Younger of Leckie*).

A memorable SNP poster (*Courtesy of Rob Gibson MSP*).

With George and Diana Younger at an exhibition to mark the centenary of the Scottish Office (*Courtesy of Viscountess Younger of Leckie*).

NUM pickets and mounted police clash at Ravenscraig (© *The Scotsman Publications Ltd*).

Mrs Thatcher under fire as she visits Falmer Jeans in Cumnock (*Courtesy of STV*).

Supporters greeting Mrs Thatcher at the 1986 Commonwealth Games in Edinburgh (© *The Scotsman Publications Ltd*).

With the new owners of the millionth council house to be sold under Right to Buy (© *Press and Journal/Evening Express*).At the 1988 Scottish Conservative conference with Ian Lang and Malcolm Rifkind (*Courtesy of The Herald & Evening Times picture archive*).

Mrs Thatcher at her first visit to the General Assembly of the Church of Scotland (© *The Scotsman Publications Ltd*).

Mrs Thatcher delivers her infamous 'Sermon on the Mound' (© *The Scotsman Publications Ltd*).

Harry More-Gordon's watercolour of the Ceremony of the Keys (*Courtesy of Sir Charles Fraser* © Harry More-Gordon).

Kirsty Wark interviews Mrs Thatcher.

Mrs Thatcher visiting the Lockerbie crash site (© *The Scotsman Publications Ltd*).

Mrs Thatcher opens Glasgow's St Enoch Centre (© *The Scotsman Publications Ltd*).

A portrait of the Mrs Thatcher by Anne Mackintosh (*Courtesy of Anne Mackintosh*).

At a Conservative Party event in Eastwood (*Courtesy of Jackson Carlaw MSP*).

Campaigning in Scotland during the 2005 general election (© *The Scotsman Publications Ltd*).

Visiting Gordon Brown at 10 Downing Street (© *Getty Images*).Lord Forsyth and the author talking to Baroness Thatcher (*Courtesy of Steve Richmond*).

FOREWORD

By Sir Malcolm Rifkind MP

ANY ASSESSMENT OF Margaret Thatcher's Scottish legacy has to separate Thatcher's personality from her achievements. She, clearly, was the most disliked Prime Minister that the Scots were burdened with in the twentieth century but, paradoxically, also the most admired. Many loathed her during her tenure of power and her name has been used since to terrify the gullible in a manner that used to be reserved for witches and warlocks.

Yet even Thatcher the person is being reassessed in the most unlikely quarters. Tony Blair made no secret of his desire to be compared with her and that most Scottish of Prime Ministers, Gordon Brown, judged it politically advantageous to invite her for tea at 10 Downing Street. Some north of the border will have seen that latter event as comparable to 'Tea with Mussolini', but the spinners and their like clearly felt otherwise.

That Thatcher was unpopular in Scotland is hardly surprising, regardless of her policies. She was a woman; she was an English woman; she was a bossy English woman. Each was a quality that many found objectionable. Combined with the cut-glass voice and an apparently patronising manner, they were lethal.

And yet Thatcher the person was also disliked by millions of people in England, for much the same reasons apart from her nationality. Even many who voted for her south of the border had deep reservations about this domineering, intransigent and forceful Prime Minister. It was in England that she was asked whether she believed in consensus politics. She replied that she did. There should be a consensus behind her convictions.

Much of the analysis about Thatcher and the Tories in Scotland misses the point. The main reason the Scots didn't vote for her was the same reason that they hadn't voted Conservative in every election since 1955. It was the same reason that a majority of the voters in the north of England and Wales never voted Conservative. These countries and regions had been, and remained, the main sources of strength for the Labour Party because they were where working-class voters greatly outnumbered the middle classes, unlike in the south of England.

Scotland's brief flirtation with the Tories was enjoyed between the collapse of the Liberals in the 1920s and their revival, combined with the emergence of the SNP in the 1960s. There were various reasons for these political changes, but anything that happened before 1979 can hardly be blamed on Margaret Thatcher.

Nor can the collapse into temporary oblivion of the Scottish Tories in 1997 be interpreted as a purely Scottish phenomenon. Exactly the same occurred in the north of England and Wales. Indeed, to this day, there is not a single Conservative councillor in Manchester, Newcastle or Liverpool, while Tory councillors serve in Edinburgh, Dundee, Aberdeen and even Glasgow. The real political divide in the United Kingdom is not between England and Scotland. It is between the south of England and the rest of the country.

And yet while the usual analysis is simplistic and misleading, there was a Scottish dimension during Thatcher's time in office which didn't exist in regard to the north of England and which was exacerbated by her style and personality. Scotland had never been just a region. Its national identity had been recognised by the terms of the Act of Union, preserving its legal system and its church. Thatcher understood that dimension but was never comfortable with it if it seemed likely to delay the reforms that she believed were essential for the whole of the United Kingdom.

Furthermore, Scotland (and, to a lesser extent, Wales) was experiencing a growth in Nationalist sentiment which had begun in the 1960s, and which was not extinguished either by the failed attempt to introduce a Scottish Assembly by the Callaghan government, nor by the defeat of most SNP Members of Parliament by Tories in 1979 when Thatcher first came to power.

This nationalist phenomenon was not peculiar to the United Kingdom. In different forms it was to be seen in Spain with Catalans and Basques, in Belgium with Flemings and Walloons, with Corsicans in France, Bavarians in Germany and with the Northern League in Italy.

It is curious, in a way, that Thatcher was so insensitive to this political dimension. She is identified, more than any other European statesman, with battling to preserve national sovereignty from the European Union and the Brussels federalists. Yet she often seemed incapable of understanding that the British patriotism that locked her into battle with the Europeans, in the name of self-government, was seen by many Scots as not fundamentally different to the Scottish patriotism that led them to seek more self-government for Scotland either within or without the United Kingdom.

Thatcher assumed that with a United Kingdom mandate at three successive general elections her government was entitled to implement its policies throughout the country. Constitutionally she was correct, as no British government has ever limited the implementation of its manifesto commitments to only those parts of the country that had voted for them. But a constitutional mandate is not the same as a political mandate. In political terms, the weakness of the Conservative Party in Scotland, especially after the 1987 election, needed policy reforms to be implemented in a different, sensitive way that could be seen as acknowledging Scotland's special circumstances.

Thatcher found it difficult to accept this and was encouraged in this belief by some of her more right-wing advisers. Some of my disagreements with her, when I was Secretary of State for Scotland, were on just these matters. I am, here, referring to educational reforms and industrial policy. The Poll Tax was a quite different matter. The policy was hers but the political misjudgements about the timing of the introduction of the legislation in Scotland, a year ahead of England, were not her responsibility but that of George Younger and, subsequently, mine when I succeeded him at the Scottish Office.

Interest in devolution would have revived without Thatcher, and the creation of a Scottish Parliament was, probably, inevitable given the historic changes both in the United Kingdom, and in Europe, that had been developing for fifty years. But Thatcher's unpopularity, and the political potency of the argument that she was forcing unwanted reforms on Scotland without a political mandate, crystallised the constitutional arguments, ensured a large majority in the referendum, and made it impossible for the Labour Party to withdraw (as Tony Blair would, probably, have preferred) from its pledge to create such a parliament in Edinburgh as one of the first priorities of his government.

So much for the effect of Thatcher on Scotland. What about the effect of Thatcherism? Her own verdict is summed up in the title she chose for the relevant section in her memoirs. It is headed 'Thatcherism rebuffed'. While her critics in Scotland would be quite happy to endorse this verdict, both they and she are quite wrong if one goes beyond her inability to persuade the Scots to vote for her party.

Scotland, itself, was as much transformed as England and the rest of the United Kingdom as a result of the 11 years of her premiership. That transformation was overwhelmingly to Scotland's benefit even accepting the pain and distress in traditional mining, steelmaking and other heavy industry communities. Few seriously doubt that these industries would have declined or disappeared even if the Thatcher government had never existed, but their decline would have stretched out over many more years and their replacement by new investment, by modern businesses and by new opportunities for employment, would have taken far longer to materialise.

By the time Margaret Thatcher left office in 1990 Scotland had been economically transformed and was out-performing most of the English regions. Scotland was a Mecca for overseas investment and thanks to the Right to Buy legislation, home-ownership had gone from one of the lowest levels in Europe to one of the highest. Far from council tenants rebuffing Thatcherism they embraced it with great enthusiasm, buying their homes against the advice of both the Labour Party and the SNP.

Privatisation, too, had become as dominant in Scotland as south of the Border. The South of Scotland Electricity Board, the North of Scotland Hydro Board, Kvaerner Govan Shipbuilders and the Scottish Bus Group were all household names that had moved to the private sector, and Scots seemed no less keen to buy the shares of privatised utilities than their fellow citizens elsewhere in the kingdom.

Thatcher's own view that 'Thatcherism' had been rebuffed in Scotland was significantly influenced by the difficult relationship that she and I had when I served as Secretary of State for Scotland between 1986 and 1990. She was entitled to believe that I was not unequivocal in implementing Thatcherite reforms in Scotland.

I shared her strategic objectives but I resisted cuts to Scottish public expenditure that were not to be implemented in parallel in England. Although Scottish expenditure was, and remains, higher than in England, any changes should only be made as a result of a proper Needs Assessment Study for the whole of the United Kingdom. This was resisted by her Treasury ministers. Likewise, her enthusiasm for self-governing Scottish state schools was admirable but I had to point out that without any tradition of governors in Scottish state schools the reforms would take far longer and needed to start with the creation of school councils.

She was disappointed that on several occasions I preferred to give priority to my assessment of Scottish interests when they conflicted with her preferred agenda. In resenting this she revealed one of the reasons why she did not fully understand the Scottish dimension. It was precisely because of the Union and because we were a unitary state that any Scottish Secretary had to give priority to representing Scotland in the Cabinet rather than representing the Cabinet in Scotland. Most of the time there was no conflict between the two but when, in the Scottish Secretary's judgement, Scottish interests required different solutions it was the Secretary of State's duty to point that out to the Prime Minister and to the Cabinet. This could, sometimes, be a lonely task.

There was much controversy over her 'Sermon on the Mound' and the introduction of the Poll Tax. So far as the former is concerned her critics would be well advised to read it again or, perhaps, read it for the first time. I was present when she addressed the General Assembly of the Church of Scotland and I have just reread her remarks. While Gordon Brown may not have made such a speech in 1988 it is virtually identical to the speeches he has been making as Prime Minister, stressing the need for people to work rather than rely on welfare, and the social objective of accepting personal responsibility for one's family and one's actions. Margaret Thatcher's sin was not to be found in the content of her 'Sermon', but in the fact that she dared to express these sentiments in the General Assembly at a time when she was politically unpopular.

Her enthusiasm for the Poll Tax was a quite different matter. It was and remains the greatest political mistake of her premiership. But there, too, to see it in anti-Scottish terms is absurd. Its implementation in Scotland was unpopular but it was in London, not in Glasgow, that it caused riots in the streets.

Both she and her Scottish Office colleagues assumed that any alternative would be preferable to the hated domestic rates. It was a major blunder to introduce the Poll Tax a year earlier in Scotland than in England. But that was never Thatcher's proposal. The earlier introduction was because Scottish

Office ministers wanted to get rid of the rates as quickly as possible and saw no need to wait until England was ready for its own similar reform. It is ironic that the SNP government has made the same mistake in proposing a Scottish local income tax in order to get rid of the much disliked council tax. As Edmund Burke remarked: 'To tax and to please is a power not given to man.'

I have no doubt that history's verdict on Margaret Thatcher will be favourable and that, even in Scotland, it will be recognised that she was a remarkable, courageous Prime Minister whose reform programme was as necessary as it was unavoidable if Scotland was to adapt to a changing world.

Some of Thatcher's contemporaries were less than flattering. Denis Healey, with characteristic charm, called her 'Attila the Hen'. President Mitterrand said she had 'the eyes of Caligula and the mouth of Marilyn Monroe'. One of Margaret Thatcher's more endearing qualities is that she would, probably, take both these descriptions as a compliment. She asked for no quarter and she gave none.

Sir Malcolm Rifkind MP
Secretary of State for Scotland 1986–90

FOREWORD

By Brian Wilson

I REMEMBER EXACTLY where I was when I learned that Margaret Thatcher had emerged as leader of the Conservative Party. (It was the main railway station in Oslo, since you ask, and the information was transmitted through the front page of the *Daily Mail*). This cameo has remained with me as a useful reminder of how fallible my political judgment has often been. For my first reaction was to rejoice in the fact that the Tories had preferred Thatcher to Willie Whitelaw and had thereby – surely – consigned themselves to certain electoral defeat. Britain would never vote for the shrill, suburban milk snatcher!

One-third of a century later, Margaret Thatcher has long since gone, having led the Conservative Party to three general election victories and bequeathed her husband's name to a harsh political creed. In Scotland, the legacies of her 11 years as Prime Minister live on in many forms. She can be held responsible, to lesser or greater degree, for the much reduced circumstances of the Scottish Conservative and Unionist Party; the very existence of a devolved Scottish Parliament; the degree of anti-Englishness that permeates Scottish society; the continuing social problems which flow from a generation of mass unemployment and industrial collapse; and much, much more. Her admirers could doubtless add balance to the list.

It is impossible to separate into neat, measurable strands the forces which contribute to change within any society or shift of political power. So there is no fixed answer to the question of how much difference Thatcher and Thatcherism actually made. Whether one is contemplating the strange death of Tory Scotland or the steady decline of manufacturing industry, it is pretty clear that her role was to accelerate these processes rather than initiate them. Equally, it is a mistake to exaggerate the degree of well-being that existed within Scottish society before Mrs Thatcher got her hands on it. She did not invent poverty or social injustice.

The Scottish Tory Party that she inherited was already well into long-term decline for reasons that could be seen in microcosm in North Ayrshire, part of which I later represented in Parliament. One of my predecessors had been Sir Fitzroy Maclean, war hero, toff, not very political and all-round good egg.

This was the kind of person around whom the Scottish Tory success had been built in the post-war decades. But by the 1970s, they were a dying breed. The Tories were fast running out of people who could draw on a constituency that extended far beyond a natural class base. As it happened, there was also a significant Orange Tory vote in that part of Ayrshire but it too was in rapid decline as a significant political factor. Throw in the unpopularity of Edward Heath and the oil-fuelled rise of Scottish Nationalism and it is no surprise to find that by the time Mrs Thatcher became leader of the Scottish Tories, their share of the vote in October 1974 was down to less than a quarter.

Within that cocktail, the advance of Nationalism should have served as a warning to the Tories of what was to follow. Although the SNP's rhetoric was often of the pseudo-left, their electoral success came almost exclusively in traditional Tory areas such as the fishing constituencies of the north-east and the small-town rural seats of Perthshire and Angus. These were the places where their couthy remedies and populist slogans were best received by people who had voted Tory more out of habit than conviction. In the face of opposition in places where they had never experienced it before, the ageing Scottish Tory Party had very little idea of how to respond. For a brief period, the advent of Mrs Thatcher's leadership actually improved their standing rather than undermine it. The Scottish Tories performed well in her first General Election in 1979. Ironically enough, their lifeline proved to be the SNP's decision to vote with Mrs Thatcher in the confidence vote which led to the downfall of the Callaghan government. If the Nationalists thought this would stand them in good stead in their Tory heartlands, if nowhere else, they were very much mistaken. Even the first Thatcher term was far from being a disaster for the Scottish Tories. There were plenty in Scotland who saw the need for radical economic reform and were not particularly enamoured of trade union power, the performance of the state-owned industries or indeed Michael Foot as an alternative Prime Minister. And there has always been a market in Scotland for a patriotic war so that, in spite of Tam Dalyell's best endeavours, the Falklands adventure worked for Mrs Thatcher in Scotland as elsewhere. The Tories retained 21 seats at the 1983 general election.

While Mrs Thatcher's hard-line approach to industrial closures and apparent disregard for their social consequences had already alienated much of the Scottish public – exactly as it had done in other comparable parts of the UK – it was really only the events between 1983-87 that turned Thatcherism into a reviled creed. I believe that the single most important episode in creating that change of mood was the handling of the miners' strike. Whatever the complexities of that dispute or the failures of leadership which led the gallant miners straight into Thatcher's trap, it developed into a straight choice of 'which side are you on?'. The miners' strike became a powerful symbol of a fractured society and the vast majority of people decided that, on the whole, they were on the side of the financially-stricken miners, proud communities and the dignified Mick McGahey, rather than of their strident oppressor.

It was around the same time that Mrs Thatcher's leading apostles in Scotland became more blatantly in her own image. The emollience of George Younger and Hector Monro gave way to the zeal of Michael Forsyth and, it must be said, of Malcolm Rifkind for as long as his job depended on it. These were not sympathetic figures and the most prominent members of their supporting cast in the House of Commons were a distinctly odd-ball crew. The Scottish Tory Party, ageing and disorganised in the constituencies, took on the air of a political freak show in its public demeanour – and an increasingly hard-hearted, right-wing one at that. Mrs Thatcher's anointment of Michael Forsyth as the true face of her government in Scotland was one of her biggest provocations.

Out of this maelstrom emerged the Poll Tax. I may be the last person in Scotland – or certainly the last non-Tory – who does not believe in the conspiracy theory that the Poll Tax was a premeditated experiment visited upon the people of Scotland by a malevolent political witch. Unfortunately, however, my recollection of events does not support that view of history. The truth was far more reactive and pragmatic and the origins of the Poll Tax lay in the rather prosaic fact that Scotland, unlike the rest of the UK, was obliged by law to have rating revaluations every five years. Elsewhere, it could be postponed indefinitely according to political expediency. When the results of revaluation became known in 1985, the Scottish Tories were hit by a tidal wave of protest from their own supporters since the effect of revaluation would have been to double and treble domestic rates bills at the higher end of the property market.

I remember these events very well because they marked the moment at which I became prospective Labour candidate in the Tory-held seat of Cunninghame North. It was an unexpected bonus to find the good burghers of Largs and West Kibride in a state of insurrection against their political representatives over the issue of domestic rates and revaluation. Whichever party had been in power would, in the face of such hostility from its own core support, have been obliged to act. The problem was that there was no easy answer for the Scottish Tories. They could not cancel the revaluation exercise, which would have been the most attractive option. And the only immediately available alternative was the Community Charge, a flat-rate tax which had been devised by a right-wing pressure group a few years earlier when the advent of Mrs Thatcher' leadership opened the door to such radical possibilities. It was at this point that Mrs Thatcher's trust in Michael Forsyth and his associates, to the point of adopting their preferred solution, sowed the seeds of her eventual undoing.

At first, the 'abolition of rates' was hailed as a political masterstroke. But it did not take long before the full horrors of the Poll Tax with all its administrative absurdities and gross inequities became apparent. For the Tories' opponents in Scotland, it was manna from heaven. It conveniently encapsulated the contempt in which the Thatcher regime held any remotely egalitarian principle such as 'ability to pay'. Its introduction was an act of political triumphalism in which an all-powerful government would steam-roller over all rational arguments in order to create a system which revelled in its own inherent unfairness. And while I can just about understand why, in extremis, Mrs Thatcher opted for its introduction in Scotland given the prevailing circumstances, I have always marveled at its subsequent extension to the rest of the UK as an act of complete political lunacy.

The Poll Tax left many myths in its wake. According to one, it was brought down by non-payment which was certainly not the case. Indeed, non-payment played into the hands of the Tories since the last thing they were interested in was the security of local councils' revenues. Neither was it rioting in Trafalgar Square that eventually killed the Poll Tax. Far more powerful in concentrating the minds of Tory MPs was the straightforward threat of electoral disaster and that is what impelled them to get rid of both the Poll Tax and Mrs Thatcher in time for the following general election. But long before then, the Poll Tax had left its own unpleasant marks on Scottish society – and sounded the death-knell for the Scottish Tories as a substantial political force.

Above and beyond any other factor, it was the Poll Tax that legitimised in many Scottish voters' minds the concept of tactical voting – in other words, anything to get a Tory out. The sheer immorality of the Poll Tax (in the context of everything else that was going on in Scotland at that time) seemed to create a collective moral imperative to defeat the authors of these injustices in all places and at all costs. That is a terribly dangerous place for any political party to find itself and it really was the beginning of the end for the Scottish Tories. In 1987, their representation in the House of Commons was reduced to ten MPs, with complete wipe-out to follow a decade later.

Personally, I was never comfortable with the incitement to 'make Scotland a Tory-free zone'. For one thing, it acted as a stalking horse for the equally reactionary creed of Nationalism to reassert itself in those parts of Scotland where it was the principal alternative to the Tories. Second, it gave rise to the insidious equation of the Conservative Party with 'England', thereby identi-fying it as an alien force within Scotland. This seemed to me grossly and dangerously unfair to the hundreds of thousands of decent Scots who, even at their party's lowest ebb, continued to identify themselves as Tories. The Scotland I have lived in all my life is not a Tory-free zone, far from it indeed, and the distortion of a nation's political complexion, for reasons of short-term advantage, carries its own dangers. There was little place for such sentiments in Scotland, however, during the late 1980s and early 1990s. For most people, Mrs Thatcher had simply put the Tories beyond the pale. There was far too much evidence of her government's handiwork in every community, whether epitomised by the dereliction of former workplaces or the hopelessness of unemployed youth. Just as in much of England and Wales, the masses wanted her out for these reasons. And in the same way as I remember exactly where I was when I first learned of her election as Tory leader, so I recall the moment I heard about her removal from office. It was in Paisley and I was canvassing in a double Parliamentary by-election. Loudspeaker vans toured the streets with the glad tidings and people stopped to wave and cheer.

One of Mrs Thatcher's most paradoxical achievements was to guarantee the creation of a devolved Scottish Parliament. Her 11 years in office did not lead to an upsurge in support for Scottish independence but it did encourage many people to believe that protection was needed against the possibility of Scotland ever again getting something so entirely different to what it voted for. This mantra became the obsession of the political and chattering classes. Crucially, it was embraced by the Labour Party in Scotland so that constitutional reform became the be-all and end-all of its objectives, to the exclusion of any more profound vision and analysis. For better or worse, Scotland now lives with the consequences and it wouldn't have happened without Mrs Thatcher.

Brian Wilson
Labour MP for Cunninghame North 1987–2005

Chapter 1

WHAT IS THATCHERISM?

TOWARDS THE END OF HER premiership Margaret Thatcher was interviewed by BBC Scotland's Kirsty Wark. It was not the Prime Minister's finest
hour. Under enormous political pressure from the Conservative Party over
Europe, the Poll Tax and the economy, she appeared tired and defensive.
Some of Mrs Thatcher's chosen phrases were also unfortunate, most famously her references to 'we in Scotland'.[1] It made her sound imperious and
distant, consolidating the impression of Scottish television viewers that
Thatcherism operated in what the academic David McCrone had described
in a 1989 essay as a 'cold climate'[2].

Thus the title of this book, but what precisely is 'Thatcherism'? Arguably, it
is a concept that billows beyond the word which represents it, and for the past
30 years it has been notoriously difficult to define. The former Conservative
minister Kenneth Baker characterised it as a series of instincts: less power for
the state, more for the individual; state spends less, individual spends more;
state owns less, individual owns more; and so on. To the academic Robert
Skidelsky, meanwhile, it suggested 'both a set of beliefs and a momentum to
reorder society according to those beliefs, driven by the commitment of a
remarkable political personality'.[3]

The former Chancellor of the Exchequer, Nigel Lawson, claimed to have
coined the term in a 1981 speech to the Zurich Society of Economics entitled
'Thatcherism in Practice', although he later learned that the journal *Marxism
Today* had christened it, in an ideological sense, prior to the 1979 election. Mrs
Thatcher used it herself, albeit in a humorous context, when she remarked in
March 1975 that to 'stand up for liberty is now called a Thatcherism',[4] a sly
dig at critics who had begun characterising the new Conservative leader as an
extremist.

It is Lawson, however, who perhaps came closest to capturing the essence

---

[1] 'The Margaret Thatcher Interview' (BBC Scotland) 9/3/1990.
[2] *Radical Scotland* June/July 1989.
[3] Skidelsky, *Thatcherism*, 2.
[4] Speech to Conservative Central Council, 15/3/1975, MTF.

of Britain's most famous political 'ism'. ' "Thatcherism" is, I believe, a useful term, and certainly was at the time,' Lawson reflected in his memoirs. He continued: 'No other modern Prime Minister has given his or her name to a particular constellation of policies and values. However it needs to be used with care. The wrong definition is "whatever Margaret Thatcher herself at any time did or said". The right definition involves a mixture of free markets, financial discipline, firm control over public expenditure, tax cuts, nationalism, "Victorian values" (of the Samuel Smiles self-help variety),[5] privatisation and a dash of populism.'[6]

Lawson's is also the most useful definition when it comes to examining Thatcherism (also referred to as the 'New Realism' and the thinking of the 'New Right' throughout the text) in a Scottish context, for several of his elements – particularly free markets, Nationalism, 'Victorian values' and the 'dash of populism' – arguably provoked a specific response in Scotland, as did the 'remarkable political personality' identified by Skidelsky. For the purposes of this book, 'Thatcherism' will be taken to mean any major policy associated with Mrs Thatcher since her election as Conservative leader in 1975.

Equally useful is a working summary of why Scotland apparently rejected Mrs Thatcher and Thatcherism. The 'two fundamental reasons' were perhaps best defined by the cleric Canon Kenyon Wright:

> First we perceived that she was imposing on Scotland not just policies broadly rejected and even detested . . . but worse was the imposition of an alien ideology that rejected community and expressed itself as an attack on our distinctive systems of education and local government . . .The second reason was even deeper – the grim centralisation of power . . . this made us see with a clarity that we had never had before, that we could never again rely on the British state or live comfortably with its constitutional doctrines.[7]

But are either of Kenyon Wright's 'fundamental reasons' an accurate reflection of Scottish public opinion throughout the Thatcher decade? There is certainly no convincing case to be made that the majority of Scots liked Mrs Thatcher personally, or approved of Thatcherism in general. Whether measured by general election results, local government elections or opinion polls, relative to Wales and comparable regions of England, Scotland and its inhabitants regularly put two fingers up to 'that woman' in Downing Street. In that context, Scotland certainly constituted a cold climate for Thatcherism.

Nevertheless that reaction, both then and now, is perhaps the most interesting thing about Thatcherism and Scotland. Indeed, Mrs Thatcher

---

[5] Samuel Smiles (1812–1904) was a Scottish author and reformer from Haddington in East Lothian. He was best known as the author of books extolling the virtues of self-help, as well as biographies chronicling the achievements of Victorian engineers.

[6] Lawson, *The View from No. 11*, 64.

[7] Devine, *The Scottish Nation*, 606–07.

recognised herself that Scots responded in a distinct way to her premiership. '[T]here were regional exceptions, most notably Scotland,' she wrote in the first volume of her memoirs, *The Downing Street Years*. 'There was no Tartan Thatcherite revolution.' She went on: 'It had been a country humming with science, invention and enterprise – a theme to which I used time and again to return in my Scottish speeches. But on top of decline in Scotland's heavy industry came socialism – intended as a cure, but itself developing quite new strains of social and economic disease, not least militant trade unionism.'[8] Mrs Thatcher's attempt to explain away her lack of political prowess in Scotland, however, is as unconvincing as her critics' frequent invocations of the egalitarian Scot bravely defending attacks from what Kenyon Wright called an 'alien ideology'. Neither goes the whole way to explaining the weakness of Mrs Thatcher personally, and Thatcherism in general, in a Scottish context.

Indeed, in the early twenty-first century the legacy of Thatcherism in Scotland is awash with mythology. 'I believe that the whole history of Scotland has been coloured by myth,' wrote the historian Hugh Trevor-Roper shortly before he died, 'and that myth, in Scotland, is never driven out by reality, or by reason, but lingers on until another myth has been discovered, or elaborated, to replace it.'[9] In the 1980s I would contest that the Scots discovered another such myth, that of a Mrs Thatcher who did not understand Scotland, neglected it, hated it and even sought to use it as a test bed so malicious was her vendetta against it.

It is, however, important to note that this myth-making worked both ways. As the leading Tory 'wet' Sir Ian Gilmour observed, 'in ideological as in other wars truth is the first casualty, and a rewriting of the history of the very recent past, if not of the present, was also a conspicuous feature of the Thatcher years in government'.[10] The Scots were regularly depicted by Mrs Thatcher as thrifty, enterprising and patriotic Brits, and therefore obvious candidates for enthusiastic conversion to the New Realism. In other words, Scotland had been infected with the economic and social strains of socialism and needed cured. Similarly, some of the wilder claims made on behalf of Thatcherism's achievements require re-examination.

To cut through the mythology on both sides of the Thatcher–Scotland dichotomy, the aim of this book is threefold: first, to describe what happened *vis-à-vis* Scotland and Mrs Thatcher from her election as Conservative Leader in 1975 until her resignation in 1990; second, to analyse each event in the context of the myths detailed above, busting them where necessary; and third, to assess the legacy of Thatcherism in Scotland.

Surprisingly, accounts of Scotland's recent past are few in number and have a tendency to analyse the Thatcher factor in an almost derisory way.

[8] Thatcher, *The Downing Street Years*, 618.
[9] Trevor-Roper, *The Invention of Scotland*, xx.
[10] Gilmour, *Dancing With Dogma*, 2.

Many have a tendency to be heavily biased (the historian Christopher Harvie, for example, compared Mrs Thatcher unfavourably with Edward I), selective in approach and often full of florid hyperbole.[11] Though far from hyperbolic, Carol Craig's much lauded book *The Scots' Crisis of Confidence* is a case in point. Although it contains many perceptive insights into how Scots view themselves and others, a section headed 'The Thatcher Legacy' is almost banally predictable. Mrs Thatcher, Craig informs us, 'gave a huge boost to Scottish nationalist sentiments', claimed there was 'no such thing as society', preached to an 'unimpressed', General Assembly of the Church of Scotland, and 'had long harboured the view that the Scots had a dependency culture' and therefore 'had to be made to stand on their own two feet again'. And when it came to the Poll Tax, Craig continues, many Scots were outraged at 'a policy which ran against the grain of Scottish values'. Each assertion is either incorrect or, at best, debatable.

To be fair, Craig's book also recognises the paradox that many aspects of Thatcherism 'were publicly condemned in Scotland but embraced by individual Scots'.[12] Even so, analysis of this sort arguably reinforces more myths about Scotland in the 1980s than it deconstructs. The Scots-Canadian economist John Kenneth Galbraith referred to this phenomenon as the 'Conventional Wisdom' in his 1958 book *The Affluent Society*; 'the beliefs that are at any time assiduously, solemnly and mindlessly traded between the conventionally wise'.[13]

Conventional wisdom in 21st-century Scotland has it that Mrs Thatcher wilfully stamped all over Scotland. The Scottish agriculturalist Ben Coutts recounts a story in his memoirs which helps explain how this negative perception took hold. The year was 1964, the location Kruger National Park in South Africa, and Coutts was celebrating after hearing that the Liberals had won a by-election in Caithness. 'I was full of cheer and was pouring out drinks for all,' he recalled. 'Whereupon the gentleman [next to me] announced, "My wife can't stand the Scottish Liberals or Scotland and when she comes to power she'll see that they are soundly defeated."' Coutts then asked "who is your wife?" "Margaret Thatcher," came the reply.'[14]

It is a nice story, but almost certainly elaborated beyond recognition. Not only was 'power' a distant prospect to Mr and Mrs Thatcher in 1964, but it is unlikely that Mrs Thatcher – not yet a senior or even well-known Conservative MP – had spent much of her career dwelling on either Scottish Liberals or their native land. Yet writing his memoirs in the late 1980s, Coutts would have had no fear of contradiction. By then Mrs Thatcher had assumed mythic status in Scottish political history, a status which lingers still.

---

[11] See also Brown *et al.*, *Politics and Society in Scotland*, and the written work of Neal Ascherson. Tom Devine's historical doorstopper, *The Scottish Nation*, is, on the other hand, more balanced.

[12] Craig, *The Scots' Crisis of Confidence*, 106–07.

[13] Galbraith, *The Affluent Society*, 8.

[14] Coutts, *Bothy to Big Ben*, 111.

'She had no comprehension of Scotland,' Alex Salmond told the author when interviewed for this book, 'to her it was a faraway country of which she knew nothing, the "undiscovered country" to quote Shakespeare.'[15] Sir William Kerr Fraser, permanent under-secretary at the Scottish Office during most of Mrs Thatcher's premiership, reckoned 'God did not make her the sort of conglomerate which was likely to endear her to Scotland.'[16] Even friends of Mrs Thatcher recall events in a negative light. 'She tried everything she possibly could because she actually cared about Scotland,' said Sir Teddy Taylor in the 1990s, 'she liked Scotland and she became very depressed that she got nothing but abuse and negative responses when she came.'[17]

Abuse is certainly a good word to describe much of Mrs Thatcher's reception in Scotland. Even though the Thatcher revolution reached every corner of Scotland, changing attitudes and altering expectations of the government's responsibilities – often for the better and on occasion for the worst – the words 'Thatcher' and 'Thatcherism' entered the Scottish political lexicon, and not in a positive way.

The reasons why are certainly worthy of analysis on this, the thirtieth anniversary of Mrs Thatcher becoming the first female Prime Minister of the United Kingdom, and it is surprising that so few critiques have been produced thus far. John Campbell's otherwise excellent two-volume biography of Mrs Thatcher, for example, virtually ignores Scotland despite its author's roots, while other judicious accounts – most notably Hugo Young's *One of Us* and Sir Ian Gilmour's *Dancing With Dogma* – devote just one or two pages to Thatcherism in a Scottish context. It should be noted, however, that both volumes of Mrs Thatcher's memoirs cover Scottish issues at length and not unsympathetically.

But this is not a biography in the conventional sense. Rather it is a political and historical sketch of Scotland's reaction to a figure who continues to be as divisive as she was in 1979. It is also unashamedly parochial and makes little effort to analyse Thatcherite foreign policy or other issues which did not directly impact on the Scottish experience. I have sought to be balanced, and therefore quote Mrs Thatcher's Scottish speeches and interviews (all available online at www.margaretthatcher.org) as liberally as I do her critics. Hopefully from between the two emerges an accurate picture of a fascinating decade, mercifully free of mythology and culminating with – in the final chapter – a fair assessment of Thatcherism in a Cold Climate.

---

[15] Interview with Alex Salmond MSP, 24/6/2008.
[16] Sir William Kerr Fraser to the author, 25/7/2008.
[17] Clements *et al.*, *Restless Nation*, 98.

Chapter 2

'MRS SUPERCOOL' (1975)

We will not succeed, and would not deserve to succeed, if we sought the support of the people of Scotland by pretending to be, or seeming to be, partly a Liberal party, partly a socialist party and partly a Scottish national party. We stand as Conservatives for Conservative policies.

Speech in Glasgow, 21/2/1975

'MRS THATCHER, in her first major public appearance since being confirmed as leader of the Conservative Party, was mobbed by thousands of people in Edinburgh yesterday,' reported *The Times* with a hint of bemusement on 22 February 1975, 'and had to abandon a "walkabout" in a shopping centre. She confessed herself "totally astonished" by the reception.'[1]

Mrs Thatcher had reason to be. Six policemen accompanying the fledgling Tory leader tried unsuccessfully to hold back a crowd of more than 3,000 who packed the St James Shopping Centre at the east end of Edinburgh's main thoroughfare; at least three women fainted, and other spectators had to be guided clear. Additional policemen and Scottish Conservative representatives – including the Shadow Scottish Secretary Alick Buchanan-Smith and the Scottish party chairman George Younger – formed a protective wall around Mrs Thatcher as she retreated to a car having taken refuge in a jeweller's shop ('where I saw an opal (my birthstone) that I later had made into a ring'[2]). There were a few mischievous cries of 'bring back Ted', but her reception in the Athens of the North was overwhelmingly warm. Even the Labour-supporting *Daily Record* covered its front page with the headline 'Mrs Super-cool' the following day.

The new Leader of the Opposition had arrived at Edinburgh Airport early on 21 February to the strains of 'A Man's a Man for a' That' played by a waggish piper. 'I have never seen anything like it, anywhere,' said Mrs

---

[1] *The Times* 22/2/1975.
[2] Thatcher, *The Path to Power*, 296.

Thatcher of her rather hysterical welcome. 'It was a fantastic reception. I was not worried about myself but I was worried about the safety of people who were being pressed against the shop windows.'[3] This maternal concern for crushed shoppers was genuine, yet Scots would never quite accept her more feminine qualities. 'There is nothing that I like more than being among people, really right in the middle of a crowd talking to them,' Mrs Thatcher later said of such encounters. 'That really is when I come alive.'[4]

In retrospect, the reasons for what the *Financial Times* called Mrs Thatcher's 'over-enthusiastic'[5] reception in Scotland seem clear. First, she was a novelty. Not only was the new leader of the Conservatives doing walkabouts in Scottish cities but she was a woman, the first to lead a UK political party. Secondly, Scottish Tory activists were in dire need of a morale boost and Mrs Thatcher's flying visit provided just that. The number of Conservative MPs in Scotland had fallen to just 16 at the October 1974 general election (from 21 at the February 1974 poll) a few months before, so it was a Tory faithful eager to hear of plans to halt further decline which greeted the new Conservative leader on electorally difficult ground.

Inevitably, there was a press conference. Sporting a large sprig of heather in her buttonhole, Mrs Thatcher told reporters she would begin with questions from north of the border. The first was predictable: what did she think about devolution for Scotland? Well briefed, she replied that her Conservative Party was absolutely in tune with the 'theme' of devolution. (In fact, as we shall see, she was absolutely out of tune with it.) As for the details, she stood by the last party manifesto and denied any change of view on her part. Further queries on the details were fudged, a subtlety journalists present would have done well to note.

What about the party's performance in Scotland? Mrs Thatcher replied that ten days in the job was not enough time to produce major policy decisions. 'You would be the first to jump down my throat if I did come up here with ready-made solutions', she said. 'I will be back again, soon.' Instead the Conservative leader attacked the SNP (whom she dismissed in a radio interview as a 'Snap, Crackle and Pop'[6] party), noting that its MPs had voted inconsistently at Westminster and not always in the best interests of Scotland. Another reporter asked whether her answers meant she would take a less positive line towards Scotland as leader. 'You must regard it as willingness to learn and listen,'[7] Mrs Thatcher replied, and peremptorily brought the press conference to a conclusion.

Following her hectic walkabout at the St James Centre, Mrs Thatcher addressed about 600 party officials, MPs and supporters at a luncheon in Edinburgh. 'From the moment I set foot on your soil today', she told them,

---

3 *The Times* 22/2/1975.
4 Interview for *Aberdeen Press and Journal*, 30/4/1990, MTF.
5 *Financial Times* 22/2/1975.
6 *Radical Scotland* June/July 1985.
7 *The Times* 22/2/1975.

'I have been given the most marvellous welcome that any politician could ever have been given anywhere in the world.' As they cheered her loudly, Sir William McEwan Younger, the Scottish Tories' former chairman, commented: 'You would never have seen a reception like that for Ted.' He noted the number of young people present and added: 'The question is whether we can convert all this into votes.'[8]

Mrs Thatcher then headed west for a rally in Glasgow. There, her reception was even more tumultuous. More than 1,800 people stood and cheered as she entered the City Chambers and another 600 in two overflow halls heard her speech relayed by loudspeakers. Later, those in the main hall swept her along – surrounded by a ring of Glasgow policemen – to a hotel for tea. She shook scores of hands and even signed autographs. For a visiting UK party leader, this was unprecedented.

In Glasgow, Mrs Thatcher loosened up a little when asked about devolution. A Scottish Assembly, she said, must be a top priority to ensure that more decisions affecting Scotland were taken in Scotland by Scots. 'But let there be no doubt that any such change must be within the framework of preserving the unity of the United Kingdom,' she added, signalling the start of an important qualifying theme. 'We want British influence in the world, and if we were to fragment Britain, that influence would diminish, and the influence of each part of the United Kingdom would diminish together with the contribution we can make to world affairs.'

Mrs Thatcher said the Conservatives had always been British nationalists. In Scotland there was a hard battle ahead for the party, but she was convinced they could win. 'We will not succeed,' she continued, 'and would not deserve to succeed, if we sought the support of the people of Scotland by pretending to be, or seeming to be, partly a Liberal party, partly a socialist party and partly a Scottish national party. We stand as Conservatives for Conservative policies.'[9]

Ten years later, and after six as Prime Minister, Mrs Thatcher looked back on her first visit as she addressed the Scottish Conservative conference in Perth. 'I shall never forget the warmth of that reception,' she gushed. 'Overnight, I became "Maggie"! And I've been Maggie ever since.'[10]

In truth, 'Maggie' was an unknown quantity in Scotland, a country to which she had seldom been. Mrs Thatcher's only Cabinet post to date, that of Education Secretary from 1970 to 1974, had mainly been concerned with England and Wales, although her remit did extend to Scottish universities ('I had only very limited responsibility here, as the Scottish Office Ministers constantly reminded me.'[11]), while her infamous decision to end free school milk in primary schools also had a knock-on effect in Scotland. So it was as

---

[8] *Financial Times* 22/2/1975.
[9] *The Times* 22/2/1975.
[10] Speech to Scottish Conservative conference, 10/5/1985, MTF.
[11] Speech in Glasgow, 21/2/1975, MTF.

'Mrs Thatcher, milk snatcher' that most Scots knew the new Conservative leader, if at all. But then the same could have been said for much of the United Kingdom.[12]

As for Mrs Thatcher's attitude towards Scotland, one of her biographers summed it up thus:

> Mrs Thatcher never understood Scotland, though she liked to think she did. She fancied she had a special affinity with the Scots, whom she imagined as thrifty, enterprising and inventive, a mixture of Adam Smith, George Stephenson and David Livingstone, hardy pioneers who had made the industrial revolution and built the British Empire. The reality was a persistent disappointment to her. Most Scots turned out to be unreconstructed working-class socialists with an egalitarian culture of public housing and an inbred hostility to Thatcherism; or tartan Tories, patrician, feudal, paternalistic and equally disdainful of her sort of southern stridency.[13]

That 'southern stridency' had also been noticed by the United States embassy in London. 'Her immaculate grooming, her imperious manner, her conventional and somewhat forced charm, and above all her plummy voice stamp her as the quintessential suburban matron, and frightfully English to boot,' observed a perceptive briefing note destined for Washington. 'None of this goes down well with the working class of England (one-third of which used to vote Conservative), to say nothing of all classes in the Celtic fringes of this island.'[14]

During her first visit to the north-eastern part of that Celtic fringe, Mrs Thatcher was at pains to talk up her party's past Scottish influences. 'It was the Conservative Party, under the leadership of Harold Macmillan, which led by establishing the Post Office Savings Bank headquarters in Glasgow,' she reminded activists in Glasgow. 'We also led the field on devolution by setting up the committee under the chairmanship of Sir Alec Douglas-Home.'[15] Although the gentrified grandson of a crofter and the former 14th Earl of Home (recently re-ennobled as Lord Home of the Hirsel) were hardly representative of Scotland in 1975, Mrs Thatcher was at least trying. Neither Macmillan nor Lord Home, meanwhile, could be said to share their successor's political instincts. Indeed, in economic terms the last truly 'dry' Tory leader in the Thatcher mould had been Andrew Bonar Law, a Canadian Scot. Despite sharing Bonar Law's status as a political outsider, however, Mrs Thatcher in no way resembled Tory leaders past.

---

[12] 'It was an absurd issue on which to enter the national demonology,' wrote Hugo Young. 'Plenty of free milk had already been cut by Labour governments.' (Young, One of Us, 73)

[13] Campbell, The Grocer's Daughter, 397.

[14] 'Margaret Thatcher: Some first impressions', 2/1975, MTF.

[15] Speech in Glasgow. Home's committee proposed the creation of a 'Scottish Convention' with approximately 125 members to consider the second reading and committee stages of all exclusively Scottish Bills.

Mrs Thatcher had first been a minister, at the UK Ministry of Pensions and National Insurance, when Macmillan was Prime Minister in 1961, and she admired his drive for improved standards of living (summed up by Macmillan's rallying cry, 'you've never had it so good'). '[H]e had the people *with* him,' she explained to STV's Colin Mackay on her visit to Glasgow. 'He was working *with* the instincts of the people.'[16] Mrs Thatcher liked Lord Home, on the other hand, simply because he was a nice person. As Lord Dunglass he had been Mrs Thatcher's first guest during her presidency of the Oxford University Conservative Association, while in 1975 Home tutored her in foreign affairs, an act of kindness she never forgot. In a peculiar twist of fate, he had also revised the Conservative Party's leadership election rules – requiring a first ballot win of 50 per cent plus 15 per cent of all Tory MPs – just weeks before Mrs Thatcher defeated Heath. In another twist of fate, that same system would also lose her the leadership nearly 16 years later.

Both Macmillan and Home, however, were male. Later in Mrs Thatcher's interview with STV there was a hint of the sexual iconoclasm which would accompany her leadership of the Conservative Party. 'To be the first woman at it [the leadership] is quite a responsibility,' she told Mackay. 'But after all, you know, the men haven't made such a success of it all the time. So, to yesterday's men, tomorrow's woman says "hello".'[17]

In 1975 most Scots would have welcomed the backing of 'tomorrow's woman' for a devolved Scottish Assembly, or at least so the political classes believed. And while Harold Wilson's Labour Party had only converted to devolution in July 1974 out of political expediency, the party Mrs Thatcher now led had been committed since Ted Heath's Declaration of Perth in May 1968.[18] As Prime Minister from 1970 to 1974, however, devolution had hardly been a priority for Heath, and his enthusiasm for it only seemed to increase after he ceased being leader.

But, as an instinctive Unionist or 'British nationalist', Mrs Thatcher was uncomfortable with the devolution commitment she had inherited, telling Patrick Cosgrave (a sympathetic journalist and early Thatcher groupie) that she was 'worried about it' in late 1973. And just a month before she was elected Conservative leader, Cosgrave claims Mrs Thatcher told a Scottish Tory MP: 'It must be stopped, really, or it will break up the kingdom.'[19]

In reality, devolution for Scotland was a policy which Mrs Thatcher had barely considered over the past seven years.[20] In her first Scottish television

---

[16] Interview with STV, 21/2/1975, MTF.

[17] Conservative party political broadcast, 5/3/1975, MTF.

[18] 'I was never happy with the policy and there was little enthusiasm for it among English Tories,' Thatcher recorded in *The Path to Power*, 321. 'But Ted pressed on.'

[19] Cosgrave, *Thatcher: The First Term*, 58–59.

[20] The Labour MP Tam Dalyell recalled questioning two of her advisers about her views on devolution shortly after she was elected Conservative leader. He was told it was one issue she did not fully understand, 'but that instinctively and temperamentally she had "little sympathy at all" with the idea of a Scots Assembly'. (Dalyell, *Devolution*, 169)

interview she again reiterated the Assembly pledge, but hedged it with caveats which belied her real views. 'You know it's very interesting that some of the letters I have had from Scotland, from the north, say "look, we feel sometimes just as remote from Edinburgh as we do from London"', she told Colin Mackay. 'What they want is *real* devolution, not just from one capital to another, but to wider and wider centres in the country and people taking their own decisions.'

Again, this quickly became a standard Thatcherite argument when faced with questions about devolution. 'How far do you think that English members simply just want to get rid of Scotland quietly?' added Mackay provocatively. 'They're making so much trouble . . .' 'Oh never,' Mrs Thatcher interrupted sharply. 'Never never never. We're all part of the United Kingdom, and for any one part to go would diminish us all.'

This burst of passion enlivened an otherwise pedestrian interview. Still raw as a television performer (she was renowned for her reluctance to do on-camera interviews), Mrs Thatcher had yet to benefit from a make-over which would smarten her appearance and soften her occasionally grating accent. 'How do you think you can identify with the voters of Scotland?' Mackay then asked her, alluding to her Home Counties image. She replied:

> Well, you know there are suburbs in places other than the Home Counties. But I am not really a suburban person at all. I am a lass, born and brought up in a small town and very glad that I was because I know what it's like to be a part of a community where you all know one another and you have a community life, as well as your own life. I think the way in which I was brought up was the way in which many of my Scottish friends were brought up. One was brought up to work hard, to put a lot of stress on education, and to get on as a result of your own efforts.[21]

This 'Lincolnshire lass' analogy was one to which Mrs Thatcher would often return on visits to Scotland, and it always sounded – rightly or wrongly – as it did on STV in 1975: clumsy, mildly patronising and unconvincing. As the journalist Hugo Young observed in his probing biography of Mrs Thatcher, *One of Us*, she 'was born a northerner but became a southerner, the quintessence of a Home Counties politician'.[22] As the young Margaret Roberts gravitated towards London and the world of Westminster, much of her 'Lincolnshire lass' persona had deliberately been left behind.

'Today, I thought, as I was going round among the people,' the *Scotsman* reported Mrs Thatcher as saying of a successful day's campaigning, 'we are

---

[21] Interview with STV.
[22] Young, *One of Us*, 28.

on our way back to an increasing Conservative Party in Scotland and an increasing number of Conservative members at Westminster.'[23] She was correct, at least in the short term. 'It all began so well,' wrote the Gershwins of another doomed love affair, 'but oh, what an end', an appropriate refrain for Mrs Supercool's maiden visit to Scotland.

---

[23] *Scotsman* 22/2/1975.

Chapter 3

'LANCING THE BOIL' (1975-79)

As an instinctive Unionist, I disliked the devolution commitment. But I realised that so much capital had by now been invested in it that I could not change the policy immediately. Had I done so, there would have been resignations which I simply could not afford. For the moment I would have to live with the commitment.[1]

Margaret Thatcher, *The Path to Power*

DESPITE HER RAPTUROUS reception in Scotland, Mrs Thatcher was acutely aware that all was not well with Conservatism north of the border. 'I believe that the problem is the same as further south', she wrote to the Scottish Tory chairman, George Younger, shortly after becoming leader, 'people lost *faith* in us and our job is to restore it.'[2] And to Priscilla Tweedsmuir (a Scottish Tory peeress) Mrs Thatcher admitted frankly: 'We seem to have problems in Scotland and the difficulty from my point of view is to get agreement on how to reorganise and with whom.'[3]

To that end a committee to 'consider all aspects of the Party in Scotland'[4] had already been established a few months before Mrs Thatcher became leader. Younger spoke optimistically of the party arising phoenix-like from the ashes of two electoral defeats, but in reality resources were tight, morale dangerously low and prospects gloomy. So in 1976 Mrs Thatcher set up a second committee of inquiry chaired by the MP for West Aberdeenshire, Russell Fairgrieve.

Scottish policy-making had long been the preserve of grandees like Fairgrieve, responsibility having been devolved northwards – much like the powers of the Scottish Office – since the 1920s. Scottish Unionist Party (the name Conservative was only adopted in 1965) intellectuals like Walter

---

[1] Thatcher, *The Path to Power*, 322.
[2] MT to GY, 16/2/1975, George Younger Papers. 'I shall need a lot of advice about Scotland', she also told Younger, 'but am ready and willing to take it.'
[3] MT to Lady Tweedsmuir, c2/1975, Acc 11884 f283, Tweedsmuir Papers.
[4] Minute dated 1/11/1974, GYP.

Elliot, Scottish Secretary from 1936 to 1938, flourished as a result. Elliot later contributed to the nationalistic party document, *Scottish Control of Scottish Affairs*, which appeared in 1949. Its central recommendations – additional Scottish Office ministers and a Royal Commission into Scottish affairs – trumped a centralising Labour government and all were implemented when Sir Winston Churchill returned to Downing Street in 1951.

Mrs Thatcher was reluctant to overturn this autonomy, not least because she had no convincing alternative, but nevertheless her presumption was towards further integration between Scottish Tory headquarters in Edinburgh and Conservative Central Office in London's Smith Square. When Fairgrieve's committee reported in April 1977, that was exactly what he proposed. Although the post of treasurer was to be maintained, the Scottish party's finances were to be controlled from London, something only reversed by another Thatcher-backed review ten years later. There were also positives: Scottish constituency associations could for the first time send delegates to the UK party conference, while Scottish HQ was beefed up with the appointment of Graham Macmillan (the party's high-flying agent in Yorkshire) to the new post of director. But on internal party organisation, as in general policy matters, Mrs Thatcher's instincts were centralist.

Nothing embodied these instincts more than the thorny issue of devolution. By the time Mrs Thatcher was elected leader of the Conservatives, every major party in the House of Commons was committed to the creation of devolved assemblies for Scotland and Wales (and the restoration of devolution to Northern Ireland). This was, in the case of Labour and the Conservatives, a rather cynical response to the rise of the SNP in the two general elections of 1974, while for the Liberals it reflected a long-standing commitment to federalist constitutional reform.

Despite this broad consensus, however cynical, devolution was fast becoming a millstone around the Labour government's neck. Whips struggled to persuade backbenchers to support planned legislation while many ministers, including the Prime Minister James Callaghan, were less than enthusiastic. The Conservatives also tried to paper over the cracks of internal division. Many in the parliamentary party were opposed to Heath's Declaration of Perth, fearing devolution would constitute the 'slippery slope' towards full independence. More tactically minded Tories, meanwhile, saw obvious advantages in stepping up the pressure on Labour by opposing it.

Mrs Thatcher essentially agreed with this analysis but feared, as the historian Chris Collins has observed, 'that a sudden reversal of policy would cause internal divisions, particularly with those still loyal to Heath and in Scotland where the whole party establishment was strongly devolutionist'.[5] The fact that Heath's renewed devolution push following the February 1974 election defeat had resulted in even fewer Scottish Tory MPs at the October poll simply deepened Mrs Thatcher's cynicism. As far as she was concerned,

---

[5] www.margaretthatcher.org.

the SNP should not be pandered to by the Unionist parties via proposals for devolution.

Mrs Thatcher, therefore, decided to play a long game. When her adviser Patrick Cosgrave presented her with a draft speech for her first Scottish Conservative and Unionist Association conference (hereafter referred to as the Scottish Conservative, or Tory, conference) as leader, which expressed unequivocal opposition to devolution, she rejected it, saying, quite gently, 'No. I will retreat, but I do not want to bang the drums too loudly.'[6] Instead, Mrs Thatcher repeated the commitment to an Assembly 'as briefly as [she] decently could' while gathering support behind the scenes for a change. 'Talking to people at the Conference brought home more clearly than ever the fact that there were some Scottish Tories who bitterly disagreed with their leaders about the whole question,' she recalled in her memoirs. 'My unease grew – and so did that of many other people.'

An important factor fuelling Mrs Thatcher's unease was growing discontent among English Tory MPs. Regular meetings with backbenchers told her that opinion in that quarter was overwhelmingly hostile to a Scottish Assembly. 'At the same time Alick Buchanan-Smith and Malcolm Rifkind [the Shadow Scottish Secretary and his deputy respectively], getting ever more out of touch, were flirting with the idea of a separate Scottish executive,' she later wrote. 'This went yet further beyond the Home proposals and took us well into Labour territory.'[7] The Home proposals had merely recommended a consultative assembly, while the 'idea of a separate Scottish executive' was the part Mrs Thatcher objected to most. She wanted the Scottish Secretary to remain the *de facto* 'Scottish executive' at Westminster, while she also refused to budge on calls for elections to the Assembly to be conducted by proportional representation. Backed by figures like George Younger and Buchanan-Smith to act as a check on a likely SNP advance, the idea soon fell by the wayside.

There was even speculation towards the end of 1975 – when the government's white paper on devolution was due to appear – that Mrs Thatcher would whip her troops to vote against any devolution Bill instead of offering qualified support. Consequently, the Conservative leader had to wade through a steady stream of letters for and against such a move. She agreed with a letter from Nigel Lawson that 'the demand for devolution has come because governments have taken too much power themselves',[8] while her reply to a letter from Malcolm Rifkind gave an even clearer insight into her thinking: 'We have not yet decided – but I am more and more doubtful about the possibility of drafting an amendment which will suit all our people. We *are* committed to an Assembly and there will be an Assembly. We must take those factors into account.'[9]

---

[6] Cosgrave, *Thatcher: The First Term*, 59.
[7] Thatcher, *The Path to Power*, 323.
[8] MT to Nigel Lawson, 30/12/1975, MTF.
[9] MT to Malcolm Rifkind, c12/1975, MTF.

One correspondent Mrs Thatcher took seriously was the former (and future) Lord Chancellor, Lord Hailsham, who wrote to her as a 'convinced devolutionist'. 'If we had only *come to terms* with devolution in the 1880s,' he argued, 'we might still have a totally united U.K. and no Ulster problem on our hands today.' In any event, Hailsham concluded, 'I would hope that we will avoid another fiasco like the Home proposals for an assembly without powers.'[10] Ultimately, however, Mrs Thatcher acquiesced, perhaps sensing it was too soon to act in the face of pro-devolutionists like Hailsham and Rifkind. As she explained in the second volume of her memoirs:

> Ted had impaled the party on an extremely painful hook from which it would be my unenviable task to set it free. As an instinctive Unionist, I disliked the devolution commitment. But I realised that so much capital had by now been invested in it that I could not change the policy immediately. Had I done so, there would have been resignations which I simply could not afford. For the moment I would have to live with the commitment.[11]

When MPs returned to Parliament after the Christmas recess, they were faced with a four-day debate on the government's white paper, *Our Changing Democracy: Devolution to Scotland and Wales*. Mrs Thatcher's speech emphasised that any changes ought to be made on a 'sound constitutional footing' and with clear knowledge about 'where they will take us'. 'After all,' she said, quoting a favourite line from Robert Burns, ' "The best-laid schemes o' mice an' men gang aft a-gley," I was going to stop at that line, but I am tempted to go on: "And leave us nought but grief and pain, For promised joy." '[12]

Later in the debate Willie Ross, Labour's caustically effective Scottish Secretary, commended Mrs Thatcher's temerity in quoting the Scottish bard. In particular, Ross noted the expression on the face of the Glasgow Tory MP Tam Galbraith when she mentioned a legislative assembly, again wielding Burns to comic effect:

> But Maggie stood right sair astonish'd,
> Till, by the heel and hand admonish'd,
> She ventur'd forward on the light;
> And, vow! Tam saw an unco sight![13]

Mrs Thatcher essentially regarded devolution as an 'unco sight' and accordingly hedged her continuing support for a Scottish Assembly with caveats and reservations. Her objections at this stage were threefold: the

---

[10] Lord Hailsham to MT, 6/11/1975, MTF. Mrs Thatcher underlined 'come to terms'.
[11] Thatcher, *The Path to Power*, 322.
[12] Hansard 903 c229.
[13] Ibid., c1056.

existence of 'rival Executives' would lead to 'maximum conflict, friction and argument' between the Assemblies, government and Parliament; there would be a 'massive extension of bureaucracy'; and finally the 'reduced status' of the Secretaries of State for Scotland and Wales would 'diminish the voice of Scotland and Wales in the affairs of the United Kingdom'.

Mrs Thatcher proposed a constitutional conference as an alternative, followed by the application of 'some of the good things in a federal system' to a devolution statute. She said the Conservatives would also 'prefer that an Assembly should not have a separate Executive'. 'A statutory relationship monitored by the courts, with fundamental safeguards, would be more likely to be stable than that which the Government propose,' she argued. 'I do not believe that this scheme will stand the test of time. Its constitutional basis is too flimsy . . . The devolution scheme which is eventually enacted must both conserve and enhance that union.'[14]

The detail of the Thatcher alternative, however, remained ill-defined, something that infuriated many pro-devolution Scottish Tories. Mrs Thatcher's over-arching aim in all of this, however, was to slowly chip away at a distasteful relic of the Heath era while maintaining party unity. At the Scottish Tory conference in May 1976, for example, she praised delegates for expressing 'understandable differences of opinion' over devolution without any 'personal rancour'. This was ironic considering the debate had ended in a near riot when the chairman declared that a show of hands had endorsed the pro-Assembly line. Even so, Mrs Thatcher added, 'we will oppose any Bill based on their [the government's] White Paper or which goes further than their White Paper'. This hardly left much likelihood of Tory support at the next parliamentary stage, yet still she emphasised that 'it remains our policy . . . that there should be a directly elected Scottish Assembly'. 'We believe that the Union is more likely to be harmed by doing nothing,' Mrs Thatcher explained, 'than by responding to the wish of the Scottish people for less Government from Westminster.' This minimalist pledge also appeared in *The Right Approach*, a seminal statement of Conservative thinking which appeared that autumn.

Mrs Thatcher was also, not unreasonably, cynical about the widespread belief (which surfaced again 20 years later) that the creation of a Scottish Assembly would somehow become a panacea for all of Scotland's ills. 'The machinery by which we are governed is of less consequence than the purpose of those who are elected to govern,' she argued. 'Any machine can be used well, or ill. It can be designed with an honourable or a malevolent intent. It can be used to preserve or to destroy freedom.'[15] Although Mrs Thatcher reluctantly acknowledged that Scots did feel remote from government at Westminster – the existence of 11 SNP MPs meant she could hardly dispute it – she believed (as outlined in *The Right Approach*) this was 'partly the result of

---

[14] Ibid., c229–41.
[15] Speech to Scottish Conservative conference, 15/5/1976, MTF.

economic difficulties'.[16] A largely institutional response, therefore, made little sense in Mrs Thatcher's mind.

The issue came to a head again at the end of 1976 when the government's Scotland and Wales Bill reached its second reading in the House of Commons. Once again, senior Conservative figures sensed their leader pondering what to do. One suggestion came, remarkably, from the Scottish National Party. A Conservative Whip, Jack Weatherill (later Commons Speaker) was secretly approached by the SNP MP Hamish Watt, who wanted to urge Mrs Thatcher not to vote against the second reading on the basis that if 'she does it will be impossible for the SNP to have any working arrangements with us'.[17] According to the note, Watt – who was a former Conservative parliamentary candidate – saw common ground between the two parties, particularly if, as many expected, the Conservatives were to become the next UK government with a much bigger group of SNP MPs in Scotland. Watt was almost certainly acting on his own initiative; certainly there is no evidence in Mrs Thatcher's opposition papers of a formal response, let alone a deal. His motivation was to achieve devolution at whatever cost.[18]

Mrs Thatcher, of course, did not share Watt's desire and her opposition continued to harden. She dined with the constitutional lawyer Professor David Yardley, and also discussed the government's legislation with the constitutional scholar Nevil Johnson. 'The more I heard and the more closely I read the Bill,' she remembered later, 'the more dangerous it appeared to the Union. It was a prescription for bureaucracy and wrangling, and the idea that it would appease those Scots who wanted independence was becoming ever more absurd.' Furthermore, a private poll towards the end of 1976 showed that Scottish opinion was heavily fragmented. Consequently, Mrs Thatcher realised that her party's 'position could be fudged no longer'.[19]

By now, the lady was certainly for turning. After no fewer than four long and difficult discussions in the Shadow Cabinet in late November/early December, Mrs Thatcher imposed her will – with the crucial support of the Anglo-Scot Willie Whitelaw[20] – and dictated that the party should vote against the Bill's second reading on the basis that it supported devolution in principle, just not the government's scheme. The party's Shadow Scottish Secretary, Alick Buchanan-Smith, warned that this subtlety would be seen in Scotland as an abandonment of devolution itself. Instead he proposed a 'reasoned amendment', but when this was rejected he and Malcolm Rifkind, his deputy, had little

---

[16] *The Right Approach*, 48.

[17] Memo by Jack Weatherill, 12/1976, MTF.

[18] In the 1979 no-confidence motion, for example, Watt argued that the SNP should support Callaghan's government on this basis.

[19] Thatcher, *The Path to Power*, 324. The opinion poll (dated 1/12/1976) found that the majority of electors in England favoured some form of self-government for Scotland, together with three-quarters of Scots, although there was disagreement as to what form this should take.

[20] Whitelaw was a protégé of Churchill's chief whip, James Stuart, who was also Scottish Secretary from 1951 to 1957.

choice but to resign, although the pair delayed their departure for a week in the hope that they might be able to negotiate a right to abstain on the key vote.

Mrs Thatcher later met a deputation putting the case for this so-called 'conscience clause' in which Tory MPs who felt unable to vote against the white paper would be paired with a Labour Member. 'Four other front benchers wanted to go,' she recalled in *The Path to Power*, 'but I refused their resignations and even allowed one of them to speak against our line in the debate and vote with the Government. No Party leader could have done more.' In fairness, Mrs Thatcher worked hard at damage limitation, reassuring Scottish colleagues that she remained committed to an Assembly and even expressing the hope that Buchanan-Smith would return to the front bench. In truth, however, Mrs Thatcher never forgave him nor he her, and although Buchanan-Smith did become Minister of State for Energy in her first government, he never gained promotion to the Cabinet – the final insult being Mrs Thatcher's request that he serve as Rifkind's deputy at the Scottish Office in 1987 (which Buchanan-Smith refused).

Despite Mrs Thatcher's best efforts, however, the Scottish party – and to a lesser extent the party in England – did split. 'I had no illusion that this could be done without some resignations,' recalled Mrs Thatcher. 'I wanted to minimize them, but not at the expense of failing to lance the devolution boil.' She did, however, manage to satisfy a noisy band of English backbenchers – led by Julian Amery (son of Leo) and Maurice Macmillan (son of Harold) – who opposed devolution, noting with satisfaction in her memoirs that the 1922 Committee loudly cheered the new whipping arrangements. Lord Hailsham, on the other hand, came close to resigning, telling Mrs Thatcher that he 'regarded the 3-line whip on devolution a folly, not merely of tactics'.[21]

But while the Shadow Cabinet decision was an important victory for Mrs Thatcher, the devolution boil was far from fully lanced. It is often overlooked that the Tory line remained supportive of a 'directly-elected Scottish Assembly', and indeed this caused problems when it came to finding a replacement for Buchanan-Smith as Shadow Scottish Secretary. The account in Mrs Thatcher's memoirs skirts over the difficulties she faced. 'To replace Alick Buchanan-Smith I moved Teddy Taylor, whose robust patriotism and soundness had long impressed me,' she wrote, 'from Trade to become Shadow Scottish Secretary.'[22] In fact Mrs Thatcher's first choice had been the Renfrewshire East MP Betty Harvie Anderson, a staunch anti-devolutionist with whom she had once shared a Commons office. But despite their friendship, Harvie Anderson declined, explaining:

You expressed to me your belief that I have been right . . . in my opposition to a directly elected Scottish Assembly, [so] it will not have surprised you that I

---

[21] Lord Hailsham diary entry dated 20/12/1976, MTF. Hailsham had that year warned of an 'elective dictatorship' if the UK constitution was not reformed.
[22] Thatcher, *The Path to Power*, 325.

had to refuse to place myself in a position where I should have to subscribe to a decision of Shadow Cabinet to which I was not party, and to agree wording which included the very words – directly elected – which in my view lie at the heart of the deep division of opinion with which we are faced now.[23]

In light of later criticisms that Mrs Thatcher (as Prime Minister) did little to further the careers of female Conservative MPs, her attempted promotion of Harvie Anderson is a hitherto unknown point in her favour.

It had been figures like Harvie Anderson and Teddy Taylor who had convinced Mrs Thatcher that devolution in general, and a separate executive in particular, constituted a slippery slope towards independence. Harvie Anderson had been involved in the anti-devolution 'Scotland is British' group, while her agent James Goold (Mrs Thatcher's future Scottish party chairman) was part of the 'Keep Britain United' group. Later, Harvie Anderson and Taylor were also key players in the 'Union Flag Group' which sought tacit anti-Assembly alliances with dissident Labour MPs. Mrs Thatcher never discouraged such activities, and indeed she indicated in late 1976 that party discipline would slacken, benefiting anti-devolution groupings more than adherents of the official line.

'Here's my Christmas present for Scotland'

---

[23] Betty Harvie Anderson to MT, 8/12/1976, MTF.

So Teddy Taylor, whose 'robust patriotism' undoubtedly impressed Mrs Thatcher, was actually her second choice as Shadow Scottish Secretary, largely because he (unlike Harvie Anderson) was content to follow the line on having a directly elected Assembly. Whatever his faults – Taylor's highly strung nature crops up regularly in George Younger's diary during the late 1970s – his political instincts were good and his flair for publicity often inspired. Everything to Taylor was a scandal, an outrage or a disaster, and while not necessarily Thatcherite, he was certainly very fond of his party leader. To him, the devolution argument 'represented the divide between the Heathite policies and the Thatcherite policies', Heath's 'people believing that a sensible and agreeable compromise was the best way of solving problems, while the Thatcherites believed in fighting their own corner against the enemy'.[24]

Mrs Thatcher wrote her own speech for the second reading debate on 13 December 1976 ('exactly the sort of forensic operation that I enjoyed'[25]) following further talks with Professor Yardley. It was indeed a forensic performance, although at points it was difficult to believe Mrs Thatcher believed in any sort of devolution:

The Government have chosen a completely wrong approach to and wrong structure for the Scottish Assembly. They have chosen to make it separate but supervised. That is giving power with one hand and taking it back with the other. It will satisfy no one and will lead to the very discord and conflict which it is our purpose to avoid. It will be used as a basis of agitation and eventually as a basis to try to fragment the unity of the kingdom.[26]

To Bernard Donoughue, a senior policy adviser to James Callaghan who was watching the debate, it was actually the Conservative leader's tactics which threatened to fragment the Union. 'Mrs Thatcher put on a remarkable performance,' he recorded in his diary. He went on: 'A brilliant barrister's dissection of our bill . . . But in the end she did not say where she stood on Scotland and devolution. She said what was wrong with our bill, but not what she would replace it with. It is not even clear whether or not she opposes devolution totally. She simply hopes to bring down the government on devolution. Then the Scot Nats will take Scotland, and she will take power as the largest English party.'[27]

Donoughue's assessment was perceptive, although inaccurate regarding the SNP. 'The more I consider the devolution proposals the more I am sure that what Alec Douglas-Home proposed is about as far as we can possibly go,' Mrs Thatcher wrote to James Goold, 'without jeopardising the future of the

[24] Taylor, *Teddy Boy Blue*, 173.
[25] Thatcher, *The Path to Power*, 325.
[26] Hansard 922 c1001–07.
[27] Donoughue, *Downing Street Diary*, II, 120–21.

U.K. – and that we must not do.' She then added: 'I do not agree with the argument that this bill was about the *principle* of devolution; it is not; it is about a particular *method* of devolution with which we wholeheartedly disagree.'[28]

At the final division on the Bill's second reading, 42 Conservatives, including Edward Heath, Russell Fairgrieve and George Younger, either abstained or were paired under the 'conscience clause' sanctioned by Mrs Thatcher. Five – including Buchanan-Smith and Malcolm Rifkind – voted with the government. Labour was just as divided, with 29 of its MPs abstaining and ten even voting with the Conservatives. Overall there was a 45-vote majority for the Bill, but an awful lot more unhappiness on both sides. But although Mrs Thatcher had been superficially effective in criticising the government's plans during the debate, it became increasingly obvious she could offer no constructive alternative, as Donoughue had observed, to what she labelled a 'thoroughly bad Bill'. 'Our proposals lack credibility because . . . they have not been sold,' concluded a briefing from the Conservative Research Department. 'In addition, there is a widespread belief that not even the leadership of the Party really believes in them.'[29]

Luckily for Mrs Thatcher, fallout from the split – beyond the resignations of two front benchers – was limited, largely because the Scotland and Wales Bill was withdrawn when the government lost an essential procedural vote in February 1977. Mrs Thatcher now appeared to be drawing tangible benefits from Labour's divisions and could claim vindication for her December U-turn. In the no-confidence debate that followed in March, the government was expected to be defeated and forced to go to the country.

Defeat did not come, at least not yet, and instead the Conservatives eroded further their devolution commitment with a proposition for an all-party convention on constitutional reform. A compromise pushed by the devolution spokesman Francis Pym (about which Mrs Thatcher was not enthusiastic), it conveniently avoided scrutiny of the Conservatives' own proposals. And by the time of the Scottish Tory conference in May 1977, Mrs Thatcher was feeling even more confident. 'I felt able to alter some policies which I had inherited and to set out my own views more clearly on others,' she recalled. 'I took advantage of the Scottish Party Conference in May effectively to jettison the commitment to devolution, which passed off remarkably quietly.'[30] 'Effectively' was a crucial qualification. In fact the devolution commitment remained, just in an increasingly less credible form.

Perhaps influential in that respect was the Scottish Labour MP and academic John P. Mackintosh. He and Mrs Thatcher had become friendly in the 1960s despite obvious political differences. The two remained on warm, some might even say affectionate, terms ('Having presumed to give you advice in the past,' Mackintosh wrote on one occasion, 'I feel I may as well

---

[28] MT to James Goold, 5/1/1977, MTF.
[29] CRD 4/15/11, 20/12/1976, CPA.
[30] Thatcher, *The Path to Power*, 396.

compound the presumption') even after Mrs Thatcher began eroding her party's commitment to devolution, the political cause closest to Mackintosh's heart. He wrote her a long note ahead of her 1977 Scottish conference speech, urging her to leave 'room for manoeuvre' should she end up as prime minister with around 30 SNP MPs in Scotland.

> It would not be difficult for you to write a speech blaming centralisation, too much government, mostly from London for the rise of the SNP. This, you can say, you will remedy. Conservatives believe in less government and what there is must not be Whitehall dictating to Scotland or anywhere else. While you will attack these symptoms at their root, you recognise that the political feeling that has been around has a real base inside all the parties as well as in the SNP and you will meet this in a way which recognises realities, eradicates causes and provides remedies for genuinely felt wrongs.[31]

Mrs Thatcher certainly concurred with Mackintosh's analysis if not his conclusion, although she must have admired his intellectual rigour, and he hers. After Mackintosh died prematurely in 1978 a close friend wrote to Mrs Thatcher about his last conversation, in which Mackintosh 'spoke in the warmest manner about the qualities of sincerity and courage which he believed that you have brought to the British political scene. It was these qualities which (party differences aside) he regarded as essential to the survival of British parliamentary democracy.'[32] High praise indeed from a political opponent, and a devolutionist to boot.

The whole devolution episode was instructive both in terms of Mrs Thatcher's tactical style and her approach to Scottish politics. To Patrick Cosgrave, it offered fascinating insights into 'the fashion in which she uses advance, withdrawal and cunning to achieve her aims'. He wrote:

> From the very beginning she set out to scupper the whole project. She was convinced that nationalism could not, ultimately, be appeased, and that devolution was merely the first step down the road to the break-up of the United Kingdom. She was convinced, moreover, that if only the whole business could be protracted, and a suitable mechanism built into the referenda arrangements, then disaster could be averted. But she would not tackle the issue head on, nor as a matter of principle.[33]

---

[31] John P. Mackintosh to Margaret Thatcher, 10/5/1977, Churchill College.

[32] Professor Alan Thompson to Margaret Thatcher, 24/8/1978, Churchill College. 'For your own private information I had quite a long talk with him about 3 months ago before his death,' Mrs Thatcher replied to Professor Thompson. 'His comments were invaluable. I still have several of his lectures and articles and could commend them to any true Conservatives!' (Margaret Thatcher to Professor Alan Thompson, 4/9/1978, Churchill College)

[33] Cosgrave, *Thatcher: The First Term*, 29 & 59.

Mrs Thatcher had deftly manoeuvred the party from a position of support for devolution to one of outright opposition in all but name, although the government's difficulties had made this transition easier than anticipated. She overruled leading members of the Scottish party and bravely tackled the prevailing devolution orthodoxy head on, subtly encouraging anyone who would reinforce her instinctive view. It was the kind of iron-willed determination Mrs Thatcher would later demonstrate as Prime Minister in other policy areas.

Although Mrs Thatcher's actions hinted at things to come, there is little evidence the gradual U-turn went down badly with Scots, although it undoubtedly caused dismay among many Scottish Tories. Given the likelihood of a Tory government at the next election, the whole episode had been closely followed by the Scottish press, but never in a hyper-critical way. The *Glasgow Herald* flagged up the 'dangers of delay'[34] in implementing devolution while the *Scotsman* urged a free vote. So Mrs Thatcher's opposition to devolution was not yet seen as dogmatic and anti-Scottish, as arguably it would be a decade later, largely because her opposition to devolution remained selective rather than unequivocal.

THE RIGHT APPROACH TO SCOTLAND?

Ironically, devolution of power could easily have slotted into the then emerging set of ideas which became known as Thatcherism, it was simply the case that its eponymous leader did not like the idea. When a Shadow Cabinet meeting on 11 April 1975 broke decisively with the party's Heathite past, devolution was still on the agenda. As it was when *The Right Approach* was published in late 1976, albeit couched in rather vague terms.

The key document in policy terms, however, was *The Right Approach to the Economy*, edited by the Tory grandee Angus Maude and published in 1977. Only the section on regional policy specifically mentioned Scotland. 'Many of the worst discouragements to enterprise are still to be found in the development areas – in Scotland, Wales, the North East and Merseyside as well as in Ulster,' it asserted. 'These policies must be modified . . . We must ensure that expenditure on regional development is effective, or it will end by destroying more jobs than it promotes.'[35]

While that objective was certainly bold, what the journalist Hugo Young found striking about this early programme was 'its modesty, even its lack of confidence'. Privatisation was a distant ideal and public spending not the bogeyman it later became. In that sense, an unpublished document called *Stepping Stones* was more important still. Strongly anti-trade union, 'Its essential objective was a change in public attitudes,' wrote Young, 'asserting that the election presented Britain's last chance to eliminate socialism and prepare for a world without North Sea oil.'[36]

---

[34] *Glasgow Herald* 2/12/1976.
[35] Maude, *The Right Approach to the Economy*, 44–45.
[36] Young, *One of Us*, 108 & 115.

An outstanding Conservative pledge on setting up an oil development fund, however, did not make it into the only specifically Scottish policy document of the late 1970s. Instead, in 1978's *Onward to Victory: A Statement of the Conservative Approach for Scotland*, the commitment was downgraded to a 'sensible and judicious use of revenues from North Sea oil'. (Teddy Taylor, who drafted the original pamphlet, had wanted to call it *The Right Approach to Scotland*.) Otherwise *Onward to Victory* reflected both the earlier *Right Approach* documents in stressing a more balanced regional policy while easing the transition between Scotland's old and new industries. 'It is no good keeping declining, unprofitable firms going for ever, soaking up resources which could be used elsewhere,' it declared. 'There is equally no point in making things that people do not want to buy.' It also concluded with a resolutely Thatcherite refrain: 'It is only the people of Scotland themselves who can pull our country up by its bootstraps. What is needed is a government which will give them the chance to do so – the freedom to succeed.'[37]

It was often said that the government that did was imbued with an ideology alien to Scotland. Yet in terms of Thatcherism's development as an ideology, as the academic David Seawright has written, 'It may be argued that Thatcherism owes more to St Andrews University Conservatives than to Friedman or Hayek.'[38] Certainly the debt owed to that sleepy corner of north-east Fife was recognised by Sir Keith Joseph, the Tory MP acknowledged as a driving ideological force behind Mrs Thatcher. Allan Stewart, later a Thatcherite minister at the generally anti-Thatcherite Scottish Office, remembers Sir Keith asking him which university he had attended. When Stewart said St Andrews, Sir Keith perked up and declared: 'That's where it all started.' Indeed, it could be said that in Scotland Thatcherites predated Thatcherism.

Sir Keith was probably referring to Ralph Harris, a former Scottish Unionist parliamentary candidate, Glasgow-based journalist and lecturer in political economy at St Andrews University. He became the first head of the Institute for Economic Affairs (IEA) in London, where he argued the case for the free market and was encouraged by Friedrich Hayek to debunk the Keynesian orthodoxy that unemployment could be kept low through high public spending. Joseph would also have been aware of the St Andrews graduates Eamonn Butler and Madsen Pirie, who had founded another think tank called the Adam Smith Institute (ASI) in 1977. (Also influenced by the ASI was Michael Forsyth. Equipped with formidable right-wing credentials having served as chairman of the Federation of Conservative Students from 1976 to 1977, Forsyth was elected to Westminster City Council in 1978 with Mrs Thatcher's blessing.) But it was Sir Keith's own think thank, the Centre for Policy Studies, that was closest to Mrs Thatcher and which 'became the furnace in which the new economics was forged'.[39] It is also

[37] Taylor *et al.*, *Onward to Victory*, 56 & 16.
[38] Seawright, *An Important Matter of Principle*, 37–39.
[39] Ridley, *My Style of Government*, 8.

fair to say that the so-called St Andrews 'school' owed more to a chance gathering of like-minded economists than any distinctly 'Scottish' tradition of thought.

The school's later incarnation, the ASI, did, however, supply Mrs Thatcher with the example of the Scottish philosopher-economist Adam Smith, which allowed her to try and persuade Scots that her radical brand of conservatism was a native, rather than an alien, ideology. This attracted inevitable criticism. 'The Adam Smith Institute and Margaret Thatcher portray a deracinated caricature of Adam Smith and other Enlightenment thinkers,' wrote the academic James Mitchell, 'on close examination, "Thatcherism" is seen to be tawdry, far from coherent and fails to measure up to the traditions and values of the Scottish Enlightenment.'[40]

While Mrs Thatcher's attempts to marry Smith's economically liberal policies with Scottishness often sounded clumsy, her understanding of his work was not limited to prudent finances. 'Smith was particularly important for Thatcher because he was, as she was keen to point out, a "moral philosopher" and not simply an economist,' observed the academic E. H. H. Green. 'She felt that Smith's pattern of thought anticipated her own in so far as she had indicated that free market economics were necessarily linked to broader social and cultural principles.'[41]

Indeed, much of what Smith wrote in *An Inquiry into the Nature and Causes of the Wealth of Nations* would have struck Mrs Thatcher as eminent good sense. 'Little else is requisite to carry a State to the highest degree of opulence from the lowest barbarism,' Smith argued in a lecture, 'but peace, easy taxes, and a tolerable administration of justice; all the rest being brought about by the natural course of things.'[42] Couched in different language, Smith had unwittingly supplied a prescient definition of Thatcherism.

Another indirect Scottish influence was the little-known Tory MP Noel Skelton, who had espoused embryonic Thatcherism in an engaging 1924 pamphlet called *Constructive Conservatism*. Attacked at the time as pseudo-Marxist, in Skelton's emphasis on individual responsibility, widespread share-ownership and what he famously called a 'property-owning democracy',[43] there was much Mrs Thatcher would instinctively have supported, although perhaps not Skelton's emphasis on the role of the state.

Skelton's pregnant phrase allowed Mrs Thatcher to link her political vision to an enduring principle of Tory philosophy which extended back to Lord Salisbury's premiership. It reached her via one of Skelton's most famous protégé's, the future Prime Minister Anthony Eden. At the first Conservative Party conference attended by Mrs Thatcher in 1946, Eden revived central elements of Skeltonian philosophy in a landmark speech calling for the creation

---

[40] Mitchell, *Conservatives and the Union*, 123.

[41] Green, *Thatcher*, 30.

[42] Hamilton, ed., *The Collected Works of Dugald Stewart*, 68.

[43] *Spectator* 12/5/1923.

of a 'nation-wide property-owning democracy'.[44] Mrs Thatcher began using
the phrase in speeches and also recalled Eden's rallying cry in her own first
conference oration as Conservative Party leader, which took place in the same
Blackpool venue. 'You will understand, I know,' she said, 'the humility I feel at
following in the footsteps of great men like our Leader that year, Winston
Churchill . . . In the footsteps of Anthony Eden, who set us the goal of a
property-owning democracy – a goal we still pursue today.'[45]

Scotland, with its relatively high proportion of council housing, presented Mrs
Thatcher with an ideal case study. 'How does the proportion of home-ownership
in Scotland compare with that in other Western European countries?' she asked
rhetorically at the 1976 Scottish Tory conference. 'The answer is Scotland has a
lower proportion of home-owners than England and Wales, Belgium, West
Germany, Italy, Luxembourg, the Netherlands, Ireland and Denmark. Scotland, in fact, has less home-ownership than any EEC country.'[46] To that list
she could also have added any Eastern European state, a point frequently
made by Malcolm Rifkind and later Michael Forsyth at the Scottish Office.
Together with a commitment to abolish the rating system, 'which has been
creaking at the joints for years',[47] what became known as the 'Right to Buy'
was the first legislative experience Scotland would have of the Thatcherite
revolution a few years later, although in itself the policy was neither
Thatcherite nor particularly right wing (council house sales were also
proposed by Labour policy-makers). The other pledge, abolition of the rates,
took rather longer and, like the Right to Buy, was implemented in Scotland
first. The results of that reform were disastrous, of which more later.

In most other policy areas, there was little by way of distinctive policy
development for Scotland. In fact, Mrs Thatcher was generally hostile
towards otherwise popular Scottish initiatives being undertaken by the then
Labour government. A case in point was the interventionist Scottish Development Agency (SDA), which in 1975 she dismissed as 'a sort of tartan
Wedgwood Benn'.[48] Mrs Thatcher also resisted attempts by her own MPs to
support dispersal of civil service jobs to Glasgow, while the precious funds
'being squandered on the nationalisation of Scottish shipbuilding [in 1977]
and shiprepairing companies could be used infinitely better on new investment by private industry: on creating real jobs instead of pandering to the
out-of-date and irrelevant doctrine of nationalisation'.[49]

The hostility towards the SDA lingered well into Mrs Thatcher's premiership, tempered only by George Younger's gentle persuasion from the Scottish
Office. But as the 1979 general election approached, Mrs Thatcher's tone
mellowed. 'We want to see the SDA doing what it can to help the Scottish

---

[44] *The Times* 4/10/1946.
[45] Speech to Conservative Party conference, 10/10/1975, MTF.
[46] Speech to Scottish Conservative conference, 15/5/1976, MTF.
[47] Speech in Aberdeen, 8/9/1975, MTF.
[48] Speech to Helensburgh Conservative rally, 18/4/1975, MTF.
[49] Speech to Scottish Conservative conference, 15/5/1976, MTF.

economy,' she said, 'not acting as a vehicle for further nationalisation.'[50] Far more important for the financial aspects of Thatcherism, however, was the production – beginning in the year of her election as leader – of North Sea oil, or so-called 'Black Gold'. To Mrs Thatcher, the boom town of Aberdeen was a shining beacon of private enterprising triumph. 'Of course, if it had been left to the planners,' she told Scottish Young Conservatives in 1978, 'the oil would still be at the bottom of the ocean and Aberdeen would still be back in the 1960s while the rest of the world is moving into the 1980s.'[51]

Labour's response was to create a Glasgow-based British National Oil Corporation (BNOC), which allowed the government to take a controlling stake in North Sea oil production. Mrs Thatcher was appalled. Not only was the cost 'alarming', but 'the new B.N.O.C. spells socialism in every sense. It gives the Corporation far reaching powers which enable them to do virtually everything from running petrol stations to owning fleets of giant tankers.'[52] Visiting British Petroleum's exploration rig *Sea Quest* during the 1975 summer recess, Mrs Thatcher did not hesitate in pledging to denationalise BNOC. On that, she was true to her word; on another outstanding pledge, to set up an oil development fund, she was not.[53]

DEVOLUTION REDUX

'History repeats itself,' said Karl Marx, 'once as tragedy, and again as farce.'[54] Whereas the Labour government's first piece of devolution legislation – the combined Scotland and Wales Bill – had been tragically killed by guillotine, its successor – the standalone Scotland Bill – ran into almost immediate, and farcical, problems. 'Now Banquo's ghost came back to haunt the Labour Government,' recalled Mrs Thatcher in her memoirs. 'Devolution, which they had embraced solely as a means of staying in power with support from the Scottish and Welsh Nationalists, turned to grimace and gibber at Jim Callaghan at his lowest point.'[55] When the Tory leader met James Callaghan to discuss devolution on 7 March 1977, proceedings were 'polite and bland'. 'She did not show her hand at all,' recorded Bernard Donoughue in his diary, 'and the PM did not press her as hard as he had pressed the Liberals and the Nationalists in his earlier meetings.'[56]

When Callaghan lost his parliamentary majority just weeks later, however, Labour backbenchers began to press his government to ditch the whole

---

[50] Speech to Glasgow Conservatives, 19/1/1979, MTF.
[51] Speech to Scottish Young Conservatives, 1/9/1978, MTF.
[52] Speech to Scottish Conservative conference, 17/5/1975, MTF.
[53] The October 1974 manifesto said a Conservative government would 'establish a Scottish Development Fund. This will provide immediate cash help to solve the problems created by oil development, but beyond that it will lay the foundation for Scotland's long-term economic prosperity.'
[54] Marx, *The Eighteenth Brumaire of Louis Napoleon*, 3.
[55] Thatcher, *The Path to Power*, 430.
[56] Donoughue, *Downing Street Diary*, II, 157.

devolutionary experiment. One amendment came from George Cunning-ham, a Scottish-born English Labour MP, stipulating that referendums to approve assemblies for Scotland and Wales should require support from 40 per cent of the electorate. Government whips failed to prevent the amendment being passed, and the so-called '40 per cent rule' became another unexpected stroke of luck for Mrs Thatcher in her crusade against devolution. So when her old ministerial boss, Lord Boyd-Carpenter, wrote to her in November 1977 suggesting the Conservatives amend the Scotland Bill in the Commons or Lords to extend the referendums UK-wide (or at least Great Britain-wide), Mrs Thatcher was attracted by the idea, believing it might draw support from Labour dissidents such as Tam Dalyell. But she was also shrewd enough to anticipate objections from certain colleagues. Indeed, Teddy Taylor immediately spotted the pitfalls in English votes being seen to have scuppered devolution in Scotland and the idea was not pursued. Maintaining party unity remained crucial to Mrs Thatcher's approach, even when everything appeared to be going her way.

She had good reason to be cautiously positive when it came to Scotland. In the regional council elections of 1978 the Conservatives gained more seats than any other party except Labour. It seemed support for the SNP had peaked, and Taylor gleefully reported moderate Labour-to-Conservative swings to Mrs Thatcher. The UK picture was also brighter, albeit in negative circumstances. In 1976 Callaghan was forced to negotiate a massive loan from the International Monetary Fund (IMF) and impose brutal spending cuts as a quid pro quo. Trade union pay demands then led to an outbreak of strikes which culminated in the so-called 'winter of discontent'.

This context probably led to a degree of hubris in the Thatcher camp. 'Mrs. T. said that if Scotland rejects the Assembly we would have to try to be as helpful as possible,' George Younger recorded in his diary following a Shadow Cabinet meeting in late 1978. 'But if Scotland chose an Assembly they would get nothing. That just shows the attitude of hostility we now have to counter.'[57] The remark also indicated just how hurt Mrs Thatcher was by the whole devolution saga. Perhaps a contributing factor had been the Berwick and East Lothian by-election a few months earlier. Although Scottish Tories had anticipated victory on the back of a Thatcherite bounce, Labour held on, demonstrating that despite UK-level difficulties and the decline of Nationalism, the onward march of Labour continued north of the border.

By the time of the referendums in March 1979, according to Patrick Cosgrave, 'Mrs Thatcher had demonstrated a hitherto unsuspected capacity to play a waiting game'.[58] Part of that waiting game involved convincing all Scottish Conservatives to vote 'no', even those whose natural inclination was to vote 'yes'. The result was a contrived 'no-but' position, a disingenuous plea that voting 'no' would not mean an end to devolution. A campaigning visit to

---

[57] Diary entry dated 4/12/1978, GYP.
[58] Cosgrave, *Thatcher: The First Term*, 60.

Scotland by Mrs Thatcher was set for 19 January, while party strategists also 'agreed that a recommendation to vote No on the part of Lord Home would carry great weight in Scotland'.[59]

Home duly obliged in a speech at Edinburgh University, later telling the *Scotsman* that 'a No vote does not and need not imply any disloyalty to the principle of devolution',[60] while he was certain the next Conservative government would bring forward a better Bill. Many believed this intervention eroded fatally support for the 'yes' campaign.[61] The Scottish Labour Party MP Jim Sillars remarked caustically that having begun his career by helping to betray Czechoslovakia, Lord Home had ended it by betraying his native land.[62] 'I suppose the truth is that he felt that he had to respond to an appeal from Margaret Thatcher to come to the aid of the Party,' judged the Nationalist diplomat Paul Henderson Scott. Nevertheless, he thought, Home had been 'manipulated and misled'[63] by Mrs Thatcher. 'I am absolutely devoted to Alec Douglas-Home,' she gushed in 1990. 'I think he is one of the most marvellous men I have ever met.'[64] Looking back to his treatment in 1979, many activists thought she had a funny way of showing it.[65]

What made the 'no-but' approach even more cynical was the fact that Mrs Thatcher herself carefully avoided any mention of bringing forward a better Bill, merely promising that a 'no' vote would 'open the way for all parties to explore together a lasting alternative arrangement'.[66] Above all, she argued, the Conservatives wanted a decisive 'no' vote because 'we believe in the overriding value of the Union to all its citizens'. Her pitch was to reject the Assembly and instead back a Conservative government: 'We in the Tory Party are advocates of what I would call true devolution. Not the bogus devolution which imposes yet more layers of government. But devolution in the fundamental sense of dispersing power from government to the individual by returning choice and independence to him. Give us the mandate to release the people of Scotland from these trammels; and I believe you will surprise yourselves by the vigour of your response.'[67]

She was essentially arguing that the Thatcherite revolution would itself be a substitute for devolution, the legislative manifestation of which she depicted as nothing more than a cynical compromise to keep Labour in power and

[59] CCO 20/11/86, CPA. Sir Alec Douglas-Home had returned to the House of Lords as Lord Home of the Hirsel following the October 1974 general election.

[60] *Scotsman* 15/2/1979.

[61] Thorpe, *Alec Douglas-Home*, 456. Home later defended his move rather equivocally. 'The Act as drafted was divisive,' he said in 1995. 'I'm sure it was right to vote against it.' (*The Times* 10/10/1995)

[62] As Neville Chamberlain's parliamentary private secretary Home had supported appeasement and the Munich agreement which granted Hitler large tranches of Czech territory.

[63] Henderson Scott, *A Twentieth-Century Life*, 149 & 268.

[64] Interview for *Scotland on Sunday*, 13/9/1990, MTF.

[65] Private information.

[66] Message to Russell Sanderson, 27/2/1979, MTF.

[67] Speech to Glasgow Conservatives, 19/1/1979, MTF.

appease the SNP. 'It would do nothing for the real problems of Scotland which, like inflation, unemployment and social problems, are common to the whole of Britain,' Mrs Thatcher argued. 'And it shows little enough promise of making an impact even on the devolved matters like health and housing whose problems, too, are echoed in the south.' Ultimately, she concluded, 'A "No" vote on Thursday will ensure that we spend the 1980s together.'[68]

The referendum campaign could be seen as the last example of a distinctly Scottish approach taken by the Conservative Party for what would be more than a decade, albeit one that caused severe strains internally. Those in the party inclined towards legislative devolution emphasised Francis Pym's all-party conference commitment, while the uncompromising Teddy Taylor barely mentioned it at all. The Federation of Conservative Students, then perhaps the only branch of Scottish Conservatism to have fully embraced New Right thinking, was even more strident. Its then chairman, Brian Monteith, launched the 'Student Campaign Against the Devolution Act', while Alick Buchanan-Smith and Malcolm Rifkind openly canvassed for a 'yes' vote. A Conservative Yes Campaign, meanwhile, was only hastily established as a direct response to Lord Home's intervention.

When the referendum vote finally took place on 1 March (St David's Day), a bare majority of those voting said 'yes', although the number was well below the required 40 per cent of the total electorate. The government's unpopularity had had an undeniable impact on the result, coming as it did in the middle of the winter of discontent, and with the Conservatives then polling on a par with Labour in Scotland, its tactics had an important impact. 'For the moment,' recalled Mrs Thatcher in her memoirs, 'devolution was dead; I did not mourn it.'[69] A brief statement issued from her Finchley constituency could barely conceal her glee. 'When only one-in-three Scots favour the Government's proposals for an Assembly,' it read, 'surely this is no basis for implementing the Scotland Act. This has been a good day for the United Kingdom.'[70] In her memoirs she was even more blunt: 'Although I had not publicly campaigned for a "No" vote in the referenda in Scotland and Wales, that was the result I wanted.'[71]

Mrs Thatcher's reaction was understandable. Although instinct had driven the change of policy in December 1976, she was aware that it carried risks. The referendum result, although inconclusive, removed most of that risk and was seen by many of her acolytes as a vindication of her entire approach to devolution. She also interpreted the Scottish result (the Welsh vote needed little analysis) as confirming her suspicion that most Scots did not really want devolution. 'In Scotland, of those who voted, almost as many were opposed to the Assembly as favoured it,' Mrs Thatcher explained the day after the result

---

[68] *Sunday Post* 25/2/1979.
[69] Thatcher, *The Path to Power*, 430.
[70] CCOPR 315/79, CPA.
[71] Thatcher, *The Path to Power*, 430.

was announced. 'And if you count the abstentions as NO votes – and that's how Labour were describing them in the campaign – then you can only conclude that the Scottish people rejected Labour's plans decisively.' She even listed some regional results for added emphasis. 'Dumfries and Galloway said NO. Shetland said NO. Orkney said NO. The Borders said NO. Tayside said NO. Grampian said NO.'[72]

Parliamentary horse-trading soon began, although the Scotland Act required the government to repeal the legislation following the unsuccessful referendum vote. Privately, Callaghan believed the best outcome for his government was for it to have appeared to try and devolve power, but failed. In the interim he tried to buy time. Mrs Thatcher, however, scented blood, and although the parliamentary session had only a few months left, the tactical advantage of bringing down the government through a vote of confidence was obvious. After listening to Callaghan's devolution statement on 22 March, in which he called for all-party talks on the way forward, Mrs Thatcher tabled her no-confidence motion (after the SNP had tabled one of its own), arguing that the government's proposals for the implementation of devolution were 'not for a dying Parliament but for a new one'.[73]

The no-confidence debate on 28 March turned out to be one of the most dramatic Commons debates in years. Callaghan famously described SNP support for the Tory motion as 'the first time in recorded history that turkeys have been known to vote for an early Christmas',[74] while Michael Foot wound up for the government with typical eloquence. The Leader of the House teased Mrs Thatcher for leading 'her troops into battle snugly concealed behind a Scottish nationalist shield, with the boy David [Steel] holding her hand'. 'She [Mrs Thatcher] has no proposals for a Scottish Assembly or any form of devolution or progress in that direction,' he added. 'If that is her course, she has come round in a big circle. I will not say full circle, because she has never been very much in favour of devolution.'[75]

Mrs Thatcher used her speech to pillory the government not only for what she called its 'inept' handling of devolution, but also its stewardship of the British economy. 'No Government can protect yesterday's jobs for ever,' she said ominously. 'They can postpone the day of reckoning, but they cannot escape it. They can ease the transition from one job to another, but this Government try to protect yesterday's job without facilitating the growth of new industries. That is a policy for penury and unemployment, from which the regions suffer most of all.'[76]

One of those 'regions' was about to suffer badly from Mrs Thatcher's own policies, yet Scotland and Scottish issues were almost non-existent during the

---

[72] Speech to Conservative Local Government conference, 3/3/1979, MTF.
[73] Hansard 965 c462.
[74] Ibid., c471.
[75] Ibid., c577 & c579.
[76] Ibid., c465.

election campaign which followed the government's defeat. 'London politicians who came north of the border likely sensed a different political climate in Scotland,' observed one commentator. 'However, the Scottish dimension remained elusive, ignored by the English electorate, recognised but scarcely understood by English politicians, and perhaps something of a mystery to the Scots themselves.'[77] The Conservative manifesto included a bland commitment to hold 'discussions about the future government of Scotland' with no mention of an Assembly, but the failure of the referendum had given Scottish Tories a useful boost as campaigning got under way.

Interestingly, SNP candidates in the election fell victim to perhaps the earliest form of political smear by association with Mrs Thatcher. Despite having voted fairly even-handedly with both the Labour government and the Conservative opposition since 1974, Labour began referring to the Nationalists as 'Tartan Tories', a tag which stuck in the wake of the no-confidence debate in which the SNP's 11 MPs voted against the government. In his Stirlingshire West election address, Dennis Canavan said that 'from their voting record, it seems the SNP would rather have Scotland ruled by the Thatcher government in London', while in the Western Isles the Labour candidate urged: 'Remember, Mrs Thatcher's extra vote was Donald Stewart's [the SNP MP]'.[78] Callaghan's government had, of course, fallen by just a single vote.

Mrs Thatcher travelled north to address a rally in Edinburgh on 25 April, boasting that it was her fourteenth visit to Scotland since becoming leader of the Conservative Party. She began by declaring that she was a Unionist, but also took care to allay any fears as to her intentions towards Scottish governance. 'When we take office,' she stated confidently, 'we shall start talks with all the interested parties, to see how you in Scotland can have more say in the management of your affairs . . . And however we proceed, I give you this promise: we will never be party to a scheme which lumbers the Scots with fresh and costly layers of bureaucracy.'

Few other Scottish pledges were reiterated, although the sale of council houses at 'a very good discount from market value' featured prominently, 'and that prospect alone is a threat to the true Socialist promised land, a land of dreary uniformity, in which the only freedom is the freedom to do as the man in St Andrew's House or the City Chambers orders'. Mrs Thatcher also mocked Labour ministers for being forced to 'beg for loans, more loans, to pay for their wild extravagances' from the IMF. Many of these debts, she added, were 'not paid off even yet, despite the windfall of North Sea Oil'.[79] With the previous election's pledge of an oil development fund now jettisoned, it was a windfall of which Mrs Thatcher would soon take full advantage.

---

[77] Butler & Kavanagh, *The British General Election of 1979*, 98.
[78] Lynch, *SNP*, 141.
[79] Speech to Conservative rally in Edinburgh, 25/4/1979, MTF.

Importantly, at this stage in her relationship with Scotland Mrs Thatcher was still considered an asset to the Scottish Conservative Party as it sought to improve its electoral showing on the October 1974 debacle. 'Although she was on the "no" side in the devolution debate her opposition wasn't seen as dogmatic at that time,' recalled David McLetchie, who stood in Edinburgh Central and went on to become leader of the Scottish Conservatives in the Scottish Parliament. 'There was also no sense that the 1976 U-turn was damaging in Scotland. She was definitely an asset at that time because she was a novelty, there was no hostility to her – as there was later on – as "that woman".'[80]

Always conscious of her gender, Mrs Thatcher also played up to her unlikely image as a thrifty housewife during the campaign. 'I was brought up to believe that it was unforgivable to acquire debts you can't repay and dishonest to make promises you can only keep at other people's expense,' she said at the Edinburgh rally. 'And to my mind, there is no essential difference between that old-fashioned family morality and the way in which govern-ments ought to conduct national business.'[81]

The conduct of national business in Scotland, and indeed in the UK, was about to change irrevocably. For more than 30 years Labour and Con-servative governments had operated within the constraints of the post-war consensus, an approach to economic management which was essentially a trade-off between unemployment and inflation, a belief that the former could be reduced by cutting taxes and boosting government spending. By the late 1970s, however, even Labour began to doubt this consensus. 'I tell you in all candour', James Callaghan told the Labour conference in 1976, 'that that option no longer exists.'[82]

It certainly did not exist for Mrs Thatcher and, in that context, the referendum result can be seen a turning point in Scottish and UK constitu-tional history. Instead of the state beginning to devolve power away from the centre, it began – under Mrs Thatcher – to centralise strongly, away from local government, and even Whitehall departments, to an increasingly powerful Prime Minister in Downing Street. The referendum result also set in stone Mrs Thatcher's attitude to devolution, and therefore to an extent the Scots, believing it to have been a hyped-up desire with no real foundation. In the short term this view paid dividends, but some party grandees believed she was making a colossal long-term blunder. There was a story, probably apocryphal, that when she asked the former Tory Chancellor R. A. Butler (also Alick Buchanan-Smith's cousin) for advice in 1978, he reportedly took out a piece of chalk and wrote on the chest of his suit the word 'Scotland'. 'Mary died with the word "Calais" written on her heart,' he told her. 'You will die with the word "Scotland".'[83] Given that Butler was a principal

[80] Interview with David McLetchie, 6/10/2008.
[81] Speech to Conservative rally in Edinburgh.
[82] Morgan, *Callaghan: A Life*, 535.
[83] Pearce, *The Lost Leaders*, 6.

architect of the post-war consensus Mrs Thatcher was seeking to demolish, it is doubtful his florid warnings had much of an impact.

Ironically, Mrs Thatcher's premiership was to alter the whole nature of the devolution debate. What started life as a cynical response to Scottish Nationalism became, within less than a decade, a response to Thatcherism and its chief exponent's dwindling mandate north of the border. When polling stations closed on 4 May 1979, however, there was little indication that this would be so. Mrs Thatcher had reputedly predicted that Scotland's 11 SNP MPs would 'melt like snow in the sunshine' and indeed the Nationalists lost all but two seats. 'She had played a long hand with great skill and nerve,' concluded Patrick Cosgrave of her devolution tactics, 'and had taken the vital trick.'[84]

'Politics is not the art of the possible,' the Scots-Canadian economist John Kenneth Galbraith once told John F. Kennedy, refuting Rab Butler's maxim to the contrary. 'It consists in choosing between the disastrous and the unpalatable.'[85] To Mrs Thatcher, devolution would have been disastrous; the status quo – pseudo-autonomous rule via the Scottish Office – she very likely considered unpalatable. St Andrew's House in Edinburgh and Dover House on Whitehall had barely crossed Mrs Thatcher's radar in her four years as Conservative leader, but she would come to regard the Scottish Office – if not Scotland itself – as the northern outpost of the dependency culture she was determined to extirpate.

Although the Conservatives had helped create the Scottish Office in 1885 and played a greater role than any other party in its development, Mrs Thatcher had less sympathy for the so-called Scottish dimension than any of her predecessors. 'Thatcher had limited experience of the territorially diverse nature of the state she came to govern,' observed the academic James Mitchell. 'She represented a fairly novel strain in British political thinking as far as territorial politics was concerned: Thatcher was assimilationist.'[86] Not only that, but she was not inclined to factor the Scottish dimension into most Conservative or government policy-making.

Surprisingly, few observers appeared to anticipate a clash. The Labour MP Donald Dewar was an exception. In a curiously prescient speech shortly after the election, he predicted widespread opposition as Mrs Thatcher's first government pursued policies against the wishes of a large number of Scottish voters, many of whom would still be clamouring for self-government. 'It may be that many who did not vote No, or who abstained,' he said, 'may come to regret the indecisive result of the referendum as Mrs Thatcher's shock troops ride roughshod . . . over Scotland'.[87] With that in mind, anyone who believed that life under Mrs Thatcher's maiden administration would be politics as usual, as many in 1979 naively did, were in for a nasty shock.

---

[84] Cosgrave, *Thatcher: The First Term*, 61.
[85] John Kenneth Galbraith to John F. Kennedy, 2/3/1962.
[86] Catterall, ed., *Reforming the Constitution*, 240.
[87] Donnachie, ed., *Forward!*, 157.

Chapter 4

'WHERE THERE IS DISCORD' (1979–83)

'Where there is discord, may we bring harmony.
Where there is error, may we bring truth.
Where there is doubt, may we bring faith.
And where there is despair, may we bring hope.'

. . . to all the British people – howsoever they voted – may I say this. Now that the Election is over, may we get together and strive to serve and strengthen the country of which we're so proud to be a part.

Remarks on becoming Prime Minister, 4/5/1979

She regarded herself as an outsider in politics, from the provinces and proud of it, so she expected the Scots, Welsh and Northerners to think she was one of them . . . what she wanted to do was make life better for them by creating the circumstances and incentives to take control of their lives but although it was the right approach, if you live in a political culture where social services are a regular thing you won't like it.[1]

John O'Sullivan, Scottish adviser in the Downing Street Policy Unit

During my time as Prime Minister I was convinced that Conservative policies in Scotland must be guided by two over-arching beliefs. The first was my own passionate commitment to the Union. The second was my determination that the policies I believed were necessary to revive Britain should be applied everywhere – no part of the United Kingdom should be left behind.[2]

Baroness Thatcher, 2009

BRITAIN IN MID 1979 was to many a disquieting place, fearful of its future. Tory and Labour governments had over the past decade lurched from crisis to crisis, buffeted by inflation and industrial unrest. Allusions to 'prices and incomes policy' and 'balance of payments crises' appeared almost daily in

---

[1] Interview with John O'Sullivan, 7/11/2008.
[2] Interview with Baroness Thatcher, 20/1/2009.

British newspapers, terms which would baffle most voters just a generation later. And in Scotland there was the added uncertainty of the national question, which no one seemed to know how to handle let alone resolve. 'You know there are times, perhaps once every thirty years, when there is a sea-change in politics,' James Callaghan told his adviser Bernard Donoughue shortly before polling day. 'There is a shift in what the public wants and what it approves of. I suspect there is now such a sea-change – and it is for Mrs Thatcher.'[3]

Margaret Thatcher's emollient first words to the nation as she prepared to enter Downing Street (the prayer of St Francis of Assisi) were therefore deliberately chosen, but appeared ironic in light of subsequent events. The UK's first female Prime Minister would come to evoke devotion and antipathy in almost equal measure. To her supporters she was cutting through the country's uncertainty with practical solutions; to her detractors she was the harbinger of doom. 'The forces of error, doubt and despair were so firmly entrenched in British society,' Mrs Thatcher conceded in her memoirs, 'that overcoming them would not be possible without some measure of discord.'[4] Similarly, Baroness Thatcher reflected in 2009 that as 'the culture of dependency which had done such damage to Britain was that much stronger in Scotland, I knew that, in bringing about change, we would be challenging firmly entrenched interests'.[5]

As the dust settled on the 1979 general election results, however, the Conservatives could claim to have been restored as a major party in Scotland. Its share of the vote increased from 24.7 per cent in October 1974, just months before Mrs Thatcher became leader, to 31.3 per cent, a larger share than the SNP at its height five years before. The party also increased its tally of Scottish seats by six, mainly at the expense of the SNP in rural constituencies like Moray and Nairn and Banffshire. But it remained Labour's night. The People's Party increased its number of seats (including Glasgow Cathcart, where Teddy Taylor was defeated) and share of votes, despite the winter of discontent and the resulting decline in Labour support south of the border. If British and Scottish politics had been diverging since the two 1974 elections, then Mrs Thatcher had hastened the divergence.

'Her swing, at first sight, is as positive an affirmation of faith as the British people have contrived for three decades,' observed the *Guardian*. 'Only at a second glance do the qualifications emerge: Scotland swirling against the trend; the big cities of the north acknowledging the inevitable only at a grudging shuffle.'[6] Even in the swirl, Mrs Thatcher could point to six more Conservative MPs in Scottish seats, while in the first direct elections to the European Parliament which followed in June 1979, the Scottish Tories increased their share of the vote to 33 per cent – more than Labour's –

[3] Donoughue, *Prime Minister*, 191.
[4] Thatcher, *The Downing Street Years*, 19.
[5] Interview with Baroness Thatcher.
[6] *Guardian* 5/5/1979.

and secured five out of eight MEPs. So, at least initially, Mrs Thatcher could be said to have been electorally popular in Scotland. Indeed, many Scots voted Conservative for the first time in May 1979.

Scotland had known female politicians – even aggressive ones – in the past. Tories like the Duchess of Atholl, Lady Tweedsmuir and the tweedy yet formidable Betty Harvie Anderson, the nearly-woman of Scottish politics who was to die shortly after the election; firebrand socialists such as Jennie Lee, Peggy Herbison and Judith Hart; and more recently glamorous Nationalists in the form of Winnie Ewing and Margo MacDonald.

This monstrous regiment of Scottish female politicians had all been, however, distinctly Scottish, however anglicised they sounded. Mrs Thatcher was not only perceived as middle class, but she sounded resolutely English. An element of chauvinism towards the Conservative leader manifested itself quite early on, the Labour MP Dennis Canavan having urged his constituents not to 'let that witch hang up her curtains in Downing Street!'[7] during the 1979 election campaign. So in presentational terms at least, warming Scottish hearts was going to be difficult for the new Prime Minister.

In policy terms, however, concrete reactions of Scots to the government's programme were slow to emerge, even though Mrs Thatcher had stated her dislike of the principles of collectivism and welfare more firmly than any of her post-war predecessors. Her intentions were also outlined unequivocally in the 1979 manifesto: de-indexing of major social security benefits, pruning of the housing programme, public assets sold to the highest bidder, and not least, automatic government grants to inefficient state-owned enterprises were to cease. The Thatcherite vision of freedom also included protecting employees from monolithic trade unions, giving council tenants the right to buy their homes and granting some parents public funds to educate their children privately.

These policies not only struck at the heart of socialism but also at the middle ground in British politics. And in every area outlined above, Scotland had its stake, often disproportionately so. So discord, not harmony, was the likely consequence of pursuing such policies, particularly north of the border. Yet for much of Mrs Thatcher's first term, not only did her government successfully implement most of its manifesto (with a majority of only 44), but it did so unchallenged to any serious degree by the Labour Party, which now plunged into a civil war.

The SNP was at first stunned by the scale of its defeat (it was left with just two turkeys after voting for an early Christmas), then directed its energies inwards, engaging in the sort of factional infighting which had been hitherto been considered the special province of the Labour Party. Combined with the referendum defeat, neither independence nor devolution was any longer in the running as a panacea for Scotland's ills.

---

[7] Kemp, *The Hollow Drum*, 209.

COMMON-SENSE POLITICS

The timing of the annual Scottish Conservative conference in May meant Mrs Thatcher's keynote speech often assumed heightened significance. And so it was in 1979 when she made her first speech as Prime Minister to the party faithful in Perth. 'Life is not easy for Scottish Tories; nor was it to become easier,' Mrs Thatcher reflected of this gathering in her memoirs. 'Unlike English Conservatives, they are used to being a minority party, with the Scottish media heavily slanted against them. But these circumstances gave Scottish Conservatives a degree of enthusiasm and a fighting spirit which I admired, and which also guaranteed a warm-hearted and receptive audience.'[8]

'Well, we won', Mrs Thatcher declared before moving on to cautionary talk about the perils of inflation, a new figure of 10.1 per cent having been published that day. 'The evil of inflation is still with us,' she warned. 'We are a long way from restoring honest money and the Treasury forecast when we took over was that inflation was on an upward trend . . . But little can be achieved without sound money. It is the bedrock of sound government.'

The Prime Minister also took care to discuss the Scottish question and explore why the Conservatives were still 14 short of a majority in Scotland despite the UK-wide election victory. 'Is it that our policies are not so popular in Scotland? Of course not,' she asked, and answered, rhetorically. 'Every opinion survey . . . shows us that our main policies are overwhelmingly popular'. That was hardly surprising, Mrs Thatcher continued, as the 'Scots have always prided themselves on common-sense politics – and that is exactly what we have been offering them – action on law and order to make our streets safer, tax cuts, incentives for small businesses, a drive for higher standards in schools.' She went on:

> So why hasn't the Conservative Party been even more successful in the polling booths? Above all, I believe, because so many people have been conditioned by years of Socialism, locally and nationally, that they have come to accept that we cannot do any better than we have in the last few years. There are lingering doubts about anyone who says – 'Yes, we can do better and we will do better if only we can do things in a different way'.

Mrs Thatcher then moved on to the ill-fated Scotland Act. 'We will ask Parliament to repeal it,' she declared. 'But we have made it clear that we shall initiate all-party discussions aimed at bringing government closer to the people.'[9] Arguably, this was an empty promise and the prospect of all-party talks a charade. When Malcolm Rifkind, newly installed as an under-secretary at the Scottish Office, wound up the repeal debate for the government on 20 June (which struck some observers as a strangely efficient performance for someone who had voted 'yes' in the referendum), he said it was the beginning of

---

[8] Thatcher, *The Downing Street Years*, 35–36.
[9] Speech to Scottish Conservative conference, 12/5/1979, MTF.

a new phase of devolution. But this new phase was clearly going to be non-legislative, and the ill-fated Scotland Act – with the Assembly it was supposed to create – just an unpleasant memory. The devolution boil had finally been lanced through a parliamentary vote, at least in the short term.

Over the next decade or so a mythology built up about who was to blame for the failure of the original Scotland Act. One theory had it that by helping to bring down the Callaghan government it was the SNP who had ushered in a Thatcher government and therefore killed devolution; another account had it that the Tories needlessly repealed the Scotland Act in order to spite the opposition. In other words, it was everybody else's fault except Labour's. 'Within days of Mrs Thatcher's coming to power', wrote Gordon Brown in his polemic *Where There is Greed*, 'hopes of a Scottish Assembly were betrayed.'[10] Both myths were propagated by Labour politicians but, in truth, it had been compromising amendments from Labour's own backbenchers and repeal provisions in the Scotland Act itself which compelled the incoming government to remove the legislation from the statute book.[11] The worst Mrs Thatcher and her ministers could be accused of was zealousness in doing so.

The government's proposals for improvements to the government of Scotland were predictably cosmetic, but continued a long tradition of Unionist tinkering with what was known as administrative devolution. When the Leader of the House, Norman St John Stevas, unveiled his list of new Select Committees to scrutinise government departments in June 1979, one monitoring 'Scottish Affairs' was notably absent; in fact it was being held in reserve, to be produced at a later date as if it were a concession from the government following the promised all-party talks, which the SNP boycotted.[12] The committee had previously existed, created by Harold Wilson in the late 1960s in a similarly cynical attempt to appease calls for devolution. But while a useful tool for parliamentary and departmental scrutiny, it was difficult to imagine that a Select Committee was what Lord Home had in mind when he urged Scots to vote 'no' for a better form of devolution.

To Mrs Thatcher, it was undoubtedly a better option, as was the Scottish Grand Committee (SGC), reconstituted and allowed to meet in Edinburgh for the first time. While meetings of the SGC could be boisterous, ironically the Select Committee, deftly chaired by the laconic Labour MP Donald Dewar, soon lapsed into the sort of consensual backslapping so despised by the Prime Minister. One committee member, the Scottish Tory MP Iain Sproat, instinctively Thatcherite in a way which aroused hostility from his wetter colleagues, tried unsuccessfully to wrestle the chairmanship from

---

[10] Brown, *Where There is Greed*, viii. Brown dedicated the book to the constituents of Dunfermline East, 'who have more reason than most to look forward to the end of the Thatcher era'.

[11] Even in 2008, when the SNP revoked a rule preventing coalition agreements with Conservatives, one Scottish Labour MSP told the author that the no-confidence vote was evidence of pernicious 'Tartan Toryism'.

[12] Mrs Thatcher later regretted their creation at all. A second Stevas reform in October 1980 made it possible for these expert committees to act legislatively as well.

Dewar and transform the Select Committee into a public sector watchdog, rooting out waste, clipping the distastefully interventionist wings of the Scottish Development Agency,[13] and promoting Thatcherism by stealth.

Meanwhile, bruised and battered devolutionists began to regroup. On 1 March 1980, exactly a year after the referendum defeat, 400 people gathered at the Edinburgh Trades Council Hall to launch the cross-party Campaign for a Scottish Assembly (CSA). Jimmy Milne of the Scottish Trades Union Congress (STUC) argued that a year of Thatcherism had strengthened rather than diminished the case for home rule, while a sole Tory representative called Helen Millar drew cheers for ironically asking an absent Lord Home how his 'better Bill' was coming along.

Although the CSA lacked influence, it at least kept the devolution issue alive. Indeed, a Scottish Conservative Party memo noted in 1981 that if 'Scotland is seen to be doing badly in economic terms'[14] then interest in devolution might be revived. Mrs Thatcher also feared that James Prior's efforts to establish an Assembly in Northern Ireland following his exile to the province in 1981 would set an undesirable precedent for Scotland and Wales. Scotland's radical left, meanwhile, 'made Thatcher its anti-heroine', largely on the basis of her opposition to home rule. 'Every issue, thought, action, is an anti-Thatcher issue, an anti-Thatcher thought, an anti-Thatcher action,' read an editorial in the polemical journal *Radical Scotland*. 'All thought of self-government is postponed, joyfully so by some, in pursuit of the devil queen.'[15]

THE INVISIBLE HAND

The devil queen's first speech as Prime Minister was followed by another Scottish visit, a much-needed holiday. 'I go there for pleasure too', Mrs Thatcher often said of Scotland, 'not only for work.'[16] In fact she liked to visit Scotland socially most years during her premiership, a routine that received curiously little publicity. Her husband Denis also enjoyed the jaunts, although the abundance of golf probably explained his enthusiasm. The businessman Hector Laing often hosted the Thatchers at his home near Forres, while much later on she stayed regularly with her protégé Michael Forsyth near Stirling. The Prime Minister liked big houses and weekends away; not for nothing did the Tory toffs Peter Morrison, Mark Lennox-Boyd and Archie Hamilton serve as her parliamentary private secretaries – one of their jobs was to fill the weekend diary.

The destination for this particular weekend in August 1979 was an estate on the Isle of Islay, owned by Peter Morrison's father Lord Margadale. A former chairman of the 1922 Committee and party string-puller *par excellence*, in 1972

---

[13] Iain Sproat believed that had he and Teddy Taylor ended up at the Scottish Office instead of George Younger, the SDA would have been abolished.

[14] CRD 4/15/17, 3/3/1981, CPA.

[15] *Radical Scotland* Spring 1980.

[16] Speech to Parliamentary Press Gallery, 5/12/1979, MTF.

Margadale reportedly told one of his sons: 'Mark my words, Margaret Thatcher will be the next leader of the party,'[17] prescience later talked up, to Mrs Thatcher's irritation, by Margadale's son Peter. Peter's brother Charles (also a Tory MP), by contrast, approved of neither Mrs Thatcher nor Thatcherism. 'They were hardly her sort of people,' wrote the journalist Hugo Young of the Margadales, 'but they had entertained many leaders before her. Besides, she took her own company.'[18]

Despite doing so (Young was referring to Leon Brittan), Mrs Thatcher's visit to Islay could not be considered a success. 'It was hearty Scotland, shooting snipe and all of that,' remembered Archie Hamilton, 'it wasn't really her game.'[19] With a latent inability to relax, it is difficult to imagine Mrs Thatcher enjoying island life. That said, local press photographs show her apparently relishing the Argyll Conservative ceilidh at the Bruichladdich Village Hall, an occasion complete with pipers and local schoolchildren. The Prime Minister also visited the local Conservative agent, Danny Campbell, at his shop on Islay. When he offered to cut her a pound of butter she said 'no, let *me* cut *you* a pound', which she proceeded to do so precisely that Campbell jokingly offered her a job lest her present occupation not work out. 'Mrs Thatcher told Danny she was also an expert at filling one or two-pound bags of sugar,' remembered the local activist Betty Waddell, 'as she used to do it in her father's shop.'[20]

Mrs Thatcher was fond of recalling her days living above the shop, and this Islay anecdote was typical of her small-shop-on-the-corner talk of not spending money you have not earned, not to mention her hatred of waste. 'There is no better course for understanding free-market economics', she once said, 'than life in a corner shop.'[21] It also chimed with her rather idealised view of Scotland as a nation of thrifty, disciplined characters, an impression perhaps gleaned from an Edinburgh schoolmistress who had taught her Latin in Grantham.[22] That teacher probably also conformed to a Victorian stereotype, and indeed Mrs Thatcher had a rose-tinted view of Victorian-era Scotland as a period of unbridled enterprise and innovation. She enjoyed drinking malts, always with soda water or 'British' sparkling water, and liked Queen Victoria's sketches, particularly those of the Scottish Highlands. Inevitably, this perception was reinforced by trips to other-worldly places like Forres and Islay. The Queen's home at Balmoral must have had a similar effect. A devoted monarchist, Mrs Thatcher's relationship with the Queen was the focus of much speculation. On her annual visits to Balmoral

---

[17] *Daily Telegraph* 8/4/2003.

[18] Young, *One of Us*, 335.

[19] Interview with Lord Hamilton, 6/5/2008.

[20] Interview with Betty Waddell, 27/5/2008.

[21] *London Review of Books* 10/12/1998.

[22] Although Mrs Thatcher often mentioned this teacher, Dorothy Gillies (who was in fact headmistress of Kesteven and Grantham Girls' School), positively in Scottish speeches, she had refused to teach the young Margaret Roberts Latin and also discouraged her from applying to Oxford. 'You are thwarting my ambition,' Mrs Thatcher reputedly told her. (Campbell, *The Grocer's Daughter*, 42)

courtiers spoke of the difficulty of finding 'something to do in the afternoon',[23] although this was easily solved by placing the Prime Minister in front of a red box. 'She loathed going to Balmoral,' wrote Simon Jenkins, 'with its long picnics, boring people and cold walks.'[24]

George Younger, who became Mrs Thatcher's first Secretary of State for Scotland, belonged to the fringes of that world. The eldest son of a viscount and an Old Wykehamist like his Cabinet colleagues Willie Whitelaw and Sir Geoffrey Howe, Younger was as emollient as Teddy Taylor was combative. 'Teddy Taylor's defeat was a bitter blow,' the Prime Minister had lamented at the Scottish Tory conference in May 1979. 'We lost our standard bearer at the hour of victory.' Taylor attributed the loss of his Cathcart constituency to a combination of demographic change, the collapse of the SNP vote, a strong Labour campaign and Tory complacency. 'The House of Commons is a poorer place without you, Teddy,' Mrs Thatcher added, 'but you will be back, and in no long time.' The pugilistic Taylor did indeed come back, winning Southend by a whisker in a by-election the following year, although he never again won preferment from Mrs Thatcher. To his critics, who breathed a sigh of relief at the loss of his seat, Taylor was a loose cannon who would have been a disaster at the Scottish Office; but to his supporters he was a nearly man who might have redefined Thatcherism in distinctly Scottish terms.

Younger, unlike Taylor, had acquiesced over devolution in 1976, which made him a more palatable second choice for the Scottish Office than Alick Buchanan-Smith. Although certain strands of the Thatcherite agenda – abolition of the rates and council house sales – naturally appealed to Younger, he had been at odds with Mrs Thatcher over dispersal policy and the SDA, both of which he supported as essential platforms of a regional policy, that bulwark of the post-war consensus distrusted by the Prime Minister. Younger's tone was also markedly different, less strident than Taylor's and more conciliatory than Mrs Thatcher could manage. A balancing act between the harsh realities of Thatcherism and what Younger judged to be the expectations of the Scots was to be a persistent theme of his unprecedented seven-year stretch as Secretary of State.

The appointment of Younger also demonstrated Mrs Thatcher's even-handedness when it came to assembling her Cabinet, a pragmatic approach which lasted until she was toppled from power 11 years later. Indeed it surprised many commentators that the Prime Minister gave most of the 1976 devolution rebels high-profile jobs in her first government, while natural acolytes such as Iain Sproat and the Perth and East Perthshire MP Bill Walker got nothing. Even Malcolm Rifkind, who had resigned alongside Buchanan-Smith over devolution, was not considered indispensable and joined Younger at the Scottish Office as the administration's youngest minister aged only 32. The epitome of a Tory meritocrat, Rifkind was also sharp, media-friendly and a

[23] Young, *One of Us*, 490.
[24] Jenkins, *Thatcher & Sons*, 108.

talented debater. Alex Fletcher and Russell Fairgrieve, the other MPs appointed to the Scottish Office, were also not exactly true believers. The former
at least had meritocratic credentials, having progressed from being the son of a
shipyard worker to qualifying as an accountant, while the latter was a typical
rugby-loving Borderer. In fact, all in all Mrs Thatcher had few natural
supporters among the Scottish Tory intake of 1979.

'It should not go unnoticed that as well as picking an excellent Scottish
Office team led by George Younger,' Mrs Thatcher boasted, 'I have also
chosen men like Alick Buchanan-Smith, Hamish Gray and Hector Monro for
important tasks in the United Kingdom Ministries.'[25] There was never any
love lost between Buchanan-Smith and Mrs Thatcher, but nevertheless he
became Minister of State at the Ministry of Agriculture, Fisheries and Food,
while Hamish Gray went to the Department of Energy, also as Minister of
State, a crucial posting given the importance of North Sea oil. Hector Monro,
meanwhile, became Minister for Sport, although he fell out with Mrs
Thatcher over the Moscow Olympics and was dropped from the government
in 1981. Another Scot the Prime Minister might have added to her list was the
Home Secretary, the Nairn-born Willie Whitelaw, who turned out to be the
lynchpin of her first administration.

This period marked an unusual phase in the history of the Scottish Office.
Throughout its 94-year existence, both Labour and Tory governments had
championed administrative devolution and presented each additional responsibility for St Andrew's House as a major victory for the Scots. Under Mrs
Thatcher, however, the Conservatives propagated this pattern while singularly
failing to capitalise upon it. As discussed in the previous chapter, she had an
innate suspicion of the department, although made a point of visiting it on her
grand tour of Whitehall shortly after reaching Downing Street. Mrs Thatcher hit
Whitehall, wrote the academic Peter Hennessy, 'with the force of a tornado'.[26]

'You're all right,' a colleague at the Department of Energy told Sir William
Kerr Fraser, permanent under-secretary at the Scottish Office since 1978,
'being 400 miles away.' In fact the department was second on the Prime
Minister's list and the tornado soon hit Scotland. 'She was with us from 8 a.m.
to 4 on one day,' recalled Sir William. He went on:

> Fishery Cruiser, police HQ, hospital, Ethicon Sutures [appropriately, this
> made wound-closure devices], lunch with Heads of Departments [at St
> Andrew's House] and coffee with groups of staff. My recollection is that
> she was a big hit with all she met. The impression we wanted to convey was the
> comprehensive nature of the [Scottish] Office's coverage, and I think we
> succeeded, but I have no idea what stuck in her mind – apart from what she
> later described, not very favourably, as my 'beautiful room'.[27]

[25] Speech to Scottish Conservative conference, 12/5/1979, MTF.
[26] Campbell, *The Iron Lady*, 38.
[27] Sir William Kerr Fraser to the author, 25/7/2008.

What also stuck in the Prime Minister's mind was the number of Scottish Office ministers, not to mention the size of their staff. On coming to power Mrs Thatcher deliberately reduced the ministerial team by one and made it clear New St Andrew's House (where most Scottish Office civil servants were based) would not escape her proposed 'efficiency savings', otherwise known as cuts. Scotland, however, got off relatively lightly, with the department expected to shed 10 per cent of its staff as compared with a 14 per cent average for other Whitehall departments. But although Mrs Thatcher clearly perceived the Scottish Office as a problem, there was not at any stage a serious prospect of it being abolished and integrated into the rest of Whitehall, as some purists at the Adam Smith Institute would have liked.

Instead, George Younger subtly modified fledgling Thatcherism for a Scottish audience in three ways: first, he sought compromises over certain privatisations or threatened closures; second, he strove to protect historically high public spending levels in Scotland; and third, but by no means least, Younger presented it differently. Gentleman George, as he became known, never sounded harsh or dictatorial, but was instead smooth and reassuring.

The Scottish Secretary scored an early victory in this respect when the government decided to sell the National Enterprise Board's (NEB) 50 per cent stake in the electronics company Ferranti, which employed 7,000 workers in ten Scottish plants. Fearful that one of Scotland's most successful companies would be gobbled up by a competitor (most likely GEC, one of its main rivals) in an asset-stripping coup, Younger and Alex Fletcher, the industry under-secretary, bounced Sir Keith Joseph, the Industry Secretary, into a compromise whereby the NEB would place its 50 per cent shareholding with Scottish financial institutions rather than the highest bidder.

Had Younger lost the Ferranti battle he would have been branded a Cabinet weakling, while the episode also demonstrated that the Scottish Office was prepared to act as an 'invisible hand' pulling the levers of the Scottish economy. It may not have been what Adam Smith had in mind, but as a form of 'constructive interventionism' it produced a few notable victories during Mrs Thatcher's first government. The Weir Group, a Glasgow-based engineering company, was saved after Younger authorised the SDA to underwrite a rights issue, while the Scottish Office lobbied against two separate bids to take over the Edinburgh-based bank Royal Bank of Scotland. In referring the bids to the Monopolies and Mergers Commission (MMC), John Biffen, the Secretary of State for Trade, made it clear he had taken into account both the importance of Edinburgh as a financial centre and of retaining a strong Scottish banking system. With two notes of dissent, the MMC found that 'either merger may be expected to operate against the public interest'[28] and recommended that neither should be permitted.

Although the Scottish Office selected carefully the issues over which to fight, this 'Scotland first' approach created a long-term fissure in the

---

[28] Cmnd 8472.

Thatcherite revolution. To Younger's paternalistic guard, ministers were repackaging Thatcherism and trying to preserve the party's precarious support, while to their right-wing opponents they were depriving Scotland of the full benefits of the New Realism and therefore achieving exactly the opposite in electoral terms. 'If you run a large organisation you can't have one branch running a different policy – say it was Marks & Spencer – from the rest of the branches in the country,' recalled the right-wing Scottish Tory MP Bill Walker. 'By conviction I was a monetarist and I found it uncomfortable pretending we were being monetarist in Scotland when we weren't.'[29]

Whatever the government's willingness to compromise in Scotland, even by the end of 1979 a perception had developed that the Conservatives in general and the Prime Minister in particular, were 'anti-Scottish'. 'There is a feeling among Scotch MPs', stated a journalist after Mrs Thatcher had addressed the Parliamentary Press Gallery in December 1979, 'that because . . . they [the government] find a Labour majority in Scotland, that the Prime Minister has not all that [much] sympathy on Scottish issues.' This provoked a rather sharp response. 'Absolute nonsense,' Mrs Thatcher snapped, 'I spent a good deal of my time on them and I think possibly visit Scotland as a part of the UK more than anywhere else.'[30]

This was to become a standard exchange of the Thatcher era in Scotland: accusations that the Prime Minister did 'not care' rebutted with counter-accusations that Scots had simply failed to notice just how much she *did* care. Crucially, this exchange was seen through the prism of the national question, a view skewed by the government's relatively weak mandate. 'We have got a better majority than Robert Mugabe', said the Scottish Labour MP Dennis Canavan in March 1980, 'and we are completely over-ruled by the dictates of the Iron Lady and her tin men at St. Andrew's House.'[31] More temperate Labour figures like Donald Dewar regarded this constitutional argument as quasi-nationalist; nevertheless, the notion that Scottish election results should be regarded separately from those in the UK slowly began to take hold. Ironically, the 1978 Scottish Tory pamphlet *Onward to Victory* had indulged in similar logic, arguing that 'Labour has betrayed Scotland – the more so because without its majority in Scotland it would never have formed the government of the United Kingdom as a whole in 1974.'[32]

THE CATHCART MEMORIAL CLAUSE

Two manifesto pledges were among the first implemented during the fledgling weeks of the Tory government, and constituted symbolic exemptions from the Thatcher axe then falling on every other area of the public

[29] Interview with Bill Walker, 2/6/2008.
[30] Speech to Parliamentary Press Gallery, 5/12/1979, MTF.
[31] Conference speeches 9/3/1980.
[32] Taylor, *Onward to Victory*, 1.

sector. Not only were the Edmund Davies Committee's recommendations on police pay implemented in full by the Home Secretary, Willie Whitelaw, Francis Pym at the Ministry of Defence (MoD) also fulfilled a similar promise in relation to Armed Forces pay, with the increase even backdated by a month.

Mrs Thatcher was unapologetic that policing and defence should have escaped the cuts. 'Every Police Force in Scotland has been expanded, and all save one today is up to strength or better,' she boasted to the 1981 Scottish Conservative conference. 'Notwithstanding the vital need to curb our over-spending, we have increased resources for defence, and we are proud to give a lead to the whole [NATO] Alliance.'[33] The MoD's responsibilities in Scotland were one disproportionately high spending commitment the Prime Minister was not only prepared to tolerate, but actually increase.

Both pledges had obvious political value in terms of shoring up the Conservative's credentials on law enforcement and national defence. The Criminal Justice (Scotland) Bill, meanwhile, proposed new police powers to 'stop and search' individuals for weapons. This had been a hobby horse of the defeated Teddy Taylor, and the stop-and-search provision soon became known as the 'Cathcart Memorial Clause' by Labour MPs. Taylor had a rather romantic view that it would enable policemen to search randomly wild youths in the dance halls of Glasgow, but on top of allowing officers to question suspects for six hours without charge at a police station, the Bill also provided for an unlimited number of six-hour extensions at the whim of a legal warrant. Lord McCluskey denounced it as reminiscent of South Africa, but there were no fewer than six advocates on the Scottish Tory benches to argue the contrary, including the flamboyant Nicholas Fairbairn, the recently appointed Solicitor-General for Scotland.

Mrs Thatcher had a soft spot for Fairbairn, whose political outlook was a paradoxical combination of libertarianism and disciplinary zeal. He argued that violent crime required unpleasant remedies, while Labour warned of fragile relations between the police and local youths as a result of the new provisions. The result created an impression that Thatcherism was not only harsh economically, but inclined towards draconian legal measures at the expense of, ironically, individual liberty. This impression was not helped when Bill Walker, soon to develop a reputation for his unpredictable brand of right-wing fervour, introduced a clause to bring back the birch despite instructions from Downing Street to desist.

Ultimately, however, fears that increased police powers would be abused came to nothing. There was also notable success in tackling violence during football matches by banning the sale of alcohol in stadiums and on coaches and trains carrying fans to games. 'So often a Saturday afternoon's entertain-ment at a Scottish football match had been marred by the drunken and violent behaviour of a hooligan minority,' Mrs Thatcher said in 1983. 'The

---

[33] Speech to Scottish Conservative conference, 8/5/1981, MTF.

crowds dwindled. Some responsible fans stayed away. We took firm action. Its success is plain. The cans and bottles left after a match are now no more than a handful. The disruptive behaviour has strikingly diminished.'[34] Indeed, the Prime Minister praised regularly Scottish football fans for being better behaved than their southern counterparts. 'The Scots seem to have much more pride in the game than the English', she said in 1989 following violence by English fans in Stockholm, 'and we must analyse their success and try to emulate it.'[35]

The Criminal Justice Bill also led to another, unplanned, reform. A talented Scottish Labour backbencher called Robin Cook tabled an amendment to bring Scotland's laws on homosexual practice into line with England and Wales, where private homosexual acts between consenting adults had been decriminalised in the late 1960s (a move supported by Mrs Thatcher). Malcolm Rifkind had long argued that such a disparity was legally, if not morally, indefensible, and although Cook found support on the government benches, most Scottish Tory MPs were reticent and George Younger even urged caution in supporting it. Nevertheless, the amendment passed easily and although the Prime Minister was personally blind to the sexual proclivities of MPs and her staff, this incident – together with the later controversy over the Section 28 ban on 'promoting' homosexuality in schools (known as Section 2A in Scotland) – did little to encourage Scotland's gay community to become ready supporters of the otherwise libertarian Thatcherite revolution.

A PROPERTY-OWNING DEMOCRACY

The first substantial application of Thatcherism to Scotland was the pregnantly titled Tenants' Rights Etc (Scotland) Bill. Indeed, the so-called 'Right to Buy' came to be seen as one of Mrs Thatcher's few enduring achievements in Scotland and was happily sustained by Labour-led governments, both UK and devolved, long after she left Downing Street. Only in 2007 was the policy altered following the election of a minority SNP government in Scotland. But although undeniably popular, the sale of council housing stock at a massive discount had both positive and negative consequences which remained apparent in the early twenty-first century.

'We will give to every council tenant the right to purchase his own home at a substantial discount on the market price and with 100 per cent mortgages for those who need them,' Mrs Thatcher declared during the debate on the Queen's Speech shortly after her election victory. 'This will be a giant stride towards making a reality of Anthony Eden's dream of a property-owning democracy. It will do something else – it will give to more of our people that freedom and mobility and that prospect of handing something on to their

---

[34] Ibid., 13/5/1983, MTF.
[35] *Dundee Courier* 8/9/1989.

children and grandchildren which owner-occupation provides.'[36] Rather than being Anthony Eden's, however, the dream was actually Noel Skelton's. Appropriately, when the Prime Minister boasted each year to Scottish Tories of how many council houses had been sold, she did so in Skelton's former constituency of Perth.

As with the Criminal Justice (Scotland) Bill, many of the provisions in the Tenants' Rights Bill, a deliberately political title insisted upon by Malcolm Rifkind instead of the usual catch-all 'Housing Bill', were neither new nor distinctly Thatcherite. Some council housing stock had been sold under Edward Heath's premiership, while Labour's 1977 green paper on Scottish housing had advocated measures to sell more in controlled circumstances.

Unlike Labour, however, Mrs Thatcher actively disliked council housing. (She once informed the journalist Simon Jenkins there was no such thing as a 'good' housing estate). Housing associations, which fared well throughout the 1980s, were another matter, but as far as the Prime Minister was concerned there was no need to pussyfoot around the issue of council house sales, particularly in Scotland, for 'nowhere else in the United Kingdom are so many people locked into local government tenancies with no present possibility of escape'. Indeed, she became positively evangelical at the 1980 Scottish Tory conference:

> Let no-one say they do not want it. Since we published our proposals last summer, 1,500 tenants in Scotland have bought their own homes, and at this moment another 12,000 applications to buy are being processed. But these are the lucky ones; they are tenants of local authorities – mostly Tory – which are willing to recognise their entitlement to become home-owners. There have been, to date, another 18,000 enquiries from would-be purchasers. Many of them will be frustrated in their ambitions until our Bill gives them the right which Labour councils are denying them. We shall not betray them.[37]

Mrs Thatcher liked statistics, and those relating to housing explained why she believed Scotland to be a nation of aspirant home-owners. When she came to power in 1979, 53 per cent of all household tenants in Scotland were in the public sector, compared with only 28 per cent in England. Scottish council tenants also enjoyed rent levels which were, on average, 30 per cent lower than their English counterparts. Scotland, therefore, had more than its fair share of UK public expenditure on housing and less, as a consequence, than its fair share in terms of Mortgage Interest Tax Relief, one subsidy the Prime Minister defended strongly. The rapid extension of the property-owning democracy was therefore seen as an electorally beneficial means by which to redress the balance.

---

[36] Hansard 967 c73–87.
[37] Speech to Scottish Conservative Party conference, 9/5/1980, MTF.

Predictably, Labour did not share Mrs Thatcher's zeal. The MP Norman Buchan called the Tenants' Rights Bill a 'dangerous and nasty piece of legislation',[38] while more than half Scotland's local authorities refused to take action on a pre-legislative circular, including many councils in Tory-voting rural areas, even though revenue from Scottish sales went back into house building, unlike in England. In essence, critics argued that Right to Buy undermined the whole structure of public sector housing built up, or as the Tories might have argued propped up, by Labour councils. In attacking the likely side effects rather than the ideological thrust of property ownership, however, Labour left itself vulnerable to Tory counterattacks of denying to their own supporters the perfectly legitimate opportunity of owning a home, an aspiration many natural Labour supporters undoubtedly held.

In this sense Mrs Thatcher was a good Marxist, engaging in subtle class warfare of divide and rule to hive off aspirational socialists. 'Council houses were municipal socialist Scotland at its very worst,' admitted Kenny Mac-Askill, then a left-wing SNP activist. 'Labour controlled where you lived, where you worked, what colour you painted your front door. It created some of the best things in Scotland but also some of the worst; the worst were the things that had to change.'[39]

Right to Buy certainly constituted a change, but although the government's commitment to the policy was, if anything, greater in Scotland than in England, the pace of sales was initially slower north of the border. When Mrs Thatcher became Prime Minister in 1979, Scottish local authorities owned 892,000 houses; by the 1983 general election they still owned 875,000. 'It soon became clear, however, that the upgrade from proletariat to property-owner had not changed their politics at all,' observed the Scottish political commentator Neal Ascherson of those who took advantage of their Right to Buy. 'Families on Scottish council estates who had bought their homes continued to vote Labour. In fact, they were slightly more inclined to vote Labour than they had been before. It was the Tory vote which continued to shrivel.'[40]

This widely espoused view, however, that the Conservatives gleaned no political reward from Right to Buy does not quite tell the whole story. At that election in 1983, 47 per cent of owner-occupiers in Scotland voted Tory, so the political advantage of underwriting an extension in property ownership could not be underestimated, especially given that no fewer than 38 of the 41 seats won by Labour had a majority of council tenants. Indeed, the Conservatives' biggest increase in its share of the vote was in Livingston, a New Town in which council house sales were an attractive proposition. Nevertheless, the upwardly mobile, home-owning middle class which formed Mrs

---

[38] *Glasgow Herald* 25/1/1980. *Radical Scotland* dubbed it 'The Nae Rights (Tenants) Bill'. (*Radical Scotland* Spring 1980)
[39] Interview with Kenny MacAskill, 19/5/2008.
[40] Ascherson, *Stone Voices*, 150.

Thatcher's natural support base in England was a much smaller proportion of the population in Scotland. As the academic Ivor Crewe concluded, tenants purchasing their council houses were inclined to vote Conservative even before they became property owners.

The Prime Minister was clearly disappointed by Scotland's sluggish response to her housing bonanza. 'Since 1979 some 50,000 council tenants in Scotland have taken advantage of our legislation to become the owners of their homes,' she said at the 1983 Scottish Tory conference. 'And another 13,000 sales are in the pipeline. That's good, but it's not good enough. For so far only one in twenty council tenants have taken advantage of the offer. South of the border, it's about one in nine. So go out and spread the good word. Those who own their homes have taken the first all-important step in becoming independent men and women of property.'[41]

In 1982 Mrs Thatcher introduced 90 per cent home-improvement grants in a further bid to woo owner-occupiers. Not surprisingly, these proved popular; and although home owners in Glasgow constituted less than 1 per cent of the UK total, they managed to claim more than 8 per cent of the available grants. These were dumped after the 1983 general election, although the Tenants' Rights Etc (Scotland) Amendment Bill further extended Right to Buy while Labour continued to squirm, having hinted before the campaign that its all-out ideological opposition might be diluted. Meanwhile, the popularity of, and controversy surrounding, Mrs Thatcher's flagship policy had successfully distracted attention from savage cuts to Scotland's Housing Support Grant (HSG).

The nature of Scotland's public sector building programme made it administratively easy to cut, and cut it was. In 1979/80 the HSG amounted to £765 million in Scotland; by 1983/84 it was expected to fall to around £450 million, pushing up rents as a result. To be fair, the cuts had begun under the previous Labour government, but Mrs Thatcher accelerated it even further. Meanwhile, grants to the private sector for house building and improvements increased by 364 per cent to £114.6 million between 1979 and 1983. While in 1975 approximately 12,300 local authority houses had begun construction, in 1980 that number had fallen to 2,800. With much of local councils' best-quality housing stock sold off and little new being built, Shelter Scotland found that those on waiting lists grew from 144,000 in 1981 to 156,000 in 1982, with the brunt of the problem impacting on rural areas.

Nevertheless, the policy made Labour uncomfortable. When the journalist Kenneth Roy challenged John Smith about the fact that Mrs Thatcher appeared to have tapped into a conservative instinct in many of Labour's natural supporters, he could almost see the future Labour leader squirm. 'Yes, many working people are socially conservative,' Smith replied reluctantly. 'And she's given them their council houses,' said Roy. 'They've really done rather well out of . . . Mrs Thatcher.' 'I don't fully understand this,'

---

[41] Speech to Scottish Conservative conference, 13/5/1983, MTF.

responded Smith. 'It's not a phenomenon I've noticed much in Scotland. If people in my constituency choose to buy their council house, they don't on the whole change their vote as a result.'[42] Smith's analysis neatly sidestepped the question of whether or not he agreed with what many of his constituents were doing.

Other opposition politicians were more even-handed. To the SNP MP Donald Stewart, it 'was an intelligent idea, had it not been followed by a freezing of moneys for the building of new homes'.[43] This pithily summed up the retrospective view of the Right to Buy in Scotland. Over time the principle of property ownership in Scotland came to be embraced by everyone except those on the hard left; the related erosion of Scotland's public sector housing stock and the social consequences thereof, however, was never accepted.

Like much of Thatcherism, however reluctant many were to acknowledge it, the Right to Buy did change attitudes. For Mrs Thatcher, as Simon Jenkins has written, 'home-ownership embodied all the vigorous Tory virtues: secure savings, family values, household gods, a lifetime of hard work rewarded'.[44] And for many council tenants with little or no family history of home ownership it enabled them to break free from generations of paying local authority rents. For those able to exercise the Right to Buy in Scotland (and despite the discounts many still could not), research found that it altered their whole attitude to, and expectations of, home ownership; increased their sense of freedom; increased their ability to undertake home improvements; and gave them a liberating sense of financial stability.[45] The lack of council new-builds, however, created undeniable problems later on. 'Had the sale of council houses to their tenants been combined with adequate new council building,' judged the leading Tory wet Sir Ian Gilmour, who generally approved of Right to Buy, 'the government's housing policy would have been both popular and an almost unqualified success.'[46]

'The Adventures of Auntie Maggie's Highland Hero'

[42] Roy, *Conversations in a Small Country*, 62–63.
[43] Stewart, *A Scot at Westminster*, 93.
[44] Jenkins, *Thatcher & Sons*, 125.
[45] Government Social Research, Research Findings No. 235/2006.
[46] Gilmour, *Dancing With Dogma*, 176.

'EXCESSIVE AND UNREASONABLE'

Mrs Thatcher's antipathy towards council housing was matched by her disdain for local government. Just as she believed there was no such thing as a good housing estate, she could not believe there was any such a thing as a well-run council. Her election as Conservative leader had coincided with a major reorganisation of Scotland's councils, from a confusing myriad of local bodies into a two-tier system of powerful regional authorities and relatively weak district councils. Following the regional elections of 1978 the Conservatives controlled two of the nine regions, while the 1980 district elections left the governing party in charge of seven out of 53 districts.[47]

The relative weakness of municipal Conservatism in Scotland probably made Mrs Thatcher's assault on local government spending – on the pretext that it was a 'runaway train' – less risky north of the border and therefore all the more intense. While Labour ministers had been almost apologetic in cutting local authority spending, their Conservative successors were not. And even though the image of spendthrift Labour councils was certainly exaggerated by the government, it was fuelled by militant authorities like Greater London Council and Liverpool District in England, and the ostentatiously left-wing Lothian Region and Stirling District in Scotland.

There were also other, specifically Scottish, factors at play. Not only was central government spending on local government disproportionately higher north of the border, structurally, like the HSG, it was also easier to cut. There was no equivalent of the HSG in England, while the introduction of the so-called Barnett Formula in 1978 allowed the Scottish Office much greater discretion over allocation of expenditure than the Department of Environment (which had responsibility for local government in England). Notably reticent about other aspects of the Thatcher revolution, Younger had no qualms about leading the way on the local government front.

And lead the way the Scottish Secretary did. The blandly named Local Government (Miscellaneous Provisions) (Scotland) Bill was the opening salvo in this battle, enshrining in legislation the fundamental division between Labour and the Conservatives over the level of public expenditure in Scotland. Using this new Act in conjunction with existing powers under the Local Government (Scotland) Act of 1966, Younger was able to penalise authorities deemed to be indulging in 'excessive and unreasonable' expenditure. In doing so he appealed directly to local ratepayers' sense of outrage over what the Scottish Secretary called 'a totally intolerable burden'. The government, he claimed, had inherited a 'totally unrealistic' public expenditure programme and was now trying to 'get the runaway train under control'.[48] Furthermore, the 1982 Local Government and Planning (Scotland) Act compelled councils

---

[47] District elections during Mrs Thatcher's premiership took place in 1980, 1984 and 1988; regional in 1982, 1986 and 1990.

[48] *Scotsman* 16/6/1981.

to directly reimburse individual ratepayers. To an extent, Mrs Thatcher and Younger were appeasing their troops. Having retreated from her election pledge to abolish the rates, the Prime Minister needed to offer 'her people' an alternative.

'We need your help as local electors and ratepayers to insist on better housekeeping from the town halls and the regional headquarters,' Mrs Thatcher told the 1981 Scottish Conservative conference. She went on:

> It can be done: and the figures prove it. This spring Tory-controlled Scottish district councils raised their rates by 14½ per cent, and Tory-controlled regional councils raised their rates by 23 per cent. That is far too much. And you and we will expect them to do better in future. But look at Labour. Labour regions and districts raised their rates by 39 and 40 per cent respectively. Such extravagance is totally unnecessary, and we have got to bring it under better control.[49]

In truth, however, Mrs Thatcher's fledgling Conservative government did not fully understand the system of local government funding it now controlled. Small increases in the Rate Support Grant (RSG), particularly during a period of high inflation, resulted in a 'gearing effect' which led to a high grant-to-rates ratio of 80:20 in Scotland (lower in England) which pushed up rates regardless of Labour councils' spending priorities. Lothian and Strathclyde Regions, for example, increased their spending by 2 per cent in real terms but increased their rates by 41 per cent and 39 per cent respectively.

Nevertheless, on 21 July 1981 Younger moved orders to cut the RSG to Lothian by £47 million, Dundee District by £2 million and Stirling District by £1 million. Lothian was told to give £30 million back to its ratepayers or face the cut, but on 11 August 1981 the council defied the government and Younger made the unprecedented move. By the end of that month Lothian's grant had been almost halved, with £1.4 million a week being clawed back by a confident Scottish Office. There were, however, political exceptions. Despite high spending, Shetland Islands Council escaped government action because of its strategic importance in the production of North Sea oil.

So government policy was unashamedly geared towards ratepayers, then a significant minority in Scotland. In doing so, Mrs Thatcher polarised the debate. While many home owners undoubtedly applauded government attacks on their local authorities, scores of council tenants faced cuts in much-valued local services as a result. But, as the local government specialist Arthur Midwinter observed, 'the government soon realised that a cut in real terms wasn't going to work, so they then moved to a cut in the share of GDP, then a cut in the rate of growth, and finally to the Community

---

[49] Speech to Scottish Conservative conference, 8/5/1981, MTF.

Charge'.[50] Not for nothing did Scottish local government depict itself as at the forefront of the battle against Thatcherism throughout the 1980s. Indeed, in November 1981 the *Financial Times* observed that Scotland had become 'a test bed for the Government's offensive against local authority spending'.[51]

THE PARENTS' CHARTER

Education, alongside Scots Law and the Church of Scotland, represented Scotland's troika of distinct institutions preserved in the 1707 Acts of Union. The Scottish education system was also the basis of the developing argument that Scots were distinct from their English brethren. More egalitarian and less deferential, most Scots apparently eschewed the public-school culture of England and were instead given a superior education at a network of local state schools.

Or so ran the popular myth. In fact, as the historian James Scotland pointed out, 'much of Scotland's pride in her educational tradition is unreasoning and unreasonable'.[52] Not only that, but Scotland's exam results hardly supported many of the wilder claims made about the supposed superiority of the traditional Scottish dominie. Furthermore, education was the only policy area in which Mrs Thatcher had direct ministerial experience, having served as Education Secretary in Heath's government. At the Department for Education she had continued zealously Labour's comprehensive school programme to the detriment of many English grammar schools. Mrs Thatcher's emphasis on granting schools freedom from state control, therefore, could be regarded as a kind of penance.

Like the Tenants' Rights Bill, the Education (Scotland) Bill, unveiled by Alex Fletcher in March 1981, reversed trends accepted in Scotland for decades and therefore faced stiff opposition. Fletcher argued that falling school rolls offered an opportunity to relax school catchment areas and widen parental choice, chiefly through the Assisted Places Scheme (APS, whereby the state paid for bright pupils to be privately educated) and mechanisms which enabled parents to 'choose' between public sector schools. Indeed, the Educational Institute of Scotland said the APS was 'socially divisive and almost entirely irrelevant', while the Parents' Charter favoured the 'well-to-do at the expense of the under-privileged'.[53] Fletcher also invoked the beneficial consequences of market forces, asserting that the 'consumer interest is fundamental to the maintenance and provision of educational standards'.[54] The government, meanwhile, hailed the Bill as 'the biggest initiative in Scottish education since the Education (Scotland) Act 1945'.[55]

[50] Interview with Arthur Midwinter, 17/11/2008.
[51] Mitchell, *Conservatives and the Union*, 116.
[52] Scotland, *The History of Scottish Education*, 257.
[53] Stewart, 'Challenging the consensus', 179.
[54] *Scotsman* 13/5/1981.
[55] Drucker & Drucker, eds, *Scottish Government Yearbook 1982*, 5.

Labour, however, dubbed it the 'Edinburgh Plan', the implication being that ministers were legislating for the benefit of middle-class parents in the Scottish capital, not to mention other towns and cities with prestigious educational institutions. Certainly the 40 schools due to participate in the scheme constituted a roll-call of the educational establishment, ranging from grant-aided secondaries like George Heriot's and Dundee High, to independents such as Gordonstoun, Edinburgh Academy and Fettes, the last of which had bid farewell to a young Anthony Blair a decade earlier. Indeed, Tony Blair's first government would promptly abolish the APS in 1997, as the Shadow Scottish Secretary Bruce Millan promised in 1980 the next Labour government would do.

If the Right to Buy symbolised the property-owning aspirations of Thatcherism, then the Education Bill represented its educational ambitions. Again, many Labour councillors and MPs were in a quandary. The MP for Argyll, John MacKay, himself a former teacher, capitalised on this discomfit by accusing his Labour opponents of deserting their working-class constituents by criticising the APS. 'It was very easy at the time to look at the whole raft of policies and just brand them all as anti-working class,' said John Mullin, a Strathclyde councillor in the 1980s, 'but there were a number there which did allow people to break away from what was a very traditional municipal offering in terms of housing and education. We did have members who aspired to own property, and who naturally wanted to make sure their children took advantage of opportunities they themselves hadn't.'[56]

Like the Right to Buy, many Scots took advantage of their new rights courtesy of the Education (Scotland) Act. The number of transfer requests doubled from 10,456 in 1981–82 to 20,795 in 1984–85, although – as with council house sales – the scheme's take-up varied across Scotland. Demand was predictably higher in urban areas, less so in rural parts of the country, and in island communities virtually non-existent. And although the number of requests increased steadily in the first few years of the Act, from the mid 1980s the number of primary school requests levelled off while those for secondary schools actually declined.

Nevertheless, the move was undeniably radical, as had been the Tenants' Rights, Criminal Justice and Local Government Acts. Together they constituted a broadly Thatcherite agenda with some distinctly Scottish elements, and all, therefore, were opposed bitterly by Labour and earmarked for repeal. This belied an element of complacency on the Labour benches, no doubt aided by the widespread belief that come the next election Mrs Thatcher and her Scottish 'governors' would be swept from office. If the first year or so of the Thatcher revolution in Scotland could be regarded as the phoney war, however, a bloodier and more sustained battle was to follow. In 1980–81 the government's popularity sank to a new low with at one stage less than one Scot in six declaring enthusiasm for Mrs Thatcher's administration. Support

---

[56] Interview with John Mullin, 18/6/2008.

for Labour, meanwhile, in stark contrast to its showing south of the border, carried on rising.

Much of this unpopularity could be explained by the effect of growing unemployment and the deepening recession on Scotland, but then many regions of England were as badly affected by both but continued to poll positively for the government. So even early on in her premiership there seemed to be specific Scottish factors making Mrs Thatcher unpopular north of the border. Michael Ancram, then chairman of the Scottish Conservative Party, almost seemed to acknowledge this in a circular to constituency chairmen at the end of the government's first year in office. 'In truth we are now on a hard course to which there is no true alternative – certainly none have been forthcoming from any of those who oppose us,' he wrote in stirring prose. 'Like a long-distance runner we are meeting the pain barrier. When we break through it we will find an easier run ahead.'[57]

VICTORIAN VALUES

A lot of this pain was arguably caused by Mrs Thatcher's economic radicalism. And when that radicalism came under attack a favoured defence was to invoke the spirits of the Scottish economist Adam Smith and the moral philosopher David Hume. 'It was Adam Smith, after all,' the Prime Minister told the Glasgow Chamber of Commerce in early 1983, 'who said that the two foundations of a sound national economy are hard work and the particularly Scottish quality of thrift.' And, she added, 'we are going to keep the nation's finances in excellent shape. Not for us the accumulation of debt of which that great Scottish philosopher, David Hume, complained. He wrote: 'The source of degeneracy which may be remarked in free Governments consists in the practice of contracting debt and mortgaging the public revenue, by which taxes may in time become altogether intolerable.'

Although Mrs Thatcher stopped short of calling the Scots, as she later did northerners, 'moaning minnies', the Prime Minister cautioned that then and now, 'you do not get anywhere by blaming your own lack of progress on others'. ' "It's all the fault of the multinationals" is a fashionable excuse,' she continued. 'Yet it was Scottish trading houses, Scottish banks, Scottish shipping lines and Scottish engineers who were among the first and greatest of the multinationals.'

Even more revealing was the Prime Minister's reference to a recent television interview:

I was asked whether I was trying to restore 'Victorian values'. I said straight out, yes I was. And I am. And if you ask me whether I believe in the puritan work ethic, I'll give you an equally straight answer to that too. I believe that

---

[57] Acc 12514 (1), 13/8/1980, SCUAP.

honesty and thrift and reliability and hard work and a sense of responsibility for your fellow men are not simply Victorian values. They do not get out of date. They are not tied to any particular place or century. You could just as well call them 'Scottish Values' or 'English Values'. They are part of the enduring principles of the Western world. And if we just write them off and wave them goodbye, we are destroying the best of our heritage.[58]

It could have been said, of course, that Mrs Thatcher' new values – those of Friedman-esque austerity and monetarist ideology – had themselves done a pretty good job of destroying the best of Scotland's industrial heritage. 'I remember going to a party at Downing Street', recalled the journalist Magnus Linklater, 'and her saying to a group of us, "Come on you Scots, where are your big projects? Come up with some; you built all these bridges in the old days."' By the 'old days' Mrs Thatcher meant the Victorian era in which Scots ruled the industrial world and Scottish national identity was conveniently suppressed within a 'North British' mindset. So it was not just the Prime Minister's opponents who mythologised the Scotland of old but the Prime Minister herself. 'Of course the flip side of all this unfettered Victorian capitalism was grinding poverty,' added Linklater, 'a parallel Mrs Thatcher would not have liked.'[59]

---

[58] Speech to Glasgow Chamber of Commerce, 28/1/1983, MTF.
[59] Interview with Magnus Linklater, 3/6/2008.

Chapter 5

'LAME DUCKS IN A GROUSE MOOR SANCTUARY' (1979–83)

Do we have to roam the world
To prove how much it hurts?
Bathgate no more
Linwood no more
Methil no more
Irvine no more

'Letter From America', The Proclaimers (1987)

All this played to a particular part of the Scots psyche, what I call, but no one else does, the 'Letter from America ideology', where distant figures seek to impose an alien ideology – often a free market one – on Scotland. Whether this was the Hanoverian monarchs, the Highland Clearances, or 'Lochaber no more', there was a pre-existing narrative into which Mrs Thatcher was unwittingly slotted.[1]

Michael Gove MP

Increasing international trade and competition were already leaving Scottish industry well behind and no amount of public subsidy could alter the facts – although too many people remained in self-denial. By broadening the base of the economy and by promoting enterprise, Scotland rose to the challenge. New businesses emerged and outside investment increased – particularly in the financial services sector and in electronics and other high-tech areas.[2]

Baroness Thatcher, 2009

MRS THATCHER WOULD LATER reflect in her memoirs that the 'balance sheet of Thatcherism in Scotland [was] a lopsided one: economically positive but politically negative'.[3] By the end of her first term as Prime Minister,

---

[1] Interview with Michael Gove MP, 28/7/2008.
[2] Interview with Baroness Thatcher, 20/1/2009.
[3] Thatcher, *The Downing Street Years*, 623.

however, it looked negative in both respects. In the recession that began in late 1979, the remnants of Scotland's old industrial structure were swept away. What was more, the New Realism decreed that the life-support of state financing had to be switched off, or at the very least used selectively. The burgeoning North Sea oil industry mitigated the worst effects, as it did throughout the UK in terms of the nation's balance of payments, but it was not until the end of the decade that the performance of the Scottish economy (an abstract concept first mooted in the planning mindset of the 1960s) began to converge with that of England.

Economic management was therefore central to the Thatcher revolution, both its stated aim and the record upon which it came to be judged. On becoming Prime Minister Mrs Thatcher was determined to mount an immediate assault on public spending and the trade unions, both of which she considered responsible for Britain's economic decline. This meant Scotland was vulnerable for several reasons. Not only did its public sector constitute a higher proportion of GDP and employment than in the UK as a whole (even beyond the relatively narrow remit of St Andrew's House), it also depended upon a disproportionate share of largely unprofitable nationalised industries, namely shipbuilding, steel and coal. The composition of Scottish public expenditure also added to this vulnerability. Spending was high on programmes such as housing and regional aid, which the government intended to cut for both ideological and budgetary reasons. So if Mrs Thatcher was going to roll back the state, it was inevitably going to be rolled back to a greater extent north of the border.

In that context, Sir Geoffrey Howe's first budget was a bold statement of political intent. Direct taxation was cut (the basic rate of income tax fell from 33 to 30 per cent and the top rate from 83 to 60 per cent), indirect taxation increased (Value Added Tax was almost doubled to 15 per cent) and exchange controls abolished, while a key departure was the adoption of the Medium Term Financial Strategy (introduced in March 1980) which deliberately trimmed expectations of how government would manage public spending.

Perhaps aware that Scotland would suffer disproportionately from her intended reforms, Mrs Thatcher did her best to sound reassuring in her first speech as Prime Minister, which happened to be in Perth. 'In parts of Scotland you have special problems of high unemployment and declining industries,' she said, and went on:

> We accept that government has a duty to mitigate the effects of industrial change. While we see no benefit in pouring vast sums of taxpayers' money into firms or industries which have no future, or which lack the will to adapt to the new demand of their customers, we will certainly not turn a blind eye to industries which need assistance to overcome the problems of transition – we will be prepared to help them along the way as long as there is a real prospect of success.[4]

---

[4] Speech to Scottish Conservative conference, 12/5/1979, MTF.

This commitment to aiding industrial transition, with the crucial caveat of economic viability as outlined in *The Right Approach to the Economy* in 1977, was certainly followed through but, as with so many elements of Thatcherism, events did not fully match the rhetoric. Some 'successful' Scottish companies nevertheless collapsed during the 1980s, while others with no 'real prospect of success' – most notably the British Steel Corporation's (BSC) Ravenscraig plant – continued to benefit from 'vast sums of taxpayers' money'.[5] As Hugo Young observed, 'The refusal to prop up lame ducks with public money was one of the most aggressively stated of Tory policies, but large exceptions were made in practice.'[6]

Guiding the Treasury was a relatively new economic model called 'monetarism', in simple terms the belief that by controlling the money supply (loosely termed M3) a government could also control inflation. This notion struck even many Tories as economic lunacy (Sir Ian Gilmour called it 'the uncontrollable in pursuit of the indefinable'),[7] but it was nevertheless pursued zealously by Mrs Thatcher and certain colleagues, who sold monetarism as a 'good housekeeping' approach to the ailing British economy. As with Thatcherism in general, there was a convenient Scottish antecedent. Nigel Lawson, the Chief Secretary to the Treasury, quoted frequently the Scottish philosopher David Hume as having first defined the process which linked the money supply to inflation. Lawson could also have cited the Labour Chancellor Denis Healey, whose successful restraint of public spending through cash limits and tax rises (an achievement unmatched by Mrs Thatcher) had also hinted at monetarism during the ill-fated Callaghan government.

Did Mrs Thatcher understand the technical details of monetarism? It is generally accepted that she did not. In his memoirs Edward Heath called it 'perhaps the most deceptively simplistic of all economic theories'. 'As such, it was always likely to be especially attractive to those whose understanding of economics was limited.'[8] The new Prime Minister had no formal training in economics, and in wrongly measuring the money supply, Mrs Thatcher's governments ended up pursuing erroneous monetary targets. And although the policy did not survive the duration of the 1979–83 Parliament, its impact on Scottish manufacturing in the interim was savage. While the recession had been caused by decreasing international demand, it was arguably made much worse by a squeeze on the domestic economy caused by monetarism, not to mention a high exchange rate fuelled by the effect of North Sea oil on the UK's balance of payments.[9]

With UK production therefore uncompetitive *vis-à-vis* other countries, a lot of it moved abroad. So instead of galvanising 'hitherto complacent businessmen into dramatic entrepreneurial activity',[10] company profits fell, as did

[5] Supporters of Ravenscraig argued, correctly, that the plant was one of the BSC's least subsidised.
[6] Young, *One of Us*, 318.
[7] Ibid., 203.
[8] Heath, *The Course of My Life*, 576.
[9] The pound was around $1.60 in 1977, and reached a high of $2.44 at the end of 1981.
[10] Gilmour, *Dancing With Dogma*, 21–22.

output, and unemployment rose along with interest rates. Desperate for the cash necessary to survive, Scottish firms cut back on investment, reduced stocks and laid off staff. Even then, many did not succeed. Formal advice on how to avoid the ill effects of what was now a petrocurrency, specifically an oil fund to invest oil revenue overseas, was ignored.[11] To Alex Salmond, Mrs Thatcher's early economic policies 'were potty'. 'You could make a case for some of the structural changes in terms of the relationship between trade unions and public services,' he conceded, 'but the essence of monetarism and Thatcherism wasn't anything to do with that.'[12]

But Mrs Thatcher, contrary to popular belief, was not blind to the devastating effects of the recession and her economic policies on Scotland, she simply believed with the zeal of a Scottish missionary bringing Christianity to Africa that the pain was necessary. 'The Government's strategy of economic realism, looking not just to the problems of the present but to the opportunities of the future, offers the only way ahead for Britain,' she told Scottish Tories in 1980. 'And because some of Scotland's problems are of longer standing and are more deep-rooted than those of the south-east, it is even more important that they should not be dealt with on a basis of short-term expediency.' Realism, Mrs Thatcher continued, 'can be painful now; but without it the eventual revival will be even longer delayed. When it comes, the skills and the labour resources of Scotland will find opportunities they have for too long been denied.'[13]

In the long term there was a lot of truth in this analysis, but during the medium-term horror of rising unemployment and industrial decline it was an understandably difficult dose of Thatcherite medicine for Scots to swallow. And as nurse Thatcher dispensed that foul-tasting medicine from Downing Street, there was less of the usual sugar – in the form of regional aid – to help it go down. The Prime Minister even cheerfully admitted that Labour *and* Tory governments had been culpable in taking too much from the public purse to pay for spoonfuls of sugar in the past, but she was determined to overturn yet another fixture of the post-war shopping basket. Inevitably, this harsh yet realistic view confirmed many Scots' perception of the Prime Minister as a typical southerner, uninterested in industrial Britain and particularly uninterested in Scotland. This disguised, however, the uncomfortable reality that deindustrialisation was already well under way by the time Mrs Thatcher reached Downing Street in 1979. Scotland's manufacturing sector had declined by 4 per cent since 1975; employment in Scottish shipbuilding had declined drastically during the 1970s, while previous Labour governments had already begun closing less profitable coal mines in what the National Coal Board called its 'Scottish Area'.[14]

---

[11] This advice came from the Scottish Office economist Gavin McCrone, both before and after the 1979 general election.

[12] Interview with Alex Salmond, 24/6/2008.

[13] Speech to Scottish Conservative conference, 9/5/1980, MTF.

[14] Scotland was home to more than 100 coal mines in the early post-war years, a figure reduced to about 13 by the mid 1970s.

Paradoxically, and despite all the rhetoric to the contrary, Mrs Thatcher did nothing to erode seriously the fact that identifiable public expenditure per head in Scotland was consistently about 21–24 per cent above the UK average, more than in Wales but lower than in Northern Ireland. Nevertheless, Labour attacked what they crudely called 'cuts'. 'In Mrs Thatcher's housewife-stateswoman's book of sins there can be few worse than waste,' sneered Gordon Brown in his 1989 polemic, *Where There is Greed*, 'yet the policy of her government towards the regions is characterised by a wastefulness that beggars description.'[15] Brown, in common with many Labour MPs, naively believed that mass unemployment would propel his party back into government.

Opposition politicians such as Brown could be very eloquent in articulating damning critiques of Thatcherism, but for much of the 1980s alternative economic strategies limped lamely behind the rhetoric. There was vague talk from some trade unionists about pursuing limited reflation, but such an approach was ideologically unthinkable for the government and was not even taken seriously by Labour. Mrs Thatcher's mantra that 'there is no alternative' (often shortened to TINA) may have been dogmatic, but – as Hugo Young observed – it also 'became a beautiful propaganda weapon'.[16] Opponents failed to produce anything that came close to contradicting its central thrust, while, as the historian Tom Devine pointed out, there 'was precious little discussion of the deep-seated weaknesses in several Scottish industries which were the major long-term causes of their collapse'.[17] This ideological vacuum frustrated many on Scotland's left. 'For Labour to win back and expand popular support', wrote Doug Bain in *Radical Scotland* following the 1983 general election, 'means much more than dreaming up a shopping list of goodies to bribe back the skilled worker, the youth etc. It means more than getting the manifesto across better next time. It means investing Left politics with a moral meaning, legitimising our programme as part of a democratic, caring, liberal and tolerant tradition.'[18] 'Government policies have robbed Scotland,' wrote the academic Henry Drucker with similar bewilderment, 'and yet, there is the curious incident of the guard dog in the night-time. The dog did nothing in the night-time. It neither bit nor barked.'[19]

The Scottish Trades Union Congress (STUC) certainly barked, but it lost the night-time battle. Jimmy Milne, its general secretary, cursed George Younger's 'feebleness' following a meeting to try to save one doomed factory, but union officials were often privately dismayed at the lack of fight evident among their members. 'Such was the ferocity of the recession that workers seemed oddly fatalistic about redundancy,' observed Keith Aitken in his

---

[15] Brown, *Where There is Greed*, 69.
[16] Young, *One of Us*, 204–05.
[17] Devine, *The Scottish Nation*, 594.
[18] *Radical Scotland* August/September 1983.
[19] McCrone, ed., *Scottish Government Yearbook 1983*, 17.

history of the STUC, 'as though they believed the government's message that the surgery was traumatic simply because it had been too long postponed. TINA persuaded more than just the supporters of Margaret Thatcher.'[20]

BLACK GOLD

Cushioning the worst effects of the recession, however, was an economic boon from the north-east coast of Scotland. On the face of it, the North Sea oil industry was a model of Thatcherite economics. With minimal state control, companies from all over the world had converged upon Aberdeen since the mid 1970s to make their fortunes. It also made the Treasury a fortune, which during a period of rising unemployment, was fortuitous to say the least. It was, as Hugo Young observed, 'the greatest uncovenanted economic blessing the country had ever enjoyed'.[21]

Until the 1970s the Scottish oil industry, if there was such a thing, was synonymous with the company Burmah Oil.[22] Founded in Glasgow in 1896 to develop oil interests on the Indian subcontinent, it was initially expected to play a leading role in the development of oil production in Scotland but collapsed in 1974. Most of its North Sea interests were transferred to the newly formed British National Oil Corporation (BNOC), a Glasgow-based government agency which marketed up to 51 per cent of all crude oil extracted from the North Sea.

In opposition, Mrs Thatcher had pledged full privatisation of BNOC; in government, the true-believing Energy Secretary David Howell was charged with implementing it. Although the government retained control of the BNOC's trading arm, its exploration and production functions were transferred to a new subsidiary called Britoil. In 1982 Nigel Lawson, Howell's successor as Energy Secretary, authorised the first Britoil share issue on the London Stock Exchange. The SNP spent most of the 1970s and 1980s arguing that Britoil was actually Scottish, but the only concession to national sentiment Mrs Thatcher was willing to make was the habitual appointment of a Scot to the Department of Energy. The first Minister of State was the Ross and Cromarty MP Hamish Gray, succeeded in 1983 by Alick Buchanan-Smith.

Although the first barrel of oil – nicknamed Black Gold – had been received onshore by the Labour Energy Secretary Tony Benn in 1975, by the time Mrs Thatcher reached Downing Street more than 1.7 million barrels a day were coming ashore with annual sales totalling £2,800 million and another 11 fields, in addition to the 12 already functioning, due to come on-stream by 1983. 'You have shown that new technology is the true friend of full

---

[20] Aitken, *The Bairns O' Adam*, 268–69.

[21] Young, *One of Us*, 144.

[22] Burmah Oil's board included Denis Thatcher until June 1975, an association which nearly caused an early political scandal for his wife.

employment,' the Prime Minister gushed on opening the Shell UK Exploration Centre in September 1979, 'the indispensable ally of progress; and the surest guarantee of prosperity.'[23]

Reality was not quite so rosy, however large the related tax revenues. North Sea oil revenue certainly improved the UK's hitherto volatile balance of payments, benefited to an extent Edinburgh's financial services, and ensured that Grampian region became one of the wealthiest in the UK, but it also boosted foreign demand and therefore the exchange value of sterling, which in turn made output from an already precarious manufacturing sector even less competitive. In June 1980 the UK became a net exporter of oil for the first time, while three years later it was producing 50 per cent above its requirements.

So instead of the natural-resource bonanza of oil improving Scottish and UK living standards, it actually reduced them. An economic affliction nicknamed 'Dutch disease' by *The Economist* in the 1970s, it described the travails of manufacturers in the Netherlands following the discovery there of natural gas. Dutch disease duly hit the UK in the early 1980s, although Mrs Thatcher's first government relied upon North Sea oil revenue to fund rising social security costs as a result of the recession. In other words, Scotland was Mrs Thatcher's banker or, as Alex Salmond later put it, North Sea oil revenue was 'used to bankroll monetarism'.[24] Indeed, as John Campbell has written, 'the impact of the recession would have been a great deal worse, and maybe politically unsustainable, had it not been for the fortuitous subsidy that Britain's independent oil supply gave to both government revenue and the balance of payments'.[25] And although the fortuitous subsidy did create jobs, affluence and self-confidence, it did not, as anticipated, transform Scottish industry. Only a few domestic concerns like the Scottish-owned Wood Group thrived as a result of its engineering and drilling expertise. Otherwise, as the academic W. J. Pike observed, 'In the volatile international market, they [North Sea oil producers] simply could not afford the luxury of waiting for a suitable infrastructure to develop in Scotland.'[26]

The SNP made much of this sense that Scotland was losing out while revenue flowed into the Treasury in a memorable poster depicting Mrs Thatcher as a black-caped vampire with oil dripping from her fangs. 'No wonder she's laughing,' read the poster's caption. 'She's got Scotland's oil.' With a minority of Scottish seats the SNP's argument was easily dismissed by the government. Scotland was part of the UK, Mrs Thatcher would respond, and as the revenue was an integral part of the UK Treasury then every part of the country would benefit. Indeed, the Treasury milked North Sea oil profits through successive budgets, the supplementary petroleum duty levied in 1981 being but one example.

---

[23] Speech opening Shell UK Exploration Centre, 7/9/1979, MTF.
[24] *Truth, Lies, Scotland and Oil* (BBC Scotland) 4/6/2008.
[25] Campbell, *The Iron Lady*, 7.
[26] Devine, ed., *Scotland in the 20th Century*, 31.

'She's got Scotland's oil'

What of the Conservatives' 1974 pledge to establish an oil development fund? Unlike a promise from the same year to abolish the rates, Mrs Thatcher did not feel similarly bound by the oil fund commitment. 'Should we heed the advice of those who would have us turn it [North Sea oil revenue] into a Government-directed investment fund?' she asked in 1980. She continued: 'But when we reflect upon the record, can we really be sure that politicians make the best investment decisions? Were the millions spent by our predecessors on Portavadie,[27] or on the ships the Poles will be happily using to undercut our shipping lines, really examples of money wisely put to use? It hardly looks that way to me.' As the winning of North Sea oil was 'a miracle of free enterprise investment' (it in fact received £310 million in government cash via regional aid from 1979 to 1987), Mrs Thatcher argued, 'we must use its proceeds to create more wealth to sustain us long after the oil has been depleted. Just as free enterprise created this opportunity, so given the chance it will find the investments of the future.'[28]

It was a neat argument, but arguably Mrs Thatcher missed a trick in not establishing some sort of oil endowment.[29] Gavin McCrone submitted a paper to the Cabinet in 1976 which urged exactly that, but although discussed by ministers before the 1979 election it did not progress any further. As Sir Ian Gilmour observed, 'North Sea oil could have been used to finance a massive increase of investment in industry and in the infrastructure; the social repercussions of economic change could have been cushioned, and industry restructured and made more competitive.'[30] In other words, instead of

---

[27] The Portavadie complex was built in Argyllshire on the basis that oil had been discovered on the west shores of Loch Fyne. There was never any evidence for this, but the onus was to construct platform-building yards in return for huge government subsidy. The site was never used.

[28] Speech to Scottish Conservative conference, 9/5/1980, MTF.

[29] Shetland Islands Council did manage to negotiate the creation of an oil fund, a by-product of the control it exerted over terminal facilities at the Sullom Voe oil terminal which opened in 1981.

[30] Gilmour, *Dancing With Dogma*, 56.

suffering disproportionately from Thatcherism, Scotland could have benefited from it to a greater extent than England and Wales.

North Sea oil revenue peaked in 1986, at about the same time unemployment in Scotland reached an all-time high. Meanwhile, Norway prudently
invested its oil revenue in a large stabilisation fund which reduced pressure on
the krone's exchange rate after it rose sharply in the late 1970s. By the
beginning of the twenty-first century the fund was worth more than £350
billion. Perhaps Mrs Thatcher regretted missing the trick. Andrew Marr has
pointed out in his *History of Modern Britain* that she barely mentions the
importance of North Sea oil in her memoirs. It was almost as if she wanted to
pretend the Thatcherite revolution had occurred without the aid of Black
Gold.

SOFTLY, SOFTLY

Within months of Mrs Thatcher winning the 1979 general election she faced a
UK-wide steel strike and industrial action at British Leyland (in another non-
Thatcherite move, Leyland was ultimately 'bailed out' to the tune of £450
million). The government simply sat the steel strike out, which lasted from
January to April 1980, eventually settling below the going public sector rate at
14 per cent. The future of the Scottish steel industry was to become a running
sore for Mrs Thatcher in Scotland, and although nothing compared with the
winter of discontent that marred Callaghan's final months in office, it was
hardly a helpful beginning to her promised era of harmony where once there
was discord.

There was another portent of industrial strife to come, when in 1981 the
government initiated the closure of putatively uneconomic coal mines, including several in Scotland. Sensing that, at that particular moment, any clash with
the miners could not be won by the government, Mrs Thatcher reluctantly
engaged in a tactical retreat and the plans were abandoned. A year later, Arthur
Scargill was elected president of the National Union of Mineworkers (NUM).
His deputy was the Scottish communist Mick McGahey. The battle lines were
set for the central conflict of the Thatcher era.

The best-known industrial body in Scotland was then, as now, the STUC.
Founded in 1897, this had a long tradition of independence from the British
Trades Union Congress and controlled the most heavily unionised region of
the UK. Under Mrs Thatcher's governments, however, the STUC lost
influence it had long taken for granted. Regular meetings with the Prime
Minister – *de rigeur* with Harold Wilson – were now out of the question, and,
instead, meetings were restricted to the Industry and Employment Secretaries, Sir Keith Joseph and Jim Prior respectively, and later Scottish Office
ministers, a deliberate snub given that industrial power still resided in
Westminster. And although it got buckets of charm from George Younger,
the STUC found the doors of most Whitehall ministerial suites firmly closed
for the first time since the First World War.

Mrs Thatcher regarded trade unions, whether Scottish or British, with barely concealed contempt.[31] Within days of becoming Prime Minister, she signalled bluntly to Jim Prior that she had no intention of formulating a wages and income policy, hitherto a staple feature of the post-war consensus. Prior was well known for his desire to pursue a 'softly-softly' approach to trade union reform, but both the Prime Minister and New Right MPs were impatient for immediate action to neuter union power. The party's folk memory was still fresh. The unions had at first forced Ted Heath into a U-turn and then rewarded his flexibility by bringing down his administration. History, dictated true believers, should not be allowed to repeat itself.

It was, therefore, all the more remarkable that Prior's 1980 Employment Bill largely implemented his preferred softly-softly approach. It removed legal immunity from most secondary action and all secondary picketing, banned some forms of closed shop, and made unions liable for unlawful acts by their officials. In correcting the most obvious abuses highlighted during the winter of discontent, it kept right-wingers at bay without totally alienating the unions. In doing so, Mrs Thatcher extended to regulated employment the same rhetoric she had used for Right to Buy. Ordinary workers were now 'free to choose' whether or not to join a trade union. None of this, however, washed with the STUC. Willie Dougan of the Boilermakers' Union described the Bill as 'the most serious attack on fundamental trade union rights since the last Tory government introduced its Industrial Relations Act'.[32] But while 20,000 took to the streets of Glasgow (12,000 in Edinburgh) on 14 May 1980 to protest against the Employment Bill, the turnout was disappointing.

Once again, Mrs Thatcher had tapped into a rich vein of popular feeling that proved to be electorally rewarding, at least in England. Sufficiently emboldened, the government followed the Employment Act with death by a thousand cuts for organised labour in the UK. Legislation in 1984 meant ballots were obligatory to authorise industrial action, elect union executives and approve the use of political funds; a 1986 Act saw workers below the age of 21 lose the protection of wages councils; 1988 legislation gave strike breakers the right to sue their unions for taking disciplinary action against them, outlawed more aspects of the closed shop and tightened up ballot procedures; and in 1989, paid time off for union officials was restricted to specified activities. The 1990 Employment Act – passed in the last year of Mrs Thatcher's premiership – ended the closed shop in any form, held unions liable for unofficial action by their members, authorised selective dismissal of workers taking unofficial action, and made all secondary action unlawful. If this was Conservative payback for the unions' destruction of Heath's government in 1973–74, then it was prolonged and largely successful. Furthermore, it appeared to be effective. Between 1980 and 1982 the number of working days

---

[31] This feeling was not limited to Mrs Thatcher. Willie Ross, the long-serving Labour Scottish Secretary, used to witheringly refer to the 'Scottish Trades Union Congrouse'.
[32] Aitken, *The Bairns O' Adam*, 261–62.

lost to industrial action in Scotland fell from 1,447,000 to 634,000, a figure still above the UK average.

Rising unemployment was the main factor. From 1979 to 1987 the number of STUC-affiliated members fell from 1,090,000 to 910,942 and trade union density from a peak of 55 per cent of employed workers to just over 40 per cent. In the Borders textile industry, the Scottish Carpet Workers Union saw a decline in membership of more than 80 per cent. Public sector unions proved more resilient, remaining steady at around 80 per cent, while the National Association of Local Government Officers (NALGO) continued to grow steadily despite the government's attacks on Scottish local authorities. Most relevant unions amended their rules to enable them to follow their members into the private sector, but increases in self-employed workers, those working part-time, rising female employment and the growth of the service sector inevitably meant declining trade union membership, as did the largely foreign-owned, and therefore non-unionised, employers of Silicon Glen. When the Norwegian shipping magnate Fred Olsen met George Younger to give him bad news about his Timex plant in Dundee, for example, he bluntly informed the Scottish Secretary that if its workforce wanted to be part of the electronic age then they would have to end restrictive practices.

While Mrs Thatcher did not purposefully seek the widespread destruction of Scottish manufacturing – although a certain degree of 'shake-out' was considered both inevitable and beneficial – she did seek to further erode trade union membership by other means. Contracting out cleaning and catering services in the National Health Service, for example, was calculated to weaken the influence of health service unions (the number of STUC nominees on Scotland's health boards also fell from 32 in 1979 to none in 1991), and likewise with Compulsory Competitive Tendering in local government.

The result was a radical shift in the onward march of Labour. No longer were set-piece confrontations between the STUC and government about advancing pay and conditions, but rather about safeguarding jobs. As if to compensate for declining relevance in the industrial life of Scotland, the STUC sought actively to shore up its political relevance by continuing to advocate devolution even when most mainstream politicians abandoned it. Indeed, by the early 1990s leading Scottish trade unionists even liked to claim the STUC had played a prominent role in forcing Mrs Thatcher to resign.

'KEYNESIANISM NORTH OF THE BORDER'

Another regular feature of the rhetorical battleground in the 1980s was regional aid, almost as anathema to Mrs Thatcher as the word 'planning'. Using taxpayers' money to aid depressed areas and lure foreign business to the regions was another fixture of the post-war consensus, although aspects of it had been in place since the depression of the early 1930s. And as the Prime Minister regularly acknowledged, Tory governments had been as guilty as Labour in promoting regional aid as a cure for the nation's economic ills.

In Scotland, as in the rest of the UK, regional aid had three main sources. The Industry Act of 1972 had introduced two, Regional Development Grants (RDG) and Regional Selective Assistance (RSA), while the third came via the European Regional Development Fund, which doled out cash to Scotland's Assisted Areas. Another feature of regional policy was the deliberate 'dispersal' of government projects, agencies and jobs to the regions, most commonly Wales (the Driver and Vehicle Licensing Agency (DVLA) for example, and the Royal Mint) and Scotland (the National Savings Bank). Mrs Thatcher had inherited a pledge to disperse Ministry of Defence (MoD) and Overseas Development Agency (ODA) jobs to Glasgow and East Kilbride, respectively, although she had done her best in opposition to jettison it. The divide over this was more political than ideological. Both Teddy Taylor and George Younger, for example, supported dispersal while their English colleagues opposed it, fearing the policy would erode fragile majorities in constituencies where largely Tory-voting civil servants originally lived.

George Younger had fought to preserve the line at a December 1978 meeting of the Shadow Cabinet ('A very anti-Scottish attitude was shown',[33] he recorded in his diary), pointing out that work was already well advanced at East Kilbride and in Glasgow. Eventually, Mrs Thatcher agreed not to abandon the principle but review the detail of which departments would go. Three months after the 1979 election this review was complete. 'Four weeks ago she [Mrs Thatcher] heard me talking about it to Christopher Soames, and snapped, "You're not going to get it, none at all",' recorded Younger in his diary. 'However we have got it, the key was a deputation of Scots Tory MPs led by [Iain] Sproat who came to see her 2 weeks ago. She was so impressed that in Cabinet she backed me all the way.'

This episode demonstrated Mrs Thatcher's ability to compromise ('after hammering at you for an hour in a very aggressive way,' observed Younger, 'she can see your point of view and even change her own'), not a trait she liked to publicise, although this particular compromise was far from a victory for Younger et al. Only 1,400 MoD personnel were to be dispersed from London to Glasgow, together with 650 ODA posts to East Kilbride, just a third of those originally planned. Even so, as Younger acknowledged, 'Looking back over three months Scotland has done well in very bad circumstances.'[34]

Accompanying this reassessment of dispersal had been a general review of regional policy. To Mrs Thatcher the problem and solution were clear, and both were firmly set within her wider economic philosophy. The arguments for retaining regional aid, she decided, were social rather than economic, and although the policy would be sustained it would, like everything else, be cut down to size. In 1979 regional aid was worth £251 million for Scotland and the whole country had long been designated an Assisted Area. The chief

---

[33] Diary entry dated 4/12/1978, GYP.
[34] Ibid., 26/7/1979, GYP.

architect of the New Realism, Sir Keith Joseph, wanted to remove from that category much of the Borders and Grampian, as well as cities like Edinburgh, Aberdeen and Perth. By the time the Scottish Secretary's invisible hand had gone to work, however, most parts of Scotland were instead downgraded to Intermediate Status, the lowest possible category, and would only cease to be classified as Assisted Areas in August 1982.[35] Nevertheless, Mrs Thatcher essentially presided over a transition from generous *carte blanche* regional aid towards specific assistance. 'We say: "Yes, we do want you to go to the regions and we will give incentives for you to go to the regions. Here are the incentives.",' she explained in 1988. 'But that is totally different from [giving] incentives . . . so they choose [where] they want to go, from saying: "No you cannot go where you want to go, you must go where you do not want to go." '[36]

Usefully, Younger was able to mitigate the worst effects of this transition by alternative means. 'I was lucky in that I had the Scottish Development Agency with its own funds and we found many ingenious new ways to help industry,' he remembered in 1993. 'Margaret was suspicious of the SDA but I persuaded her to accept it by turning it into a strongly private-enterprise-orientated body. All it did was complemented by participation by private enterprise which multiplied many times the public money involved.'[37]

It was difficult to travel far in Scotland south of the Highland line (north of it a separate and older agency, the Highlands and Islands Development Board, held sway) without catching sight of the distinctive blue bow-shaped logo of the ubiquitous factory-builder, site-clearer, developer, sponsor and general refurbisher of the urban environment – the SDA. And although Mrs Thatcher's hostility to this corporatist relic of the Wilson era had cooled since she dismissed it in 1975 as a 'tartan Tony Benn', many of her acolytes remained wary. What particularly offended right-wingers were its significant powers of investment, otherwise known as intervention, while many English Tory MPs would have preferred to see it abolished altogether, jealous that their southern region did not enjoy similar benefits. New ministers like Alex Fletcher were initially also sceptical about the SDA's investment functions, although he soon realised that it played a valuable role in channelling financial assistance to small firms and in leading employment regeneration initiatives in areas hard-hit by major closures.

The Prime Minister herself set the tone at the Scottish Conservative conference in May 1979. 'It can provide temporary help for firms which have been brought low by the nation's economic ills, but which have a viable future,' she explained. 'The SDA can also help in providing finance for new businesses. We would prefer to see them grow up – as their predecessors did – independently, individually, without State aid and certainly without State interference. [But] the confidence, the cash resources, and the vitality of the

---

[35] Intermediate Status also afforded continued access to European structural funding.
[36] Interview for *Glasgow Herald*, 31/10/1988, MTF.
[37] *Scotland on Sunday* 17/10/1993.

private sector have suffered. Until we can restore them, there is a gap which the SDA can fill.'[38] The word 'until' was important. Mrs Thatcher had effectively given the SDA a temporary reprieve, and indeed it would be abolished, or rather replaced, by the time she left office 11 years later.

Meanwhile new guidelines were issued, trimming rather than abolishing the SDA's investment functions by reducing its capacity to take equity shares in industry. Younger also appointed a new chief executive by the name of George Mathewson. A Nationalist by inclination, Mathewson had a successful background in the electronics sector and recognised the importance of promoting advanced technology in collaboration with the private sector. Under his charge, the SDA's small business advice and investment activities expanded rapidly, something of which Mrs Thatcher must surely have approved. His stewardship also demonstrated the Agency could back entrepreneurship via its New Ventures Unit. 'My goal at the SDA was creative, catalytic and commercial,' Mathewson recalled, 'to make sure the government got enough punch for its money and to move it towards output as opposed to need.'[39]

In 1982–83, the SDA received £100 million in government funding, and its Highlands equivalent close to £30 million. Importantly, this was in addition to already high levels of regional aid in Scotland, comprising £287 million in RDGs and some £20 million of RSA. It was, therefore, not surprising that one Cabinet minister told the *Daily Telegraph* that George Younger was practising 'Keynesianism north of the border'. This was probably stretching a point, but conversely it was surprising that Mrs Thatcher did so little, relatively speaking, to prevent it. Therein lay one of the paradoxes of Thatcherism as applied to Scotland: even when the government did not act in a strictly Thatcherite way, its ideological and rhetorical antipathy to policies like regional aid prevented it reaping political benefits. 'The biggest problem was that because we were seen to be ideologically opposed to state intervention,' reflected David McLetchie, 'we didn't take credit for steps we were actually taking and therefore allowed Labour to lead the debate and present it otherwise.'[40]

Edward Heath used to distinguish between productive and non-productive public expenditure and the SDA certainly fell into the former category. It was just that Mrs Thatcher did not want to brag about it. It therefore became a cliché of the Thatcher years that economic and social ills could not be cured simply by 'throwing money at them'. But far from providing proof that Keynesianism flourished north of the border, the SDA simply demonstrated how limited Scottish Office control of central government policy actually was. Keynesianism required control over the level of demand in the economy, a power the SDA could hardly claim to possess.

---

[38] Speech to Scottish Conservative conference, 12/5/1979, MTF.
[39] Interview with Sir George Mathewson, 22/5/2007.
[40] Interview with David McLetchie MSP, 6/10/2008.

'HONG KONG ECONOMICS'

Mrs Thatcher was fond of harking back to the days when enterprising Scots led the way in industrial and business innovation, the implication being that this spirit had been stifled by socialism but could be reawakened by the freedoms and choice of Thatcherism. 'For you helped to create the industrial revolution in this country, and elsewhere,' she enthused in 1985. 'You sent engineers, scientists and businessmen the world over in pursuit of business opportunities.'[41]

Some seasoned commentators, however, believed the Prime Minister had fundamentally misunderstood the nature of Scotland's brand of enterprising initiative. 'This small nation has bred plenty of spectacular entrepreneurs, and has seen plenty of colossal advancements,' wrote Neal Ascherson in *Stone Voices*. '[But] in Scotland . . . there is an instinct that conspicuous personal success must involve some loss of Scottishness. The young are urged to "get on", but never quite forgiven for having got on.' He continued: 'With a few exceptions, Scottish enterprise has never been individualistic. On the contrary, it has been a matter of small, authoritarian oligarchies, tightly controlling their own recruitment and run as disciplined collectives for the benefit of a group – usually a family, sometimes a particular district, and often both. The internal principles on which these private partnerships were run had little to do with open competition.'[42]

This was a convenient, and arguably romanticised, view of Scottish enterprise. Perhaps shaping Mrs Thatcher's views to the contrary was her friendship with the Scottish businessman Hector Laing,[43] a UK Tory Party treasurer whom she admired both for his entrepreneurial flair and charitable deeds. First as managing director and then as chairman, Laing had turned United Biscuits into a dynamic international food group operating in 22 countries, with sales worth more than £1.5 billion. Helpfully, he also donated more than £1 million to Conservative Party coffers during Mrs Thatcher's leadership. Other successful Scottish businessmen were also naturally sympathetic to the Thatcherite project, most notably the industrialist Sir Norman (later Lord) Macfarlane and the merchant banker Angus (later Sir Angus) Grossart.

Second only to the City of London in UK terms, Edinburgh in the 1980s fast became a financial centre of European stature. Finance houses in the Scottish capital had £1.6 billion under management, and fund managers increasingly specialised in Japan, the USA, North Sea oil and high technology. 'The financial services sector in Edinburgh in the late 1970s was minute,' recalled the Dutch-born financier Peter de Vink. 'Looking back they fitted together incredibly well [Mrs Thatcher and Edinburgh's financial sector] and anyone in business was

---

[41] Speech to Scottish Conservative conference, 10/5/1985, MTF.
[42] Ascherson, *Stone Voices*, 176 & 238–39.
[43] He later became Sir Hector, and finally Lord Laing of Dunphail in Mrs Thatcher's resignation honours list.

absolutely full square behind the Conservative Party. It was unthinkable that any chairman of a substantial company would have voted socialist.'[44]

Powerful Scottish businessmen, however, were still capable of forcing Mrs Thatcher to compromise. Peter de Vink had been involved in resisting attempts by the HSBC and Standard Chartered to take over the Edinburgh-based Royal Bank of Scotland (RBS), despite Mrs Thatcher's better instincts, while high-profile lobbying ensured that instead of grouping a regional network of Trustee Savings Banks (TSB) into one, Great Britain-wide TSB, Scotland retained its own prior to its sale.[45] As the Thatcher revolution gathered pace, these banks, not to mention Scotland's other financial institutions, began to thrust themselves at potential borrowers, offering mortgages, credit or personal loans, thereby fuelling the consumer boom which became a hallmark of the 1980s.

Scottish entrepreneurs also benefited from the government's emphasis on helping small business start-ups. As the former Scottish Tory MP Anna McCurley noted in 1989, Glasgow was 'a city which has not got one single Conservative MP, and yet the entrepreneurship has just mushroomed. And the funny thing is it's mushrooming in the 25 to 30 year old category who wouldn't think in a million years of voting Tory. Yet they are the Thatcher children.'[46] As Mrs Thatcher told the Glasgow Chamber of Commerce in January 1983, 'small businesses are vital to the health of Scotland's future'.[47]

'I saw no reason why, in the long run, the Scottish people would not once again embrace the spirit of free enterprise which Adam Smith had espoused first in the eighteenth century and which had put Scotland at the forefront of economic progress,' recalled Baroness Thatcher in 2009. 'I was convinced that the people of Scotland were no less entrepreneurial than those south of the border given the right opportunities.'[48]

Yet throughout the 1980s Scotland consistently lagged behind England in terms of new business start-ups, a problem which persisted into the 1990s and beyond. The economist Brian Ashcroft attributed this 'deficiency of enter-prise' to Scotland's relatively low wealth, an under-representation of manage-rial and professional skills, and a plant structure which to some extent militated against workers gaining experience of small firms. '[I]f the govern-ment is serious about raising firm formation rates in Scotland,' Ashcroft concluded in 1990, 'it would do better to focus on certain aspects of the regions' economic structure than on repeated exhortations to local residents to embrace the "enterprise culture".'[49]

So it was in financial services rather than new business that Thatcherism really succeeded in Scotland, constituting a small but influential part of Mrs Thatcher's Scottish support base which probably helped Edinburgh constituencies like

[44] Interview with Peter de Vink, 13/6/2008.
[45] The Scottish TSB, however, finally succumbed on merging with Lloyds in 1995.
[46] Campbell, *The Iron Lady*, 245.
[47] Speech to Glasgow Chamber of Commerce centenary, 28/1/1983, MTF.
[48] Interview with Baroness Thatcher, 20/1/2009.
[49] Ashcroft et al., *New Firm Formation*, 19–20.

Malcolm Rifkind's Pentlands seat remain true blue until 1997. Perhaps with this in mind, the Prime Minister regularly applauded the financial sector in her Scottish speeches, while the likes of Peter de Vink reciprocated by raising millions of pounds for the Scottish Conservative Party. Despite their enthusiasm, however, few Scottish businessmen actually believed that Adam Smith's 'invisible hand' could alone do the job and most were interventionist with a small 'i', as evidenced by the fight to save Ferranti and RBS. The invisible hand, they believed, needed just a little bit of guidance.

Meanwhile, the Chancellor Sir Geoffrey Howe was determined to encourage latent Scottish entrepreneurialism by other means. Originally proposed by Professor Peter Hall in 1977, the concept of Enterprise Zones (EZs) had been embraced by Sir Geoffrey in opposition. He was impressed by the argument that urban economic decline was due to the state stifling entrepreneurial initiative through taxation, state intervention and planning restrictions. By contrast, EZs would be free from the usual planning procedures, rent controls and certain business rates and taxation. The genial Sir Geoffrey cited Hong Kong in his favour, not to mention ghettoised Huguenots, Jews and Irish immigrants whose latent entrepreneurial and capitalist instincts were unleashed within certain geographical constraints.

Initially, England was to get three or four EZs, while Scotland, Wales and Northern Ireland were to get one each. Mrs Thatcher unveiled the locations in July 1980. 'We are creating an opportunity unequalled in modern times,'[50] she declared, announcing that Clydebank near Glasgow was to be the first part of Scotland to emulate Hong Kong Island. Yet the anticipated 'Hong Kong economics' did not work out quite as planned. In terms of attracting industry Clydebank was certainly a success; by April 1984 229 companies had moved to premises in the zone with a projection of 2,577 jobs. Fifty-eight of those companies, however, were relocations, existing firms (the best known of which was Radio Clyde) simply moving to take advantage of the EZ's concessions. On the other hand, 1,551 jobs were created in new companies, although the vast majority were provided in SDA premises. So far from vindicating the free market, the whole exercise underlined the importance of public intervention in persuading entrepreneurial capitalism to settle in otherwise barren parts of Scotland's former industrial heartland. By April 1984, £19.5 million of public money had been invested in the Clydebank EZ compared with £16.25 million from the private sector.[51]

Enterprise Zones also became an unintentional extension of the government's scaled-down regional policy. Clydebank had been chosen in the wake of the closure of its Singer factory, and additional EZs soon followed similar industrial setbacks in Dundee (after the demise of Timex) and Invergordon (where the aluminium smelter closed in 1982). This led to inevitable confusion over whether the Zones were actually capitalism at work or simply old-

---

[50] Hansard 989 c1313.
[51] Keating & Boyle, *Re-making Urban Scotland*, 58.

fashioned interventionism. Nevertheless, a fourth Scottish EZ, in Inverclyde, was designated in March 1988.

'LAME DUCKS IN A GROUSE MOOR SANCTUARY'

The Invergordon crisis presented another example of Mrs Thatcher's willingness to compromise on long-held principles. Its closure was an unhappy side effect of the recession coupled with financial problems at British Aluminium, and despite initial reluctance to bail out the Highlands' aluminium smelter, the Prime Minister relented in face of pressure from the Scottish Office and coughed up a temporary £5 million subsidy which, in the event, was never taken up. Despite strenuous efforts to find another buyer, not to mention the offer to Alcan – which had just bought British Aluminium – of a rescue package worth £25 million over five years, by mid 1982 George Younger was forced to concede that one could not be found.

Central government cash also magically appeared when rumours surfaced in early 1981 that the automobile company Peugeot-Citroen wanted to close its Talbot car factory at Linwood and instead concentrate its car manufacturing activities in France. Younger offered it £40 million in grants to remain in Scotland, but on 11 February the closure of Linwood with a loss of 4,800 jobs was confirmed, provoking widespread political fury but curiously little fight from its traditionally militant workforce. With such handouts seemingly on offer to failing Scottish industries despite the recession, there was predictable southern resentment. One headline in the *Daily Telegraph* even referred sardonically to 'Lame ducks in a grouse moor sanctuary'.[52]

Despite the offered bailout, Linwood to Mrs Thatcher was the ultimate symbol of previous Conservative governments' folly in terms of regional policy. 'Eighteen out of nineteen years in which that factory was at Linwood it made a loss,' she stormed in 1988. 'Now you cannot go on making a loss, but it was even worse than that in a way because when it started there, all the wages became much higher than they were locally and therefore all your small local businesses could not compete for the labour and therefore they went out of business.'[53] The Prime Minister could also have added appalling labour relations and a string of unsuccessful models to Linwood's litany of woes.

Linwood and Invergordon, however, were not the only flagship developments from the Macmillan era that failed during the recession. The pulp mill at Corpach also closed during 1981, as did the British Leyland commercial vehicle plant at Bathgate, depriving the Ravenscraig steelworks (itself a flagship) of another much-valued local customer. 'I think it was actually the closure of Scotland's more recent industries which caused the most resentment,' recalled the journalist Keith Aitken. 'There was a feeling that they had come to Scotland as of right.'[54]

---

[52] *Daily Telegraph* 21/3/1984.
[53] Interview for *Glasgow Herald*, 31/10/1988, MTF.
[54] Interview with Keith Aitken, 29/10/2008.

The sheer size of Scotland's manufacturing sector (42.4 per cent of Scottish employment was manual in 1981, compared with 38.5 per cent in England and Wales) meant that a labour shake out would have an inevitable impact on the number of Scots out of work. The problem was also compounded by a traditional reliance on overseas investment in so-called 'branch factories'. In 1980 one estimate put the number of Scottish jobs which relied on foreign owners at 100,000, or 16 per cent of the workforce, much higher than in other parts of the UK. During a slump, foreign companies instinctively cut back abroad before slimming down at home, and that was precisely what happened in Scotland. In 1979 alone a significant number of branch factories shed labour or closed down in Scotland, leading to some 28,000 job losses within months of Mrs Thatcher's election victory. It was therefore natural for the closures to be associated with the beginning of her premiership, when in fact many owed more to the onset of an international recession than to nascent Thatcherism.

Singer had been the first to go, closing down its sewing machine plant at Clydebank with the loss of 4,500 jobs. This was followed swiftly by Monsanto in Ayrshire, Pye TMC at Livingston, Wiggins Teape at Corpach, VF Corporation at Greenock and Massey Ferguson at Kilmarnock. These were not small factories and employed hundreds, if not thousands, of people. 'One of the dangers now facing Scotland is that the new industries coming to replace the old will be in the same position in 10 or 20 years time', was the gloomy assessment of Ray Perman at the *Financial Times*, 'and today's bright hopes on the frontiers of technology will be tomorrow's peripheral plants with high overheads to be closed down when world capacity has to be cut back.'[55]

This assessment was prescient (see Chapter 9), but instead of encouraging mobility such closures bred defensiveness and resistance to change. After each, the Scottish Office press team would send out a short expression of regret coupled with the explanation that it had been a 'commercial decision'. And in speech after speech ministers emphasised that Scottish industry was part of a UK economy going through a structural change, while warning that government intervention would only act as, at best, a palliative.

Although arguably true, this approach smacked of insensitivity towards those suffering the distress of losing their jobs. Even Robin Duthie, the SDA's chairman, reflected elements of public opinion when he likened monetarism to a 'blunt instrument',[56] and implied that those in the south-east of England did not appreciate just how serious the problem of unemployment was in places like the west of Scotland. He even doubted the wisdom of reducing capacity at the cost of so many jobs, a point which to true believers was close to heresy.

Despite the considerable autonomy of the Scottish Office and the spending power of the SDA, however, the machinery of Scottish government could achieve little beyond damage limitation. Major decisions were taken by the

---

[55] *Financial Times* 9/11/1979.
[56] Drucker & Drucker, eds, *Scottish Government Yearbook 1982*, 170.

Department of Industry in Whitehall, although Scotland did have advantages in terms of cash and administration. 'Your reporter recently went to see how the West Midlands were coping with the same kind of trouble,' observed *The Economist*. 'The comparison – through no fault of the Midlanders – is overwhelmingly in favour of the Scots.'[57]

It is also unlikely that Labour, despite all its protestations, would have been more successful in staving off what seemed, in retrospect, inevitable. Peugeot-Citroen was a prime example. Despite the offer of substantial financial assistance, its owners pointed out that even if the government paid the full cost of the tooling and production of every new model at Linwood, the plant would still lose money.

Inevitably, the blame was personalised. Noisy crowds of demonstrators greeted Mrs Thatcher whenever she visited Scottish factories, including her tour of the Falmer clothing factory in Cumnock, the UK headquarters of which was located in her Finchley constituency. 'There were coachloads of demonstrators, some of them hurling eggs,' Denis Thatcher recounted to the newspaper editor John Junor. 'At one stage, when Margaret went to her car, she discovered it locked and the chauffeur absent having a cup of tea . . . an egg was thrown and deftly caught by one of her police bodyguards.' By the time the Prime Minister left Falmer a crowd of about 1,000 had gathered to boo and whistle as her car departed for a weekend at Balmoral. When her entourage stopped in Inverness a man carrying a sheaf of papers burst through a security cordon and got within 15 feet of Mrs Thatcher before being thwarted by a policeman's flying rugby tackle.

Instead of colouring Mrs Thatcher's view of working-class Scots, however, the Falmer episode induced a crisis of confidence in the Prime Minister. 'It had clearly had an effect on her,' judged Junor having visited the Thatchers at Downing Street shortly after the Prime Minister returned from Scotland. 'She wondered just how popular she was with people.'[58] Clearly, public reaction, and therefore Scottish public opinion, mattered to Mrs Thatcher, whatever the popular perception.

By early 1982, there were glimmers of hope that the economic tide had turned, the recession having peaked, or at least so Mrs Thatcher claimed, in 1981. A small but perceptible increase in output did occur in the third and fourth quarters, while business optimism also improved. But in August of that year, Scotland's oldest manufacturing company, Carron (founded in 1759), fell into the receiver's hands. Indeed, between 1979 and 1981 Scotland lost close to 11 per cent of its industrial output and 20 per cent of its industrial employment, a fall dramatic enough to constitute full-scale deindustrialisation.

Mrs Thatcher, however, dismissed curtly calls for economic retreat. 'You turn if you want to,' she declared at the 1980 Tory conference. 'The lady's not

---

[57] *The Economist* 10/9/1983.

[58] Junor, *Listening for a Midnight Tram*, 262. The local Labour MP, George Foulkes, had leaked details of Mrs Thatcher's visit to the protestors.

for turning.'[59] Sir Geoffrey Howe's 1981 budget indicated that she was serious. By implementing yet more cuts to an already depressed economy, Cabinet wets geared up for open revolt amid public furore. 'However beautiful the strategy,' Sir Ian Gilmour reputedly remarked at one meeting, quoting Churchill in protest, 'you should occasionally look at the results.'[60] Meanwhile 364 academic economists argued in a letter to *The Times* that further deflating demand had 'no basis in economic theory'.[61]

When, in the months following the budget, output began to rise while inflation and interest rates started to fall, it appeared that Sir Geoffrey's brave gamble had paid off. And while claims that the recession was over sounded hollow in Scotland, Mrs Thatcher's speech to the Scottish Tory conference more than a month later on 8 May continued to list selectively engineering triumphs and new factories. 'I could go on,' she said:

> But every single one of these achievements – and many others that I have not mentioned – have one thing in common. They mean jobs for Scotland. Jobs which earn their keep. Jobs which make a real and a lasting contribution to the national balance sheet. Jobs which help to pay for better living standards, and better services for all our people, in the years to come. Jobs won not by Government purchase, and therefore extra tax on successful Scottish businesses. But by the resource, the perseverance, and the aggressive salesmanship of Scottish firms and Scottish people. More power to their elbow!

As for the 364 academic economists, 'Their confidence in the accuracy of their own predictions' left the Prime Minister 'breathless'. 'But having myself been brought up over the shop,' she continued, 'I sometimes wonder whether they back their forecasts with their money.'[62] On the budget, however, Mrs Thatcher was evasive. The government, Hugo Young thought she appeared to claim, 'was grappling with global forces, as well as past cowardice and folly. Public spending was up, so it had to be prudently paid for. That was the reason for the tough budget. The pain, she implied, was good for you. And it was already showing its therapeutic effects.'[63]

Those therapeutic effects were slow to manifest themselves in Scotland. A high pound (which, John Campbell asserts, Mrs Thatcher believed 'was a good thing'[64] for patriotic reasons) fuelled by North Sea oil exposed Scottish companies to an unprecedented onslaught of takeovers. One was Chartered Consolidated's 1983 bid to take over Anderson Strathclyde, which manufactured underground coalmining machinery. The invisible hand of the

---

[59] Speech to Conservative Party conference, 10/10/1980, MTF.
[60] Gilmour, *Dancing With Dogma*, 46.
[61] *The Times* 30/3/1981.
[62] Speech to Scottish Conservative conference, 8/5/1981, MTF.
[63] Young, *One of Us*, 217.
[64] Campbell, *The Iron Lady*, 79.

Scottish Office again went to work, lobbying for the bid to be referred to the Monopolies and Mergers Commission (MMC) on the grounds that such a move would prove detrimental to the Scottish economy. When the MMC concurred, its recommendation was promptly overruled by the government. Norman Tebbit, the Industry Secretary and a cynic when it came to ring-fencing Scottish companies, then issued a statement saying that future takeover bids would only be referred to the MMC on competitive grounds.

Yet despite these widespread changes to the Scottish economy, industrial and employment structures were transformed with relatively little fuss and attention. As factory after factory closed there were numerous, but ineffective, protests and few repeats of the 'work-in' spirit of the early 1970s (the 1981 Lee Jeans occupation in Greenock was a rare, and successful, exception). Opponents crudely depicted government policy as being driven by market forces, while Labour claimed increased state intervention would stimulate development not only in Scotland but in the inner cities of the south. Even so, many people found it difficult to believe that the devolutionary panacea of a Scottish Assembly could have mitigated any of the recession's worst manifestations. The argument that the Scottish economy could develop 'not by the invisible private hand of Adam Smith,' as the Labour Chancellor Hugh Dalton once remarked, 'but by the visible public hand of the Labour Party',[65] now sounded both anachronistic and unrealistic.

At the Scottish Conservative conference in Perth each May, Mrs Thatcher's retort to Scotland's industrial woes was simple. 'That is but one side of the picture,' she reasoned, for example, in 1982. 'For while too many trades contract, some of the most famous names in Scottish industry have been proving their ability to fight back and win the vital orders in the markets of the world in the teeth of cut-throat international competition.' The examples she gave were firms like John Brown Engineering, Macfarlane Clansman of Glasgow, NEI Parsons, the Howden Group and the Borders' woollen textile industry, but there were more every year. 'These are the achievements of individual Scots,' Mrs Thatcher said. 'For jobs and markets are not won in Whitehall, nor even – dare I say it – in St Andrew's House.' She continued: 'Our task as politicians is to shape the climate in which Scottish thrift and enterprise can earn their due rewards again. And that we have done: by scrapping confiscatory taxation; by dismantling the abuses of monopoly; by better balance in the books of public spending; and, above all, by the steady restoration of more honest money.'[66]

Despite Mrs Thatcher's roll-call of success at each conference, the over-riding impression during the 1980s was of job losses and factory closures. It is possible that the editorial instincts of the Scottish media, naturally inclined towards bad news, helped reinforce that impression. 'Our narrative was one of devastating industrial decline and Government heartlessness,' recalled

---

[65] Dalton, *High Tide and After*, 153.
[66] Speech to SCUA Centenary, 26/11/1982, MTF.

BBC Scotland's business and economics correspondent Robin Aitken, who began reporting in 1981. 'But . . . if BBC impartiality meant anything, we would have balanced our story by emphasising the growing banking, oil and electronics industries. Instead, we constantly lamented the closure of shipyards and fretted about the ailing Ravenscraig steelworks.'[67]

Fretting about the ailing Ravenscraig steelworks near Motherwell occupied a lot of ministerial time during the 1980s, and in many respects sums up the paradoxical nature of Thatcherism in Scotland. At face value, Ravenscraig was the archetypal lame duck, a colossal testament to the ability of the postwar consensus to contrive industrial jobs in an area hundreds of miles from its main market. Although Ravenscraig could produce 3 million tonnes of steel a year, demand in Scotland never exceeded 2 million; and while this surplus steel was often of very good quality, trying to sell it in competition with foreign plants and other state-run steelworks in Wales was hopeless. So to Mrs Thatcher Ravenscraig should have been a prime candidate for early closure.

Yet for almost the whole of the Thatcher decade Ravenscraig represented a line the Prime Minister would not cross, much like the NHS, rail privatisation and Mortgage Interest Tax Relief. Twice, in 1982 and 1985, she granted it three-year reprieves at taxpayers' expense, buying into the Scottish Office argument that a steel industry was essential to the Scottish economy and that such a loss of jobs, estimated at more than 10,000, would simply be unacceptable.

So instead of dispensing with Ravenscraig, Thatcherism formed a protective barrier around one small corner of industrial Scotland. Indeed, it became a test of the government's commitment to what remained of Scotland's traditional manufacturing sector. Nevertheless, in the first three years of Mrs Thatcher's premiership, the workforce at Ravenscraig fell by 2,000 to 4,400, and in 1982 it was announced that its fate would be determined by the Cabinet. There was also a European context. In August 1981 the European Commission ordered the phasing out of government subsidies for steel, a policy Britain attempted to implement – unlike most of its fellow member states.

The Scottish Lobby also kicked into gear to prevent its closure. George Younger even pre-empted the Cabinet's decision during a speech in Peebles in which he asserted that it was 'our duty to see that our steel industry survives in a condition ready to take advantage of the economic recovery', although he conceded that 'trimming and reorganization'[68] would be necessary. Gavin Laird, general secretary of the Amalgamated Engineering Union, and more importantly Tommy Brennan of the steel union, were on side, as was the Industry Secretary Patrick Jenkin. (Ferdinand Mount in the Downing Street Policy Unit also strongly argued for it to be kept open for as long as possible). Only a few Tories on the fringes of the party, like the journalist and

---

[67] *Mail on Sunday* 17/2/2007.
[68] *The Times* 6/12/1982.

prospective candidate Michael Fry, said openly that it should be allowed to close. For Younger to have accepted that inevitability, however, would have looked like surrender, while an impending general election also focused ministerial minds as the Cabinet worked towards a decision. The Scottish Secretary indulged in a tried-and-tested Scottish Office trick by hinting at resignation even though it was unlikely to be carried through. 'Mr Younger can be relied upon to do the decent thing,' judged *The Times*, 'and resigning over Ravenscraig would not be at all decent.'[69] But at the decisive Cabinet meeting in December 1982 it was the Prime Minister's voice which proved crucial in saving, or rather reprieving, the steelworks for three years. In Scotland, politics beat economics more often than Mrs Thatcher would have liked to admit.

THE ECONOMIC MIRACLE OF SILICON GLEN

Scotland's growing electronics industry, the so-called 'Silicon Glen', was, along with Edinburgh's financial sector and Aberdeen's North Sea oil industry, a favourite economic refrain of Mrs Thatcher's, proof that all was in fact well in the land of Adam Smith. A 70-mile-wide corridor stretching between Ayrshire and Tayside, which at its height employed around 40,000 people in microelectronics, Silicon Glen was indeed a rare economic success story for Scotland in the 1980s, albeit one which proved to be a medium-term mirage.

Companies such as IBM, Honeywell, Ferranti and Burroughs had been in Scotland since the 1940s, but by the early 1980s few major manufacturers of computers and semiconductors were not represented on the Scottish roster. Ironically it was state aid rather than free enterprise which attracted most employers. A plentiful supply of cheap, mainly female, semi-skilled labour was another factor, while European tariffs also made access to the European market desirable.

'National Semiconductor – investing over £100 million at Greenock,' recited Mrs Thatcher at the 1985 Scottish Tory conference. 'Hewlett-Packard – spending £10 million on its plant near Edinburgh. Motorola £22 million at East Kilbride.' She went on:

And a Japanese Company Shin-Etsu are [*sic*] investing £35 million at Livingston. And, this very week, another Japanese firm at Livingston – Mitsubishi Electric, the first ever Japanese video assembly factory outside Japan. Then there's IBM – £8 million at Greenock . . . Now, why? Why are they coming to Scotland? Are they coming to Scotland out of public duty? Or because perhaps in some cases some of their forebears came from Scotland?

---

[69] *The Times* 10/12/1982.

Or, in the Japanese case, is it a yen for access to the best golf courses in the world? As Eliza Doolittle might have said, but didn't – not remotely likely.[70]

Humour, especially with a Scottish audience, was never Mrs Thatcher's forte. But while George Younger's jaunts to the land of the rising sun were popular with the media and sometimes yielded results, the aim was frequently quixotic and did not quite tally with the Prime Minister's stated aims. The financial inducements required to attract inward investment were often substantial, and could not ensure that once foreign companies had set up shop in Scotland's Central Belt, that they did not leave as soon as cold economic winds began blowing across the glen.

Even so, the government pursued zealously inward investment, not least because it was easier to get substantial projects from abroad than stimulate them domestically. The result was exactly the kind of short-termism Mrs Thatcher claimed to despise. Although by 1996 Silicon Glen produced 35 per cent of Europe's personal computers, by the beginning of the twenty-first century more than 10,000 workers had been made redundant as many foreign giants scaled back their overseas commitments.

Younger even rebranded existing promotional efforts to form the enticingly named agency 'Locate in Scotland', in order to give Scotland the edge in attracting overseas business. Again, this perceived favouritism upset English right-wingers, while a Scottish Affairs Select Committee report even argued that the Scottish effort cut across the United Kingdom initiative and should be closed down. Norman Tebbit agreed, but when Whitehall hostility was leaked to the press in 1984, it simply strengthened the Scottish Lobby's hand in rebuffing assimilation within a UK-wide promotional campaign.

'SCOTLAND IS NOT THE ONLY COUNTRY'

'It would overstate the case to argue that Thatcher and her close colleagues planned for mass unemployment,' assessed the academic E. H. H. Green, 'for it beggars belief that any politician or any government could have embraced the idea of the economic losses and social hardship that accompanied the joblessness of the 1980s.'[71] Nevertheless, the first Thatcher government's approach to unemployment was certainly different, redefining what was considered by the public and Parliament to be an acceptable level.

In Scotland, that definition was sharply revised upwards. The double whammy of monetarism and the recession pushed Scottish unemployment to levels not seen in 50 years. Even as early as February 1980 the jobless total reached its worse level since the outbreak of the Second World War, having averaged 6.4 per cent between 1973 and 1979. In 1981 it was even worse.

---

[70] Speech to Scottish Conservative conference, 10/5/1985, MTF.
[71] Green, *Thatcher*, 69.

'With 250,000 Scots on the dole and declining industrial production it is little wonder that the Iron Lady does not want to meet the people,' declared the 79 Group, a left-wing sect of the SNP. 'The Scottish Resistance to Thatcher has begun in earnest.'[72] Mrs Thatcher protested, correctly, that unemployment was not a problem specific to any one part of the UK. 'England is not the only country, nor Scotland, nor Wales, nor indeed, the whole of Great Britain, which has suffered from much much higher unemployment,' she told STV in 1986. 'It has afflicted the whole of Europe, as we know, and it is one of the problems of the European Economic Community.'[73]

Claims that Thatcherite economics were exacerbating a north–south divide drew an equally sharp response. 'Some of the most prosperous areas of the United Kingdom are in Scotland and the manual wages in Scotland are the second highest,' the Prime Minister told regional lobby journalists in 1985. She continued: 'There are quite a lot of long-term unemployed also in the south-east and of course in the south-west where unemployment has always been considerably high. So just do not say north–south divide. Do not imagine some line drawn across and everything north of that is very difficult and everything south of that is all right. That is an oversimplification of the problem.'[74]

Even if talk of a north–south divide was an oversimplification, Scotland also appeared to be experiencing an east–west split. While North Sea oil had a major impact on the economies of Shetland and the North East, and stimulated financial institutions in Edinburgh, Glasgow and much of the west coast continued to experience decline. The growth of Silicon Glen cut across all of this, but for a nation which liked to present itself as a cohesive social and political entity bravely battling against Thatcherism, the fact that many Scots were enjoying highly paid jobs while others queued up at the dole office was an uncomfortable contrast. Scottish Office ministers frequently pointed to the West Midlands, where unemployment was much worse.

Again, Mrs Thatcher tried to inject some realism into the criticism high unemployment levels attracted. 'We are not going to rid Scotland or Great Britain of the scourge of unemployment by mouthing empty slogans,'[75] she cautioned in 1981. The figures emanating from the Scottish Office indicated that, in any case, 'empty slogans' would have been an inadequate response, although Mrs Thatcher's habit of tinkering with the method by which unemployment was measured did not help her case.

Although the decline in industrial production in Scotland was not quite as bad as that in the UK as a whole, total employment in that sector fell until September 1980 by 77,000, 61,000 of which was from manufacturing. A month earlier the *Daily Record* had emblazoned its front page with the

---

[72] *79 Group News* 5/1981. The headline was: 'Thatcher puts Scotland on the dole'.
[73] Interview with STV, 4/9/1986, MTF.
[74] Press Conference for regional lobby correspondents, 10/6/1985, MTF.
[75] Speech to Scottish Conservative conference, 8/5/1981, MTF.

headline: 'WANTED: prime minister urgently required to take over from failed incumbent. Must care about people, find jobs for two million (241,267 in Scotland). Salary £30,430.'[76] Another bitter pill for those out of work had been the government's decision to end the index-linking of benefits and pensions to average earnings, and instead peg them to the retail price index. 'The system of social benefits we inherited was telling young people that living on benefit was an acceptable substitute for being in work,' the Prime Minister explained in a 1988 Scottish speech. 'So some young people were choosing to be idle. That was wrong – so we stopped it.'[77] From Mrs Thatcher's experience at the Ministry of Pensions in the 1960s, wrote John Campbell, 'she retained the conviction that the benefit system was a wasteful mechanism for recycling money from the hard-working to the lazy'.[78]

Every sector of Scottish employment, meanwhile, was proportionately affected, the greatest hit being textiles, engineering and metal manufacturing, but also smaller drops in construction due to massive cuts in government capital expenditure and house building. By May 1981, total registered unemployment reached 288,200. Central and southern Scotland bore the brunt, although the Western Isles saw the largest proportional increase. Decreasing demand for food and drink accounted for the loss of 6,000 jobs during 1981, while many whisky distilleries – which supplied Mrs Thatcher with her favourite tipple – either worked short-time or closed down completely. Ministers pointed to global recession and the need to fight inflation, but even accepting that, the UK, and particularly Scotland, still had proportionately higher unemployment than comparable countries on the continent and beyond. All industrialised countries may have been in the same boat, but the British boat was sinking much faster than the others.

Still the numbers rose. 'The Government's economic policy', lamented the academic Henry Drucker, 'which has led to a doubling of unemployment – to 324,709 in May 1982 – has not produced any coherent response from Labour.'[79] Indeed, Labour was then so distracted by internal ideological disputes that it failed to articulate a united critique of rising unemployment, let alone propose a solution. It seemed that Scotland, much like the rest of the UK, had come to see mass unemployment as an unavoidable fact of modern political reality. As Hugo Young observed, 'How to stop worrying and live with unemployment was one of the principal lessons Thatcherism administered to the country, and it achieved a permanent social shift in the process.'[80]

Again, it was difficult to pin rising unemployment exclusively on the actions of Mrs Thatcher and her government. Although it made sense for Labour to

---

[76] *Daily Record* 8/1980.
[77] Speech to Scottish Conservative conference, 13/5/1988, MTF.
[78] Campbell, *The Iron Lady*, 173–74.
[79] McCrone, ed., *Scottish Government Yearbook 1983*, 24.
[80] Young, *One of Us*, 534.

designate 1979 as year zero in social and economic terms, Scottish unemployment had in fact been increasing, in fits and starts, since the mid 1960s, and had for long outstripped that of England, reflecting long-term problems with traditional heavy industry. Labour and the Conservatives had also sought to outdo the other in attacking benefit fraud and 'voluntary' joblessness, with the effect that blame shifted steadily from government to the victims of unemployment.

The Conservatives, however, brought a particular zeal to these arguments. 'I grew up in the '30s with an unemployed father,' Norman Tebbit told the 1981 Tory conference. 'He didn't riot. He got on his bike and looked for work, and he kept looking 'til he found it.'[81] Although Tebbit was arguing that the jobless should follow new jobs, he failed to recognise that in many parts of Scotland the unemployed could have cycled for days and not found any. Even so, the combined employment growth provided by Silicon Glen, the financial services sector and North Sea oil did prevent a fall in Scotland's total employment figures between 1983 and 1987, a phenomenon which surprised even Gavin McCrone at the Scottish Office.[82] Thousands of jobs may have gone in manufacturing, but a related broadening of the Scottish economy had replaced a lot, if not all, of the employment lost in traditional industries.

Fear of unemployment, however, often proved as damaging to self-confidence as unemployment itself, particularly for Scotland's younger workforce. The 'baby boom' of the early to mid 1960s had produced a bulge in new entrants to the labour market and in the midst of a recession the inexperienced and unskilled were at a considerable disadvantage. The result was youth unemployment on an unprecedented scale. By 1983 a third of male, and half of female, under-25s in Scotland were without work.

Because youth joblessness rose even faster than overall unemployment, it posed a particular problem for the government. The responsibility for tackling this resided with the Manpower Services Commission (MSC), established in 1974 as a Great Britain-wide body. Its initial response was something called the Youth Opportunities Programme, rechristened the Youth Training Scheme in 1983, the acronym 'YTS' becoming playground shorthand for 'out of work'. Older workers in Scotland fared little better. At one point more than one in five unemployed men in their fifties had been out of work for more than two years, while by January 1981 120,000 Scots had been jobless for more than six months, and nearly 60,000 for more than a year. Even the resources designated to help both young and old find work were cut back. In its Scottish plan the MSC began shedding job-centre staff even though its budget in Scotland, control of which had been transferred to the Scottish Office in 1977, actually increased.

Long-term and youth unemployment inevitably impacted on many of

---

[81] *The Times* 16/10/1981.

[82] The figure remained static at 64 per cent, whereas the UK figure increased from 68 per cent to 70 per cent.

Scotland's most deprived areas, usually dominated by dilapidated peripheral housing estates later captured so effectively by the Scottish writer Irvine Welsh in his novel *Trainspotting*. The presence of a so-called 'underclass' in Scotland was nothing new, but it undeniably grew much larger as a result of Thatcherism. The link between high unemployment and social disruption was only reluctantly acknowledged by the Prime Minister following riots in London, Liverpool and other English cities in the summer of 1981. But while Michael Heseltine bounded around Liverpool dispensing charm and government grants, George Younger engaged in less ostentatious attempts to regenerate Scotland's potential trouble spots, most notably in Glasgow's Merchant City and the waterfronts of Dundee and Leith.

Again, there were longer-term factors at work. Although it has often been claimed that Mrs Thatcher destroyed community cohesion in Scotland, the profusion of badly constructed peripheral housing schemes which characterised Labour's approach to urban planning in the 1960s and 1970s arguably played a part. 'What started the break-up of the old community and its close-knit spirit was the redevelopment plans of the 'Sixties,' wrote a Gorbals doctor, Patrick Connolly, in 1982. 'Despite the promises of a new home in their own area, many of my patients found themselves being posted out, like wagon-train settlers, to schemes on the periphery of the city. People now look towards the State as a prop rather than their family or their neighbours. The old way of working-class life has gone for ever.'[83] The thoughtful Labour MP Frank McElhone also believed that the creation of New Towns had increased the problems of communities like Glasgow's East End by drawing away the more aspirational elements of the city's working class.[84]

Whatever the long- and short-term trends behind deindustrialisation and mass unemployment in the three years from 1979 to 1982, it was undoubtedly a traumatic period in modern Scottish history and, as Tom Devine concluded, 'in large part fuelled popular hostility to the Thatcher governments, on whom fell the blame for the series of economic disasters'.[85] Thatcherite measures to regenerate the British economy, argued the writer Allan Massie, also 'contributed to the political disenchantment with Scotland's position in the United Kingdom'. 'It was harsh medicine, a purgative, and although eventually it might be argued that the patient recovered, emerging from the experience with an economy better suited to the modern age, the treatment had been so painful that the Scottish electorate deserted the party responsible for administering it.'[86]

Sir Ian Gilmour reckoned that Scotland was treated rather like an intermediate institution, 'suffering from the centralizing urge of Thatcherism'. Mrs Thatcher's first government, he thought, 'should have treated

---

[83] *Sunday Standard* 7/3/1982.
[84] The journalist Harry Reid remembers McElhone articulating this theory.
[85] Devine, *The Scottish Nation*, 594.
[86] Massie, *The Thistle and the Rose*, 266.

Scotland, which was far from holding Thatcherite views and elected a
dwindling number of Conservative MPs, with some care. Such sensitivity
was aggressively absent.'[87] 'There is no alternative,' Mrs Thatcher would
claim as she wielded her public spending axe or stood by as yet another
factory closed, but for many Scots there did seem to be a constitutional
alternative in the form of independence or devolution, not to mention
political alternatives come polling day. Thatcherism in a cold climate was
about to be put to the test at its first general election, but only after a war in a
faraway island of which most Scots knew nothing.

---

[87] Gilmour, *Dancing With Dogma*, 270–71.

Chapter 6

THATCHERISM CONSOLIDATED
(1982–83)

So tonight we go forth from Perth to battle. Great things are expected of us.
If we keep our standards and our vision bright, what we have begun here
tonight in Perth, will end not only in victory for our Party, but in fulfilment,
of our nation's destiny.

Speech to Scottish Conservative conference, 13/5/1983

THE WHOLE FOCUS OF Scottish and British politics was changed by the
Argentine invasion of the hitherto little-known Falkland Islands in the South
Atlantic. Although the islands had served as a whaling base for a Scottish firm
(the Tory-inclined Christian Salvesen) and one of its villages was called Leith,
events there had little to do with Scotland or with the Scottish dimension in
British politics. They had everything to do, on the other hand, with the
nationalistic aspect of Thatcherism. Furthermore, the Falklands episode
demonstrated that Anglo/British nationalism could be every bit as potent,
if not more so, than Scottish Nationalism.

Ironically, therefore, the government's foray into the South Atlantic during
the spring and summer of 1982 was a rare example of Mrs Thatcher
capturing the Scots' imagination. As the Labour MP and academic John
P. Mackintosh once pointed out, the Scots possessed dual nationality –
Scottish and British – and switched between the two when it suited them.
During the Falklands War the motifs and symbols to hand were those of
Britain, not Scotland. 'I remember going into a Glasgow pub during the
Falklands,' recalled the Conservative MSP Bill Aitken, then a city councillor,
'and a hush fell over the place as soon as soon as news of the war appeared on
television.'[1]

On this occasion, the Scots had opted to be British, although with some
qualifications. While the Scottish media backed the Task Force and supported a

---

[1] Interview with Bill Aitken MSP, 20/6/2008.

military victory, the mass-selling *Daily Record* took a markedly less jingoistic line than the *Sun* in England. The STUC and the General Assembly of the Church of Scotland, meanwhile, were at best lukewarm in their support. Some also maintained that any enthusiasm Scots had for the conflict was restricted to the Scots Guards and Scots-based Commandos fighting there. In other words it had more to do with 'supporting our boys' than the government.[2] Nevertheless, the war displaced the entire political agenda. Items which were already low, such as devolution, disappeared, and politicians associated with them also seemed to shrink. Others increased in stature, not least the Prime Minister, who had been until then languishing in the polls and seemingly headed for electoral disaster.

There were, however, Scottish voices in the rhetorical mix. The Scottish Labour MP Tam Dalyell emerged during this time as one of Mrs Thatcher's most persistent critics, while his colleague George Foulkes (the MP for South Ayrshire) rebelled against his party's line and spoke out against any military involvement. By contrast, the right-wing Tory MP Bill Walker strenuously defended Maggie's war and later attributed his increased majority after the 1983 election to what became known as the 'Falklands Factor'. Foulkes and Walker even co-hosted a Radio Clyde phone-in programme for 14 consecutive weekends, giving many Scots an opportunity to air their views on the conflict. Politically, however, the government enjoyed wide support. Even the SNP, although largely anti-war, offered qualified support largely because Donald Stewart's Western Isles constituency enjoyed links with the distant islands; he had persistently warned of the likely Argentinian threat.

Just a week before the Argentinians invaded the islands on 2 April 1982, the Conservatives lost their last foothold in Glasgow when the former Labour Cabinet minister Roy Jenkins (once considered by Mrs Thatcher as a possible Chancellor despite his party allegiance) won the affluent Hillhead constituency in a by-election for the SDP/Liberal Alliance. Although a symbolic defeat for a party which once held the majority of Glasgow constituencies, Jenkins' victory was soon overshadowed by international events.

Conducted under the shadow of battle, May's Scottish regional council elections were one of the first tests of the so-called Falklands Factor. Turnout was low and Labour remained the largest party, with the Conservatives losing more councillors and sinking to just over a quarter of the vote, although they managed to regain control of Grampian and Tayside Regions. On Lothian Region – the focus of recent spending battles – there was a tie between Labour and Brian Meek's[3] Tory group at 22 seats each. An informal pact with the Alliance gave Meek control of the council, an important boost for George Younger's hard-line approach to 'excessive and unreasonable' council expenditure. To Tory activists like David McLetchie in Edinburgh this marked

---

[2] Interview with Tam Dalyell, 26/7/2008.

[3] Meek's enthusiasm for devolution had lost him the nomination to succeed Betty Harvie Anderson in Renfrewshire East in 1979, the candidacy instead going to the devolution-sceptic Allan Stewart.

the 'high watermark' of Thatcherism in Scotland, although it quickly receded. The new coalition moved swiftly to shut local schools in order to save money, cuts on the ground which probably did a lot to turn Lothians voters against Mrs Thatcher. The important contrast, however, was with simultaneous local government elections in England. There, in the north and south, voters moved towards the Conservatives. MORI polls also showed the Falklands Factor to be only half as strong in Scotland as in England, while on the basis of System Three polls it was virtually non-existent north of the border.[4]

Just days later, on 14 May 1982, the Scottish Conservative conference again became unintentionally significant. Mrs Thatcher delivered a barnstorming performance, talking quietly and movingly about the dangers which lay ahead. It clearly caught the mood of activists. 'We must uphold their right to live their lives in their way,' she said of the 1,800 Falkland islanders. 'We must respect their loyalty, the wonderful loyalty they have shown. Their freedom of choice and their independence of spirit. After all, Mr President [of the SCUA], that's what being Scottish and British is all about.'

It was very much a speech intended for UK, if not international, consumption, and Scottish references were kept to a minimum. 'But there are even larger issues at stake,' Mrs Thatcher continued. 'The right to self-determination is enshrined in the United Nations Charter. If that right is weakened, small countries the world over would be at risk.' It said a lot about the Prime Minister's confidence in the wake of war that she could talk of upholding the rights of small nations with no fear of contradiction, particularly in Scotland. She continued:

I don't want to see one more life lost in the South Atlantic, whether British or Argentinian, if it can be avoided. But I should not be doing my duty if I didn't warn you in the simplest and clearest terms that for all our efforts, those of Mr. Haig [the US Secretary of State], and those of the [Javier Perez de Cuellar] Secretary General of the United Nations, a negotiated settlement may prove to be unattainable. Then we should have to turn to the only other course left open to us.

Mrs Thatcher was making it absolutely clear she would be no walkover. For a premier with the stated aim of making Britain great again, the timing was perfect. The conflict allowed her to project Thatcherism beyond the UK to the international community and redefine notions of 'One Nation'. 'Ever since I was given the trust to lead our Government it has been my purpose to set a course that both friend and foe may understand and that we may adhere to,' she explained. 'And that purpose is the same at home as it is overseas. To uphold certain principles and values which some had thought that we could live without.'[5]

---

[4] Miller, *Testing the Power of a Media Consensus*, 23.
[5] Speech to Scottish Conservative conference, 14/5/1982, MTF.

The Prime Minister finished her speech to a tremendous ovation, a reaction she later said 'gave a great boost to my morale'.[6] David Steel, the Liberal leader, accused Mrs Thatcher of jingoism, and even George Younger later told the journalist Hugo Young that her reception at conference reminded him 'of the Nuremberg Rally'.[7] Even beyond the Westminster village, commentators observed that in Scotland 'feelings were noticeably less fevered and jingoistic than in the south'.[8] 'I'm not claiming that "Dalyell not getting flak" reflects Scottish public opinion,' reflected Tam Dalyell, 'but while I wasn't howled down during Scottish meetings about the conflict, I was in Birmingham Town Hall.'[9] Others emphasised Mrs Thatcher's financial priorities. 'If the rights of 1,800 Falkland Islanders are worth spending £3 billion on,' commented the STUC's general secretary Jimmy Milne, 'the rights of 350,000 unemployed Scots are worth spending some on too.'[10]

Mrs Thatcher certainly milked the conflict, and especially its successful resolution, for all it was worth, but that was simply shrewd politics. Her transformation was complete. From being the most unpopular Prime Minister on record that spring, she had become the most popular by the summer. And having reinvented herself as Britannia personified (an image encouraged by *Sun* cartoons), the Scottish dimension had to play second, if not third, fiddle. Later the Prime Minister would use the conflict as an example of what bound Scotland and England together, remembering in 1989 that 'it was as a part of the United Kingdom Armed Forces that the Scots Guards fought and won at Tumbledown Mountain'.[11]

Although not a 'Scottish' politician in the narrow sense, Tam Dalyell proved a fascinating nemesis for Mrs Thatcher then, and in the years ahead. If Dalyell, a student Tory at Oxford, had followed the Conservative path instead of Labour he might even have ended up in her government as a favoured Old Etonian grandee. Instead he latched on to Mrs Thatcher's actions over the *Belgrano* – which was sunk by a Clyde-based submarine – and almost obsessively pursued a justification, if not an apology. Even then, he could not help but separate the private woman from the public persona.

'I've always got time to see the awkward squad!' Mrs Thatcher declared, having agreed to see Dalyell as the Task Force steamed towards the South Atlantic. 'The lady I saw in her room on 21 April [1982] was worried sick about what might happen to many young Britons in the task force,' he later recalled. 'My instinct tells me that Mrs Thatcher was, in her private moments, more deeply touched by the deaths, burns and maiming that she felt it prudent to publicly reveal.'[12]

---

[6] Thatcher, *The Downing Street Years*, 221.

[7] Young, *One of Us*, 273.

[8] Donnachie, ed., *Forward!*, 161.

[9] Interview with Tam Dalyell.

[10] Press release dated 22/6/1982, STUC.

[11] Speech to Scottish Conservative conference, 12/5/1989, MTF.

[12] Galbraith, *Inside Outside*, 181–82.

With shared instincts on devolution, the two were more similar than they might have cared to admit. In Mrs Thatcher Dalyell detected essential human decency, while in Dalyell Mrs Thatcher must at least have admired his dogged persistence.

MODERATING THATCHERISM

Despite Mrs Thatcher's initial unpopularity across the UK, looking back in 1983 some Scottish commentators believed the government had had a good first term. It had behaved like a good general, knowing when to advance (Right to Buy) and retreat (Ferranti) in good measure, and almost all its radical legislative programme had gone through Parliament despite vociferous opposition from Labour. 'Whatever the more blinkered critics say, Thatcherism has not had a free run in Scotland,' wrote Allan Massie in the *Spectator*, a few months before the 1983 general election. He went on:

In each of the critical decisions – Linwood, The Royal Bank, Invergordon, Ravenscraig, Anderson Strathclyde – George Younger and the Scottish Office have been found articulating the need to protect Scottish interests against the free play of market forces. That they have lost more often than they have won is not the point. What they have done in every case is to set a perceived Scottish interest against the economic theories of the government which presumably represented the government's view of British interests.

Inevitably this meant Younger had to speak the language of the 'wets' while implementing the policies of the New Right. A Tory Secretary of State in Mrs Thatcher's Britain also had to answer the Labour jeer that he had no mandate in Scotland, although the opposition's ongoing civil war meant this was far from a unified criticism.

In his speech to the 1979 STUC congress, Tony Benn had signalled some of the civil strife to come by calling for power in the Labour Party to be transferred from its parliamentary representatives to constituency organisations. Although Scotland proved generally resistant to the worst extremes of the subsequent Trotskyite Militant Tendency entryism which threw various English seats into turmoil, it was not immune to the consequences. The result was fragmentation on not just the left of the Labour Party in Scotland, but also on its right. When the Gang of Four formed the Social Democratic Party (SDP) in 1981, there were two Scottish defections, Bob Maclennan in Caithness and Sutherland and Dick Mabon in Greenock, while one of the Gang – Roy Jenkins – later captured Glasgow Hillhead in the aforementioned by-election.

The SDP's appeal was obvious, pitching itself some way between Thatcherism and socialism, but somehow its pledge to break the mould of British politics did not quite capture the imagination of Scots. Its cool suburban rationalism seemed somehow as English as Mrs Thatcher – even though it was committed to devolution – and, instead, Scotland seemed more inclined to stick with the small party it new best, David Steel's (or Russell Johnston's in Scotland) Liberals. When asked how the SDP would sustain itself as a party, Dick Mabon was only half-joking when he replied: 'God shall provide by-elections.'[13]

'Parties which "seem" English generally have a hard row to hoe in Scotland,' observed Keith Aitken in his history of the STUC. 'The biggest loser of all from that was Margaret Thatcher whose hectoring Home Counties bray, to her lasting mystification, grated as savagely on Scottish voters' ears as on their traditions of collectivism.' He continued: 'While their southern neighbours fell heart and soul for the saloon-bar swagger of Thatcherism or the suave reason of the SDP, Scots continued doggedly to vote Labour, turning to the Liberals or the SNP when moved to express exasperation. Conservatism in Scotland, as the decade wore on, took on the trappings of an alien occupying force.'[14]

It was the SNP which did most to depict Thatcherism as an alien ideology seeking to impose itself on a defenceless Scotland, but somehow it failed to capitalise significantly on the ostentatiously English flavour of the first Conservative administration as a result. So extreme was the Nationalists' dislike of not just Mrs Thatcher but the Conservative creed in general, that it voted to prevent its elected representatives forming coalitions with compliant Tories at local authority level. But, like Labour, the independence movement was not in good shape as polling day approached in June 1983.

Following near electoral wipe-out in 1979 (only two of the party's 11 MPs survived the election) the SNP turned in on itself, concentrating its energies on arcane debates about how best to achieve independence instead of focusing on tactical rejuvenation. The former Labour MP Jim Sillars, who defected to the SNP before marrying one of its most prominent members, Margo MacDonald, in 1981, was influential, and pledged direct action to occupy, among other things, the proposed site for the Scottish Assembly on Edinburgh's Calton Hill.

Sympathetic Nationalists, who included future Scottish Government ministers Kenny MacAskill, Stewart Stevenson and Alex Salmond, called themselves the '79 Group and advocated not just independence but a Scottish socialist republic. The right of the party (led by Winnie Ewing), meanwhile, responded by setting up another faction. This forced the hand of Gordon Wilson, the SNP's conservative (with a small 'c') convenor, and in a conference speech which anticipated Neil Kinnock's purge of the militants several years later, Wilson gave notice that his leadership would not tolerate internal groupings.

Another such grouping was *Siol nan Gaidheal* (Seed of the Gael) whose

---

[13] Private information.
[14] Aitken, *The Bairns O' Adam*, 264.

members regularly burned the Union Jack and wore tartan regalia. They also chanted anti-Thatcher slogans and came face to face with their nemesis when the Prime Minister arrived in Perth to attend the 1982 Scottish Tory conference. She looked relaxed until she noticed a dozen *Siol* members charging down the street towards her. Graham Macmillan, the party's Scottish director, pushed Mrs Thatcher through the door of the conference venue but got kicked by one of the protestors. The Prime Minister's departure from the hall following her speech was just as undignified. The *Siol* supporters again made to charge and a waving Mrs Thatcher was hustled into the rear seat of her car by police officers. Her husband, Denis, was also bundled into the front seat of the Jaguar, and the car drove off at speed with his leg flapping from the open door. From 1983 onwards, security at the Scottish Tory conference was noticeably stepped up.

As for Mrs Thatcher's view of Scottish Nationalists, it is probably fair to say she filed them under 'c' for contempt, alongside trade unionists and consensualists. Teddy Taylor once told the *Glasgow Herald* editor Arnold Kemp that although Mrs Thatcher wanted to destroy the SNP she had no such ambition for the Labour Party. Even she recognised that a parliamentary democracy needed them as much as it did the Conservatives. The SNP's civil war simply made the task easier. As Andrew Marr wrote, 'Mrs Thatcher was lucky in her enemies and the Scottish Nationalists were yet another good example.'[15]

'GO FORTH FROM PERTH TO BATTLE'

Parliament was dissolved on Friday 13 May 1983. 'The next day I flew to Scotland to address the Scottish Conservative Party Conference in Perth,' recalled Mrs Thatcher in her memoirs. She went on: 'The hall in Perth is not large, but it has excellent acoustics. It is one of the best places to speak anywhere in Britain – perhaps only Blackpool Winter Gardens is better. In spite of a sore throat from the tail-end of a heavy cold, I enjoyed myself. Not only do I always recall that this is the nation of Adam Smith, the romantic strain of Scottish Toryism appeals to the non-economist in me too.'[16]

Indeed, there was a certain romantic lyricism to the Prime Minister's speech that day – perhaps the conference venue reminded her of Methodist halls from her Grantham childhood – which effectively launched the UK Conservative election campaign. She spoke of uprooting 'the thickets of bureaucracy' in Whitehall and in town halls, while offering the party faithful the opportunity to 'banish from our land the dark divisive clouds of Marxist socialism'. The Liberals were dismissed for having 'propped up the most illiberal Government of modern times', and the SDP's leading lights were accused of having fostered a 'misleading permissiveness' prior to their split from Labour.

---

[15] Marr, *A History of Modern Britain*, 447.
[16] Thatcher, *The Downing Street Years*, 291.

Predictably, Mrs Thatcher also praised Scotland for battling 'through recession with determination and enterprise'. She continued:

> Scottish enterprise and overseas investment here are leading to recovery. But your Scottish Ministers have also played a crucial role. They have helped to capture orders for such famous names as John Brown Engineering, Babcock Power, the Weir Group, and Ferranti. Indeed, time and again, the Scottish Ministerial team have richly earned the collective title which I believe some jealous Sassenachs imposed upon them – that of the Tartan Mafia. And I must say that George Younger makes a most benevolent 'Godfather'.

'So tonight we go forth from Perth to battle,' Mrs Thatcher concluded, indulging in Churchillian rhetoric. 'Great things are expected of us. If we keep our standards and our vision bright, what we have begun here tonight in Perth, will end not only in victory for our Party, but in fulfilment, of our nation's destiny.'[17] 'As always after visits to the Scottish Conference,' she later recalled, 'I returned to London encouraged and in fighting spirit. The atmosphere had been one of buoyant enthusiasm – a good omen for the campaign.'[18]

It was indeed a good omen for the Conservative election campaign, yet again it was one strangely lacking in a Scottish dimension. 'The most remarkable feature of the campaign in Scotland is how similar it has been to that being fought in England and Wales,' noted the *New Statesman*. 'It has the same idiosyncrasies, the same preconceptions, and the same truisms. It has been less distinctly Scottish than on previous occasions.'[19]

Mrs Thatcher's only night out of London during the campaign was at the Station Hotel in Inverness. As Carol, who was keeping a diary of the campaign, and her mother left the town's airport Jimmy Anderson, a well-known local press photographer, collapsed on the kerb and died of a heart attack. In a typical gesture, the Prime Minister sat down and wrote a note of condolence to his widow. 'She was a woman, with a woman's concern for those around her and a most assiduous attention to the details of their lives,' observed Hugo Young. 'The contrast was much to be remarked between this attractive trait and the inability she constantly manifested to register the same quality of caring for the nation at large.'[20]

There was also a detectable sense of humour, although the Scottish Tory MP Ian Lang remembered this being 'very on-off'.[21] Lord McAlpine, the

[17] Speech to Scottish Conservative conference, 13/5/1983, MTF.
[18] Thatcher, *The Downing Street Years*, 291.
[19] *New Statesman* 10/6/1983.
[20] Young, *One of Us*, 159. Mrs Thatcher also had a woman's eye for interior furnishings. 'Are you wise to have no curtains?' she asked the Scottish Tory official Graham Macmillan on touring party head-quarters during the election campaign. 'People can see in from across the street.' (*Scotsman* 1/6/1983)
[21] Interview with Lord Lang, 11/11/2008.

Conservative Party treasurer, recalled it being very much 'on' as Mrs Thatcher prepared to address an industrialists' conference in Glasgow during the early 1980s. The Prime Minister had a cold, and as she waited behind the stage before getting up to speak, Jim Prior remarked: 'I heard you on the radio last night Margaret; you were very good. You sounded very sexy – have you got a cold?' Apparently Mrs Thatcher looked him straight in the eye and replied: 'Jim, I don't need a cold to sound sexy.' Prior, recalled McAlpine, did not know how to respond. 'She knew how to play the female part,' he added, 'she played it unmercifully on occasion.'[22]

After polling stations closed on 9 June 1983, the outcome in Scotland was something of a surprise. The SNP performed badly, polling only 12 per cent, while Labour lost three seats. The Conservatives, meanwhile, retained their 21 seats (down from 22 in 1979 because of the Hillhead by-election) and achieved a small swing of 1.7 per cent against Labour, narrowing the opposition's lead of 10.1 per cent four years earlier to just 6.7 per cent. But the total Tory vote in Scotland still fell as it did in the rest of the UK. Labour's vote share, however, fell by twice as much, from 42 per cent to 35.1 per cent.

Labour did attract more votes in Clydeside, where after four years of Thatcherism even the longest suicide note in history (as Gerald Kaufman described the Labour manifesto) seemed attractive, but surrounding it was a ring of seats that swung to the Conservatives, while even in hostile territory like Coatbridge and Airdrie the governing party's small but loyal vote appeared to have held up. The SDP also did relatively well in Scotland – its best result outside the south-west of England – with a 17 per cent vote share, more than the Liberals but not enough to prevent the defectee Dick Mabon losing to the moderate Tory Anna McCurley (the only female Scottish Tory MP during Mrs Thatcher's premiership) in Renfrew West and Inverclyde. There, the SDP split the opposition vote to the benefit of the Conservative candidate, a psephological occurrence that added to Labour's woes all over the country. As Hugo Young observed, 'To the survival of Thatcherism, both the phenomenon and its heroine', the defection of the Gang of Four had been 'among the most decisive contributions'.[23]

Despite the Conservatives holding on to all their Scottish seats and all but 1.6 per cent of its vote share, Mrs Thatcher did not share the jubilation of many Scottish Tories. 'She thought she was going to get 30 or 40 seats,' recalled Quintin Jardine, who then worked as a press officer for the party, 'but I don't know what was going through her mind. All I know is that we went in with 21 and came out with 21; we lost two and gained two, it was a bloody good result as far as we were concerned.'[24] Indeed, having endured a

---

[22] *Thatcher: The Downing Street Years* (BBC) 8/10/1993.
[23] Young, *One of Us*, 293.
[24] Interview with Quintin Jardine, 9/3/2007. The two losses were Hamish Gray in Ross and Cromarty and Iain Sproat in Roxburgh and Berwickshire; the two gains were Anna McCurley and Michael Hirst in Strathkelvin and Bearsden.

crippling recession and massive unemployment as a result, it is remarkable that a greater number of Scots did not turn decisively against the Conservatives on polling day. Nevertheless, had the Falklands Factor been felt in Scotland then Mrs Thatcher would have welcomed at least seven new Scottish MPs to Westminster. So the result in Scotland, although superficially impressive, was the first indication that Conservative MPs were about to become an endangered species north of the border.

'As usual, Scotland is distinctive and different,' observed the *Scotsman*'s post-election editorial. 'Here in Scotland . . . the Conservative Party . . . has fallen below 30% of the vote . . . how many Scots can believe that they are being fairly treated when they get a Government which has only 21 of the 72 Scottish MPs?'[25] The *Glasgow Herald*, meanwhile, noted that '70% of the Scottish vote was for non-Government candidates, and almost by definition this must bring the Scottish dimension to the fore again'.[26]

The Scottish dimension, however, did not return to the fore and Labour continued to be reticent in pursuing the 'no mandate' argument against Mrs Thatcher in Scotland. Scottish Labour MPs such as John Maxton and George Foulkes, for example, pursued it all the same, the latter issuing a memo advocating 'immediate parliamentary action', and more drastic measures like 'token strikes' and possible legal challenges.[27] Newly elected members such as the future Prime Minister Gordon Brown did not approve and, together with the Greenock MP Norman Godman, he tried to nudge the Scottish Labour Party towards a more coherent anti-Thatcher position based around a devolution commitment. But with many in the Labour Party still unenthusiastic about a Scottish Assembly, much of the 1980s became a long hard slog for devolutionists like Brown. 'The prospect of five years of Thatcherism has a demoralising, indeed a paralysing effect,' noted an editorial in *Radical Scotland*. 'If the Left is to recover, it cannot condemn itself simply reacting to various ramifications of her [Mrs Thatcher's] policies. A positive identity and alternative has to be offered – a self-government campaign is our best bet.'[28]

An internal paper by Labour's Scottish research officer, Murray Elder, ranked self-government fifth in a list of immediate priorities following the election defeat. 'Electoral reality dictates that our central appeal *must* be directed to both traditional working class people *and* what has come to be termed the new working class,' Elder observed. 'This means that, if we seek to protect the disadvantaged in our society, we *also* have to appeal to those whose social advantages (largely as a result of Labour Movement successes),

---

[25] *Scotsman* 10/6/1983.

[26] *Glasgow Herald* 10/6/1983.

[27] Foulkes also co-authored a paper entitled 'Defending Scotland Against Thatcher: An Action Plan for the Labour Movement' along with four other Scottish Labour MPs. This discussed 'establishing a Scottish Assembly as a defensive bulwark against Thatcher', using parliamentary and extra-parliamentary action to 'outflank the Nationalists, and highlight the divisions in the Alliance on this issue'.

[28] *Radical Scotland* August/September 1983.

include more secure employment, educational attainment, home-ownership and wider social horizons for themselves and their children.' Thatcherism consolidated had nudged even the Labour Party's Scottish Council into a reality check. 'If we are serious about the pursuit of power,' the paper asserted, 'this strategic imperative should underlie our every action.'[29]

The Scottish Office team, meanwhile, was subject to a minor reshuffle. George Younger reluctantly remained as Scottish Secretary while the promotion of Allan Stewart, a product of St Andrews University, gave the department a more ideological edge. Hamish Gray, a wetter MP who had lost his Highlands constituency in the wake of the Invergordon closure, also returned to St Andrew's House, but via the House of Lords. 'This action of Thatcher's outraged democracy, not to mention Highlanders,' stormed the SNP MP Donald Stewart in his memoirs. 'The offence was compounded by Lord Gray being appointed at the same time to the Scottish Office as Minister responsible for the Highlands and Islands!'[30]

But such was the Prime Minister's authority, even in Scotland, that she could afford to dismiss such criticism with a careful turn of her finely coiffured head. Even though her election result could hardly have been interpreted as a great vindication of Thatcherite policies, the Falklands Factor had turned it into a triumph. Mrs Thatcher's successful Falklands gamble also overshadowed some unhelpful economic statistics. For all the government's talk of cutting taxes and public spending, the overall tax burden had actually risen during 1979–1983 from 34 per cent of GDP to nearly 40 per cent, while government spending rose to 44 per cent of GDP, breaking the Prime Minister's target of reducing it to 40 per cent. Nevertheless, the 1983 general election was significant in consolidating the Thatcherite revolution and allowing it to continue for at least another four years. This was as true in Scotland as in England. 'The Conservatives won less than a third of the votes at the election,' observed the journalist James Naughtie of the Scottish result, 'but the foundations of the Scottish Office have not yet begun to tremble.'[31]

---

[29] Labour Party Scottish Council paper 'Facing the Future'.
[30] Stewart, *A Scot at Westminster*, 77.
[31] McCrone, ed., *Scottish Government Yearbook 1984*, 35.

Chapter 7

THATCHERISM IN A COLD CLIMATE

(1983–87)

Mrs Thatcher evidently cares for Scotland. Her pattern of travel within the United Kingdom has made Scotland a more favoured destination than other more populous regions . . . But does Scotland need special treatment within the United Kingdom? . . It would do the Conservative cause at large no good and would insult the tradition of Scottish Unionism [for] government ministers . . . to try to purchase political peace with public money.

The Times 8/5/1985

We are in politics because we care. It is because we care that we don't care for Socialism. It is because we care that we are Conservatives.

Speech to Scottish Conservative conference, 16/5/1986

Mrs Thatcher respected Scotland enormously . . . for having its own history and traditions and institutions. She had a sort of regard for Scotland: grand families, grand estates, that sort of thing. But she didn't really have a view of Scotland as a separate area in policy terms. I didn't feel that there was a great emphasis on Scotland as such.[1]

Lord Griffiths, head of Downing Street Policy Unit 1985–90

THE SECOND THATCHER government was the zenith of Thatcherism in England, or more accurately in the south-east; an era of economic prosperity, privatisation, 'yuppies' and the Big Bang. In Scotland things looked very different. The recession lasted until 1986, unemployment continued to rise as manufacturing declined even further, and the Big Bang could barely be heard despite Edinburgh's growing financial sector. In England the second term culminated in another landslide for the government; in Scotland the

---

[1] Interview with Lord Griffiths, 1/12/2008.

Conservative Party lost more than half its MPs. While socialism appeared to have been defeated in the south; north of the border the onward march of Labour continued apace. Common UK experiences were largely negative. The miners' strike, and later the teachers' strike, united north and south.

'The election showed that something remarkable has happened in this country,' Mrs Thatcher told the Conservative Party conference a few months after the election. 'I believe we have altered the whole course of British politics for at least a generation.'[2] The 1983 Conservative manifesto, however, lacked a truly radical edge, and many Thatcherites came to regard the period from 1983 to 1987 as a wasted opportunity. As John Campbell has observed, 'Contrary to collective memory, the Thatcherite revolution did not carry all before it, even in 1983–87'.[3]

In Scotland, too, right-wingers were frustrated at a perceived lack of progress, to them all the more sluggish in the collectivist north. There, the Scottish Secretary George Younger became as much a victim of events as the Prime Minister. The Scottish Office led the reforming agenda in just one, ultimately disastrous, respect: abolition of the rates and the introduction of the Poll Tax. Although this was a reform championed by Scottish right-wingers like the newly elected Stirling MP, Michael Forsyth, and the Glenrothes councillor Douglas Mason, it did not feature in the ominously named *Omega Report: Scottish Policy*, published by the Adam Smith Institute (ASI) in January 1984.

Designed to stimulate political debate in Scotland following four years of Thatcherism, the *Omega Report* had shades of a document produced by the Central Policy Review staff at Downing Street shortly after the Falklands War. That, as Andrew Marr has written, constituted 'Margaret Thatcher unplugged'.[4] It recommended an end to state funding for higher education with student loans replacing grants; a break in the link between benefit payments and inflation; and the replacement of the NHS with a system of private health insurance, including charges for doctors' visits and medicines. Mrs Thatcher was personally enthusiastic but the rest of the Cabinet horrified. Details were deliberately leaked to the press and the report shelved.

In that context, the equally radical conclusions of the *Omega Report* stood little chance of being adopted. 'In Scotland, the way to political reform is blocked by dissensions,' it declared, 'but the path to *economic* reform is still open.' To that end most functions of the Scottish Development Agency ('the embodiment of corporatist thinking that has typified Scottish policy for the last forty years') were to be undertaken by the Confederation of British Industry and the Scottish Council for Development and Industry; regional aid ('distorting') was to be phased out; development rights to North Sea oil and gas fields auctioned to the highest bidder; and Scottish banks cut loose from the Bank of England and allowed to circulate their own currency.

---

[2] Speech to Conservative Party conference, 14/10/1983, MTF.

[3] Campbell, *The Iron Lady*, 210.

[4] Marr, *A History of Modern Britain*, 406.

Other recommendations, however, would later become policy: an end to the monopoly of British Gas; privatisation of Scotland's electricity boards; an end to the solicitors' monopoly on conveyancing; contracting out of local services; and the ability for Scottish schools to opt out of the state education system. If all this took place, the report declared, the desire for a devolved Scottish Assembly would simply disappear. 'The demand for devolution, after all, arose in part because many Scots resent the all-pervading influence of a distant and insensitive bureaucracy,' it argued. 'Cut back that pervasiveness, and it will become obvious that there is enough variety and vitality in Scottish institutions, and the Scots people, to produce a social and economic renaissance which the present enforcement of a dreary conformity makes impossible.'[5]

The *Glasgow Herald* deemed the *Omega Report* 'the prescription as preached by Mrs Thatcher rather than practised',[6] but it met with a more sympathetic reaction in the *Spectator*. To its reporter, Allan Massie, the report was evidence that the Scottish right was 'stirring, [and] that it has got itself out of its dull statist and unionist trench'.[7] There is little evidence, however, that Mrs Thatcher shared this sentiment, or indeed, even read the report. Although one of its authors was the Prime Minister's protégé Michael Forsyth, Brian Griffiths, later head of the Downing Street Policy Unit, does not remember a single ASI document making it to her boxes for diligent perusal. He recalled that the ASI was regarded by some Conservatives as a bit cranky; a think tank not to be taken seriously, a perception perhaps fuelled by its president, the permanently bow-tied Madsen Pirie.

'A great psychological benefit would flow from the abolition of automatic subsidies to Scotland,' concluded a key passage of the *Omega Report*. 'They have fed the delusion that she is a special case, somehow incapable of facing and overcoming economic change – when all experience up to this century pointed to precisely the opposite conclusion.'[8] Indeed, the belief that Scotland was a 'special case', or a 'more equal' society than England, was regularly asserted but rarely tested during the 1980s. The notion was problematic, not least because there were significant regional variations even within Scotland and differing levels of Tory support as a result. In towns like Perth and Ayr, the Conservatives were seen as protectors of a way of life, while in most of Glasgow and cities like Dundee, they were perceived as a threat to another, altogether different, way of life. 'We asked at the time whether, for example, Aberdeen was more "community-minded" than, say, Bolton, or whether Edinburgh was more "community-minded" than, say, Birmingham,' recalled Malcolm Rifkind's special adviser Graeme Carter. 'It seemed to me to be an over-generalisation to claim Scotland had a markedly different cultural outlook to the rest of the UK.'[9]

---

[5] *Omega Report: Scottish Policy*, 1–2.
[6] *Glasgow Herald* 12/1/1984.
[7] *Spectator* 14/1/1984.
[8] *Omega Report*, 3.
[9] Graeme Carter to the author, 27/8/2008.

It would have been more accurate to claim that Scotland's cultural outlook differed from that in the south of the UK, but not necessarily from that in the north of England. As the British Social Attitudes survey of 1988 discovered, on attitudes towards the role of the state in society, how the economy should be run, moral issues and the welfare state, what divided north and south (the division being the Humber and Mersey rivers rather than Hadrian's Wall) were all issues which stressed the need for greater economic equality in society. In general, those in the 'north' were more likely to favour government action to reduce inequality. Not all northern attitudes, however, depicted Scotland in a good light. The percentage of Scots taking a libertarian view on homosexuality, gay teachers in schools and the liberalisation of divorce and abortion laws, for example, were markedly fewer than in London and the south of England.

This feeling of 'difference', however, was inevitably harnessed by the Scottish media and became the criterion by which every Thatcherite act was judged. 'We were fed a lot of this stuff about there being an inbuilt tradition, nation of equality, lad o' pairts, and all of that,' recalled the former *Scotsman* editor Magnus Linklater. 'This bred a society which was offended by the Thatcherite philosophy and I remember writing a lot of stuff at this time which followed this line; that the reason we were anti-Thatcher was because she offended this great tradition.' But, in retrospect, 'I think on the whole that was a lot of tosh. The more I look back the more I feel slightly embarrassed and ashamed at a failure to challenge that conformity.'[10]

But, as the Conservatives' support in Scotland receded – not, at this stage, so much in the House of Commons but certainly in local government – the language, expectations and understanding of what constituted legitimate government began to change. After the 1983 election, opposition charges that Mrs Thatcher had 'no mandate in Scotland' became part of the rhetoric of Scottish politics with obvious consequences. One Labour MP even suggested the Prime Minister had 'no moral mandate'[11] north of the border. Consequently, a new form of civic politics began to gather force, one which contrived to assert Scotland's apparent collectivist traditions in conscious defiance of the cult of individualism which it alleged underpinned the Conservative government's thinking. And crucially, it was a civic coalition that did have a mandate, be it moral or political. So when Mrs Thatcher later declared that there was no such thing as society,[12] civic Scotland replied 'yes there is – the churches, unions, professionals, artists and thinkers – and here we are waving banners'.

---

[10] Interview with Magnus Linklater, 3/6/2008.
[11] *Glasgow Herald* 12/9/1983.
[12] The actual quote was: 'There is no such thing as society. There is living tapestry of men and women and people and the beauty of that tapestry and the quality of our lives will depend upon how much each of us is prepared to take responsibility for ourselves and each of us prepared to turn round and help by our own efforts those who are unfortunate.' (*Woman's Own* 23/9/1987)

Coalitions sprang up not only to advocate change (devolution), but oppose specific aspects of the government's programme (health service reforms, educational changes and, most notably, the Poll Tax), but the common theme was Scotland against Thatcherism. 'Such power as they had was symbolic, not executive,' observed Keith Aitken in his history of the STUC. 'It lay purely in the consensus they represented: by accentuating the majority, they further isolated the minority.'[13]

That minority was the Scottish Tory vote, but other commentators took a more sanguine view of this developing sense of national character. 'The construction of the idea of civic Scotland', concluded the academic Richard Finlay, 'was a polite way of saying that the Scots hated Thatcher.'[14] Similarly, the writer Tom Nairn reckoned it was careless to identify 'this Caledonian institutionalism . . . with "socialism", and sometimes with an imagined native (or even clannic) propensity towards the collective'. He continued: 'These supposed traits are then depicted as the cause of a supposed anti-individualism in Scottish society – distrust of success and personal wealth, and unwillingness to take initiative. During the period of Thatcherism this kind of critique naturally gained in popularity. As one government after another tried to make capitalism more popular, and to instil an entrepreneurial outlook, it became tempting to ascribe their failure to some sort of inherited recalcitrance or incapacity.'[15]

Intriguingly, therefore, this notion of Scotland being different from England, whether real or imagined, suited both sides in the Thatcherite battle for Scottish hearts and minds. Civic Scotland presented it as a reason why Scots would never accept Thatcherism, while the government used it to explain away the opposition with which it was regularly confronted.

This perception of Scotland standing united against the New Right also conveniently papered over the rather obvious fact that Labour and the Scottish National Party hated each other, even if both also hated Mrs Thatcher. The SNP attacked Labour's Scottish MPs (dubbed the 'feeble 50' following the 1987 election) as incapable of protecting Scotland from Thatcherism, while Labour attacked the SNP as 'Tartan Tories', little Scotlanders with the same right-wing instincts as Mrs Thatcher's Conservatives. If this was Scotland united, it was a bitter sort of unity.

The dynamic also fuelled a growing perception that individual government policies were somehow 'imposed' on Scotland, regardless of the constitutional and legal legitimacy underpinning the Conservatives' UK-wide mandate. The counter argument was, of course, that Scotland – in 1979 and again in 1983 – had rejected Mrs Thatcher's government by the only democratic means available to it, a general election. Again, this was a convenient position. Not only did it not make any sense within the context of a unified

---

[13] Aitken, *The Bairns O' Adam*, 292.
[14] Finlay, *Modern Scotland*, 367
[15] Nairn, *After Britain*, 238–39.

state, but it was hardly a new phenomenon. Scotland had voted over-whelmingly Liberal in the late nineteenth century and been rewarded with Unionist governments, while in the late 1960s Labour's UK majority relied upon MPs elected in Scotland and Wales.

'From the particular resentments of Scots . . . grew a more general dislike, shared by many Scots, of Mrs Thatcher's insistence that she knew best,' observed the former *Glasgow Herald* editor Arnold Kemp. 'She attempted to impose her policies rather than convince Scotland of their merit . . . she decided that Scotland was wrong because she had to be right, and Scotland found itself, as a result, with much reduced political leverage.'[16] Again, it seems odd to criticise a Prime Minister who did not believe that he or she generally 'knew best'. It is not odd, however, to see how this view of Mrs Thatcher as a 'bossy woman' was encouraged by certain aspects of her character and personal style. Indeed, many Cabinet colleagues believe Mrs Thatcher grew increasingly inflexible during her second term, and irretrievably so during her third.

Edward Heath once remarked, when questioned about his poor approval ratings as Leader of the Opposition, that 'popularity isn't everything',[17] yet his successor found that individual unpopularity was a large part of the problem for her party north of the border. Whereas in Mrs Thatcher's first term opposition was largely restricted to those on the left and trade unionists, in her second it extended even to natural Tory voters. Furthermore, the Prime Minister's personal unpopularity began to erode the fortunes of the once mighty Scottish Conservative and Unionist Party to a much greater extent than in had in the 1970s and early 1980s. She had given the party a new lease of life in 1979; more or less sustained it in 1983; but now appeared to be presiding over a year-on-year decline, which would culminate in the election result of 1987.

It was during the second Thatcher government, therefore, that the perception of the Prime Minister as a hectoring woman who did not care about Scotland, or its economic and social problems, became widely ac-cepted. Furthermore, Mrs Thatcher was seen to be ignoring aspects of Scotland which were distinct from England. Whatever the rights and wrongs of this impression, it quickly became the prism through which every aspect of the Thatcherite revolution was judged north of the border. And almost without exception that judgement was negative.

CUTTING SCOTLAND DOWN TO SIZE

Six months after the 1983 general election the government unveiled its plans for further changes to regional policy, a pillar of the post-war consensus which had survived, despite heavy cuts, in 1979. Although Gavin McCrone, chief

---

[16] Kemp, *The Hollow Drum*, 209.
[17] *Britain Today* (BBC1) 24/6/1969.

economist at the Scottish Office, and George Younger fought hard to convince the Treasury-led review that regional policy remained important, the *Regional Industrial Policy* white paper proposed further cuts and in November 1984 orders were placed before Parliament to implement them.

Scotland fared relatively well compared with other regions of the UK. It was to receive £41.6 million in Regional Selective Assistance in 1985/86, and £107.5 million via a new system of Regional Development Grants, which were to be abolished in March 1988. The latter still applied to 50 per cent of Scotland's working population, despite a reduction in the proportion of the country classified as Assisted Areas from 71 to 65 per cent. Critics argued that communities such as Glenrothes, which had been successful at job creation, were now being punished by having their Assisted Area status removed. In effect, however, the government was concentrating aid on areas of specifically high unemployment, which after the recession of 1979–82 were not exactly small in number. This continued a key shift of emphasis from generalised regional policy to concentrated urban policy which reached its high watermark after the 1987 general election.

There was also some good news, relatively speaking. The Scottish Development Agency (SDA) and Highlands and Islands Development Board (HIDB) – long the objects of right-wing Tory suspicion – once again survived, while the area covered by the latter (as well as the Intermediate Areas) continued to qualify for funding from the European Regional Development Fund. In 1986 Scotland also received £14 million from the European Social Fund, more than any other region in the UK. Ironically, while with one hand Mrs Thatcher took away government funding from the regions, with the other it was handed back via the European Commission in Brussels. Nevertheless, the response from civic Scotland was largely negative. 'The only comment that can be made about the changes in regional policy is that they will achieve the Government's main objective – saving money,' noted the *Scottish Government Yearbook*. 'This will be a matter for some congratulation inside the Cabinet but whether it will do anything to help reduce the regional imbalances within the national economy is quite a different matter.'[18]

In spite of these cuts to regional aid, however, Scotland continued to benefit from disproportionately higher levels of public spending per head than elsewhere in Great Britain (in Northern Ireland identifiable levels were higher still). A situation formalised, rather than inaugurated, by the so-called Scottish Block Grant/Barnett Formula system created in 1978, that it endured despite a recession and, more to the point, the election of a government determined to cut the state down to size, was remarkable. Together with big infrastructure programmes (road building and maintenance, and dozens of new hospitals) driven by the Scottish Office, the interventionism of the SDA and the paternalism of the HIDB, government in Scotland remained omnipresent.

English Tory backbenchers – to whose views the Prime Minister always paid

---

[18] McCrone, ed., *Scottish Government Yearbook 1986*, 211.

close attention – began muttering that if Thatcherism could be stopped at the Tweed, then why not also at the Tyne and the Mersey? Indeed, English resentment at perceived special treatment for the Scots was a curious side effect of the Thatcher decade. It began with a little good-natured envy in the 1960s when the Labour Scottish Secretary Willie Ross ratcheted up public spending levels by warning of Nationalist gains; grew into ill-tempered jealousy during the 1970s with the creation of the SDA and the promise of economic growth fuelled by devolution; but developed into lingering resentment only in the 1980s as Scotland seemed to escape the worst falls of the Thatcher axe.

That, of course, was the perception, particularly among long-serving Tory MPs in the south-east, reinforced by newly elected Conservatives from the Midlands and northern constituencies with wafer-thin majorities, poor economic prospects and unemployment levels akin to that in Scotland. Their resentment was justified to a degree. While regional aid was cut across the UK, it decreased by less in Scotland, and while regeneration in the Midlands and the north was administered by the Department of Industry in Whitehall, Scotland enjoyed additional resources and hefty budgets administered by the SDA and HIDB. At the other end of the political argument was the SNP, who claimed that in relation to the amount of revenue flowing into the Treasury courtesy of North Sea oil, Scotland was getting relatively little in return.

The complaints of English Tories most likely found a sympathetic ear in Number 10 and at the Department of Trade and Industry where Norman Tebbit had been installed in 1983. Yet despite their better instincts, little was done by senior ministers to redress the financial balance in favour of comparable English regions. Instead, Mrs Thatcher appeared almost to pander to regionalism and endorse the profligacy of her Scottish lieutenants. Many true believers could be forgiven for being puzzled by this apparent gulf between Thatcherite rhetoric and Scottish reality, especially given that it was a gulf which appeared to produce little electoral reward north of the border.

Nick Edwards, the Secretary of State for Wales from 1979 to 1987, could only watch and wonder as his main territorial rival in Cabinet (the Northern Ireland Office was a special case for obvious reasons) emerged triumphant from proposed cut after cut, and recalls in his memoirs a widespread feeling among English ministers that Scotland was over-resourced via the Block/ Formula system. 'About every two years the subject would be raised in Cabinet', recalled Edwards, 'and on each occasion the Secretary of State for Scotland would threaten political disaster if the system was changed and the topic would be quickly dropped.' He went on: 'During the early part of her administration, Margaret Thatcher usually gave her support to the Scots very early in the discussion and that shortened the proceedings: she was very sensitive about Scotland! However, as the years passed and, despite the increasing transfer of resources from south to north, the Tory vote in Scotland declined, the Prime Minister began to be doubtful.'[19]

---

[19] Crickhowell, *Westminster, Wales & Water*, 54.

Away from the Cabinet room, however, New St Andrew's House faced an annual (rather than bi-annual, as Edwards remembered) autumn battle over its 'Block', or budget. The first joust in 1980, an update of a year-old Needs Assessment Study (which reviewed territorial expenditure under Barnett in 1979 but was never implemented), was instigated by Edwards on the basis that he received disproportionately less than his Scottish and English ministerial colleagues. In response, the Treasury advocated moving some cash from the Scottish Block to Wales and England, while the Scottish Office argued that Wales should simply take additional resources from the Treasury's Contingency Reserve. Thereafter, however, the Treasury initiated each assault on supposed Scottish largesse. These attacks undoubtedly had support from the Prime Minister. 'The pride of the Scottish Office', she later sneered in her memoirs, 'whose very structure added a layer of bureaucracy, standing in the way of the reforms which were paying such dividends in England – was that public expenditure per head in Scotland was far higher than in England.'[20]

To an extent this was normal government behaviour. Whitehall has an innate desire to save money, but over time it became a well-orchestrated and deeply absorbing civil service game of statistic and counter-statistic. It also happened to fit in with the prevailing Thatcherite orthodoxy of restraining public expenditure. The Prime Minister herself had a well-known distaste for the Scottish Block, particularly its embarrassing disparity between per capita spending in England and Scotland. This disparity was presented to Mrs Thatcher as a taper, something that would converge with England over time. But with the Scottish population falling year on year, not to mention reductions to English departmental budgets, this anticipated convergence proceeded at glacial speed. And despite Mrs Thatcher's sensitivity about Scotland, as identified by Edwards, figures like Norman Tebbit ensured the disparity was brought repeatedly to her attention. 'In 1979 I had no desire to re-open this thorny problem,' Thatcher reflected in 2009, 'at least for the time-being.'[21]

For the Scottish Secretary, on the other hand, the Block/Formula system was a boon. Not only did George Younger avoid lengthy negotiations over individual spending programmes, he could also distribute cash within the Block – as determined by the Barnett Formula – across specifically Scottish spending areas without further recourse to the Treasury. This flexibility came in especially handy over 'excessive and unreasonable' expenditure by local authorities, but also had drawbacks. Younger came under growing pressure from the Select Committee on Scottish Affairs (encouraged by its specialist adviser David Heald) and a group of media experts, who kept the arithmetic of the Block/Formula system under constant scrutiny.

Meanwhile, the Treasury and the Prime Minister also kept up the pressure. Scottish Office officials conducted several exercises to appease the latter, while endeavouring to avoid the worst-case scenario of permitting a fresh

<hr>

[20] Thatcher, *The Downing Street Years*, 619.
[21] Interview with Baroness Thatcher, 20/1/2009

Needs Assessment Study. New St Andrew's House did lose some ground. Automatic increases related to pay and price inflation were abolished (for all government departments) by Sir Geoffrey Howe in 1981–82, while in 1984 Younger's department endured a particularly fierce attack from the Welsh-born Peter Rees, Chief Secretary to the Treasury since June 1983.

Rees's opening salvo must have sent shivers down the spines of Edinburgh mandarins. 'With the Prime Minister's approval I am taking a fresh look . . . at a number of areas of public expenditure which lend themselves to indepth review,' he wrote to Younger in June 1984. 'One area where I see a good case for this is the block budgeting regime for Scotland, Wales and Northern Ireland.' Armed with an internal Treasury needs assessment, Rees claimed nearly £900 million more than necessary had been allocated to Scotland in 1983–84, and stated his intention to claw back about a seventh of that figure in future spending rounds.

Accustomed to such attacks, the Scottish Office dusted off some old battle plans. The Treasury's needs-assessment methodology was questioned ('not an appropriate base'), the sanctity of the Barnett Formula upheld, and Younger's resignation hinted at. There were also other, more overtly political, bargaining chips. 'The continuing decline in heavy industry is still generating acute political difficulties', argued Younger during a face-to-face meeting with Rees. 'Any disproportionate reduction in Scotland's share of public spending would quickly be seized upon by our opponents and presented as a cause of further industrial difficulties that may arise.' Rees acknowledged this, but argued that a reduction could be made to the Block's 'baseline' without anyone noticing.

On the contrary, said Younger, such a reduction would leave him 'uniquely exposed' to attack from Scotland's opposition parties. He said there were signs 'that a renewal of interest in devolution is beginning to consolidate and the changes would undermine one of the main arguments which we have consistently deployed to dampen down enthusiasm for it – namely that Scotland would fare worse with an Assembly of its own than under the present system'. Cutting the baseline, added Younger, would have a 'horrific'[22] effect on health spending, which constituted around a quarter of the Block. His clincher was to remind Rees of the Prime Minister's words during a general election rally in Edinburgh the previous year. 'I have no more intention of dismantling the National Health Service', she had assured local activists, 'than I have of dismantling Britain's defences.'[23]

Scottish Office defences were again battered in the autumn of 1985, a particularly fierce attack which left Younger peculiarly isolated. A Scot, John MacGregor, had succeeded Peter Rees as Chief Secretary and was even more engaged with Barnett than his predecessor. Through sheer frustration, Downing Street asked Brian Unwin, then Deputy Secretary to the Cabinet, to put territorial expenditure on an objective footing in order to settle the ongoing dispute once and for all. Unwin's inter-departmental working party,

---

[22] SOE 6/1/1708–9 Scottish Public Expenditure 1984–1987, NAS.
[23] Speech in Edinburgh, 31/5/1983, MTF.

however, came up with relative expenditure levels not dissimilar to Barnett, although it also recommended transferring responsibilities for the Scottish Arts Council and Scottish universities to the Scottish Office without additional cash in order to 'bleed the block'. This happened a few years later, but in the meantime, his findings were agreed and the resulting 'Unwin Report' was thereafter wielded by the Scottish Office as the definitive justification for higher per capita spending north of the border.[24]

When Michael Heseltine stormed out of the Cabinet on the morning of 9 January 1986, and Malcolm Rifkind succeeded Younger as Scottish Secretary, the dynamic changed. While Willie Whitelaw had always seen Younger right if public expenditure disputes reached his so-called 'Star Chamber' (serviced by Brian Unwin), Rifkind had no such protection. When the new Scottish Secretary subsequently held out stubbornly over some small sums of cash, Mrs Thatcher and Whitelaw demanded that he settle. And in the autumn of 1986, John MacGregor tried again. 'On this occasion the Chief Secretary, as always seeking economies, produced a paper designed to show that Scottish provision had increased since the late 1970s,' recalled Nick Edwards, 'that there should be an adjustment for population; and that at some stage it would be necessary to carry out a needs study.' He went on:

> Malcolm Rifkind argued that in terms of need measured by such things as gross domestic product and unemployment, the gap between Scotland and the rest of the UK had widened; but for the first time in my memory of any such discussion he quite quickly drew down heavy fire from the Prime Minister, who said that it was all very well talking about Scotland, but what concerned her was what was happening in the north-east. Thus encouraged, ministers from south of the border entered the fray . . . A proposal that there should be an adjustment for falling population provoked the Scottish Secretary into vigorous counter-attack with the argument that it had never been part of the calculation, and that in turn prompted one colleague to ask whether, if there was nobody left in Scotland, the Scottish Office would still want the same resources!

'Your argument is losing sympathy', Edwards remembered the Prime Minister telling Rifkind; 'my hackles are raised.' Uncharacteristically, even Whitelaw joined in the attack by warning Rifkind that by resisting an adjustment for falling population the Cabinet would have to demand a second needs assessment, the worst-case scenario in the eyes of the Scottish Office.

But Whitelaw, it emerged, was playing devil's advocate. 'Think of England a bit,' said Mrs Thatcher, interrupting the discussion again, 'otherwise you won't have a Government at all.' Whitelaw suggested a compromise in the form of a proportionately lower increase in the Scottish Block rather than a straight-

---

[24] Unwin understood the consequences of what he was proposing, warning that the problem was 'both presentational and practical'. ('Territorial Expenditure', Treasury files 16/4/1986)

forward cut. 'For once the Scottish Secretary knew that he had been in a fight,' observed Edwards, 'although the result was no more than a marginal reduction in the increased funding which the formula would otherwise have provided.' He went on: 'Indeed, the reduction had to be sufficiently marginal to ensure that it could not be recognized outside! The political consequences were still considered paramount. There may have been good practical and social arguments for providing Scotland with all this additional money; but seldom has such large-scale expenditure produced such a poor political dividend.'[25]

That, later in the 1980s if not at the beginning of the decade, essentially summed up the attitude of Mrs Thatcher and several of her ministers. Nevertheless, the Scottish Block/Formula system survived the 1980s intact, although the Scottish Office was finally forced to agree to an adjustment for falling population in 1992.

THE BIG BANG

Remarkably, few of these Whitehall battles found their way into Scottish newspapers. Even if they had, it is unlikely the decline of the Scottish Conservative vote might have been halted. In Scotland's 1984 district council elections, the Conservatives even lost control of local authority strongholds like Edinburgh and Eastwood, while in the European Parliament elections that same year, the party reversed its 1979 result to emerge with just two MEPs compared with Labour's five and the SNP's one. Madame Ecosse, otherwise known as the SNP's Winifred Margaret Ewing, had long practised a highly effective form of Scottish nationalism in Brussels in stark contrast to what was seen as Mrs Thatcher's increasingly divisive English Nationalism.

George Younger's response was to ramp up the neo-nationalist rhetoric, something Scottish Unionists had excelled at between the wars. At the May 1984 Scottish Conservative conference he pointedly told delegates that Scotland was run from Edinburgh, not London. At a time when the cry 'Whitehall knows best' was echoing around Westminster, the Scottish Secretary was saying openly and to the contrary that 'Edinburgh knows best'. But still there was muttering from right-wingers. The Scottish Office was 'wet' they claimed, if not the 'wettest' department in Whitehall. While Younger's aggressive policy of clawing back money from high-spending local authorities was welcome, his industrial policy and rhetoric certainly was not.

Yet despite the seemingly patriotic behaviour of the *ancien régime* in protecting Scotland against the revolutionary forces of Thatcherism, it was also becoming increasingly clear that the Scottish Office, on a whole range of fronts, was failing to gain even a grudging acceptance of policies from what later became known as 'stakeholders', let alone Scots voters. Part of the reason was, as ever, economic. Although both the Scottish and UK economies had shown positive growth since the recession of 1979–81, by 1986

---

[25] Crickhowell, *Westminster, Wales & Water*, 54–55.

the relative performance of the Scottish economy continued to deteriorate as
manufacturing shed jobs at an alarming rate, pushing up unemployment to
an all-time high of 358,988 in July 1986. The price of North Sea oil also
slumped to $10 a barrel that year, wreaking havoc in a hitherto growth
industry lauded by Mrs Thatcher during every Scottish visit. As the UK oil
supply sector was principally located in Scotland, it therefore suffered
disproportionately, particularly in the Grampian region where oil development accounted for, directly and indirectly, a quarter of all employment.

The timing could not have been worse. On the eve of Mrs Thatcher's arrival
in Scotland in September 1986, Britoil – privatised by her government –
announced the loss of 750 jobs as a result of the oil slump, 600 of them at its
Glasgow headquarters. In the 18 months to follow various forecasts predicted
that between 10,000 and 17,500 further jobs would be lost as a result. The
electoral backdrop to the Prime Minister's visit was also bleak. In May's local
elections the Scottish Tory vote had again plummeted, while a recent opinion
poll suggested that 16 of the Conservatives' 21 constituencies in Scotland would
fall in the next general election, among them those of Rifkind and Younger.
Many commentators spoke solemnly of Conservative fortunes in Scotland
having reached their lowest ebb since Mrs Thatcher became Prime Minister.

The first day of that year's Scottish Tory conference had been dominated by
shipyard closures, including Ailsa in Younger's constituency, while Scott
Lithgow faced the New Year with an empty order book. Guinness, meanwhile,
was rationalising whisky production and the Black and White plant at Stepps
was due to close. In January 1987 Guinness merged with United Distillers and
the Tory-supporting Glaswegian businessman Sir Norman MacFarlane became chairman. Ernest Saunders, Guinness's former chief, had promised to
establish the new company's corporate headquarters in Edinburgh but few
believed the promise would be honoured (it was not). The STUC calculated
that the capital value of Scottish-owned industry fell by more than half in the
two-year period 1985–86, from £4.7 billion to £2.3 billion, the cumulative
result of Guinness, Arthur Bell, House of Fraser and Coats Paton passing into
foreign ownership. In contrast to the booming south, Scottish service sector
employment increased by just 1.1 per cent between 1980 and 1986.

Even the much-vaunted Silicon Glen was not immune to this second wave
of recession in which Scottish employment remained static at 64 per cent
while the UK figure increased from 68 to 70 per cent (a significant gulf also
emerged between average Scottish and British earnings). Burroughs announced the closure of its Cumbernauld electronics plant, while Caterpillar
moved to shut down its Uddingston factory just weeks after Malcolm Rifkind
had trumpeted a new investment programme. Given the Conservatives'
position in the Scottish polls and the prospect of a general election, the
Scottish Secretary had no choice but to describe a sit-in by workers at the
factory as 'spirited and determined'.[26] What the Prime Minister thought of

---

[26] McCrone & Brown, eds, *Scottish Government Yearbook 1988*, 274.

this pronouncement was anybody's guess. 'Today, ours is a fearful, anxious, nail-biting nation ruminating on Burns's salutation to human despair,' wrote Jim Sillars in his 1986 book, *The Case for Optimism*, capturing the gloomy atmosphere, ' "An' forward tho' I canna see, I guess and fear".'[27]

But although Conservative politicians lined up on platforms to support the Caterpillar workers, there was little the Scottish Office could do about the economic woes afflicting Scotland. The Scottish Lobby tried to fill the void by convening the grandly titled Standing Commission on the Scottish Economy in November 1986. Running along the lines of a Select Committee it was to present its case after taking evidence from a variety of organisations, institutions and individual experts. Sir Kenneth Alexander, then the left-leaning chancellor of Aberdeen University, said it would be 'hungry for ideas, suggestions, information and research in any area relevant to its work'.[28]

Surprisingly, the Scottish Office did not dismiss it out of hand and instead welcomed any realistic proposals it might offer to tackle Scotland's economic problems. But there was still no guarantee it would succeed where many other well-intentioned inquiries had failed. Sir John Toothill's influential report of the early 1960s had at least been seized upon by an expansionist Tory government which directed more industries north as a result. Back then, the creation of Ravenscraig and a generous regional policy were means by which a Tory government hoped retain its electoral hold on Scotland, but by the 1980s the economic orthodoxy belonged to Mrs Thatcher, not Harold Macmillan, and the Conservatives no longer seriously believed they could win elections in such hostile territory.

The apex of that new economic orthodoxy was reached on 27 October 1986 in the City of London. The distinction between stockjobbers and stockbrokers was removed; electronic, screen-based trading replaced open outcry; and fixed commission charges were abolished. The London Stock Exchange (LSE) was transformed overnight. Dubbed the 'Big Bang', this package of financial deregulation became one of the key events in Mrs Thatcher's reform programme. It was also distinctly un-Conservative. Elitist City networks were held responsible for the decline of London as a financial centre, and the transformation of the LSE into an egalitarian melting pot was a stated aim of the financial explosion.

The Big Bang was certainly heard in Edinburgh, where an expanding financial services sector was now a major employer (Scottish Financial Enterprise had been established that year to promote Scottish financial companies abroad), while the impact on consumers was also palpable. Rising wages and a boom in easy credit, symbolised by the appearance of automated teller machines on High Streets in the mid 1980s, indicated that Scots had

---

[27] Sillars, *The Case for Optimism*, 1.

[28] *Scotsman* 17/11/1986. When the Standing Commission reported after the 1987 election, it blamed the Conservatives' 'polarised "market versus intervention" view of industrial policy' for undermining the Scottish economy.

more disposable cash than ever. As Chancellor since the 1983 election, Nigel Lawson had continued his predecessor's emphasis on indirect taxation by increasing personal tax thresholds, taking 850,000 low earners out of income tax altogether, and extending VAT to takeaway food and building repairs. Lawson also wanted to abolish the anomalous Mortgage Interest Tax Relief (as did Michael Forsyth), although this was vetoed by Mrs Thatcher, fearful of the response from 'her people'.[29] There was a down side to this growing sense of personal affluence. Britons, and indeed Scots, began spending more money than they earned. Ironically, Mrs Thatcher disapproved both of this, people living beyond their means (thus why she always approved of statistics showing Scots to be a nation of savers), and of city traders making money from money. 'It's perfectly true that the PM gets very emotional about the plastic cards', admitted the former Scottish Tory MP Jock Bruce-Gardyne in 1989, 'and she thinks it's all very damaging and dangerous.'[30]

The Scottish left, meanwhile, considered the whole thrust of the Big Bang to be damaging and dangerous. 'These values which now seem to hold sway to such an extent in the south should concern us deeply,' cautioned an editorial in *Radical Scotland*. It went on:

> With Scotland seemingly ready to branch out into an era when consideration for *all* the population should become the norm, when caring and sharing could replace the rat-race and the mega-salaries, we are faced with not just a political and constitutional problem but a complete clash of cultures in the broadest sense of the word . . . we can all be quite clear in our minds that, as far as Thatcherism is concerned, we want none of it.[31]

Scottish Tory MPs like Michael Forsyth and Allan Stewart were determined to prove the contrary. Both signed up to the No Turning Back group, which took its name from Mrs Thatcher's 'lady's not for turning' speech and met under the chairmanship of fellow St Andrean Lord Harris of High Cross. In November 1985 they published *No Turning Back: a new agenda from a group of Conservative MPs*, in which Mrs Thatcher was implored not to lose heart and let socialism dominate the agenda. The *Glasgow Herald* editor Arnold Kemp dubbed them Mrs Thatcher's 'praetorian guard'.[32]

GARTCOSH NO MORE

The No Turning Back group were notable dissenters from the party line when it came to the future of Ravenscraig. By 1985 production was up at the

---

[29] In real terms the cost of this increased by 200 per cent between 1980 and 1990 to stand at £7 billion.

[30] *The Thatcher Factor* (Channel 4) 1989.

[31] *Radical Scotland* October/November 1986.

[32] Kemp, *The Hollow Drum*, 180.

Lanarkshire plant, although market conditions remained tough. For Mrs Thatcher, Ravenscraig remained a thorny political issue. Having publicly thanked its 4,000-strong workforce for working on in face of demands for total closure by the National Union of Mineworkers (NUM) and the dockers during the miners' strike (see below), it would have been politically damaging for her to back its closure as most of Europe struggled against a steel recession. Norman Tebbit and his junior minister at the Department of Trade and Industry, the Scots-born Norman Lamont, on the other hand, did not share the Prime Minister's sense of gratitude. They lobbied for its closure as part of something called 'Phoenix II' restructuring, and the result was a compromise that pleased no one. On 7 August 1985 the government announced that although Ravenscraig would be reprieved for another three years, its finishing mill at Gartcosh was to be sacrificed (cold rolling and steel coating were to be transferred to Llanwern in South Wales) with the loss of more than 700 jobs.

For many Scottish Conservatives, even beyond the Pyrrhic victory of another reprieve for Ravenscraig, the closure of Gartcosh was too much to bear. Iain Lawson, a parliamentary candidate, resigned, while there were threats of disaffiliation from two constituency parties in the west of Scotland. When the vote was finally taken in the Commons on 24 January 1986, however, only two Tories – Sir Hector Monro and Anna McCurley – voted against. The Scottish Affairs Select Committee launched an investigation which collapsed in acrimony as its members split along left–right lines, while in November a small group of English Tory MPs led by the Scottish Tory MP Michael Forsyth staged a remarkable putsch by ousting Sir Hector as chairman of the Scottish Conservative Backbench Committee, replacing him with the stridently right-wing Tayside MP Bill Walker. Although Monro was hastily restored when the vote was rerun, the damage to a party already reeling from a grassroots revolt over the rates revaluation (again, see below) was enormous.

On another visit to Scotland that September, Mrs Thatcher conceded frankly that any future decision on the fate of Ravenscraig would be political rather than economic. 'I have made and continue to make it perfectly clear that the future of Ravenscraig would have to come before Cabinet,' she told STV's Colin McKay. 'I am also very much aware of the importance of Ravenscraig to Scotland, to Scottish jobs.' She continued:

In a way, it is more than to Scottish jobs; it is to Scottish morale. I know that. There is a Scottish dimension as well as a steel dimension. I will not forget what Ravenscraig did and the way it stood and the way it carried on during the coal-miners' strike, but please, Mr McKay, there is no point in asking me to take umpteen decisions now. I will take them when they come up on the basis of all the circumstances. It may never come up, because the whole of the industry may improve. One just does not know.[33]

---

[33] Interview with STV, 4/9/1985, MTF.

The following day the Prime Minister met with the STUC for the first time, although the encounter at Prestwick Airport could hardly have been termed a success. Mrs Thatcher proclaimed herself 'a great fan of Ravenscraig', which cynical trade unionists interpreted as approval of those who had refused to support striking miners rather than those committed to making steel. Of the plant's steelmaking abilities, the STUC later remarked, the Prime Minister 'did not have a firm factual grasp'.[34]

Meanwhile, the Scottish Lobby was limbering up for its usual fight. George Younger – who had brokered the Thatcher–STUC meeting – went through the motions of opposing the Gartcosh closure but found himself increasingly isolated within the Cabinet. Tommy Brennan of the steelmakers' union led a march southward to lobby Parliament, and although Michael Forsyth was the only dissenter in a group of Scottish Tories who met his delegation, it was becoming increasingly clear that this was a battle the Scottish Lobby was bound to lose.

On 19 December 1985 Younger finally ruled out a reprieve, saying he had been persuaded by British Steel that the future of Ravenscraig would not be prejudiced by the closure of Gartcosh. In fact, he argued, the closure of the finishing mill might even be to Ravenscraig's long-term advantage. Few were convinced, however, and Brennan was photographed in tears as Gartcosh's fate was confirmed. Mrs Thatcher maintained that her government could not interfere with a commercial decision made by British Steel, while Younger's strategy of seeking Scottish compromises appeared to be subject to the law of diminishing returns.

The STUC's discussion document, *Scotland – A Strategy for the Future*, was published in April 1986 as a direct result of the Gartcosh closure and summed up both the strengths and weaknesses of Scotland against Mrs Thatcher. 'Despite the great concern in Scotland,' it read, 'despite the massive unity in favour of retention of the Gartcosh works, the Government has refused to listen.'[35] While the document's strength lay in drawing together otherwise disparate strands of Scottish opinion and channelling them towards a single objective, its weakness manifested itself in having produced such a woolly alternative. Not only was the assertion that public opinion should dictate the government's industrial policy positively quixotic, but the document's call for 'fresh policies' to tackle deindustrialisation sounded hollow.

This was not entirely the Scottish Lobby's fault. The government's ideological opposition to massive public subsidies for steel-making meant that opponents were forced back onto defensive arguments about saving Gartcosh or Ravenscraig, Prestwick Airport or Govan Shipbuilders, which in turn had the effect of inhibiting discussion of alternative industrial strategies which might offer a more secure long-term future for Scottish manufacturing. If the choice came down to Thatcherism or support for dying industries, therefore, more often than not the Scottish Lobby opted for the latter.

---

[34] Aitken, *The Bairns O' Adam*, 293.
[35] STUC 89th Annual Report.

Even the privatisation of the British Steel Corporation in 1988 did not diminish the symbolic potency of Ravenscraig. It had become a totem of national defiance which no number of Thatcherite reprieves and soothing words could diminish. Although the number of workers at Ravenscraig and Gartcosh was relatively small, they had disproportionate political resonance, and the impact on the wider community was always emphasised. The closure of Gartcosh had essentially marked the end of Scotland's jealously guarded status as a steelmaking nation. By removing the industry's finishing plant the government had effectively admitted that there would soon be no steel left to finish. So instead of being seen as having prolonged the life of Ravenscraig, Mrs Thatcher was perceived as its butcher.

The Scottish Lobby, or rather the STUC, fared better with its emotively titled document, *Scotland: A Land Fit for People*, which was published shortly before the 1987 general election. Its analysis of Scotland's economic problems, together with prescriptions for change, were more coherent than previous efforts, perhaps as a consequence of a certain intellectual rigour introduced by its new general secretary, Campbell Christie. Unusually committed to devolution for a trade unionist, Christie believed that an Assembly would provide Scotland with a structural context in which to reshape its industrial policies.

EDUCATIONAL THATCHERISM

'When times are hard,' noted David McCrone in the *Scottish Government Yearbook* of 1984, 'the Scots tend to have recourse to well-worn myths to protect themselves against cold and hostile winds. No set of myths comes to hand more readily than those associated with education.'[36] Those myths had already been applied in opposition to the Assisted Places Scheme and the Parents' Charter, but the story of Scottish education in the 1980s, at least in terms of funding, was effectively one of two cities. In Scotland's schools it was the best of times, while in Scotland's universities it was certainly the worst of times.

Mrs Thatcher's dislike of universities, which she considered dominated by unproductive leftist academics preaching from ivory towers, quickly manifested itself in policy terms. Indeed, the University Grants Committee wielded a Thatcherite axe with such ferocity during her first two governments (between 1980 and 1987 Scottish university funding was cut by 16.7 per cent) that Aberdeen University was forced to close six arts faculty departments and make more than 200 staff redundant. Academic supporters of Thatcherism were, therefore, a Scottish campus rarity.

Students were also hit through frozen grants and a move towards loans, although Sir Keith Joseph's attempts to introduce tuition fees were shelved following a Cabinet revolt in 1984. This assault on higher education almost certainly helped erode support for Thatcherism in Scotland's more affluent

---

[36] McCrone, ed., *Scottish Government Yearbook 1984*, 2.

communities. In Glasgow's leafy Strathkelvin and Bearsden, for example, there was an unusually high concentration of academics and families with children attending university. 'I remember well squeals of anguish from some of my well-heeled constituents over the cutting of grants,' recalled Sir Michael Hirst, the constituency's then MP. 'It demonstrated that the middle classes in Scotland were as reliant on subsidies as anyone else.'[37]

There was a happier story in terms of the number of electronics graduates leaving Scotland's universities, which increased at about 8 per cent annually, a rare case of industry and education actually working in harmony to sustain a key sector. Further down the educational ladder, however, Scottish private provision in terms of schooling continued to lag behind that in England. Whereas by 1982–83 the number of English pupils outside the public sector had increased to 6.2 per cent (from 5.9 per cent in 1979), the percentage of Scottish children attending non-maintained schools was stuck at 3.4 per cent, the same proportion as in 1979. A voucher system to stimulate demand in England and Scotland was considered, and subsequently abandoned, by Sir Keith Joseph as Education Secretary, and otherwise Mrs Thatcher simply bragged about how much more she was spending on education in Scotland than the previous Labour government. 'I could tell you that, when Labour left office, they were spending £550 on each pupil in Scotland,' she told the Scottish Conservative Party conference in 1986. 'A lot of money. Do you know how much we are spending now? Over twice as much – more than £1,200 on each pupil.'[38]

Raw statistics did not appear to impress Scotland's teachers, who were to spend much of late 1984, and most of 1985, taking part in rolling strikes. Although they accepted a 4.5 per cent pay increase in April 1984, almost half the Educational Institute of Scotland's (EIS) members had voted to reject it, so they were determined to get more in 1984–85. The EIS, together with other teaching unions, asked for an external salary review, but when the government failed to respond staff boycotted new curriculum development – most significantly the new Standard Grade exams being introduced as a result of the Munn and Dunning reports – and unions called a one-day strike to take place in December 1984.

The EIS deliberately singled out schools in Scottish ministers' constituencies for indefinite strikes, including George Younger's Ayr seat, where the union also staged a rally attended by 18,000 teachers. Mrs Thatcher visited Eastwood during the dispute, where she was greeted by a noisy EIS picket as she met the Scottish education minister Allan Stewart. The Prime Minister's response was an ill-judged homily at the 1985 Scottish Tory conference. 'I owe so much to my own teachers,' she told activists. 'I know how much I owe to my own head teacher – a Scots classicist from Edinburgh who came south to teach us English – and a lot of good Scots sense besides.'[39]

---

[37] Interview with Sir Michael Hirst, 29/7/2008.
[38] Speech to Scottish Conservative conference, 16/5/1986, MTF.
[39] Ibid., 10/5/1985, MTF.

Mrs Thatcher was mystified as to why that 'good Scots sense' seemed to have evaporated by the time she became Prime Minister. By the autumn of 1985, however, good sense also deserted teachers in England as they voted for all-out strikes and work-to-rule over their own, separate, pay dispute. In December, by which point the row affected the whole country, things were so bad that Mrs Thatcher asked a group of Cabinet ministers led by Willie Whitelaw (and including George Younger) to report directly to her with possible solutions.

Younger and Chris Patten, then Minister of State for Education in England, tried to convince the Prime Minister to change her mind about an independent review of teachers' pay as the dispute smouldered on into its third year. Mrs Thatcher, however, had an innate distaste for such inquiries, largely because they inevitably resulted in exactly the sort of pay problems which had dogged her first term (*pace* the Comparability Commission chaired by Professor Hugh Clegg). Nevertheless, the former Boots chairman Sir Peter Main was appointed by Malcolm Rifkind to examine Scottish teachers' pay and conditions. His recommendation of a 16.4 per cent increase over 18 months as a *quid pro quo* for concessions on working conditions led to a split in the Cabinet sub-committee dealing with the parallel Scottish and English disputes. Although Main would cost £234 million for Scotland, an equivalent deal in England and Wales would cost the Exchequer around £2.5 billion. Nigel Lawson, the Chancellor, vetoed both as too expensive.

As ever, tightening the nation's purse strings was the public justification for not caving in to striking public sector workers. 'They [the EIS] hooked themselves to the idea of having an independent review body', said George Younger in mid 1985, 'when they should have seen perfectly clearly there was no way this Government could ever agree to that without wrecking its entire anti-inflation policy. If we had granted one, everyone else would have wanted it too.'[40] But while in England the Interim Advisory Committee on Teachers' Pay was established in 1987 to impose pay settlements on striking teachers, there was no similar reform in Scotland, where Sir Peter's recommendations were eventually implemented.

Despite the broadly favourable outcome, the teachers' strike confirmed to many in Scotland that public sector workers, even teachers, did not feature highly in the Thatcherite pantheon. 'We were constantly alienating the middle classes in certain sectors,' recalled David McLetchie. 'It got to the stage when it would have taken a brave teacher or nurse to stand up and say "I support the Conservatives." We should naturally have been able to get professionals like teachers and doctors to support us, but instead there was a cumulative negative effect on them and their families.'[41]

In health, as in education, all Mrs Thatcher could do in Scotland was boast about how much money she was spending. 'In 1979, the amount spent on the

---

[40] *Glasgow Herald* 2/7/1985.
[41] Interview with David McLetchie MSP, 6/10/2008.

Health Service in Scotland was equal to £800 a year for every family of four,' she said at the 1986 Scottish Conservative conference. 'This year the sum is £1,500 for every family of four. An increase far greater than the rise in prices . . . 120,000 more patients have been treated in Scottish hospitals in 1984 than in 1979. That required more nurses – 7,000 more to be precise.' She went on: 'They [the opposition] will tell you of the 28 Scottish hospitals that have been closed, without telling you about the 42 hospitals and extensions which have already been opened since 1979 and the 32 further hospital schemes already under way. They will tell you of the 1,300 beds which have been lost, but not a word about the 4,200 new beds.'[42] In terms of funding the NHS, to an extent Mrs Thatcher's hands had been tied since before the 1979 general election. In addition to an agreement to honour any outstanding pay recommendations, she was also persuaded to commit to not cutting health spending in the Tory manifesto.

As a result, the NHS escaped the Thatcher axe for much of her first term – even though critics claimed annual increases were not enough to retain services at existing levels – and continued to do so during her second. The NHS had strong Scottish roots and had been governed by separate Scottish legislation since its inception in 1948. But, unlike England, it had relatively limited history of private provision before the Second World War, and as a result Scotland lagged behind its southern neighbour in terms of private healthcare throughout the 1980s. In 1979 one survey suggested that only 2.3 per cent of Scots were covered by private health insurance, a figure which had increased to just 3.8 per cent by 1984. Comparable British figures were 4.9 and 9 per cent respectively, while England also had twice the number of 'pay' beds.

In the 1970s the notion of a private hospital in Scotland would have been unthinkable, but by the mid 1980s there were several. In Glasgow, the profit-making Ross Hall competed with an older BUPA facility called Nuffield McAlpine, while in Edinburgh, Murrayfield hospital had been opened by BUPA in 1984. BUPA, whose Scottish offices also covered the north of England, almost doubled its number of subscribers in Scotland between 1979 and 1984 to around 81,000.

This growth in private provision, although relatively small, created tensions within a deeply ingrained tradition of public health in Scotland. Greater Glasgow Health Board responded by banning the use of NHS equipment for private work, while the Blood Transfusion Service refused to handle blood supplies for Ross Hall until it agreed not to charge its patients for blood. Anecdotally, staff in the private sector also reported pressure from health service unions and experiences of a highly emotive, occasionally hostile, reception from practitioners and patients.

Meanwhile, the private sector intruded nationwide through the contracting out of routine support services like cleaning, catering and hospital main-tenance. The main intellectual stimulation for this came from Michael

---

[42] Speech to Scottish Conservative conference, 16/5/1986, MTF.

Forsyth, who had been manager of a public relations firm which included among its clients Pritchards, a firm active in tendering for private contracts in England. Forsyth had published a pamphlet called *Reservicing Health*, which argued that NHS workers bullied exorbitant wage rises out of the government which in turn deprived capital projects of cash. He also pointed out that savings of between 25 and 50 per cent could be made by contracting out cleaning and catering services.

In September 1983 the Scottish Home and Health Department issued a circular asking health boards to 'test the cost-effectiveness of their domestic, catering and laundry services by seeking tenders for these services from outside contractors and comparing them with the cost of in-house services'. Response was minimal and a second circular was issued in June 1984 to 'stimulate further progress'.[43] There was a perception that it was not only health boards that were reluctant to conform to the spirit of the circulars, but the Scottish Office itself, despite all its departmental cleaning having been carried out by contractors since 1983.

Five of Scotland's health boards refused to comply, six indicated that they would while one, Forth Valley, agreed to investigate tenders but do nothing further, a course of action actually within a strict interpretation of the circulars. The not-unreasonable suspicion that contracting out had more to do with eroding the influence of health service unions than cutting costs probably explained much of this reluctance, while opinion polls showed that the majority of Scots – and even more than a third of Tory voters – were opposed to contracting out.

Contracting out had been a recommendation of a small team led by Roy Griffiths, then chief executive of Sainsbury's, to look at effective use of management techniques within the NHS. Although his remit was English, Griffiths did visit Scottish facilities and the Scottish Secretary made it clear he would seek to apply his findings north of the border. Unsurprisingly, Griffiths brought a business perspective to bear and repeatedly emphasised the similarities between NHS and business management, a view very much in keeping with the spirit of the times. Equally unsurprisingly Mrs Thatcher, the grocer's daughter, approved of a successful grocer's attempt to get the NHS larder in order.

The result in Scotland, as in England, was the introduction of general managers at both health board and unit level, an intrusion widely resented by Scottish doctors. Griffiths' intention was also to make doctors more aware of the costs they incurred each time they decided upon a course of treatment without actually confronting clinical freedom head on. But other non-structural recommendations such as performance indicators, annual review meetings and Rayner-type[44] scrutinies of particular areas of administration

---

[43] Scottish Office circulars Gen 13 and Gen 14.

[44] Sir Derek Rayner, managing director of Marks & Spencer, had headed up the Number 10 Efficiency Unit since the early 1980s. He scrutinised the working of every government department, looking for economies.

were not reproduced in Scotland with the same vigour as they took root in England.

Scarcely a week passed at the Department of Health and Social Security (DHSS) without a new reform from Norman Fowler and his deputy Kenneth Clarke, yet at St Andrew's House George Younger and John MacKay did not display quite the same reforming zeal. Oddly, despite almost a third of Scottish Office expenditure going on health and social services, the Treasury's gaze was upon the DHSS and this, coupled with a healthier resource base and higher per capita spending on health, sheltered Scotland from the full brunt of the cold winds blowing between the Treasury in Whitehall and the DHSS at Elephant and Castle. In England there were forced staffing reductions during 1983 but none in Scotland; and although there was a 1 per cent cut in resources, also in 1983, it was later reinstated. The STUC, meanwhile, argued for a real-term 2 per cent increase in spending to cover new developments and shifting demographics.

A growing challenge throughout the 1980s, particularly in Scotland, for healthcare provision was the spread of HIV and AIDS. To this, however, Mrs Thatcher responded proactively. Hysterical reactions (in July 1983 the Commons debated press reports which suggested the Edinburgh International Festival would become a 'breeding ground'[45] for the mystery disease) soon gave way to constructive action with the creation of Scottish Health Monitor – the UK's first national AIDS charity – to co-ordinate Scotland's response to the condition. When it also became clear that cities such as Edinburgh contained large numbers of injecting drug users with HIV, the UK's first needle exchange was set up in Dundee. In February 1986 the government launched its first AIDS public information campaign, publishing the message 'Don't aid AIDS' in full-page newspaper adverts. This continued in 1987 with the aggressively bleak 'AIDS – Don't Die of Ignorance' leaflet campaign, accompanied by memorable 'Tombstone' and 'Iceberg' television adverts. Initially, reported cases of HIV in Scotland rose year on year but peaked in 1986, the vast majority being associated with injecting drug use.

Despite the Prime Minister's record in this field, and her reticence when it came to tackling certain shibboleths of the welfare state, she could never understand why her government received so little credit, particularly in Scotland, for its relatively high spending levels. In that respect the NHS in Scotland was an apt microcosm for Scotland in the Thatcher era. But then the Prime Minister was seen as a warrior, as the former Health Secretary Norman Fowler has written, and not as a social reformer. Scots had for years been waiting for government to tackle rising inflation and the power of the unions, but schools, universities and the NHS were not seen as public enemies and people therefore reacted differently to assaults upon them, however soft. Mrs Thatcher herself used private healthcare, something Labour exploited as part of a wider attempt to portray her as hell-bent upon full privatisation of

---

[45] *The Times* 25/7/1983.

the NHS. Constantly rising prescription charges, not to mention charges for eye and dental checks, did not help the government's rebuttal.

Mrs Thatcher was also aware that such perceptions, however unfair she deemed them to be, contributed to a related view that she personally did not 'care'. The definition of what she did not care about was general as well as specific. Even the Queen was reported as believing the Prime Minister to be 'uncaring', while in Scotland Mrs Thatcher's lack of sympathy was associated in particular with unemployment and industrial decline, and to a lesser extent with demands for devolution. In short, the Prime Minister was believed not to care about Scottish public opinion. 'Really, do you think I would have gone through all the criticism and the flak which I have taken, and still take, if I did not care passionately about the future of the United Kingdom?' she snapped when challenged on this point by a journalist in 1989. 'Do you think I would have gone through all of the criticism of those policies if I did not care and do you think the Health Service would now be as good as it is if we did not care?'[46]

A row over distribution of the DHSS's cold climate allowance during the winter of 1985/86 did not help diminish this perception. As more and more south coast resorts qualified for the payment although temperatures stayed above zero, Scotland remained out in the cold despite enduring one of its bitterest winters in years. Tony Newton, the Social Security Minister, and ultimately the Prime Minister herself, refused to budge, leaving the indelible impression that theirs was a government that just did not care. It was literally Thatcherism in a cold climate.

'Our opponents are never slow to claim for themselves a monopoly of care,' Mrs Thatcher said at the 1986 Scottish Tory conference, attempting to tackle the perception head on. 'Surely, caring is what you do, not just what you say. And those who talk most aren't always those who do most.' She went on:

> It is because we care about the old that we have increased the old-age pension to record levels, and cut the tax on their savings. It is because we care about the disabled that we have far and away the best record of help and support of any Government . . . we are in politics because we care. It is because we care that we don't care for Socialism. It is because we care that we are Conservatives.[47]

Even Mrs Thatcher's swift appearance at the scene of two Scottish tragedies in 1988, the Piper Alpha disaster and the Lockerbie crash, did little to dispel the impression. The Labour MP and future Speaker Michael Martin even attacked the Prime Minister for not visiting survivors of a train

---

[46] Interview for *Dundee Courier*, 7/9/1989, MTF.

[47] Speech to Scottish Conservative conference, 16/5/1986, MTF. It was the Scottish Tory MP Ian Lang, an occasional speech writer for the Prime Minister, who persuaded her to actually use the word 'care' in this speech.

crash in his Glasgow constituency while simultaneously accusing her of 'ambulance-chasing'. 'The Hon. Gentleman', Mrs Thatcher retorted, 'cannot have it both ways.'[48]

Andrew Dunlop, who was the Prime Minister's political secretary at Downing Street, found the accusation that she did not care particularly perplexing. 'I used to visit my family in Scotland and get it in the neck,' he recalled:

> My brother is a doctor, the other is a lawyer, and they used to say she doesn't care about Scotland. It was stuff specific to their professions, like GP contracts and certain legal reforms . . . it used to infuriate me. Whether people thought the policies were right for Scotland or not, there was this perception that she didn't care about Scotland, which having worked for her for a couple of years I knew was complete and utter nonsense.[49]

A policy area that applied to the whole of the UK, and helped fuel this perception further, was social security. In 1981/82 expenditure in that area was running at £523 per head in Scotland, compared with £518 in England, but with some of the most deprived parts of Britain situated north of the border, this disparity was hardly surprising. The recession of the early 1980s also took its toll. From November 1979 to November 1982 the number of Scots dependent upon the old system of Supplementary Benefits rose from 450,000 to 770,000, income that was liable for tax from July 1982.

By 1985, 15.5 per cent of the Scottish population relied on government support and 45.5 per cent of Scottish households received Housing Benefit, compared with 34.7 per cent of British households. Initially cautious in this area, as in others, by the middle of the 1980s Mrs Thatcher was anxious for reform. A social security review was commissioned, followed by a green paper in June 1985. This proposed scrapping the State Earnings-Related Pension Scheme (SERPS), changing eligibility for Housing Benefit, replacing Family Income Supplement with means-tested family credit, and Supplementary Benefit with income support. When the subsequent Social Security Bill became law in 1986, Mrs Thatcher had compromised on just one component by agreeing to retain SERPS.

Although the Social Security Act did remove the worst aspects of the so-called 'poverty trap', whereby a claimant could lose more than £1 in benefits for each additional £1 of earned income, in other respects it arguably made the position of the poorest in Scotland even worse. With its emphasis on means testing and refusal to restore the link between child benefit and inflation, the number of Scottish families caught in the poverty trap actually increased. The Labour MP Gordon Brown filleted the reforms in his book,

---

[48] Hansard 148 c754.
[49] Interview with Andrew Dunlop, 16/4/2007.

entitled *Where There is Greed*, while the STUC's Campbell Christie christened the Act – which came into force in April 1988 – a 'moneylenders' charter'.[50]

The perception of an uncaring Prime Minister was also supported by opinion polls. When surveyed in 1987, 72 per cent of Scots believed Mrs Thatcher only looked after the interests of one class while 54 per cent agreed that she was uncaring. Two years later half a million Scots were in receipt of some form of benefit, and indeed the British Social Attitudes survey found that 70 per cent of Scots believed 'Benefits are too low and cause hardship'[51] (compared with 29 per cent in the south of England). As John Campbell, Mrs Thatcher's biographer, has observed, 'in the midst of rising wealth, poverty was also increasing, creating a new and permanently excluded underclass'.[52] This was most pronounced, particularly in Scotland, in terms of illicit drug use. While in 1980 there were only 58 men and 32 women in Scotland notified to the Home Office as drug addicts, by 1996 the totals were 1,032 and 431 respectively, the steepest rise having taken place between 1980 and 1986.

This world was later immortalised in Irvine Welsh's novel *Trainspotting*,[53] and many of Mrs Thatcher's critics held her directly responsible for its creation. 'We were an aspiring class which produced its own leaders via the trade union movement and in local government,' said Jim Sillars of the Scottish working class. 'The underclass doesn't aspire. These Tories gave me the impression, perhaps wrongly, that they enjoyed putting the boot into what they called the "undeserving poor". The wets were as concerned about the poor as the rich; but the Thatcherites condemned them just for being poor.'[54] Opponents also accused the Prime Minister of being insensitive to increasing inequality. 'But at the same time she also believed that inequality was not just inevitable but necessary,' wrote John Campbell, 'indeed positively beneficial, as a stimulus to enterprise, a reward for success and a penalty for failure or lack of effort.'[55] This, again, was Mrs Thatcher's Victorian incarnation to the fore, but the gap between the 'haves' and 'have-nots' was hardly a new phenomenon. As the songwriter Gus Kahn put it in 1920, 'There's nothing surer, the rich get rich and the poor get poorer'. The Prime Minister simply saw it as an inescapable consequence of her crusade to put the 'great' back into Britain.

'THE ENEMY WITHIN'

Harold Macmillan once said that the three institutions with which no Prime Minister should become embroiled were the Vatican, the Brigade of Guards

---

[50] Press release dated 11/4/1988, STUC.
[51] *British Social Attitudes 1986*, 130.
[52] Campbell, *The Iron Lady*, 247.
[53] See Chapter 8, p. 194.
[54] Interview with Jim Sillars, 9/5/2008.
[55] Campbell, *The Iron Lady*, 247.

and the miners. Mrs Thatcher followed Macmillan's advice on only two out of the three. Initially, her tactical retreat over pit closures in 1981 appeared to conform to the third, but between then and 1984 Scotland's coal mines continued to suffer from the New Realism, hinting at an inevitable confrontation. Between 1981 and 1983 Lady Victoria in Midlothian, Kinneil in West Lothian, Cardowan and Bedlay in Lanarkshire, and Sorn and Highhouse in Ayrshire all closed, reducing the number of miners in Scotland to around 14,000.

Accompanying these closures had been legislation requiring the National Coal Board (NCB) to break even by 1983/84, and repeated calls for strike action by the 'Scottish Area' of the NUM over pay claims. Dominating everything, for initially Mrs Thatcher remained aloof from the central dispute, were two very different Scots personalities. The Kinlochleven-born Ian MacGregor had recently returned to the UK from the US to head up British Steel (a transfer facilitated by Hector Laing) and now applied his cost-cutting acumen to British Coal, while Mick McGahey, National Vice-President of the NUM since 1972, was a lifelong communist.

The NCB in 1983/84 was losing £13.96 for every ton of coal produced in Scotland compared to a British figure of £6.61. MacGregor responded by preparing plans to shed 64,000 jobs at 'uneconomic' pits, and when Mortonhall in Midlothian called for strike action in response to threats of redundancies, McGahey warned the Triple Alliance (miners, steelworkers and transport workers) of 'growing resistance'[56] among pit workers which was becoming difficult to contain.

In 1984 the NCB also announced the closure of Polmaise in Stirlingshire. Despite £15.8 million having been spent on redevelopment from 1980 to 1983 and the presence of 1,350,000 tonnes of unmined coal, the NCB now argued that market conditions could not sustain such high production. Polmaise declared independent strike action in February 1984 and when the NCB announced the closure of Cortonwood in Yorkshire the following month, the seeds were sown for UK-wide industrial action. The final straw came as MacGregor unveiled plans for a 750,000-ton reduction in capacity a few days later. In response, the Scottish Area called strike action.

Arthur Scargill, the NUM's truculent president, spoke eloquently of rolling back Thatcherism and indeed, the miners' strike soon became the most violent manifestation of a long-running debate, apparently lost by Heath and Callaghan, over who governed Britain. Initially, however, Scottish pits were slow to endorse strike action. NUM policy dictated that each area had to declare for action independently, but Bilston Glen in Midlothian, Polkemmet in West Lothian, Comrie in Fife, and Barony and Killoch in Ayrshire, all voted at pithead ballots against industrial action.

In April, even after a special NUM conference lowered the national ballot requirement to a simple majority, no UK-wide vote on industrial action was

---

[56] Acc 9805/263, 29/9/1983, NUM.

held. Realising he probably could not win on a national ballot, Scargill opted instead for a domino strategy, a *de facto* national strike by the back door. McGahey famously countered criticism of this position by declaring that miners would 'not be constitutionalised out of a defence of our jobs',[57] but the NUM's flagrantly undemocratic tactics together with bad timing – strike action began with both coal stocks and temperatures running high – would undermine fatally the wider battle.

The strike also caused tension within the Triple Alliance, despite the old trade union maxim that 'unity is strength'. On 29 March Scargill asked the steelworkers' leader, Bill Sirs, to block all movements of coal into the Ravenscraig steelworks. Sirs replied firmly that he was not prepared to see his members' jobs 'sacrificed on someone else's altar',[58] fearful that compliance with the miners might give the government its desired excuse to shut the steelworks altogether. Eventually, the STUC brokered a compromise and McGahey agreed to allow two trainloads of coal a day in to keep the fabric of the plant intact.

The STUC even wrote to Mrs Thatcher in November 1984 requesting a meeting so that its general council could make the case for reopening negotiations between the NUM and NCB. The Prime Minister replied dismissively, saying that George Younger was the man they should meet. They did, on 25 January 1985, along with church representatives, an array of Lord Provosts, regional council conveners and the Scottish Council for Development and Industry (SCDI). They told the Scottish Secretary the strike was causing immense hardship and that the only way to settle it was by negotiation. 'Younger agreed,' the STUC's official history records. 'It was scarcely a breakthrough.'[59]

Even the mild-mannered Younger described the miners' strike as 'an assault on many of the things Britain stands for',[60] which demonstrated just how polarising the dispute was. To Mrs Thatcher it was a battle between 'us and them', and she even referred to the striking miners as 'the enemy within', an allusion which McGahey – whose father was a founder member of the Communist Party of Great Britain – must either have found discomfiting or construed as conclusive evidence that the class struggle was alive and kicking. Set-piece confrontations between heavily armoured policemen transported up from London or down from Scotland (avoiding their own areas to prevent conflict of loyalties) further emphasised the apparently profound nature of the dispute. Scottish policemen, always well funded by Mrs Thatcher's governments despite cuts elsewhere, appeared to have become agents of an increasingly aggressive British state.

As with the Falklands, many detected a distinctive element to the strike in

---

[57] Crick, *Scargill and the Miners*, 100–01.
[58] Aitken, *The Bairn's O' Adam*, 274.
[59] Ibid., 277.
[60] *The Times* 12/7/1984.

Scotland. Certainly the Scottish media was more sympathetic, while social support through voluntary contributions and creative local authority action attracted widespread public backing. In Strathclyde Region, for example, Fred Edwards, the council's director of social work, authorised loans totalling £191,000 to unmarried miners. The government ruled the loans illegal and threatened to hold Edwards personally financially liable. Only after a vociferous campaign and related public outcry did ministers relent.

The turning point in the strike came in October 1984, when Mrs Thatcher intervened personally to prevent the National Association of Colliery Overmen, Deputies and Shotfirers from entering the dispute. Its presence was a legal requirement when underground work was in progress, although Mac-Gregor had threatened to fire any members who refused to cross NUM picket lines – an inflammatory act the Prime Minister forced him to withdraw. By then 205 miners had returned to work at 12 of the NCB's sites in Scotland, and a November push saw that figure rise to 2,242. 'A man who decided to return to work in Scotland was very much more on his own than a man who lived in Nottingham, or next door in Derbyshire,'[61] wrote MacGregor in his memoirs, referring to the hostile attitude of Scottish miners to their more pragmatic comrades. But, on the other hand, the NCB had indulged in victimisation of its own, enforcing more ruthlessly than in any other coalfield a policy of dismissing miners for misdemeanours, great or trivial, committed during the strike.

By the time of the return to work, more than 200 of these 700 'victimised' miners were from Scotland, and many remained out of work – certainly none were re-admitted – even after Bert Wheeler, the NCB's Scottish representative, had been promoted out of Scotland. Wheeler's zeal had extended well beyond straightforward sackings. During the strike, the Bogside pit in Fife and Polkemmet in West Lothian had been allowed to flood as a result, the miners claimed, of deliberate management sabotage. The Frances colliery near Kirkcaldy, once lined up to be Scotland's showcase pit, was also badly damaged by fire. None was reopened. Detecting weakened resolve among miners, McGahey called for 'a principled negotiated settlement'[62] in January 1985.

In the last days of the strike the STUC's Jimmy Milne wrote that by 'their own exertions to save the mining industry in Scotland, by their example, they have paved the way for the salvation of the entire trade union movement'.[63] But no matter how eloquent, they were defiantly empty words from a once powerful movement of organised labour. In the next few years most of Scotland's deep mines – Bilston Glen, Seafield, Polmaise, Killoch, Barony – closed. Wheeler was said to have told colleagues shortly after the strike ended that the Scottish Area was to be reduced to just one pit, Longannet near Kincardine.

---

[61] MacGregor, *The Enemies Within*, 327.

[62] *Scotsman* 25/1/1985.

[63] Aitken, *The Bairns O' Adam*, 277.

If the miners' strike had been a battle between 'us and them', then victory indisputably belonged to the former. It was, however, victory at a cost. Although Mrs Thatcher emerged victorious, the dispute divided the nation and further consolidated the impression that her style of government was harsh and unyielding. She had also been guilty of getting carried away by her own rhetoric. Far from being 'the enemy within', the miners of Fife were nobody's enemy, as Andrew Marr has written, 'just abnormally hard-working, traditional people worried about losing their jobs and overly loyal to their wild and incompetent leader'.[64] Even workers at Ravenscraig had resisted the NUM more out of concern for their own livelihoods rather than any implicit support for the Prime Minister's attempt to rationalise the coal industry. 'I cannot forgive her for what she did during the miners' strike,' commented Tam Dalyell several years later. 'What she did, not to heal the situation in the coalfield, but to make it worse. Macmillan was a healer, Alec Home was a healer, even Heath was a healer. But not this bloody woman.'[65]

POPULAR THATCHERISM

If the miners' strike had been an important landmark on the ideological battleground of Thatcherism then privatisation marked the next stage in terms of policy development. Although selling off state-owned assets had been nothing more than a vague aim in the 1983 manifesto, a cautious Mrs Thatcher was gradually persuaded by ministers like the Chancellor Nigel Lawson, and advisers such as John Redwood, a fellow of All Souls and a future Cabinet minister in his own right, to pursue what they called 'popular capitalism'. And since Mrs Thatcher had come to symbolise a new era of British capitalism, it was inevitably offered up to voters as 'popular Thatcherism'.

In November 1981 Nigel Lawson had declared that 'No industry should remain under State ownership unless there is a positive and overwhelming case for it so doing.'[66] The first Thatcher government, however, sold off only British Aerospace, Associated British Ports (including ports at Ayr and Troon) and government holdings in Cable & Wireless and the scientific corporation Amersham International. Sir Keith Joseph also split up the General Post Office as a first step towards selling off what emerged as British Telecom (BT).

One of the first manifestations of the Prime Minister's reluctance to sell off national assets was the privatisation of Britoil. Shares had first been issued in 1982 and a second tranche was floated in 1985. Importantly, the government retained a 'golden share' in Britoil, a nominal stake which enabled ministers to outvote all other shareholders in certain circumstances, a compromise

---

[64] Marr, *A History of Modern Britain*, 416.
[65] Roy, *Conversations in a Small Country*, 7–8.
[66] Campbell, *The Iron Lady*, 97.

dreamt up by Lawson to get round Mrs Thatcher's fear that once privatised, 'her oil' might fall into foreign ownership.

The same principle applied to every major privatisation of the 1980s, which eventually encompassed everything from healthcare to forestry. The Prime Minister, however, was also pragmatic, and although she considered housing (through Right to Buy) and public utilities ripe for what she still called 'denationalisation', other state-owned assets, most notably the railways and the NHS, were off-limits. Initially viewed as simply a means by which to raise revenue, denationalisation gradually acquired ideological clothing. The transfer of public assets to the private sector would not only increase consumer choice, but reduce the state's burden in terms of expenditure, legislation, administration and direct employment.

Again, the field in Scotland was subtly different. The public sector was larger, and while the notion of a monolithic state had lost its attraction, even among some on the left and more thoughtful Scottish Nationalists, there was bound to be a degree of reluctance. When polled in 1983, only 25 per cent of Scots were found to favour more privatisation compared with a British figure of 44 per cent.[67] To get round this perceived reluctance, ministers adapted an old argument, mainly used by Scottish Unionists to oppose post-war nationalisations, that control over Scottish industry had been relinquished to government departments in London. Denationalisation, therefore, was depicted as control coming back to Scotland, albeit in private, and sometimes foreign, hands.

The British Shipbuilders Corporation (BSC), nationalised by Labour in 1977, was an emotive early example. Throughout the early 1980s its Scottish components faced stiff opposition from Japan and Korea ('if it wasn't for the nips, being so good at building ships,' sang Pink Floyd in 1983, 'the yards would still be open on the Clyde'[68]), and when the British Shipbuilders Act of 1983 privatised the BSC, which included legendary names like John Brown in Clydebank and Govan Shipbuilders, one by one they slipped away. The yards of Robb Caledon in Dundee and Leith had already closed in 1981 and 1983 respectively, while Greenock-based Scott Lithgow's individual operating companies were dissolved in 1981 and sold to Trafalgar House in 1984. Yarrow's in Scotstoun followed in 1985 when it was snapped up by GEC-Marconi; the Troon-based Ferguson Ailsa was split and sold in 1986; and Hall Russell in Aberdeen passed into A. & P. Appledore ownership the same year.

Privatised shipbuilders, however, offered no return in terms of political capital. Public utilities were a different matter, and it was only after the disposal of BT in 1984 – the first state monopoly to be sold off – that the term 'privatisation' entered the UK political lexicon. Although its privatisation had

[67] Seawright, *An Important Matter of Principle*, 160.

[68] 'Post War Dream' from the album *A Requiem for the Post War Dream* (1983). The song's refrain is 'what have we done, Maggie, what have we done, what have we done to England'.

implications for rural Scotland where telephone services generally benefited disproportionately from cross-susbsidisation, state-enforced social obligations for the newly privatised communications firm minimised any real risk of Highland disconnections.

Crucially, the privatisation of BT was a success, and dispelled any lingering doubts at Number 10. British Gas was sold off in 1986 (with an inspired 'Tell Sid' advertising campaign), while Mrs Thatcher spoke passionately of re-turning power to the people, enfranchising the many on the road to creating one nation, an aim the post-war consensus had hitherto believed could only be achieved via state-owned monopolies. Britain and Scotland did gradually become a nation of small shareholders – as Noel Skelton and Anthony Eden had long ago dreamt of – with the number of Scottish shareholders doubling from 1979 to 1988. In the UK, however, it trebled.

Skelton's 60-year-old vision of a 'property-owning democracy', therefore, came closer to reality under Mrs Thatcher than at any other point in the twentieth century. His belief that giving workers a direct stake in industry would enable them to buy into capitalism sat easily with Thatcherite ideology, and was more or less directly implemented in arrangements whereby employees of privatised state utilities, such as BT, were given a fixed number of shares to sell or invest. The central tenet of Skelton's vision, however, had been property, and to that end sales still lagged behind those in England seven years after legislation enabled the Right to Buy. Undeterred, Mrs Thatcher celebrated the sale of the UK's millionth council house at Forres in September 1986, an event captured by television cameras. Looking even more enthusiastic about the purchase than the home's new owners, the Prime Minister explored every inch of the semi-detached property. Local authorities such as Stirling District, meanwhile, tried to modify the policy by encouraging tenants to accept a buy-back arrangement, on an agreed valuation, if the owner later decided to sell.

The success of the BT sale also gave proponents of the property-owning democracy an appetite for more although not, ironically, the former Prime Minister Harold Macmillan. In a famous speech to a Tory Reform Group dinner in November 1985 Macmillan is commonly thought to have likened privatisation to 'selling the family silver'. 'First of all the Georgian silver goes,' he drawled. 'And then all that nice furniture that used to be in the salon. Then the Canalettos go.' Profitable parts of the steel industry, the railways and BT, he said, were like the 'two Rembrandts still left'.[69] Clarifying his comments in the House of Lords a few days later, Macmillan assured peers that although 'naturally in favour of returning into private ownership and private management all those means of production and distribution which are now controlled by state capitalism', what he had 'ventured to question was the using of these huge sums as if they were income'.[70] The Prime Minister was not amused. At the Scottish Tory conference two years later, she reeled

---

[69] Watkins, *A Conservative Coup*, 105.
[70] Hansard 468 c390–91.

off a list of successful sales before concluding triumphantly, 'that is selling the family silver back to the family'.[71]

It was perhaps in terms of transport that most Scots directly experienced the benefits, or otherwise, of this so-called 'popular Thatcherism'. It began with a distinctly Scottish asset sale, an attempt to sell eight airports in the Highlands and Islands owned by the Civil Aviation Authority, although that proved a flop in 1984 due to unsatisfactory bids. Norman Fowler had more success in denationalising the National Freight Corporation (1982) and the docks of the British Transport Docks Board, while regulations preventing the development of inter-city coach services were also removed.

Although the government later claimed deregulation had improved services and cut fares, the proportion of express bus services in Scotland was relatively small. The Transport Act of 1985 (to take effect from the autumn of 1986), however, went much further in removing the regulatory and licensing controls on local bus services. The industry in Scotland was dominated by the Scottish Bus Group, part of the Scottish Transport Group, and four municipal operations covering Strathclyde, Edinburgh, Dundee and Aberdeen. But the Transport Act, in some respects, stopped at the Anglo-Scottish border. The Scottish Bus Group was neither privatised nor split up into smaller units, as in England.

This concession did not please the true-believing Stirling MP Michael Forsyth, who tabled an amendment to the Transport Bill which would have seen the Scottish Bus Group join its English equivalents in motoring over to the private sector. Ultimately, however, he refrained from seeing it through, perhaps because Scotland had, as ever, a different context. While the public sector dominated bus services in its four main cities, the private sector already flourished through well-established local firms, not to forget an express market later dominated by the Perth-based Stagecoach, whose owner, Brian Souter, enthusiastically backed further deregulation despite his support for the SNP.

As with trains, which she apparently used only once as premier, the Prime Minister had an ill-disguised contempt for public transport, which she considered symptomatic of wasteful and indulgent local authorities. But while Mrs Thatcher considered bus services ripe for deregulation and privatisation, she left well alone when it came to British Rail (BR), although speculation about its possible privatisation was rarely absent from the media. Instead, some of BR's profitable, non-core, businesses were sold off, which allowed the government to contribute reduced subsidies. It began with BR's badly underinvested hotels, which included the North British (later the Balmoral) and Caledonian Hotels in Edinburgh; the Central and North British in Glasgow; Turnberry in Ayrshire; the Station Hotels at Perth, Aberdeen and Inverness; and the Lochalsh Hotel at the Kyle of Lochalsh. The world-famous Gleneagles in Perthshire, which only opened

---

[71] Speech to Scottish Conservative conference, 15/5/1987, MTF.

its doors for half the year, completed the list of some of Scotland's best-known hotels to be 'privatised'. BR's shipping line, Sealink, was also sold in 1984, although the Stranraer–Larne route constituted its only Scottish concern, while British Rail Engineering Ltd, its manufacturing business, was disposed of in 1989.

Overall, according to the railway historian Christian Wolmar, the 1980s were actually a far better time for Britain's railways than the previous decade.[72] Of benefit to Scotland, or at least those travelling between Edinburgh and London, was Mrs Thatcher's approval for the electrification of the East Coast Main Line (ECML), which had passed by her Grantham home in her childhood ('We could set our clocks by the "Flying Scotsman" as it thundered through,'[73] she recalled in her memoirs). Long delayed, work began in 1985 and was completed in late 1990, initially costing £300 million but more in the long term because the cheaply installed overhead wires were brought down so frequently that repair bills were enormous.

Sir David Serpell's 1982 report on the future of British Rail also provided a good example of Mrs Thatcher's political caution. The former civil servant's recommendations made the infamous Dr Beeching appear reticent. Sir David's so-called 'Option A' proposed reducing 10,370 route miles to just 1,630, leaving whole swathes of northern England, central Wales, the West Country and much of Scotland without a single railway line, including the ECML north of Newcastle. In clear possession of the political nous which Serpell so clearly lacked, Mrs Thatcher quietly filed his report away under political hot potatoes.

While Britain's railways would not be privatised until after Mrs Thatcher's premiership, its skies were opened up to domestic and international competition. After several reprieves, Prestwick lost its status as Scotland's sole international gateway (for long jealously guarded by George Younger, whose Ayr constituency included the coastal airstrip) in 1989, while competition was encouraged between British Airways (privatised in February 1987), British Caledonian and British Midland (and, servicing Aberdeen, Dan Air) which, anecdotally at least, led to better services.

'A LICENCE TO PRINT MONEY'

Tom Nairn's 1968 essay, 'Three Dreams of Scottish Nationalism', contained the Scottish academic's most immortalised quote: 'Scotland will be reborn the day the last minister is strangled with the last copy of the *Sunday Post*.'[74] Nairn, of course, meant ministers in the spiritual sense, and his reference to the Dundee-based *Sunday Post* newspaper was not frivolous. Essentially a conservative newspaper published by the conservative D. C. Thomson, its pithy blend of

---

[72] Wolmar, *Fire & Steam*, 294.
[73] Thatcher, *The Path to Power*, 4.
[74] *New Left Review* May/June 1968.

local news, predictable editorialising and strip cartoons epitomised what Nairn saw as the worst elements of traditional Scottish Unionism.

Thatcherism, therefore, presented a newspaper like the *Sunday Post* with certain challenges. Although her radical governments had waged war on many of the paper's traditional targets, in the process it had also produced industrial wastelands in areas from which it drew much of its natural readership. So its generally hostile coverage of the Gartcosh closure illustrated the editorial tensions this conflict produced. The 1980s, argued the former *Glasgow Herald* editor Harry Reid in his history of the Scottish press, was 'a decade when the nature of journalism was changing; it was becoming more hard-edged, more tightly subbed, possibly reflecting the harsher aspects of Thatcherism'.[75]

Overt support for Thatcher personally and her policies, however, was virtually non-existent among Scottish newspapers, unlike on Fleet Street where broadsheets like *The Times* and *Daily Telegraph*, and tabloids like the *Sun*, happily promoted the Thatcherite revolution. This had an undeniable impact on Scots perceptions of Mrs Thatcher's governments or, as Nigel Lawson put it bluntly, 'The attitudes of some Scottish people are wrong, and that is sometimes reflected in the Scottish media.'[76] It is a matter of record that Mrs Thatcher did not read newspapers, instead relying on a daily digest from her press secretary Bernard Ingham. It is unlikely, therefore, that she was aware of any Scottish coverage beyond the *Scotsman* and *Daily Record*, both available in London and therefore included frequently in Ingham's summary.

The Scottish print media was dominated throughout the 1980s by the Labour-supporting tabloid the *Daily Record*, which sold one copy for every seven people in the country, a higher penetration than the *Sun* in England and Wales, which sold one for every 13. The quality press was dominated by the Edinburgh-based *Scotsman* and the Glasgow-based *Herald*, both of which were contemplated for purchase by the Scottish Tory troika of Lord Goold (formerly Sir James, the Scottish party chairman), the senior activist Ross Harper and the former MP-turned-City-financier Iain Sproat. Their aim was to redress the balance of generally hostile coverage, usually couched in the now familiar terms of Scotland's distinctiveness from England.

Devolution was a favourite topic for erudite newspaper commentary, particularly the *Glasgow Herald*, and especially after the appointment of the left-leaning Arnold Kemp as editor. Nevertheless, Mrs Thatcher and Thatcherism put Kemp in a quandary. Despite instinctive resentment of 'the attempt to impose a narrow doctrinal mindset on a complex set of economic, social and political issues', he recognised that trade union reforms had released his industry from restrictive practices and obsolete technology. 'I also found her a personality of compelling power and charm', wrote Kemp, 'with considerable sex appeal.'

---

[75] Reid, *Deadline*, 40.
[76] *Glasgow Herald* 24/11/1987.

Mrs Thatcher's visit to the *Glasgow Herald* on the occasion of its bicentenary in 1983 was a *tour de force* in which, as Kemp conceded, she gave a 'display of personal magnetism that made us realise, if we had been sufficiently obtuse not already to have done so, that here was a politician of the highest class'. A slightly inebriated Harry Reid, Kemp's deputy and a self-confessed Thatcher fan, had been dared to kiss the Prime Minister's hand, which he did to her obvious delight. She then toured the building. 'In editorial she kicked off her shoes and chatted with the news desk, the reporters and the subs,' recalled Kemp. 'In the composing room she knocked them cold. These old trade unionists leapt around in great excitement.' He continued:

> Before she left she crushed Michael Kelly, accompanying her in his capacity as Lord Provost. One of our leader writers, Bob McLaughlan (another fan), presented her with the scholarly Glasgow University edition of Adam Smith. She said: 'Adam Smith got it right.' Kelly said Smith might have got it right then but he hadn't got it right now. She rounded on him: 'Well, laddie,' she said, 'Your lot haven't got it right yet.' Her visit was regal, more so than that of the Queen some weeks later.[77]

Kemp was bemused to receive a complaint the next day from the machine room, which had made it clear in advance of the visit that Mrs Thatcher would not be welcome in the press hall. Why, demanded the complaint, had she not visited them? 'Although Thatcherism was deeply unpopular, especially in Glasgow,' recalled Reid, 'her ebullience combined with her friendly demeanour – her style was at once familiar and regal – seemed to win most of her detractors over as she progressed from floor to floor.'[78]

Bernard Ingham used to rib Kemp, with whom he had worked at the *Guardian*, that Scotland was a less viable economic entity than Yorkshire, a view Kemp believed 'must have influenced her judgement of Scottish questions and led her to underestimate the significance of Scottish national sentiment'.[79] Indeed, Ingham saw a clear divide between what he regarded as the 'terribly partisan and parochial' reporters he encountered on Scottish jaunts with the Prime Minister and the 'sensible relationship' he enjoyed with Scottish political editors based in the Westminster lobby. 'When we went to Scotland it was as though they were defending their honour, rather like old maiden aunts,' he recalled. 'I sometimes wondered if it was because she was a woman, but even that isn't an entirely satisfactory explanation. I think it came down to a fundamental clash of values; they [the Scots] were paternalist while she was the Spartan nurse.'[80]

---

[77] Kemp, *The Hollow Drum*, 209–10.
[78] Reid, *Deadline*, 69–70.
[79] Kemp, *The Hollow Drum*, 212.
[80] Interview with Sir Bernard Ingham, 25/4/2008.

The Westminster lobby system, one example of a closed shop Downing Street not only tolerated but encouraged, came under strain in the late 1980s when the *Independent* and *Guardian* formally withdrew, objecting to the off-the-record nature of Ingham's briefings. The *Scotsman* followed suit under the editorship of Magnus Linklater, a Scottish establishment figure who had returned to Edinburgh in 1988 to edit the paper following a successful journalistic career in London. He remembers being shocked to find anti-Thatcherite sentiment in Scotland more widely entrenched than in the south-east of England, where it certainly also existed. 'Last year the Editor of the *Scotsman*, returning from exile in London,' Mrs Thatcher said in a 1989 speech to the Newspaper Press Fund, 'made the point that "while always maintaining [a] posture of healthy scepticism, we could perhaps do more to accentuate the positive, to highlight the opportunities that confront us". I agree.' The Scottish media, the Prime Minister believed, could be a bit 'dour'.[81] Indeed, the judgement of London-based Scots on Mrs Thatcher's lack of appeal in the old country often deviated sharply from the Scottish media consensus.

Andrew Neil, for example, the Paisley-born editor of the *Sunday Times*, was more of a true believer in the mould of Michael Forsyth, with whom he enjoyed friendly relations. And just as Mrs Thatcher was not afraid of alienating public sector workers with her strident rhetoric, Neil was not afraid of losing traditional readers by changing his newspaper's editorial line. He was also a key figure in the Wapping dispute of 1986, which finally broke the back of the print unions. At around the same time, Rupert Murdoch's News International group established a union-free print works at Kinning Park in Glasgow.

Sir John Junor, meanwhile, the Scots-born editor of the *Sunday Express* and a regular guest of the Thatchers at Downing Street, took an unashamedly critical view of the Thatcher–Scotland dynamic: 'If there is a dislike of Mrs Thatcher among the Scots, it's for two or three reasons. One is that the Scots are a male chauvinist race, and not any longer particularly intelligent, because most of the best people have left Scotland. They are also a whingeing people, which they never used to be. [And] they have made a mess of industry. They've buggered up shipbuilding, they've buggered up the motor car industry.' 'Margaret Thatcher's too damned good for you all,' Sir John concluded when interviewed by the journalist Kenneth Roy. 'And you resent her because she's got this upper class or simulated upper class Edinburgh accent. And you resent also the fact that she's pulling you out of the shit that you've put yourself into over so many years.'[82]

Tim (later Lord) Bell, the public relations specialist who did so much to transform Mrs Thatcher's image in England, took a similar view. As far as he was concerned there was no point developing a strategy to rescue the government's position in Scotland because, privately, 'we all considered it as socialist desert that did not believe in or agree with any of the deep-rooted

[81] Speech to Newspaper Press Fund, 3/2/1989, MTF.
[82] Roy, *Conversations in a Small Country*, 190–91.

principles of Thatcherism'. In other words, as Bell recalled, 'we knew we could win without Scotland'.

As for Scotland's broadcasters, according to Lord Bell, 'the BBC as always followed its leftist principles'.[83] Regarded with suspicion by all prime ministers, particularly Mrs Thatcher, who professed only to watch television at the weekend, the BBC did indeed have a string of left-leaning Scottish controllers during the 1980s. To Robin Aitken, appointed BBC Scotland's business and economics correspondent in 1981, this produced an editorial bias which permeated the BBC's offices at Queen Margaret Drive in Glasgow. 'The BBC in Scotland was deeply antagonistic towards the Conservative Government,' he wrote in 2007. 'In 1984 I returned to [work] after covering the Tory conference in Brighton. The IRA had come close to assassinating Margaret Thatcher with a bomb and the country was in shock. Apart, that is, from some of my BBC colleagues. "Pity they missed the bitch," one confided to me.'[84] Malcolm Rifkind and Michael Forsyth agreed with Aitken. Both attacked publicly the BBC's alleged bias in the late 1980s, echoing Mrs Thatcher's attacks on the BBC in London, and prompting BBC Radio Scotland's head of news and current affairs, Jack Regan, to argue that 'the Scottish body politic is out of kilter [with the government] and that will inevitably be reflected in our programme'.[85]

Strict broadcasting guidelines, however, meant this bias was probably less real than imagined. Mrs Thatcher also abandoned the convention of political balance in appointments to the BBC's board of governors. Tory-supporting Scots like the businessman Malcolm McAlpine and the Earl of Harewood, a former director of the Edinburgh International Festival, were installed, while the Scots-born Director-General, Alasdair Milne, repeatedly blotted his copy book and was forced to resign following a controversy surrounding the Zircon affair, in which BBC Scotland's Glasgow studios were raided by police.

True believers argued regularly that the state-sponsored BBC should be subject to commercial forces just like ITV. (Channel 4, launched in 1982, sat uncomfortably between the public and private sectors.) Sir Alan Peacock, the Edinburgh University academic commissioned to report on the BBC's future in 1986, disagreed. He recommended against scrapping the licence fee, as expected by the government, or compelling the BBC to carry adverts, while approving of what he called the 'comfortable duopoly' comprising BBC Scotland and the three ITV contractors, Grampian, STV and Border, which dominated Scottish broadcasting. STV had an obvious Labour basis, if only in terms of recruitment. Its political correspondent Fiona Ross was the daughter of the former Scottish Secretary Willie Ross, while the political producer was John Brown, brother of Gordon (who had also worked at STV in the early 1980s as a researcher-reporter). There were, however, what

---

[83] Lord Bell to the author, 6/5/2008.

[84] Mail on Sunday 17/2/2007.

[85] Macinnes, 'The Broadcasting Media in Scotland', Scottish Affairs 2 (1993), 85.

became known as 'fig leafs' – on-screen talent like the former SNP MP Margo MacDonald and the presenter Hugo de Burgh, who left STV in 1982 to contest the Coatbridge and Airdrie by-election on behalf of the Conservatives – to disguise the predominantly Labour provenance of its staff.

STV output, however, was often unavoidably hostile to the government. The *Scottish Assembly* programme, for example, aped the composition of the proposed Assembly with a representative studio audience. Week after week votes rejected Thatcherism and Thatcherite politics in Scotland. Roy Thomson, the Canadian media baron who purchased the first Scottish Television franchise in 1957, famously said it was 'like having your own licence to print money'.[86] A reference to its virtual monopoly of regional television advertising, the resulting revenue sustained high wages and restrictive practices which infuriated Mrs Thatcher. When STV's managing director, Bill Brown, tried to convince the Prime Minister that these practices (an eight-man crew to film a single interview was a notorious example) were being eliminated at ITV, she responded curtly, 'Oh come off it, Mr Brown,'[87] and turned on her heel. The Thatcherite revolution, however, did not properly interfere with commercial broadcasting until the Prime Minister's third, unhappily truncated, term in office.

THE STRANGE DEATH OF UNIONIST SCOTLAND

Although Mrs Thatcher's annual speeches to the annual Scottish Conservative conference were generally greeted with ecstatic applause from the party faithful, there were a few senior activists who, by the mid 1980s, were becoming uncomfortable with the Prime Minister's increasingly strident approach. One senior figure in the Scottish Conservative and Unionist Association recalled that this small band of doubters 'would only voice their criticisms in private and only to close friends'[88] as if they lived in fear of liquidation by a totalitarian regime.

The party's activist base, however uncritical and adoring, was also getting older (one journalist used to joke that following Mrs Thatcher's address there would not be a 'dry seat in the house'). 'The Scottish Conservative Party was a coalition of interests, all of which were diminishing,' said Michael Gove, then a student Tory but later a member of the Conservative Shadow Cabinet. 'So the party's base became more and more elderly women, the Church of Scotland and the lairds. Once they diminished to a certain level then they started to talk only to themselves and became completely divorced from the

---

[86] Braddon, *Roy Thomson of Fleet Street*, 240.

[87] This story has many versions. The exchange apparently took place in mid February 1984 when the ITV companies invited Mrs Thatcher to lunch. The Prime Minister complained that there was no good television on Saturday night and Bill Brown attempted a joke in response: 'Well, you could always watch *Union World* on Channel Four, Prime Minister.' Mrs Thatcher retaliated with what Brown later described as 'the treatment, the full laser treatment for about half a minute on the iniquities of ITV's labour relations.' (Darlow, *Independents Struggle*, 337)

[88] Private information.

reality of life in Scotland.'[89] Members of the Prime Minister's entourage gleaned a similar impression from northern jaunts. 'I remember going with her to visit a local party chairman who lived in a laird-like castle in the Dee Valley,' recalled Andrew Turnbull, a future Cabinet Secretary but then a private secretary at Downing Street. 'It was completely removed from reality. There was this strange mix of lairds and people like Bill Walker and Teddy Taylor, and it didn't really hang together.'[90]

The Scottish Conservative Party could, however, boast a lively and occasionally controversial youth wing. Although the senior Tory councillor Brian Meek was dismissive of what he called the 'crew-cropped specimens' of the Federation of Conservative Students' (FCS) Scottish contingent, they were at least energetic recruiting-sergeants for potential supporters who would otherwise have been put off by the party's anachronistic grouse-moor image.

One unlikely recruit was Murdo Fraser, the son of a car mechanic who later became deputy leader of the party in the Scottish Parliament. 'The Scottish Young Conservatives [SYCs] produced a magazine called "Boat Rocker",' he recalled. 'The joke we had was that the SYCs were rocking the boat and we in the FCS were taking an axe to the bottom of it. They thought they were so cutting edge, but they just did what the party elders told them to. We were the keepers of the Thatcherite flame.'[91] While the SYCs may have been 'Thatcher's Tartan Army', according to the press, the FCS were true believers.

These particular true believers, however, were regarded as a nuisance by Mrs Thatcher, and Norman Tebbit was eventually given the task of winding up the FCS for being, ironically enough, too right wing. One Scottish FCS pamphlet, *A Conservative Manifesto for Scotland*, illustrated why. Proposing widespread privatisation, the legalisation of drugs, and even incest between consenting adults, the document may have represented sound libertarianism but was politically explosive.[92]

Even youthful zeal could not revive the party's seemingly terminal decline, particularly at regular local government elections which always preceded awkwardly Mrs Thatcher's keynote speech in Perth. Part of the problem was that the Prime Minister simply lacked a 'feel' for Scotland and its distinctive issues. 'She was conscious for a time that Scotland was a problem politically but she didn't know what to do about it,' remembered her political secretary Stephen Sherbourne. 'She had this sense that we needed a new approach to Scotland but just didn't quite know how to fashion it. And we got distracted by other things.' This manifested itself in the annual Scottish conference speeches, 'where she always felt there was a slightly amateurish attempt to put a Scottish flavour in the speech which verged on the patronising. Michael

---

[89] Interview with Michael Gove MP, 28/7/2008.
[90] Interview with Lord Turnbull, 3/6/2008.
[91] Interview with Murdo Fraser MSP, 20/5/2008.
[92] 'As for liaison between persons within the forbidden degrees who are over 21, we are of the opinion that such relations should be treated in the same vein as the laws relating to homosexuality.' (*A Conservative Manifesto for Scotland*, 23)

Alison, her parliamentary private secretary, would occasionally throw in some Burns. "That will please them" was the thinking.'[93]

The 1985 Scottish Conservative conference was a case in point. 'It is sometimes suggested that the Conservative Party need not worry about its political strength in Scotland as its power base is south of the Border and Scotland is Labour territory,' Mrs Thatcher said. 'Nothing could be further from the truth . . . As Disraeli said, we are a national party or we are nothing. And he was referring not only to people in all parts of Great Britain, but to people from all walks of life.' She continued:

> Scotland ought to be natural Tory territory. That's the way we want to see it. We did it in the 1950s and it is time that, together, we did it again. Truly this is the way to One Nation, where all are different but all are equally important. Burns as always put it more colourfully . . . so let me say it in my English, an anglicized version of Burns: 'The rank is but the guinea stamp; the man's the guid for a' that.' All different, all equally important. And he went on: 'Then let us pray that come it may, as come it will for a' that; that sense and worth, o'er all the earth may bear the prize and a' that'. I didn't expect to find so much pure Toryism in Burns. But there it is written long before we were here.[94]

Although Mrs Thatcher genuinely liked the verse of Robert Burns (she once quoted the line 'freedom and whisky gang together' to the SNP leader Alex Salmond), invoking the Ayrshire bard in this context never came across particularly well to an external audience. Her challenge to the party to restore its position to 1955 levels of support was also quixotic, but betrayed her very real incredulity that it had slipped so far from that unprecedented – for any party, before or since – achievement of having polled a majority of votes *and* seats in Scotland.

The Prime Minister's oration the following year did not represent much of an improvement. 'Sometimes in Scotland I seem to sense that you feel that "they", "down South", in "the establishment" aren't interested,' she ventured. 'You know, that couldn't be more wrong. I could answer in figures. I could point to the fact that, of the regional aid for the whole of Britain, Scotland receives a third. Or that when it comes to spending taxpayers' money, we spend £450 more per person in Scotland than in England.' She continued:

> But there's more to it than money, I know. When I was in Grantham, I used to look at 'them', down in London, and wonder whether 'they' knew what life was like in Lincolnshire. Then I got involved and I found that they not only knew, they cared. In truth, there is no 'them'. There is only 'us'. We are all involved; we all contribute and we all share in the wellbeing of our nation. Yes, Scotland does receive special provision because of its special needs.

---

[93] Interview with Sir Stephen Sherbourne, 27/4/2007.
[94] Speech to Scottish Conservative conference, 10/5/1985, MTF.

The real problem, continued Mrs Thatcher, was that 'not enough people realise just how startling Scotland's economic transformation has been in the last decade . . . Scotland no longer depends on the heavy industry of the past, but on the enterprise culture of tomorrow'.[95] Although there was a lot of truth in this analysis – measured by GDP Scotland was consistently third in a league table of UK regions during this period – it seemed that fewer and fewer voters north of the border were listening.

Indeed, shortly before this 'Lincolnshire lass' speech Conservative fortunes had reached their lowest ebb in Scotland since Mrs Thatcher became Prime Minister. In the regional council elections of May 1986 her party managed just 16.9 per cent of the vote and 65 councillors, its poorest showing since the 1975 local government reorganisation. Even rural Scotland, deferential and aristocratic still, was no longer loyal. Tayside and Grampian Regions fell to opposition parties, as did Lothian, which the Tories had hitherto controlled as part of a coalition. A basic extrapolation of the results into parliamentary constituencies put the vast majority of Scottish Conservative MPs at risk. 'It's not just that their former voters don't like Thatcherism,' gloated an editorial in *Radical Scotland*, 'their councillors (now ex-councillors) clearly don't either.' The defeated Tory convenor in Grampian appeared to confirm this when he blamed 'decisions taken 600 miles away'[96] for the loss of the council. 'The problems facing Mrs Thatcher in her council of war with Sir James Goold and other grandees today', observed *The Times* of a post-election debriefing, 'is that despite the accommodations made with collectivism north of the border, Scottish Tories still lose elections.'[97] The Prime Minister's response was a whistle-stop tour during the long summer recess. 'She uttered barely a word that came close to being a political speech', observed *The Times*, 'as she admired computers in a high-tech factory, praised the efforts of disabled ex-servicemen making paper poppies and accepted a haggis.'

Surrounded by intense security, Mrs Thatcher kept her distance from sparse crowds and was lightly booed as she left a bakery in Hawick. An egg directed at her entourage even spattered over Denis's jacket. Bored journalists tried in vein to engage the Prime Minister on her party's prospects north of the border. 'I'm very impressed with what's happening with the development of new technology here,' she declared at Ferranti's factory in Edinburgh. Asked if she was as impressed with Scottish opinion polls, Mrs Thatcher added dismissively: 'I'm here to try and help get more jobs for Scotland, to help sell its products.'[98]

Again, the sentiment was genuine, yet Mrs Thatcher seemed singularly unable to fashion her message in a way that made it attractive to Scots. An opinion poll published in the *Daily Telegraph* on the eve of her visit showed that

---

[95] Ibid., 16/5/1986, MTF.
[96] *Radical Scotland* June/July 1986.
[97] *The Times* 16/5/1986.
[98] *The Times* 5/9/1986.

nearly four out of five Scots were dissatisfied with Mrs Thatcher personally, and of those who voted Tory in 1983 but did not plan to do so again, the Prime Minister was cited as the third most important reason for their intended defection after unemployment and pensions.

THE COMMUNITY CHARGE IS BORN

To that list would soon be added the Poll Tax. The back story was this. Heavy rates increases in 1980 and 1981 had put pressure on the government to fulfil its 1974 pledge (made by Mrs Thatcher as Shadow Environment Secretary) to abolish the rates. Its response was a 1981 green paper, *Alternatives to Domestic Rates*, which considered four possible replacements: local income tax (backed only by George Younger in Cabinet), sales tax, property taxes and a 'poll tax'. The last option had been floating around in Conservative and academic circles since the 1970s but was now considered respectable enough to be included in a government document. Influential in that respect was a *Daily Mail* article by Madsen Pirie of the Adam Smith Institute which appeared in October 1981. This proposed a per capita tax and was the result of a previous discussion at St Andrews University between Pirie and Douglas Mason, a lecturer in the university's economics department and leader of the Tory group on Kirkcaldy District Council. Mason, therefore, had a reasonable claim to being, as he later frequently claimed, the 'Father of the Poll Tax'.

Officials at St Andrew's House presciently judged that the poll tax option 'appears to carry considerable political appeal *at present* but this may dwindle on closer examination by Ministers since an increase in the number of taxes and contributors to local authority expenditure could be unpopular; administratively burdensome and uncertain in rating effects.'[99] But despite enthusiasm, ironically in light of subsequent events, from the Environment Secretary Michael Heseltine for the poll tax option, the government instead concentrated on limiting the worst aspects of the status quo through rate capping, already in place – and widely used by Younger – in Scotland. Other legislation limited the amount councils could use from rates income to subsidise rents. Only in 1984 did Whitehall follow the lead of St Andrew's House. 'As a result of Scotland's example,' Mrs Thatcher said at the 1984 Scottish Tory conference, 'good sense has begun to show in England too.'[100] Fearful about the legal consequences of the capping regime, however, ministers continued to press Mrs Thatcher for a review, and in the autumn of 1984 a 'study group' was established to take another look at the rates. Headed up by two junior Department of Environment ministers, Kenneth Baker and William Waldegrave, the latter asked Tom Wilson, a retired Glasgow University academic,[101] to join the group, which also comprised Lord Rothschild of the banking family and a QC by the name of Leonard Hoffman.

[99] SOE6/1/1109, minute dated 30/3/1982, NAS.
[100] Speech to Scottish Conservative conference, 11/5/1984, MTF.
[101] Wilson later contemplated resigning from the group when it became clear a poll tax was emerging as its favoured option.

By a process of elimination, a poll tax came to occupy the review in November/December 1984 as the favoured replacement for the rates. At around the same time the first indication of the trend of a Scottish rates revaluation came through from local government assessors. In an attempt to mitigate the worst effects, George Younger ended industrial derating, but it was too late for transitional relief or an effective phasing scheme for those affected by domestic rate increases. The last revaluation had been in 1978. The next, due in 1983, was postponed, but after that, Younger later recalled, 'we were simply running out of excuses and had to go ahead in 1984'.[102]

On 12 February 1985 the revised revaluations were published in Scotland. Although fiscally neutral overall, the rateable values of Scottish households rose by about 260 per cent; industrial values by around 170 per cent; and commercial values by somewhere between the two. After the revaluation the average domestic rates bill stood at about £406, but with all the usual mitigating factors – inflation, council spending and the size of the government grant – all pressing rate demands sharply upwards, home owners were faced with huge relative increases in their rates bills. Affluent suburbs administered by Labour-run councils were particularly badly hit. Edinburgh householders, for example, faced increases of 40 per cent. In Barnton, the city's most affluent suburb, the bill for a large, four-bedroom detached bungalow rose from £1,600 to £2,347. In Morningside, which formed part of Michael Ancram's constituency (he also had ministerial responsibility for local government at the Scottish Office), hundreds of single, elderly ladies were hit with massive bills. These 'little old ladies', be they in Troon, Bearsden or Morningside, were to become an important basis for what became colloquially known as the Poll Tax.

Local Conservative associations exploded in uproar. 'I remember in my constituency [Eastwood] it was absolutely awful,' recalled the former Scottish Tory MP Allan Stewart, 'people saying "why have we voted for a Conservative government when they raise our rates?"'[103] The Scottish Office pointed out that domestic rates bills had, on average, risen only by 17 per cent, a third of which was as a result of the revaluation, the other two-thirds being the consequence of increased spending by local authorities. But it was no use. Ratepayers blamed the massive increases on the government, not Labour-run local authorities, while Mrs Thatcher blamed two of her ministers. 'If George Younger and Michael Ancram at the Scottish Office had alerted us to the full consequences in time', she wrote in her memoirs, 'we could have introduced an order to stop it or mitigated its effects by making changes to the distribution of central government grant.'[104]

Political opponents, meanwhile, scented blood. The SNP president Donald Stewart said the process of revaluation should be shelved as it propagated the

---

[102] Butler et al., *Failure in British Government*, 62.
[103] Interview with Allan Stewart, 2/9/2008.
[104] Thatcher, *The Downing Street Years*, 647.

government's policy of using Scots 'as guinea pigs for measures which would be unacceptable in the Tory shires of the Home Counties'.[105] Indeed, *Radical Scotland* viewed the revaluation as definitive proof that Scotland was the 'guinea-pig nation', although quite what was being tested was not clear.[106] While a revaluation was necessary under distinct Scottish legislation (although there had been none in England since 1973), it is true that the government took a close interest in events up north with the Tory shires of the Home Counties firmly in mind. 'For us, south of the border,' admitted Mrs Thatcher in her memoirs, 'it was powerful evidence of what would happen if we ever had a rate revaluation in England.'[107] Indeed, as George Younger later recalled, 'Mrs Thatcher was keenly aware of what would happen if her old ladies in Finchley suddenly found themselves facing a ten-times increase in their rates bills'.[108]

Mrs Thatcher's reaction to the revaluation, however, was skewed as a result of advice from two close advisers, Sir James Goold, the Scottish Party Chairman and a golfing buddy of Denis ('nice man,' commented one party colleague of Goold, 'but knew f**k all about politics'[109]), and Willie Whitelaw, the Deputy Prime Minister. The former, having already branded revaluation 'a huge vote-loser' which meant that 'Scotland suffers, whilst England does not',[110] visited the Prime Minister in the middle of February 1985 'to describe the fury which had broken out north of the border when the new rateable values became known'.[111] The latter, shaken after repeatedly being heckled during a routine constituency engagement in Bearsden, also reported back to Downing Street that something had to be done.

There were also pressures from England. Several high-profile Labour-led councils, most notably Liverpool and Lambeth, continued to defy the government over rate capping. (In fact, considering that the Greater London Council and six English metropolitan county councils were abolished during 1986, Scotland got off comparatively lightly.[112]) So although the study group under Waldegrave and Baker would have reported in February or March in any case, the Scottish and English context lent its findings even greater urgency. Nearly half the Cabinet attended an all-day Chequers meeting on Sunday, 31 March 1985, to be briefed on the outcome. There, although Mrs

---

[105] *Scotsman* 6/4/1985.

[106] *Radical Scotland* 15 June/July 1985.

[107] Thatcher, *The Downing Street Years*, 647.

[108] *Sunday Times* 1/4/1990.

[109] Quintin Jardine to the author, 11/2/2007.

[110] *Scotsman* 6/4/1985.

[111] Mrs Thatcher later recalled the scene thus: 'Lord Goold came in on the Thursday evening and said: "I simply must see you" because the rating revaluations were going to take effect I think the following Tuesday and he said: "I do not know whether the message has got through to you or not but we simply cannot carry on" . . . I said: "But of course you cannot" and immediately we got all of the Scottish Ministers over.' (Interview for *Aberdeen Press and Journal* 30/4/1990)

[112] John Sewel, president of COSLA from 1982 to 1984, recalls a rumour that Mrs Thatcher had given George Younger the option of abolishing Strathclyde Regional Council.

Thatcher insisted that all options be discussed, 'the community charge was born'.[113] Only Nigel Lawson and the Chief Secretary to the Treasury, John MacGregor, dissented. Indeed, Lawson later circulated a paper warning that the Community Charge would be 'completely unworkable and politically catastrophic'.[114] Given that Lawson was that rare creature, a politician who actually understood local government finance, his opposition was significant, while Younger's argument for the poll tax option, according to Lawson, 'played a not inconsiderable part in sadly persuading Margaret Thatcher of its merits in general'.[115]

Speaking generally, Mrs Thatcher instinctively disliked local government, and particularly Labour-run authorities. Her experience of town hall politics went back to her Grantham childhood when her father, Alderman Roberts, was chairman of his local council's finance committee. The 'spiteful' way in which socialists had ousted her father was probably the origin of this antipathy, and perhaps in Scotland she saw too many socialist councillors of that same spiteful ilk. Even Conservative-run councils were not looked upon favourably, although London's Wandsworth Borough, which contracted out local services and kept its rates low, was singled out for regular praise. If Scotland had a Wandsworth equivalent, then it was certainly Eastwood District Council in Renfrewshire. In terms of expenditure, rate levels, sale of council houses, and its teaming up with the private sector to save a local park, the authority was a model of municipal Thatcherism. Strathclyde Regional Council, by contrast, was seen as high-spending and interventionist. Its little red book, *Social Strategy for the '80s*, even detailed extra funding for 'Areas of Priority Treatment' as a direct response to Thatcherism.

Mrs Thatcher was therefore perfectly content to let George Younger lead the way in eroding the power of local government in Scotland. The Right to Buy legislation was speedily introduced in 1979, the Rate Support Grant (RSG) cut, rates capped and the combative rhetoric ramped up, even by the usually emollient Younger. Although specific councils were targeted, such as Lothian Region and Stirling District, the result was worsening relations between central and local government which were not limited to socialist fiefdoms. Even Scotland's few remaining Tory-run authorities were resentful of continuing reductions in the RSG while Brian Meek, leader of the Conservative-led coalition on Lothian Region from 1982 to 1986, epitomised a brand of rebellious municipal Tory who did not willingly speak the language of the New Right.

The outcry from predominantly Tory-voting home owners following the 1985 revaluation was, therefore, interpreted by Mrs Thatcher as a sign that 'her people' had had enough. But while the principle of a poll tax struck the Prime Minister as a simpler, fairer, not to forget more radical, alternative to

---

[113] Thatcher, *The Downing Street Years*, 648.
[114] *Daily Telegraph* 4/3/1991.
[115] Lord Lawson to the author, 3/12/2008.

the rates, at this stage in its evolution the ideological justifications emanating from figures such as the Stirling MP Michael Forsyth and the Adam Smith Institute were less important than pressure from Younger, Whitelaw *et al.* to come up with a replacement for the rates as soon as possible. Douglas Mason's pamphlet, *Revising the Rating System*, and another by Forsyth, *The Case for a Poll Tax*, did not appear until several weeks after the crucial Chequers meeting. They did, however, help to popularise the idea in Tory circles. 'Clear accountability is the outstanding virtue of a poll tax,' Forsyth's pamphlet argued. 'The lack of an alternative has been the excuse for inaction for far too long. There is an alternative. A poll tax is clearly feasible, fair and desirable. What is needed now is the political will to introduce it.'[116]

That political will was to come from Mrs Thatcher. 'The fact is, that for far too many people, this year's rate demand has come as a thunderbolt,' she told Scottish Tories at their Perth conference in May 1985. 'And I know how commercial ratepayers feel – I spent my early years living above the shop.' She continued:

> But the underlying problem remains. I think we have reached the stage when no amount of patching up the existing system can overcome its inherent unfairness . . . Our aims are these. Any new scheme must be fairer than the existing scheme. The burden should fall, not heavily on the few, but fairly on the many. Councillors should always have to consider not only what they want to spend but also what it will cost their electors. Many Conservative councillors do this already – but many Labour councils do not.[117]

In the interim Mrs Thatcher announced an increase in financial relief from £36 million to £50 million, a degree of Treasury generosity the Chancellor, Nigel Lawson, made clear was 'exceptional'.[118] In exchange, Younger was forced to spend £5 million less on regional aid, cut the same sum off roads and transport, and separately the same again off prisons and health. Local authority housing, ironically, lost another £10.5 million. So by increasing domestic rate relief to cushion the worst effects of the revaluation, Younger was clearly redistributing the RSG away from poorer areas to subsidise Scotland's wealthier residential communities.

The behaviour of delegates at the conference, meanwhile, had further persuaded the Prime Minister that the government had to move swiftly to replace the rates. A lot of rancour bubbled below a polite veneer of loyalty during that May weekend, the cumulative result of the rates revaluation, a general feeling of being ignored by London, proposals for students' fees, milk quotas and a recent critical remark by a minister regarding the behaviour of

---

[116] Forsyth, *The Case for a Poll Tax*, 8 & 16.
[117] Speech to Scottish Conservative conference, 10/5/1985, MTF.
[118] *Guardian* 8/5/1985.

Scottish football fans. Even the otherwise popular George Younger was booed as he made his keynote speech, and Robin Harris – a close Thatcher aide who had been seconded north in April – noticed 'what a mess our relations with the Scottish Party are'. 'The way in which the rates issue has been approached in a completely different manner North and South of the Border,' he elaborated, '[and] the Scottish Office's own attitude that it wins votes for the Conservatives in Scotland [by being] seen to oppose policies agreed by the UK Government.'[119]

In the case of the abolition of the rates, if not its replacement, Scotland – via the Scottish Office – was not opposing the UK government policy, but actually compelling it to introduce a new policy. At the same conference, Younger proclaimed that 'the status quo is not an option' while Mrs Thatcher promised that proposals to rectify the 'anomalies and unfairness that are inherent in the present system'[120] would be published before the end of the year. On 20 May the poll tax proposal – at this point it was still being referred to as a 'resident's charge' – sailed through a Cabinet committee. A separate decision with important implications for the policy was also made at around the same time. The so-called '20 per cent rule', whereby every household would be compelled to pay at least 20 per cent of their local tax bill, found its way into social security reforms taking effect as of April 1988. This enshrined in statute the 'everyone should pay something' approach of which Mrs Thatcher particularly approved.

Later in 1985 the Cabinet agreed to a system of 'dual running', whereby a reformed property tax would run in conjunction with the new poll tax for a specified period of time. It was also agreed to publish a green paper in the New Year, during the drafting of which the 'resident's charge' became the 'community charge'. Younger, who was opposed to any rates element in the proposals, pushed for separate Scottish legislation ahead of a general election expected in mid 1987. 'On the strong advice of Scottish ministers, who reminded us continually and forcefully how much the Scottish people loathed the rates,' wrote Mrs Thatcher, with more than a hint of bitterness, in her memoirs, 'we . . . accepted that we should legislate to bring in the community charge in Scotland in advance of England and Wales'.[121] The Prime Minister had made the crucial mistake of confusing a disgruntled minority of Scottish Tory ratepayers with Scots in general, although to be fair her intention – but for pressure from Younger – had always been to implement the new tax across Great Britain (Northern Ireland was to retain its rates system) rather than in Scotland first.

The full Cabinet discussed the poll tax proposal for the first time on 9 January 1986, the same meeting at which Michael Heseltine resigned as Defence Secretary. It was approved in about 15 minutes and published, as

---

[119] CCO 20/11/96, 12/9/1985, CPA.
[120] *Financial Times* 11/5/1985.
[121] Thatcher, *The Downing Street Years*, 651.

Paying for Local Government, three weeks later. After summarising the new system, the green paper justified its rationale, 'to ensure that the local electors know what the costs of their services are, so that armed with this knowledge they can influence the spending decisions of their councils through the ballot-box'.[122]

Drafting legislation to make this aim a reality then fell upon officials at the Scottish Office who, it is fair to say, did not share their political masters' enthusiasm. As the draft Bill progressed more and more problems emerged, most of which were rebutted by Rifkind (the new Scottish Secretary) almost as quickly as civil servants could articulate them. Michael Ancram, on the other hand, became convinced that social security reforms compelling students and the unemployed to pay 20 per cent of the new tax would be unworkable in practice. But when he took his concerns to a Cabinet sub-committee, of which Nick Ridley (the new Environment Secretary) and William Walde-grave were members, Ancram was told bluntly to put the 20 per cent provisions back in the Bill. The suspicion was that Ancram had 'gone soft',[123] while the true-believing Ridley was reluctant to sacrifice key principles at such an early stage in the Scottish legislation.

The Abolition of Domestic Rates Etc (Scotland) Bill (abbreviated to ADRES in St Andrew's House) received its second reading in the House of Commons on 9 December 1986. By then the 'community charge' nomenclature was set in stone, as was its colloquial title of the Poll Tax, while the Bill's title gave some indication of the government's priorities. Rifkind hailed it as a 'radical reforming measure . . . to abolish a discredited and unpopular local tax'.[124] There was not a single dissenting Tory voice at the Bill's second reading or committee stage and, on 11 February 1987, MPs voted on a guillotine motion to hasten its progress. Two significant amendments were, however, accepted. First, the implementation phase was shortened from three years to a Big Bang introduction on 1 April 1989, while the Bill's ambitious provision for the designation of a 'head of the household' in order to collect the tax was sensibly dropped. The Bill then sailed through the House of Lords under the watchful eye of Lord Whitelaw.

It was at this stage the impression grew that Scotland was being used as a test bed for the reforms, although this had more to do with a rag-bag of English Tory MPs, clever opposition spin and mischievous media commentary than anything Mrs Thatcher actually believed or stated publicly. The Tory MP for Oxford East, Steve Norris, did take care to point out that 'our Scottish colleagues are trail blazers rather than guinea pigs',[125] but his colleague Timothy Raison (MP for Aylesbury) told the *Guardian* that 'as an English MP I cannot help being relieved that Scotland is to be the legislative pacemaker or guinea pig'. Similarly Sir George Young, a former minister at the Depart-

---

[122] Cmnd 9714.
[123] Butler *et al.*, *Failure in British Government*, 102.
[124] Hansard 107 c200.
[125] Butler *et al.*, *Failure in British Government*, 101.

ment of Environment, indulged in a cricketing metaphor: 'I, for one, am glad that the Scots are taking the shine off the new ball before the English go in to bat.'[126] Such remarks clearly had an effect. An opinion poll commissioned by the Scottish Local Government Information Unit at the end of 1986 found that 80 per cent of Scots were opposed to the introduction of the Poll Tax in Scotland a year ahead of England and Wales.

Other English Tory MPs and ministers were a little more sophisticated. Realising they were unlikely to win in any debate around the Cabinet table, UK ministers like the Chancellor Nigel Lawson believed that if the Scots were allowed to go first they would be given enough rope to hang themselves. As Lawson admitted in his memoirs, he hoped that early implementation in Scotland would give Mrs Thatcher 'second thoughts about its introduction in England and Wales'.[127]

'I was strongly opposed to it, full stop,' Lord Lawson recalled in 2008. 'When George Younger was adamant that he had to go ahead in Scotland, and there was nothing I could do to talk him out of this (which I tried very hard to do) I thought that at least if we waited a year to see how it worked out there, before committing ourselves to imposing it in England and Wales, Margaret might have second thoughts.' He went on:

I didn't expect this to work, but I felt it worth a try. I can understand why the fact that the Poll Tax was introduced first in Scotland may have led some to suppose that the Cabinet in London was deliberately using Scotland as a test-bed for the tax, but nothing could be further from the truth. It was the Secretary of State for Scotland who insisted on it, against everything I could do to stop him.[128]

Separate legislation north of the border also suited George Younger's old mantra, happily taken up by Rifkind, that Scotland was governed from Edinburgh, not London, although as we have already seen, when Scots went to the polls in the regional elections of May 1986 there was little sign they appreciated being at the cutting edge of rating reform.

The analysis of the result presented to the Prime Minister was convenient, to say the least. Although the rates revaluation was blamed for the poor outcome, it was interpreted as further evidence that the Poll Tax was needed to prevent even greater losses. The ADRES Bill's final parliamentary stage, however, was fraught. The Leader of the Opposition, Neil Kinnock, pledged to fight it all the way and tempers frayed when another guillotine motion left just two hours for the House to cover 132 amendments. John Home Robertson, the Labour MP for Berwick and East Lothian, even told Michael

---

[126] *Public Service in Local Government*, 1/1987.
[127] Lawson, *The View From No 11*, 580.
[128] Lord Lawson to the author.

Ancram to 'go to hell'.[129] Ancram had at least finally succumbed to calling it the Poll Tax rather than the more prosaic Community Charge, as had Mrs Thatcher in a celebrated slip during Prime Minister's Questions on 5 May.[130]

A week later, and just four weeks before the 1987 general election, the ADRES Bill completed its parliamentary stages. Days later the Prime Minister told a delighted Scottish Conservative conference in Perth that the Queen had granted the Bill Royal Assent. 'Indeed it was in response to your needs in Scotland,' she explained, 'that we finally decided on the introduction of the community charge.' It was a decision that was to haunt the rest of her premiership, and indeed her political legacy in Scotland.

THE DOOMSDAY SCENARIO

The Prime Minister also chose to launch the 1987 general election campaign in Perth, just as she had done in the wake of the Falklands victory four years before. Between England and Scotland, however, there was a problematic economic dichotomy. While in the UK as a whole the government could point to low inflation and a consumer boom as proof its policies were working, in Scotland the recession of the early 1980s appeared still to be in full swing. 'This time we want to do better still,' Mrs Thatcher informed the Scottish party faithful in Perth, 'in Britain as a whole, and here in Scotland.'[131] As if to emphasise her point, the banner on the platform behind her boasted: 'Moving forward in Scotland.'

In the light of recent opinion polls and local government elections, however, it was an unrealistic ambition. But if there were inklings in the Scottish party that the general election was not going to be a Thatcherite triumph north of the border, they were clearly not making their way back to Downing Street. By the time of the election, Malcolm Rifkind had been Scottish Secretary for more than a year. It has often been stated that Mrs Thatcher regarded the young (appointed aged 39, he was Scotland's youngest ever Secretary of State) Edinburgh lawyer with suspicion, but this has been over-emphasised. In fact she had indicated in 1982 – when Rifkind was promoted from the Scottish Office to the Foreign Office – that she regarded him as Younger's natural successor. And although he had resigned along with Alick Buchanan-Smith over the devolution U-turn in 1976, Mrs Thatcher was more than satisfied, as was Rifkind, that such undesirable instincts were nothing more than youthful folly. Only later, as Rifkind matured and the Prime Minister withdrew into a political bunker, did the relationship turn sour.

Rifkind, of course, played a prominent part in the Scottish election campaign, as did the Prime Minister herself. As with the 1983 contest, the issues to

---

[129] Hansard 116 c337.

[130] Mrs Thatcher said: 'one will pay a good deal less poll tax if one lives in a good Tory authority area than if one lives in a Labour authority area.' (Hansard 115 c574)

[131] Speech to Scottish Conservative conference, 15/5/1987, MTF.

the fore were mostly UK-wide, meaning that Mrs Thatcher was on solid ground during the campaign's more political exchanges. Defence had assumed a surprising prominence as the campaign wore on, fuelled by Labour's nuclear policy and a clumsy split in the SDP-Liberal Alliance over the same issue. The Prime Minister highlighted the potential consequences of Labour's stance at an Edinburgh rally on 2 June: Dounreay, the Highlands' third-largest employer, would have to close, as would Chapelcross in Dumfriesshire with the immediate loss of 750 jobs. 'Labour's unilateralist defence policy . . . would severely damage the economies of Argyll, Dunbartonshire and Fife by closing Holy Loch and Faslane and reversing the proposed £200 million investment in Rosyth to service Trident submarines,' she warned. 'Several thousand jobs would be put at risk by that.'[132] There was a certain irony to Mrs Thatcher warning of job losses in Scotland but it was an effective attack Labour struggled to rebut, whatever the moral and intellectual justifications for its policy.

'Made in the USA'

---

[132] Speech to Conservative rally in Edinburgh, 2/6/1987, MTF. A paper circulated to the Scottish Council of the Labour Party in 1983 had warned that the nuclear issue was an example of where 'concentrating on the moral question' had allowed the Tories 'to portray us as appeasers and job-losers'. (Labour Party Scottish Council paper 'Facing the Future')

Interviewed, once again by STV's Colin Mackay, a few days before polling stations opened, Mrs Thatcher inevitably found herself challenged about her lack of appeal in Scotland. 'Labour has many more MPs at dissolution than you have,' he reminded her. 'Why should it be that the Thatcher revolution, as it is called by Norman Tebbit, is not taking off in Scotland?' 'I ask myself the same question,' Mrs Thatcher replied, 'Scotland believes in defence . . . And Scotland, I believe, believes in the nuclear deterrent. So she should be with the Conservative Government.' She continued:

> Scotland believes in law and order . . . So again I would expect Scotland to be with us on that. Scotland I would expect to be with us on . . . the kind of property-owning democracy which we are trying to give. The Labour Party fought us all the way when we tried to give people who live in council houses the right to buy. They'll fight us all the way again. We shall continue it. They fight us all the way on denationalisation when we try to ensure that ordinary people who work in those nationalised industries . . . – and also in places like Scottish and Newcastle – have shares.

Mackay then challenged the Prime Minister about a passage in the manifesto which promised to consider further change in the good governance of Scotland. 'Would that include an Assembly?' he inquired. 'The only time we are ever asked about devolution or an assembly is when we are in a gathering of television interviewers and journalists,' replied Mrs Thatcher. 'We are not asked about it at all otherwise and I think – perhaps you may not agree – that if you go down that path what you are really doing is taking steps to separatism.'[133]

The Prime Minister's line on devolution, in other words, remained unaltered. In Mrs Thatcher's mind there was another crucial factor. Always fond of gauging public opinion by her weekly postbag, she refused to believe devolution was an issue simply because no one wrote to her about it. 'I do not myself see the demand except for something called "devolution" which has not been worked out,' she said in 1986, 'and I am not satisfied yet that there is a fundamental demand for devolution.'[134]

Scotsman opinion polls told a different story. Support for devolution went from 42 per cent to 48 per cent and 47 per cent in 1979, 1983 and 1987 respectively; support for independence from 14 to 23 and 33 per cent; and backing for the 'status quo' from 35 to 26 and 14 per cent. In general, the Conservative stance on devolution became just another shibboleth of the battle between wets and dries. Sir Ian Gilmour, in his book *Dancing With Dogma*, summed up the views of the wet faction with the assertion that if 'a large majority of Scots want a Scottish parliament (which most of the time

---

[133] Interview with STV, 3/6/1987, MTF.
[134] Ibid., 4/9/1986, MTF.

they do) I have never been able to understand why the great majority of the Conservative party should nowadays be so determined to frustrate them'.[135]

Northern Ireland, of course, was a different story, but demonstrated that Mrs Thatcher could be convinced to back bold constitutional policies and act against her Unionist instincts. Although the Prime Minister was unconvinced by various schemes for 'rolling devolution' in the Province, she realised there was no alternative and could argue convincingly that she was simply restoring an Assembly which had previously existed. This neatly avoided comparisons with Scotland, where there was no devolutionary precedent, no violence to speak of, and although there was a sectarian divide, it lacked the potency of the Falls Road. To some this was a cynical justification for not extending the same constitutional flexibility to Scotland. 'Must political imagination only arise', the academic Bernard Crick asked, 'from the unhappy stimulant of violence?'[136]

The signing of the Anglo-Irish Agreement in 1985, which gave the Republic of Ireland a direct say in the administration of the Province, also took many of Mrs Thatcher's staunchest defenders by surprise, not least her friend T. E. Utley, a blind journalist who advised her on Ireland and also, informally, on Scotland. Essentially, however, the move was a pragmatic piece of statecraft. Although Mrs Thatcher did not understand Northern Ireland's complex politics and regarded it as a drain on resources, as with devolution she realised that something had to be done. A revealing insight into her perception of the Emerald Isle came when the Irish prime minister, Garret FitzGerald, asked Mrs Thatcher (after the Agreement was signed) to lobby the European Community in order to get more funding for the Province. ' "More money for these people?" she said, waving her hand in the general direction of Northern Ireland,' recalled Fitzgerald in his memoirs. ' "Look at their schools; look at their roads. Why should they have more money? I need that money for my people in England, who don't have anything like this." '[137]

'Mrs Thatcher was always most revealing when caught off guard,' observed John Campbell. 'The people of Northern Ireland were not "her" people.'[138] Campaigning in Scotland, meanwhile, the Prime Minister was bemused by the impact of the Anglo-Irish Agreement on Scottish politics. 'I remember being quite surprised . . . when I got up there,' she recalled in 1990. 'I got the "Ulster says no" [posters] meeting me in many places in Scotland where we went round.'[139] Indeed, in Scottish constituencies where there was a sizeable Orange vote, the Anglo-Irish Agreement caused some Tory MPs acute difficulties. In Ayr, for example, George Younger ended up holding on to the seat by just 182 votes.

---

[135] Gilmour, *Dancing With Dogma*, 271.
[136] Dudley Edwards, ed., *A Claim of Right for Scotland*, 155.
[137] FitzGerald, *All in a Life*, 568.
[138] Campbell, *The Iron Lady*, 420.
[139] *Scottish Daily Express* 23/4/1990.

Hanging over that election campaign was also constant talk of what commentators melodramatically called the 'doomsday scenario', whereby the Conservative Party would increase its majority in England while losing more of its already fragile mandate in Scotland. Again it seems Mrs Thatcher was either unaware of this prospect or, more likely, simply did not believe it was possible. Sir Michael Hirst, elected to represent Strathkelvin and Bearsden in 1983, remembers attempting to emphasise this possibility when the Prime Minister had breakfast with Scottish Conservative candidates during the campaign. 'She dropped her grapefruit spoon and said "oh Micky, you don't mean to say you're going to lose your seat?"' he recalled. 'Jim Goold blustered that it was defeatist talk and that we would win 25 seats, but I said if *I'm* in difficulty then there must be at least half a dozen others who are too.'[140]

The campaign, meanwhile, oozed jingoism. One election broadcast ended with Mrs Thatcher's favourite hymn (later quoted by her to the Church of Scotland), 'I Vow to Thee, My Country', and the slogan 'It's Great to be Great Again', which even the *Annual Register* thought 'must surely have struck home like a sick joke in many parts of the country north of a line drawn from the Severn to the Wash'.[141] Conservative election rallies, including one in Edinburgh, featured Union Jacks, dry ice, laser effects, blasts of 'Jerusalem' and an Elgar-like 'coronation anthem' specially composed by Julian Lloyd Webber. The Scottish party faithful, however, did not seem to mind. After giving her annual speech to the Scottish Tory conference on 15 May, Mrs Thatcher was greeted with chants of 'Ten more years'.

During the same election campaign the Welsh Secretary Nick Edwards, who had announced his intention to leave the government after polling day, took the Prime Minister down to Cardiff Bay where they were ambushed by a small but noisy group of protestors. '[O]ne man raised his fingers in an obscene gesture,' recalled Edwards. 'The Prime Minister visibly froze, obviously offended, and turned to me saying, "Oh what dreadful people, we are really wasting our time – what is the point of all your efforts if they appreciate them so little."' He went on: 'One felt that she was not at her best and this was alien territory, far from the England that she knew and understood. In a way it was the Scottish story all over again. Her efforts to help were not rewarded; the support that she gave for her Secretaries of State was not appreciated; there was a barrier that somehow she was not able to surmount.'[142]

That barrier was certainly apparent in Scotland. 'Thatcher seemed to be hated so intensely north of the border', observed the historian Christopher Harvie in his 1987 election diary, 'because she personified every quality we have always disliked in the English: snobbery, bossiness, selfishness and, by

---

[140] Interview with Sir Michael Hirst, 29/7/2008.
[141] *Annual Register 1987*, 15.
[142] Dale, ed., *Margaret Thatcher – A Tribute*, 166.

our lights, stupidity.'[143] 'Today Scotland votes for its future', screamed the
Daily Record's front page on polling day, 'but for the Scots who have no jobs
there is no future. For them there is no future with Mrs Thatcher.'[144] As
ballots were counted on the evening of Thursday, 11 June, it quickly became
apparent that doomsday for the Scottish Conservatives was no longer a
hypothetical scenario, but an uncomfortable reality.

[143] *Observer* 26/6/1988.
[144] *Daily Record* 11/6/1987.

Chapter 8

THATCHERISM RESURGENT (1987–88)

This arch-unionist, hectoring figure has brought out the worst in Scotland in terms of our latent chauvinism, but it has also brought out something good and positive. She has forced the parties in Scotland and indeed the establishment in Scotland beyond politics to rethink its role, to rethink the system of decision-making in Scotland and hopefully she has propelled us in the direction of a legislative tier. So, irony of all time, we may yet have to raise a dram to Maggie for doing so much for us.[1]

Charles Kennedy MP, Restless Nation

The fairest way of summing up her relationship with Scotland is that Scotland did not understand her and she did not understand it. She sincerely tried to do so but nobody could give her the advice she sought which could reconcile her principles with a coherent view of the way ahead in Scotland . . . [So] she united us, in 1987, to a remarkable degree, if in a somewhat negative way.[2]

Arnold Kemp, The Hollow Drum

Naturally, I would have liked to see the stunning electoral successes south of the border which our policies delivered, similarly reflected in Scotland. But first and foremost, I was determined that we should do what we believed to be right and largely to leave the electoral arithmetic to take care of itself.[3]

Baroness Thatcher, 2009

Douglas Hurd: 'Prime Minister, I think the reason no one voted Tory in Scotland is that they felt neglected by the government.'

   Margaret Thatcher: 'Nonsense, nonsense, Hurd. What is Scotland?'
   Lord Young: 'It's that island off the Falklands isn't it?'
   Sir Geoffrey Howe: 'I thought it was a shoe shop.'
   Hurd: 'No, no, no: Scotland, it's that place up north.'

---

[1] Clements *et al.*, *Restless Nation*, 99.
[2] Kemp, *The Hollow Drum*, 212.
[3] Interview with Baroness Thatcher, 20/1/2009.

Thatcher: 'North? North? Refresh my memory, Hurd.'

Hurd: 'Here!' [pointing to Scotland on a map]

Thatcher: 'Ohhh, you mean the testing ground!' [slashing the map with bladed fingers]

Hurd: 'Testing ground?' [Hurd and Mrs Thatcher enter a laboratory]

Thatcher: 'Yes, we've we've got to have somewhere to test things out. Somewhere – a long way from my house.'

Norman Fowler: 'So we chose this . . .'

Hurd: 'Scotland.'

Thatcher: 'Yes, we've been doing it for years now, first with Lena Zavaroni and now Ridley here is testing his Poll Tax on them.'

Nick Ridley: 'You never know it might work.' [grappling with a tartan-clad rat]

Hurd: 'What if it doesn't?'

Thatcher: 'No harm done; they would have voted Labour anyway.'

Young: 'And then there's our new reciprocal fuel experiment: we take their oil; they take our nuclear waste; very successful.'

Thatcher: 'Then we're going to try out national service, the repeal of the Safety at Work Act and hanging.'

Hurd: 'For what offences?'

Thatcher: 'Isn't being Scottish enough?'

Hurd: 'I say, Maggie, there's one experiment you could try out on them.'

Thatcher: 'Yes? What?'

Hurd: 'Devolution!'

Thatcher: 'Devolution? Now where's that again?'

Howe: [Back in Cabinet room] 'It's a shoe shop isn't it?'

Spitting Image (ITV), 22/11/1987

THE RESULTS FROM Scotland haunted Mrs Thatcher's celebrations early in the morning of 12 June 1987, although their potential consequences were momentarily consumed by her landslide majority produced predominantly by the south-east of England. When the counting was finished, 11 Conservatives had lost their seats in Scotland, one more than the ten lost throughout the rest of the country. Labour were the main beneficiaries, leaving the government with just ten MPs in Scotland's 72 parliamentary seats. The *Daily Record* summed up the result thus: 'Third time lucky for Mrs T – but . . . SCOTLAND SAYS NO!'[4]

It was not just backbenchers like Michael Hirst in Strathkelvin and Bearsden who lost their seats. Michael Ancram, the housing minister; Peter Fraser, the Solicitor-General; John MacKay, the education minister; Alex Fletcher, the former trade minister; and Gerry Malone, the Scottish Tory

---

[4] *Daily Record* 12/6/1987.

Whip, were all stripped of the letters 'MP' after their names. At one point it even looked as if George Younger, the popular Defence Secretary and former Scottish Secretary, might lose Ayr, but after several recounts he scraped home with a three-figure majority.

The Conservatives' share of the vote in Scotland had slumped to 24 per cent, down nearly five points from 1983's performance, only two points ahead of the Alliance and 16 points behind Labour, which polled 42 per cent of the vote and won 50 seats, even though its vote share was the party's lowest since 1970. The SNP, meanwhile, remained stuck at 14 per cent, gaining three seats from the Tories but losing two to Labour (including its leader, Gordon Wilson, in Dundee). Although there were considerable variations in Tory support across Scotland – the best result was in Dumfries and Galloway where the party got 41 per cent of the vote – the government's vote share declined in every single region. And while tactical voting, encouraged by the *Glasgow Herald* and *Scotsman* to put a 'brake' on Thatcherism, was assumed to be behind many of the Conservative losses, there was actually only modest evidence that this was the case.[5]

Mrs Thatcher's invocation of Disraeli at the 1985 Perth conference suddenly seemed a hostage to bad fortune. If the Conservative Party was either a 'national party or nothing', then in Scotland it was perilously close to being the latter. Inevitably, the Scottish media went to town. 'In Scotland a man can buy his council house and shares in privatised industries, and continue to vote Labour,' observed Allan Massie in the *Sunday Times*. 'The upwardly mobile still vote as their parents did, encouraged by newspapers and television stations which are almost unanimously hostile to the Tories.' He went on: 'Blue-collar workers in Scotland, who still live largely in council houses, do not vote Tory to anything like the extent of their English counterparts. Even the professional classes are predominantly dependent on the public sector. Teachers, doctors and administrators see Mrs Thatcher as a threat to their way of life. As a result, the Tories have lost much of their tribal vote, while Labour has retained its.'[6]

Indeed, while the skilled working-class vote remained loyal to the Labour Party in Scotland, in England it constituted the main source of increased support for the government.[7] Mrs Thatcher merely notes in her memoirs that the Scottish results were 'disappointing', although she appeared to draw comfort from Malcolm Rifkind's assurance shortly after the election that the Poll Tax had been 'neutral' in its effect and, if anything, had at least defused unrest over the rates revaluation. Continuing gloom about the future of Ravenscraig, rather than anticipation of the Community Charge, had dominated the campaign in Scotland.

What then was the Prime Minister's explanation for Scotland's rejection of

---

[5] In Banff and Buchan, where Sir Albert McQuarrie lost out to the future SNP leader Alex Salmond, there was evidence that tactical voting had eroded the Tory majority.

[6] *Sunday Times* 14/6/1987.

[7] Scottish Tory support among the C2 social group was 23 per cent in 1979, 25 per cent in 1983 and 21 per cent in 1987. In the UK as a whole it was generally around 40 per cent.

Thatcherism? In short, it was the economy, stupid. England was booming while unemployment, which south of the border had been falling for some time, only began declining in Scotland four months before polling day. 'The real question now was whether the falling unemployment and economic recovery taking place would of themselves be sufficient to revive the Conservative Party's fortunes in Scotland,' Mrs Thatcher wrote in *The Downing Street Years*. 'I never believed that they would and this indeed proved to be the case.' She reckoned the declining Orange vote was one possible explanation, while 'whereas in the past it might have been possible for the Conservatives in Scotland to rely on a mixture of deference, tradition and paternalism to see them through, this was just no longer an option – and none the worse for that'.

Housing was another problem (Right to Buy take-up still lagged behind that in England) which, the Prime Minister believed, produced dependency ('And the conditions of dependency are conditions for socialism'). But the clincher, she thought, was that 'the power and influence of Labour' had penetrated New St Andrew's House. 'It had its arguments voiced by both Catholic and Protestant churches in Scotland and parroted in the media,' elaborated Mrs Thatcher, 'hardly any Scottish newspapers supported us and the electronic media were largely hostile.' She continued: 'The reaction of Scottish Office ministers to these difficulties had cumulatively worsened the problem. Feeling isolated and vulnerable in the face of so much left-wing hostility, they regularly portrayed themselves as standing up for Scotland against me and the parsimony of Whitehall. Yielding to this temptation brought instant gratification but long-term grief. For in adopting this tactic they increased the underlying Scottish antipathy to the Conservative Party and indeed the Union.'

In pushing for proportionately higher spending, continued Mrs Thatcher, the Scottish Office had 'effectively conceded the fundamental argument to the socialists'.[8] 'But the truth was that more public spending in a dependency culture had not solved Scotland's problems, but added to them.'[9] That the Prime Minister had herself conceded the same 'fundamental argument' following Whitehall battles over the Barnett Formula was not mentioned.

Again, however, Mrs Thatcher stopped short of significantly curtailing Scottish expenditure, which was the logical extension of her analysis. But this belief that the Scottish Office was shielding Scotland from the benefits of Thatcherism, and therefore its electoral appeal, would become a thread throughout the remainder of Mrs Thatcher's premiership. She began to try and bypass the department when it came to policy-making, and when Sir William Kerr Fraser (always proud to be the last surviving Callaghan appointment) decided to retire as permanent under-secretary in 1988, the Prime Minister sensed an opportunity to replace him with someone from outside the Scottish Office. Senior Whitehall Scots were canvassed but the Aberdonian Sir William Reid was seen in Edinburgh, where he headed up the Scottish Home

---

[8] Thatcher, *The Downing Street Years*, 618–19.
[9] Ibid., 629–30.

and Health Department, and Whitehall as the obvious candidate. But having worked with Mrs Thatcher at the Department of Education and Science (DES) in the early 1970s, he was vetoed by Downing Street. Her hostility to the civil service was, according to Hugo Young, 'a compound of suspicion, incomprehension and sheer disregard for what they were in business to be and do, [which at the DES] deepened into an indelible obsession'.[10]

Mrs Thatcher's search for a true believer to run the Scottish Office, therefore, ended up occupying an unusual amount of Prime Ministerial time, not to mention that of two Cabinet Secretaries, Sir Robert Armstrong and his successor Sir Robin Butler. 'She was looking for someone from a different stable,' recalled Kerr Fraser, 'not a political appointment but someone more Tory than Whig in spirit.'[11] Ultimately, however, and despite Mrs Thatcher displaying what Kerr Fraser called 'prejudice, conceit, suspicion – and, of course, determination',[12] the eventual candidate *was* a Scottish Office insider, Sir Russell Hillhouse, and Sir William Reid instead became Parliamentary Commissioner for Administration (and Health Service Commissioner for England, Scotland and Wales) from 1990 to 1996. The episode demonstrated that even Mrs Thatcher did not always get her own way.

Meanwhile, of the two persistent strands of Scottish Conservative thinking, less Thatcherism versus more Thatcherism, the latter became dominant while the former was reduced to carping from the sidelines. It was to prove an explosive mix. Two senior Scottish Conservatives, both of whom declined to serve at the Scottish Office following the election, appeared to represent these two conflicting positions. Alick Buchanan-Smith, who had resigned over devolution in 1976, refused Mrs Thatcher's invitation to become Minister of State, or effective deputy to Malcolm Rifkind. 'This is the moment when the losses in the election results mean that we should be looking for sensitivity on a wider front,' he argued, 'and I believe that I can better serve the Conservative Party in Scotland with the freedom to speak.'[13] Although pride probably had a lot to do with his decision (he had been senior to Rifkind on the Tory front bench in the 1970s), many believed Buchanan-Smith's absence deprived the party of a popular and moderate voice at a crucial time. Allan Stewart, meanwhile, refused to serve on health grounds but told the journalist Martin Dowle that 'the Conservatives had polled so poorly because they failed to implement Thatcherism in Scotland', and that 'since Rifkind intended to continue with an interventionist course at the Scottish Office, he could best assist his party's cause from the backbenches'.[14]

---

[10] Young, *One of Us*, 71.
[11] Sir William Kerr Fraser to the author, 25/7/2008.
[12] Ibid., 27/11/2008.
[13] *Scotsman* 16/6/1987. In his memoirs Peter Walker claims that his patronage saved Buchanan-Smith from the chop in an earlier reshuffle. 'She was not being vengeful,' he reasoned. 'If she had been that she would not have had him in the government at all, but she was not going to have him in the Cabinet.' (Walker, *Staying Power*, 147)
[14] McCrone & Brown, eds, *Scottish Government Yearbook 1988*, 13.

While these abstentions – together with the loss of two incumbent Scottish Office ministers – did not make Rifkind's job of replenishing his ministerial team any easier, talk of the government finding it impossible to govern Scotland proved premature. The defeated Solicitor-General Peter Fraser was simply kept on via a peerage; the Inverness-born English MP David Maclean was appointed Scottish Whip; while Ian Lang was promoted to become Minister of State and the affable Lord James Douglas-Hamilton made an under-secretary. By far the most significant appointment, however, was that of Michael Forsyth as Minister for Education and Health. Although he had only retained his Stirling constituency with a majority of 548, Forsyth was effectively to become Mrs Thatcher's eyes and ears in Scotland during the twilight years of her premiership.

The election result, however, did do one thing: stimulate the 'national' question and demands for home rule as never before. Rifkind, himself a former devolutionist, patiently explained that 'unilateral devolution' would not work and could only do so as part of a federal reform, while on her first visit to Scotland of the new Parliament Mrs Thatcher ruled out any concessions and told party activists that devolution was not a 'live' issue. Instead, the Prime Minister aired some familiar refrains. 'The Conservatives have got the best tunes,' she said, 'but we are just not singing them loud enough.' Furthermore, much of so-called Thatcherism was actually the philosophy of the celebrated Scottish economist Adam Smith or, as she styled it, 'Adam Smithism'.[15]

Mrs Thatcher's northern foray came less than a week after a big post-election organisational shake-up of the Scottish Conservative Party. It included the creation of a new post of chief executive, taken by the ousted MP John MacKay, while the party was to keep all money raised north of the border for the first time. There was also to be a new, more ostentatiously Scottish, logo, which reflected growing angst that the party was seen as too English-orientated. A week after Mrs Thatcher's September 1987 visit, a damning report, 'The Policies, Questions and Options: The Way Forward', was circulated to ministers and senior activists. Based on internal question-naires it concluded frankly 'that it is no use ignoring the perception that the Tories were seen as the English Party'.[16] Drafted by Michael Ancram, the report was discussed at Malcolm Rifkind's Duddingston home with each Scottish Office minister in attendance. Graeme Carter, recruited after the election as Rifkind's special adviser to supply political advice and improve communications between St Andrew's House and Scottish Conservative HQ, remembered suggesting a Scottish 'Swinton College' to revive the party's organisation.[17]

---

[15] *Aberdeen Press and Journal* 3/9/1987.

[16] *Scotsman* 10/9/1987.

[17] Graeme Carter to the author, 8/12/2008. Swinton College had been a training school for budding Tory activists and MPs.

Internal reorganisation was a standard Conservative response to electoral setbacks in Scotland, but was just one aspect of a three-pronged Tory fightback north of the border. In addition to a modernised party machine, Rikfind was to lead a promised rethink on the relevance of Conservative policies to Scotland. The third aspect was a charm offensive from the Lady herself. That Mrs Thatcher should pay more attention – or at least appear to pay more attention – to Scotland and to Scottish affairs was one of the central findings of Ancram's report, and was to an extent backed up by a *Glasgow Herald* opinion poll in October 1987. This identified an undeniable 'Thatcher factor' inhibiting Scottish Tory support. Some 84 per cent of those polled said the Prime Minister was not very or not at all sympathetic to Scotland, but when asked if she should pay more attention and visit more often, most said 'yes'. Furthermore, while 32 per cent regarded her as a good UK Prime Minister, only 9 per cent thought the same in a Scottish context.[18]

The academic A. D. R. Dickson attempted to probe Scottish attitudes a little more deeply in a 1988 study, and identified specifically Scottish insecurities in some respondents. 'We always seem to get the rough end of the stick in Scotland,' said one. 'We always seem to be forgotten about . . . That's still true today. I think even more so to do with the Thatcher Government.' Another said 'all Maggie's interested in [is] . . . the South-East of England', while one respondent reckoned the Prime Minister did not worry 'about Ravenscraig because it's so far north and she's not relying, in all honesty, on the votes in Scotland'. 'These perceptions,' concluded Dickson, 'deriving from the historical development of Scottish society and its reflections in the cultural identity of Scots, are particularly focused on the personality of the Prime Minister.' He went on:

> The public persona of Mrs Thatcher appears to many Scots to capture all the worst elements of their caricature of the detested English – uncaring, arrogant, always convinced of their own rightness ('there is no alternative'), possessed of an accent that grates on Scottish ears, and affluent enough to afford a retirement home costing around £500,000 [Mrs Thatcher had recently purchased one in Dulwich]. She is also associated with the conspicuously 'yuppie'/affluent South-East, and the City. These are bitter images for Scots, well aware of stark contrasts offered in Scotland by high unemployment, pockets of appalling social deprivation in the major urban areas, and reared in a culture where Scottish Protestantism, while not denigrating the accumulation of wealth, has always emphasised its distaste for the flouting of its manifestations.[19]

---

[18] *Glasgow Herald* 1/10/1987.
[19] Dickson, 'The peculiarities of the Scottish: national culture and political action', *The Political Quarterly* 59 (July–September 1988), 3.

Perhaps with these 'stark contrasts' in mind, Rifkind took care to acknowledge that 'the recession bit deeper in Scotland and recovery has been slower', the implication being that it was merely a matter of time before Scotland caught up with the rest of the UK. In the interim, the Prime Minister's eyes seemed to be fixed on the north, although it soon became apparent that many Scots took this heightened interest to be vindictive.

'Her court became as thick with expatriate Scots of a predatory bent', wrote the historian Christopher Harvie, 'as it was with Jews to whom the solidarity of synagogue and tailoring shop was a far-off land.'[20] One expatriate Scot who returned to the fray after the 1987 election was Sir Teddy Taylor, the nearly man of Scottish Thatcherism. He likened his return visit to addressing a Tsarist rally of Russian émigrés after the Revolution. 'What the Scottish Tories need to do', he reflected in the *Guardian*, 'is to change their policies and attitudes so that the Scottish Conservatives can be seen to be a group rather separate from the United Kingdom Tories, and seen to be a Scottish party fighting for Scotland.'[21]

But although word had gone out from Downing Street in early July that the 'Scottish problem' would have to be discussed by the full Cabinet, the same sources flatly ruled out policy changes, while making it clear that Rifkind's attitude was one of 'wait and see'.[22] Fond of quoting Disraeli, Mrs Thatcher may have been aware of his bitter assertion that the 'Scotch shall have no favours from me until they return more Tory members to the House of Commons'.[23] Following the 1987 election, however, she seemed determined not to emulate Dizzy's sentiment too closely. 'Scots look to the Conservative Party again today,' the Prime Minister wrote in the foreword to a history of the Scottish Conservative Party in early 1988, 'we will not fail them.'[24]

At Number 10, meanwhile, 'there was the sense that she was "groping" towards a solution to the Scottish problem,' recalled her political secretary Sir Stephen Sherbourne, 'which I think became much more acute following the 1987 election.'[25] Indeed, John O'Sullivan, an adviser who worked in the Policy Unit, was charged with thinking about exactly what could be done to recover the party's position in Scotland, an indication that Mrs Thatcher did not consider it beyond political reach. By contrast, the landslide in England had 'locked the Thatcher era into place,' according to Hugh Young, 'as a phase in Britain's political evolution of which the end was not in sight'.[26] In Scotland, however, there was what Neal Ascherson described as a Tory

---

[20] Harvie, *Travelling Scot*, 203.

[21] *Guardian* 22/6/1987.

[22] *Financial Times* 6/7/1987.

[23] The rest of this quote could also easily have been Mrs Thatcher's: 'and of all parts of Scotland the most odious are the Universities. They have always been our bitterest and most insulting foes.' (Massie, *The Thistle and the Rose*, 269)

[24] Warner, *The Scottish Tory Party*.

[25] Interview with Sir Stephen Sherbourne, 27/4/2007.

[26] Young, *One of Us*, 518.

counter-reformation, an attempt to reclaim 'temporarily strayed sheep'.[27] And whether Scotland's sheep liked it or not, they were about to experience Thatcherism resurgent.

RIFKINDISM

The morning after the general election Peter Walker, the outgoing Energy Secretary, received a telephone call from the Prime Minister. 'She said the party had done well in the General Election in England, but badly in Scotland and Wales,' Walker recalled in his memoirs. 'In the new Parliament, we had to put that right in the interests of the United Kingdom. Malcolm Rifkind had settled in Scotland and now had some experience behind him and she was going to ask him to continue.'[28]

There was an implied reluctance in Mrs Thatcher's reasoning for keeping Rifkind in place as Scottish Secretary, as if she suspected he was not really 'one of us'. In the wake of the election result, however, Rifkind seemed to become a born-again Thatcherite. While Peter Walker, whom Mrs Thatcher asked to be Welsh Secretary, pursued what became known as interventionist 'Walkerism' (although more a difference of presentation rather than policy), his Scottish counterpart made speeches up and down Scotland attacking dependency and extolling the virtues of free enterprise (later published as *A Vision for Scotland*), and even committed himself to eradicating the 'anti-enterprise, paternalistic, quasi-socialist culture that has been fostered in Scotland for too long'. In policy terms this meant another drive to boost council house sales, the privatisation of electricity and public transport, and a shake up of education by creating school boards and allowing individual schools to 'opt out' from state control.

Inevitably, some commentators dubbed this the 'Rifkind Revolution', or more mischievously 'Rifkindism', even though the impetus for much of this agenda came from Downing Street rather than New St Andrew's House. The Scottish Secretary even enticed Alex Pagett, formerly the Scottish Office's chief press officer, to Scottish Conservative headquarters in Edinburgh to keep journalists fully informed of Rifkindism as director of communications. But reformulating Scottish attitudes, admitted Rifkind, was 'highly controversial' and 'full of political risk', or, as he told the *Aberdeen Press and Journal*, rolling out a new wave of Thatcherism in Scotland was 'a high-risk strategy'.[29]

Rifkind, however, acknowledged publicly that Scots liked the song but not the singer, while maintaining that there was no evidence, at least in terms of take-up, that Thatcherism was unpopular in Scotland. Importantly, he enjoyed the Prime Minister's full support. 'She was deeply concerned about the result,' recalled Rifkind, 'and she and I actually got on very well for the

---

[27] *Observer* 26/6/1988.
[28] Walker, *Staying Power*, 202.
[29] *Weekend World: The Tories' Tartan Gamble* (LWT) 1/5/1988.

first six months after that election because with such a situation we had to be very robust in the face of the no-mandate argument.'

The main threat in this regard came from Labour's 50 MPs, not the SNP's three (although Alex Salmond proved personally effective at questioning the 'feeble 50's' ability to shield Scotland from Thatcherism), who were toying with deploying the no-mandate argument to much a greater extent than ever before. As an essentially Unionist party, argued Rifkind, they had no right to do so. 'The whole aim was to remove any talk of there being a constitutional crisis', he recalled, 'and indeed it faded away relatively quickly.'[30] Until, that is, the Govan by-election of November 1988, of which more later. As for Mrs Thatcher's views on the no-mandate question, 'We have had a socialist government in the United Kingdom which did not have a majority in England,' she reminded Kirsty Wark in March 1990, referring to Harold Wilson's 1964 victory. 'We did not complain, because we believe in the United Kingdom and I still believe that each and every part of the United Kingdom has done far better by being a United Kingdom.'[31]

Although it struck many as odd that Rifkind had suddenly become a true believer, including his old boss Alick Buchanan-Smith, his was a pragmatic reaction to political reality. 'By the time I became Scottish Secretary those of us who had previously not been true believers saw that by 1983–87 her general approach on tax policies was going to deliver real economic results,' he reasoned. 'So in terms of substance I think most of us felt she was winning the argument, but there remained an essentially political battle in terms of how we responded to that and represented it in Scotland.'[32]

The trouble was that many on the Conservative right were not convinced that Rifkind had fully dried out. Vociferous Anglo-Scots MPs such as Eric Forth upped the ante by attacking the 'feather-bedding' of Scotland, while English backbenchers like Gerald Howarth and Neil Hamilton demanded to know why significant progress was not being made in contracting out Scottish public services. A group even began attending the weekly Scottish Questions in the House of Commons, thus squeezing out (Scottish) Labour MPs who wished to speak. At one session, the Falkirk MP Dennis Canavan repeatedly called out 'I spy strangers' until the Speaker was forced to call a division. With Rifkind trying to present a business-as-usual demeanour in Scotland, these antics were less than helpful.

The Prime Minister, meanwhile, was busy setting out new areas for reform. One was local government finance (already dealt with, or so she thought, in Scotland), and another was the regeneration of Britain's inner cities. The government had a good record on urban renewal in Scotland, having continued Labour's regeneration of Glasgow's East End (known as Glasgow East Area Renewal, or GEAR) while initiating new schemes in Leith and

[30] Interview with Sir Malcolm Rifkind MP, 2/4/2008.
[31] 'The Margaret Thatcher Interview' (BBC Scotland) 4/3/1990, MTF.
[32] Interview with Sir Malcolm Rifkind.

Dundee. Indeed, Mrs Thatcher visited Glasgow to learn from the 'success' of Scottish urban policy. This time, however, the assumption was that the free market was best placed to finance the necessary development as opposed to the public purse.

Glasgow, and specifically its Easterhouse estate, represented the dichotomy between the two approaches. Some £300 million of public money, and an additional £200 million from the private sector, had been poured into the city's East End from 1976 to 1987. Housing was built, including some private estates, the environment improved, and a new shopping centre built on the site of the old Beardmore works at Parkhead Forge. But despite demonstrable visual improvements to the area, the impact on long-term unemployment was less impressive. In Easterhouse, meanwhile, the Reverend Russell Barr said just one word – despair – summed up life in his parish. 'The despair is tangible. It can be tasted,' he wrote in *Just Sharing*, a Church of Scotland report later presented to Mrs Thatcher. 'A little differently, one of our elders speaks of the appalling "greyness" of the people. Much of the joy and colour of life has been knocked out of them.'[33]

Brian Griffiths, head of the Downing Street Policy Unit since 1985, took a close interest in the problems of Easterhouse and personally visited the estate following the 1987 election. He returned convinced of the need for continuing intervention by the Scottish Development Agency (SDA), a view he pressed upon Mrs Thatcher, but otherwise his recommendations chimed with her instincts. In March 1988 she unveiled *Action for Cities*, while Rifkind launched the lavishly illustrated *New Life for Urban Scotland*. Essentially the new policy was to remove the state from certain urban problems and replace it with a combination of the private sector and acceptable community groups. *New Life for Urban Scotland* praised GEAR and placed great importance on initiatives in peripheral estates like Castlemilk in Glasgow, Ferguslie Park in Paisley, Wester Hailes in Edinburgh and Whitfield in Dundee, but said very little about what should be done. Rifkind hailed it as one of 'the most significant initiatives ever taken to change the face of Scotland's giant estates', but Labour MPs were scathing. 'Too little, too late' judged David Marshall, the MP for Glasgow Shettleston, while Norman Buchan (MP for Paisley South) said: 'He's given us the HP sauce but where's the bloody meat?' 'If Mr Rifkind were to announce Christmas', quipped the Tory MP for Perth and Kinross, Sir Nicholas Fairbairn, by way of response, 'the Opposition would treat it like the Crucifixion.'[34]

Tied to the publication of *New Life for Urban Scotland* was a consultation document called *Scottish Homes*. Also the name of a new national agency for housing, Scottish Homes essentially merged the Scottish Special Housing Association (the SSHA, founded by an interventionist Tory Scottish Secretary, Walter Elliot, in the 1930s) with the Housing Corporation in Scotland.

---

[33] Mitchell, *Conservatives and the Union*, 115.
[34] Brown & McCrone, eds, *Scottish Government Yearbook 1989*, 131–32.

Mrs Thatcher in Edinburgh on her first, oddly tumultuous, visit to Scotland as leader of the Conservative Party in February 1975. Alick Buchanan-Smith, the Shadow Scottish Secretary, is to her left. 'I shall never forget the warmth of that reception,' she remembered ten years later. 'Overnight, I became "Maggie"! And I've been Maggie ever since.' (© *The Scotsman Publications Ltd*)

'Mike' Forsyth, national chairman of the Federation of Conservative Students, presents Mrs Thatcher with 51 red roses on her 51st birthday in 1976. Forsyth would later become what she called the 'real powerhouse for Thatcherism at the Scottish Office'. (© *Press Association*)

Campaigning in Leith with her daughter Carol, husband Denis and Teddy Taylor, her pugilistic Shadow Scottish Secretary, during the 1979 general election campaign. Lord Sanderson, president of the SCUA, is behind Taylor. 'When we take office,' she stated confidently, 'we shall start talks with all the interested parties, to see how you in Scotland can have more say in the management of your affairs.'
(© *The Scotsman Publications Ltd*)

Watching pipers at the Argyll Conservative ceilidh with Denis during her first holiday as Prime Minister. Her host was Lord Margadale on his Islay estate. 'They were hardly her sort of people,' wrote Hugo Young, 'but they had entertained many leaders before her.'
(*Courtesy of the Churchill Archives Centre*)

Mrs Thatcher with an imposing backdrop during a speech in Scotland in 1981. Plans for a Scottish Assembly were by then dead in the water, although she had revived the Select Committee on Scottish Affairs and enabled the Scottish Grand Committee to meet in Edinburgh, which it did for the first time that year. (*Courtesy of The Herald & Evening Times picture archive*)

A regal visit to the *Glasgow Herald* on the occasion of its bi-centenary in 1983. Even its left-leaning editor, Arnold Kemp, later wrote that she gave a 'display of personal magnetism that made us realise, if we had been sufficiently obtuse not already to have done so, that here was a politician of the highest class'. (*Courtesy of The Herald & Evening Times picture archive*)

With Lord Home at a Chequers luncheon to mark the former Prime Minister's 80th birthday in 1983. 'I am absolutely devoted to Alec Douglas-Home,' Mrs Thatcher said of Home in 1990. 'I think he is one of the most marvellous men I have ever met.' (*Courtesy of Viscountess Younger of Leckie*)

George Younger talking to Lord Margadale at the same occasion. Although not instinctively Thatcherite Younger was given a relatively free hand during his seven years as Scottish Secretary. One of Lord Margadale's sons, Peter Morrison, would later become the Prime Minister's Parliamentary Private Secretary. (*Courtesy of Viscountess Younger of Leckie*)

NO WONDER SHE'S LAUGHING. SHE'S GOT SCOTLAND'S OIL.

STOP HER - JOIN THE SNP

A memorable poster from the SNP. The slogan dated from the 1970s but gained a more potent personal focus after Mrs Thatcher became Prime Minister in 1979 and North Sea oil revenue helped to sustain record levels of unemployment. She, of course, saw it very much as 'Britain's oil'. (*Courtesy of Rob Gibson MSP*)

With George and Diana Younger at an exhibition to mark the centenary of the Scottish Office in 1985. 'The pride of the Scottish Office – whose very structure added a layer of bureaucracy,' Mrs Thatcher wrote in her memoirs, 'standing in the way of reforms which were paying such dividends in England – was that public expenditure per head in Scotland was far higher than in England.' (*Courtesy of Viscountess Younger of Leckie*)

NUM pickets and mounted police clash at Ravenscraig in 1984. Not only was the future of the steel-works a running sore for Mrs Thatcher's governments in Scotland, it also caused tension within the trade union movement during the miners' strike of 1984-85. That its 4,000-strong workforce carried on working in face of demands for closure by the NUM did not prevent its privatisation as part of the British Steel Corporation in 1988. (© *The Scotsman Publications Ltd*)

A Special Branch bodyguard calmly deflects a flying egg as Mrs Thatcher visits Falmer Jeans in Cumnock. Projectile eggs and bags of flour became a fixture of such tours although the Prime Minister always managed to look unruffled. (*Courtesy of STV*)

There were not always protests. Supporters greeting Mrs Thatcher at the 1986 Commonwealth Games in Edinburgh, although there was a wider row about a boycott of the Games by 32 African, Asian and Caribbean countries because of the UK's sporting links with apartheid South Africa. (© *The Scotsman Publications Ltd*)

With the new owners of the millionth council house to be sold under Right to Buy at Forres in 1986. Although sales in Scotland were initially sluggish, by the end of the Thatcher era the policy had turned the majority of Scots into members of the property-owning democracy.
(© *Press and Journal/Evening Express*)

'Serving Scotland' at the 1988 Scottish Conservative conference in Perth with Ian Lang and Malcolm Rifkind. The latter's relations with the Prime Minister were by then strained. 'Malcolm...made some delphic remarks which were interpreted as suggesting that devolution was back on the agenda in Scotland,' she later wrote of his speech at that conference. 'He was reverting to type.'
(*Courtesy of The Herald & Evening Times picture archive*)

Mrs Thatcher at her first, lesser known, visit to the General Assembly of the Church of Scotland in 1981. Left to right, the incoming Moderator, the Rt Rev Andrew Doig, the Prime Minister, Lord Elgin, the Lord High Commissioner, and the retiring Moderator, the Very Rev Dr William Johnston. (© *The Scotsman Publications Ltd*)

Seven years later and Mrs Thatcher was invited to speak, delivering her infamous 'Sermon on the Mound'. The Rt Rev James Whyte, that year's Moderator, is in the chair. He later described the speech as 'the most extraordinary reading of scripture'. (© *The Scotsman Publications Ltd*)

Harry More-Gordon's watercolour of the Ceremony of the Keys at Holyroodhouse the evening before Mrs Thatcher's speech to the General Assembly. Left to right, Cllr Alexander; Captain of the Guard of the High Constables and Guard of Honour of The Palace of Holyroodhouse, John M. Davidson; City Officer, Charles C. Allen; Lord Lyon King of Arms, Malcolm Innes of Edingight; Lord Provost of Edinburgh, Eleanor McLaughlin; Director of Finance, Edinburgh District Council, Robert A. Marshall; Purse Bearer, Sir Charles Fraser; Lord High Commissioner to the General Assembly of the Church of Scotland, Sir Iain Tennant; Moderator of the General Assembly of the Church of Scotland,

Very Rev Duncan Shaw; Lady Margaret Tennant; Lord High Commissioner's Macer, George Davies; Master of the Horse, W. L. Sleigh; Mrs Harry More Gordon; Margaret Thatcher; Lady Fraser; Lady-in-Waiting, Mrs Angus Cheape; Lady-in-Waiting, Countess of Dunmore; Palace Superintendent, Lt Col Donald Wickes; Purse Bearer's Personal Assistant, Mrs Merle Quade; Baillie of The Palace of Holyroodhouse, Ivor R. Guild; Moderator of the High Constables and Guard of Honour of The Palace of Holyroodhouse, Dr J. D. Mathews; Palace Foreman, James L. Pollard.
(*Courtesy of Sir Charles Fraser, © Harry More Gordon*)

A celebrated encounter between Kirsty Wark and Mrs Thatcher on BBC Scotland in March 1990. It captured a Prime Minister in decline, while her references to 'we in Scotland' and being 'Prime Minister of Scotland' jarred.

A windswept Mrs Thatcher visiting the Lockerbie crash site in December 1988. Such visits seemed to do little to convince Scots that the Prime Minister actually 'cared' about Scotland. (© *The Scotsman Publications Ltd*)

Mrs Thatcher opens Glasgow's St Enoch Centre in 1990 flanked by Malcolm Rifkind and followed by Michael Forsyth at the bottom of the escalator. 'We have a long way to go', she admitted when asked about Scottish opinion polls, but the shopping centre demonstrated how far the city, not to mention the consumer society, had come since the late 1970s. (© *The Scotsman Publications Ltd*)

A portrait of the Prime Minister by the Scottish artist Anne Mackintosh. Painted in the last year of her premiership it was commissioned by the Focus in Scotland dinner, an annual fundraiser for the Scottish Conservative Party, and later gifted to Mrs Thatcher. (*Courtesy of Anne Mackintosh*)

Michael Forsyth, Lord Goold, Allan Stewart and Mrs Thatcher are all smiles at a 1991 Conservative Party event in Eastwood. The former Prime Minister had just announced her intention to leave the House of Commons at the next general election. (*Courtesy of Jackson Carlaw MSP*)

Baroness Thatcher campaigning in Scotland during the 2005 general election. 'The campaign to stop Labour's disastrous decision is a vital one,' she declared during her last intervention in Scottish politics. 'Save the Argylls and all the Scottish regiments!' (© *The Scotsman Publications Ltd*)

The grocer's daughter visits the son of the manse at 10 Downing Street in September 2007. 'I think Lady Thatcher saw the need for change,' Gordon Brown had recently declared at a Downing Street press conference. 'I also admire the fact that she is a conviction politician...I am a conviction politician like her.' (© *Getty Images*)

Lord Forsyth and the author talking to Baroness Thatcher about Scotland in October 2008. 'The culture of dependency which had done such damage to Britain was that much stronger in Scotland,' she recalled in early 2009, 'and I knew that, in bringing about change, we would be challenging firmly entrenched interests.' (*Courtesy of Steve Richmond*)

Scotland's five New Town Development Corporations were also to be wound up and their powers transferred to the new body. Labour MPs predictably attacked the plan as further eroding the influence of local authorities, a charge the government did not deny, but it enabled Rifkind to pursue new housing initiatives without recourse to fresh legislation. Usefully, it also created a new, specifically Scottish, government agency, demonstrating that even Thatcherism was not immune to nationalistic banners.

One initiative was called 'Rent to Mortgages' which allowed housing association tenants to convert their rent, less a sum for repair and maintenance, into mortgage payments. This met with some success. By December 1988, 152,000 houses had been sold to public sector tenants, almost 25,000 of which had once been SSHA properties. For the first time in decades, the public sector in Scotland made up less than 50 per cent of the total housing stock, while opinion polls showed that the vast majority of young Scots aspired to own their own home.[35] Interestingly, the 'Rents to Mortgages' idea originated with Peter Walker in Wales, and although it was enthusiastically endorsed by the Prime Minister, it ran into opposition from a senior member of the Cabinet. '[T]he immediate compromise was that we had two experiments,' recalled Walker, 'one in Wales and the other in Scotland.'[36] Oddly, however, 'Rent to Mortgages' never featured among the pantheon of government policies being 'tested' on Scotland. The Housing (Scotland) Act of 1988, meanwhile, enabled public sector tenants to change the landlords of their existing homes via the 'Tenants' Choice' scheme.

In other respects, however, the Scottish public sector reigned supreme. By 1988, one in three Scots still worked in either central or local government, so the Compulsory Competitive Tendering (CCT) introduced into the Scottish NHS in 1988, and into Scottish local government in 1989, was perceived as yet another attack on Scotland itself. The concept of CCT for the latter had first appeared in 1980 when Direct Labour Organisations (DLOs) were required to put their activities out to tender. In Scotland, DLOs had considerable success winning in-house contracts, but when the scheme was rolled out more extensively in 1989, it was attacked for leading to job losses and reducing wages. So regardless of the stated benefits, a significant portion of Scots – both professional and working class – could not be convinced that more private sector involvement was necessarily a good thing. 'The current harsh social Darwinism is not an ideology which fits well with the experience of 20th-century Scots,' wrote the Nationalist Isobel Lindsay in late 1987. 'Even in the last ten years, the best things to have happened in Scotland – environmental, cultural, recreational – have been

---

[35] This delighted Mrs Thatcher, particularly one poll showing that 80 per cent of young people wanted to own their own homes. 'This is the kind of silent revolution that has taken place,' she said. (Interview for *Dundee Courier* 7/9/1989, MTF)

[36] Walker, *Staying Power*, 215. Between 1990 and 2005, Scottish Homes transferred a further 75,000 units previously owned by the SSHA to housing associations and co-operatives.

primarily primed by public money; the worst things that have happened –
high unemployment and cuts in services – have been caused by lack of public
funding or by the ruthlessness of private institutions.'[37]

The Prime Minister, addressing her first Scottish Conservative conference
since the election, was unrepentant. 'I'm sometimes told that the Scots don't
like Thatcherism,' she said, echoing a line dreamt up the previous summer.
'Well, I find that hard to believe – because the Scots invented Thatcherism,
long before I was thought of.' She explained:

> It is more than two hundred years since Adam Smith, David Hume, Adam
> Ferguson and others first set out their ideas of a world in which wealth would be
> generated and spread ever more widely. They saw that it's not Government
> which creates wealth – it's people. That people do best when they pursue their
> own vision. And that a wise Government will harness the efforts of individuals to
> improve the well-being of the whole community. So they proposed to restrain
> Government and to liberate men and women. Mr President, those are the ideals
> I hold most dear. And they had their origins in the Scottish Enlightenment.

'Scotland,' Mrs Thatcher continued, 'is on the march again.' Another
section of her speech betrayed her growing conviction that the actions of
previous administrations, both Labour and Tory, had delayed this onward
march. 'Governments failed Scotland – not by doing too little, but by
promising too much,' the Prime Minister explained. 'Successive governments
promised to insulate Scotland from the reality of industrial change. They told
you: "You don't need to worry. We'll protect you."' She continued:

> But they couldn't – and they didn't. Shipyards closed. Factories closed. Men
> lost their jobs. Whole areas turned to wasteland. And the money that might
> have been invested in new industries, new opportunities, went instead in trying
> to keep yesterday's jobs alive. The result was that the economy fell faster,
> apathy and despair spread wider. And disillusion with Government grew
> deeper. It was as if the Scots concluded: 'If Government can't save us, what on
> earth can we do?'

Mrs Thatcher, therefore, was presenting herself – not necessarily her
government – as Scotland's saviour. The party now had to work hard, she
said, to turn the map of Scotland blue again and 'assert our Party's place in
the centre of Scotland's national life'. This means, she went on:

> I won't be discouraged by temporary set-backs. I didn't come into politics to
> take short-cuts, or court easy popularity. My principles are not at the mercy of

---

[37] *Radical Scotland* October/November 1987.

the opinion polls – neither, I am sure, are yours . . . Scottish values are Tory values – and vice versa. The values of hard work, self-reliance, thrift, enterprise – the relishing of challenges, the seizing of opportunities. That's what the Tory Party stands for – that's what Scotland stands for. And that will be our message to the people.[38]

These were noble, if somewhat hyperbolic, sentiments. The next two and a half years, however, were to represent both the high, and therefore low, point of Thatcherism in Scotland, ingraining the impression that Scottish values were about as far from Mrs Thatcher's values as it was possible to be.

THE MONSTROUS REGIMENT OF WOMEN

Although spirited, when it came to the district council elections of May 1988 – a month in which Mrs Thatcher spent an unprecedented amount of time in Scotland – it looked as if Thatcherism resurgent had achieved nothing. Already demoralised in Scotland's town halls, the Conservatives went from 189 councillors in 1984 to just 162 four years later, trailing the SNP with 19 per cent of the vote and retaining control of only three authorities in elections dominated by the imminent Poll Tax. As usual, there was no formal acknowledgement of the results by the Prime Minister as she embarked upon a trio of high-profile Scottish visits. The last of these was to be a controversial speech to the General Assembly of the Church of Scotland.

Immediately after the annual Scottish Conservative conference, however, the Prime Minister first paid homage to another national religion by attending the Scottish Cup Final at Hampden Park in Glasgow. This was the golden age of Scottish football, but predictably hostile territory for Mrs Thatcher. 'She sought my advice about what to wear when she agreed to attend the Celtic versus Dundee match,' recalled Sir Bernard Ingham. 'I said no blue or dark blue, and no green and white; she was very neutral.' Despite this sartorial caution the Prime Minister was literally shown the red card, distributed by the SNP before the match, by thousands of booing football fans. 'She took what happened in good humour,'[39] added Sir Bernard.

As if that public relations disaster had not been bad enough, the Prime Minister then prepared herself for an appearance before a theoretically more forgiving crowd, the General Assembly of the Church of Scotland, commonly known as the Kirk. Her speech, later dubbed the 'Sermon on the Mound'

---

[38] Speech to Scottish Conservative conference, 13/5/1988, MTF.

[39] Interview with Sir Bernard Ingham, 25/4/2008. There was not much good humour when the STV reporter David Whitton quizzed the Prime Minister earlier in the day about her visit. 'It appears that you are going to be even more unpopular than the referee this afternoon,' said one. 'Not as unpopular as some of you people are,' was Mrs Thatcher's response. (Remarks visiting Glasgow Garden Festival, 14/5/1988, MTF) Whitton's recollection was that she replied: 'I'm not as unpopular as some of you people think I am.'

(a soubriquet Mrs Thatcher considered tasteless), created an almost hysterical reaction and quickly became a standard reference point, if not *the* standard reference point, for the Thatcher era in Scotland.

The idea for Mrs Thatcher to address the General Assembly, something a premier can do only by invitation, actually came from Malcolm Rifkind as he searched for inspiration following the calamitous 1987 election result. He suggested it to the Prime Minister's staff at Downing Street, who then contacted Sir Charles Fraser, pursebearer at Holyroodhouse, to intimate Mrs Thatcher's intentions. Ironically, the Prime Minister's private office was acutely aware of the likely reaction to her appearance and did not want to create the impression she was asking to attend, as she had in 1981 as a spectator.[40]

'There was definitely an air of "I'm coming",' recalled Sir Charles. 'She really was a mirror image of Harold Wilson and Ted Heath [who had also addressed the General Assembly] in terms of my dealings with Prime Ministers. The arrangements for her to have her hair done while at the Palace, for instance, were considerable.'[41] A hairdresser was duly hired and attended to the Prime Ministerial hair the day before she delivered her address. Similarly, the speech itself received close attention. 'I spent Sunday at Chequers working on a speech I was to deliver to the General Assembly of the Church of Scotland,' Mrs Thatcher recalled in her memoirs; 'there was some mirth when my speech writers and I were discovered down on our knees in an appropriate posture, though drawing on the resources of sellotape rather than the Holy Spirit.'[42] But although it has long been assumed that one of those speech writers was the journalist T. E. Utley, there is no evidence he helped write it, and indeed he died shortly after it was delivered.[43] Rather it was probably Robin Catford, a devout evangelical in charge of Downing Street appointments, who prepared the text, together with input from Brian Griffiths at the Policy Unit. Mrs Thatcher liked Catford and saw him as her kind of Christian, basically low-church as well as a true believer.

'I do not generally hold with politicians preaching sermons,' Mrs Thatcher wrote in *The Path to Power*, 'though since so many clerics preach politics there seems no room in this regard for restrictive practices.'[44] Despite this wariness she had made religious speeches before, notably to St Lawrence Jewry in 1981, which anticipated many of the themes in her Church of Scotland speech

---

[40] There were protests on that occasion too. Pastor Jack Glass's followers chanted 'No popery' while several hundred Labour and trade union members shouted 'No Thatchery'. The Student Christian Movement, meanwhile, 'objected to Mrs Thatcher's attempts to give a veneer of Christian respectability to the un-Christian economic and defence policies of her Government'. (*Scotsman* 18/5/1981)

[41] Interview with Sir Charles Fraser, 26/9/2008.

[42] Thatcher, *The Path to Power*, 704.

[43] 'I remember particularly vividly our last meetings just before his death last year,' Mrs Thatcher wrote in a foreword to Utley's selected journalism, 'when we discussed at length the ideas which I intended to use in my speech to the General Assembly of the Church of Scotland.' (Moore & Heffer, eds, *A Tory Seer*, ix–x)

[44] Thatcher, *The Path to Power*, 555.

seven years later. Indeed, throughout the 1980s Mrs Thatcher became increasingly interested in the relationship between Christianity and social and economic policy, while also coming to view all churchmen as irredeemably wet. In December 1985 a Church of England report called *Faith in the City* had criticised both the established Anglican Church and the government for failing to tackle inner-city deprivation, something which confirmed rather than created that view in the Prime Minister's mind.

Raised a Methodist, Mrs Thatcher had gradually evolved – at least in terms of religious observance – into an Anglican, although her roots predisposed her to favour its evangelical wing. The Prime Minister's bedtime reading frequently included theological texts and she enjoyed the business of ecclesiastic appointments, although of course these did not extend to the Church of Scotland. And then there was her father. Alderman Roberts had been a Wesleyan lay-preacher as well as a local politician, and Margaret purposefully emulated his 'sermon voice'.

None of this seemed to matter in Scotland. From the moment it became known that the Lord High Commissioner (the Queen's representative) intended to invite the Prime Minister to address the General Assembly, some Kirk ministers whipped themselves up into an indignant fervour. The letters pages of newspapers, meanwhile, filled up with angry correspondents saying that she should not be allowed to speak. One even said that if the Prime Minister needed a biblical quotation she need look no further than Mark 4:25: 'For whoever may have, there shall be given to him, and whoever hath not, also that which he hath shall be taken from him.'

Nevertheless, as Sir Bernard Ingham recalled, 'She put an enormous amount of effort into that speech.'[45] Indeed, the so-called Sermon on the Mound was probably one of the most thoroughly prepared speeches Mrs Thatcher ever delivered. In 1558 the Scottish protestant reformer John Knox published *The First Blast of the Trumpet Against the Monstrous Regiment of Women.* By regiment he meant government, and the monstrous women he had in mind were the Roman Catholic sovereigns of the day, Mary Tudor of England and Mary Stuart of Scotland. Women in authority, argued Knox, were 'repugnant to nature'. On her arrival at the Kirk's General Assembly building on the Mound in Edinburgh, Mrs Thatcher soon discovered that the trumpet was still blasting. Not only did anti-Poll Tax demonstrators wielding more red cards harangue the Prime Minister as she entered the building, but inside the chamber five ministers argued – with Mrs Thatcher looking on from the gallery – that she should be deprived of a platform. Having failed to scupper the speech, they walked out before she had uttered a word, an astonishing act for men who claimed to support free discourse. 'There was a form of Christianity in her speech,' one of the five sarcastically conceded, 'but you could also say there was a form of Christianity in apartheid.'[46]

[45] Interview with Sir Bernard Ingham.
[46] 'The Sermon on the Mound' (BBC Radio Scotland) 7/5/2008.

Clad in blue and wearing a hat with a hint of a veil, Mrs Thatcher acknowledged that the Kirk had sprung 'from the independence of mind and rigour of thought that have always been such powerful characteristics of the Scottish people,' before adding as a joke, 'as I have occasion to know'. For her part, the Prime Minister fully realised the offence she might give and some observers thought she looked nervous as she spoke. Yet her attempt to reconcile Conservatism with the Christian gospel was sincere. 'If a man will not work he shall not eat', she said, quoting St Paul, arguing that 'abundance rather than poverty has a legitimacy which derives from the very nature of Creation'.[47] And, as Allan Massie observed, 'her suggestion that the Good Samaritan would not have been able to be of such help to the man who fell among thieves if he had not himself been a rich man was ill received, though the observation was self-evidently true'.[48]

In making the speech at all Mrs Thatcher was perhaps attempting to correct the damage done by her infamous assertion in September 1987 that there was 'no such thing as society'. The Prime Minister never exactly believed that – she simply objected to the Left's use of the term – and deliberately mentioned 'society' several times in her General Assembly speech as if to intimate a partial retreat. Few of those listening, however, picked up on this subtlety. In fact, re-reading the speech 20 years later it is striking how courteous and balanced some passages are. 'The Tenth Commandment recognises that making money and owning things could become selfish activities,' said Mrs Thatcher. 'But it is not the creation of wealth that is wrong but love of money for its own sake. The spiritual dimension comes in deciding what one does with the wealth.'[49] What Thatcherism did with the wealth is, of course, why the ideology caused such controversy, but although the speech's central assertion caused a row, noted the journalist Hugo Young, 'it wasn't greeted with incredulity. It was now fashionable to be rich not poor, to consume rather than to "care".'[50]

And contrary to popular belief, the speech was not immediately greeted with hostility. Indeed, the applause at the end of Mrs Thatcher's address was both spontaneous and enthusiastic, far from the 'stony silence'[51] often referred to. Hostility soon manifested itself, however, although it owed more to mischievous myth-making than spontaneous outrage. The first myth is that two reports presented to the Prime Minister after her speech by the Moderator – one of which was *Just Sharing: A Christian approach to the distribution of wealth, income and benefits* – were somehow an intentional rebuke. Although both reports were the most overtly critical the Kirk had ever produced, such reports were habitually presented to visiting dignitaries.

---

[47] Speech to the General Assembly of the Church of Scotland, 21/5/1988, MTF (see Appendix 1).
[48] Massie, *The Thistle and the Rose*, 280.
[49] Speech to the General Assembly.
[50] Young, *Staying Power*, 536–37.
[51] Devine, ed., *Scotland and the Union*, 164.

The second myth is that Mrs Thatcher was actually condemned during the proceedings of the General Assembly. In fact the Very Rev James Whyte, who regularly dined out on the *Just Sharing* story, only later described the speech as being 'the most extraordinary reading of scripture'.[52] Similarly, it was in a radio interview that Professor Duncan B. Forrester, who had edited the *Just Sharing* publication, informed Mrs Thatcher that the Kirk had never countenanced the idea of an 'individualist's paradise'.[53] The implication, however, was clear. The Prime Minister had hijacked Christianity in order to justify her own ideology. Coverage of the speech dominated television news that evening, and the next day the Scottish media went to town. The novelist Jonathan Raban was even inspired to pen a critique of the speech called *God, Man and Mrs Thatcher*.

The context was crucial. With constant talk of a 'democratic deficit' in Scotland, the Kirk appeared to fill that gap with its General Assembly which, although it met for less than a week each year, was looked upon by some as a surrogate Scottish parliament. It was a role the Church of Scotland – with declining membership and relevance – inevitably embraced. So by insulting Scotland's national church, by implication Mrs Thatcher had also insulted Scotland itself. 'In many ways, the event came to symbolise all that was wrong with Thatcherism in Scotland,' wrote the historian Richard Finlay. 'The fact that the Kirk, that most traditional bastion of Scottish society, had cold-shouldered the Iron Lady was taken as proof that her policies were alien even to traditional Scottish society.'[54]

This interpretation was then willingly taken up by Labour, Liberal Democrat and SNP politicians and repeated *ad nauseam*. Ironically, Mrs Thatcher's speech could barely have been classified as 'Scottish' at all beyond a few token references, yet it was widely interpreted as a wicked onslaught against Scotland. 'Christians will very often genuinely disagree,' the Prime Minister observed towards the end of her address, 'though it is a mark of Christian manners that they will do so with courtesy and mutual respect.'[55]

Ironic, then, that Mrs Thatcher's lucid, and very personal, exposition of Christianity was greeted by many with neither. Over time, however, perceptions cooled. 'As a public speaker . . . she was robust, challenging, clear, and a scourge of soft thinking and complacency,' wrote Harry Reid in his best-selling book on the Church of Scotland, *Outside Verdict*, 'and these are among the qualities that I for one would look for in a great preacher.'[56] To Sir Bernard Ingham, on the other hand, 'it was just the final conversion of the

---

[52] Roy, *Conversations in a Small Country*, 42. In fact, as Mrs Thatcher later explained to an Australian journalist, she did 'not claim any special linkage between Christianity and politics for my own party' in the speech; 'it is for each person to interpret it'. (Press conference for Australian journalists in London, 29/7/1988, MTF)

[53] Raban, *God, Man and Mrs Thatcher*, 67.

[54] Devine, ed., *Scotland and the Union*, 164.

[55] Speech to General Assembly.

[56] Reid, *Outside Verdict*, 164.

Church of England [*sic*] from the Tory Party at prayer to the Labour Party at prayer'.[57]

A month after Mrs Thatcher's trio of Scottish visits (conference, Hampden and General Assembly) the *Glasgow Herald* commissioned an opinion poll which showed support for the SNP at its highest level in a decade. 'Will the Prime Minister demonstrate her extensive knowledge of Scottish affairs,' asked its future leader, Alex Salmond, at Prime Minister's Questions after citing the poll, 'by reminding the House of the names of the Moderator of the General Assembly, which she addressed, and the captain of Celtic, to whom she presented the cup?' 'I had a very good day in Scotland,' was the Prime Minister's tongue-in-cheek reply. 'Whatever the Hon. Gentleman tries to say, Scotland's economy and people are benefiting enormously from the way in which the Government are handling them.'[58] As Salmond later reflected, 'she was much more vulnerable to humour than Nationalist arguments'.[59]

The speech's reception, however, clearly irritated Mrs Thatcher. 'I was asked to address the Scottish Assembly [*sic*], it was a great honour,' she recalled a few months after the speech. She went on:

I felt that I must devote a very considerable amount of time and thought to saying what I believed and how, in my view, politics and Christianity interwove. [So] it was Scotland asking me fully and frankly to give my beliefs, doing me the supreme courtesy and honour of asking me and listening with great attention. And if I might say, we have had more requests for copies of that speech from all over the world than any other.[60]

Indeed, 'that speech' was later included as an appendix to *Christianity & Conservatism: Are Christianity and Conservatism Compatible?*, a book co-edited by the Prime Minister's former Parliamentary Private Secretary, Michael Alison.

THE HUGHES INITIATIVE

Despite the apparent failure of May's big push, Mrs Thatcher pressed on. If the Scots could not be won over by patronage of the beautiful game and appeals to theological reason, she appeared to think, perhaps this could be achieved by other means. 'Judged by cold statistics,' she said in 1988, 'Scots enjoy greater prosperity than anywhere in the United Kingdom outside the crowded, high-priced South East.'[61] In other words, it really was the economy, stupid. After giving a prominent place to Scottish affairs at the UK

[57] Interview with Sir Bernard Ingham.
[58] Hansard 135 c566–67.
[59] Interview with Alex Salmond, 24/6/2008.
[60] Interview for *Scotland on Sunday*, 31/10/1988, MTF.
[61] Speech to Scottish Conservative conference, 13/5/1988, MTF.

Conservative Party conference that autumn, the Prime Minister relaunched her Scottish fightback.

In a new weekend newspaper, *Scotland on Sunday*, Mrs Thatcher boasted of the 'flourishing' Scottish economy while claiming credit for falling unemployment. This was true to an extent. Although Scottish unemployment dropped to 10.6 per cent in November 1988 (compared with 11.1 per cent in the north of England), it still lagged behind the UK average of 7.3 per cent. By the middle of 1987, however, the economy had picked up and, relative to other peripheral UK regions, Scotland was indeed 'flourishing', with GDP per head actually growing more quickly than the UK average. Frequent government claims that it was simply taking longer for Scotland to benefit from Thatcherism appeared to have some justification. The Scottish population, which had fallen every year under Mrs Thatcher (hence the Proclaimers' famous refrain in 'Letter from America'), began to increase, and Scots also benefited from further cuts to direct taxation as a result of Nigel Lawson's controversial 1988 budget in which the basic rate was cut to 25 per cent and all upper rates – except the 40 per cent band – were abolished. This largesse, however, also had drawbacks. The booming UK economy began to overheat, and by the end of 1988 not only had interest rates doubled, but inflation was also on the rise.

The Prime Minister emphasised only positive points in a speech to the Scottish CBI in September 1988. Manufacturing investment was rising, she said; productivity was improving; building and construction orders were up 25 per cent on the previous year; and Silicon Glen continued to attract jobs and investment from British Petroleum, British Telecom, JVC and ICI. The Scottish media, meanwhile, continued to dwell on the negative aspects of Scotland's economy, most notably a continuing decline in manufacturing employment (as opposed to investment) and, above everything else, the plight of the steel industry.

Kenneth Clarke, the Minister for Trade and Industry, had announced the government's intention to privatise the British Steel Corporation (BSC) in late 1987, and in 1988 it finally passed out of state control. Although the government maintained that, subject to market conditions, Ravenscraig would continue to operate until at least 1989, such a guarantee was essentially meaningless as BSC decided its own fate in the private sector. Also finding its own way – having been privatised in 1987 – was the British Airports Authority, which included Glasgow, Edinburgh and Aberdeen Airports.

In December 1987, a previous privatisation also came back to haunt the government. British Petroleum (BP) – itself privatised, rather unsuccessfully, that year – bid for the Glasgow-based Britoil, formerly the British National Oil Corporation. Although the government's 'golden share', which allowed it to pack the Britoil board should a hostile foreign bidder stage a raid on its shares, did not apply, the 'politics of Britoil', as Simon Jenkins has written, 'was the politics of Scotland'. Malcolm Rifkind warned the Cabinet that it was a 'sufficiently sensitive issue' to justify activating the golden share. It was duly used as a negotiating card, and although BP was allowed to take over Britoil, it only did so by agreeing to certain conditions: the government was to retain control over North Sea exploration, Britoil's headquarters was to remain in Glasgow, and BP's research and development was to move to Scotland along with 'between fifty and seventy senior executives'. 'The barter was a classic of 1970s government corporatism,'[62] observed Jenkins. Indeed, the golden share was used just once by the government, and used to buy off anticipated criticism in Scotland.

Criticism did come, however, as more job losses arose from the sale of the Royal Ordnance Factory at Bishopton in 1988, presided over by the former Scottish Secretary George Younger at the Ministry of Defence. 'There probably will be some redundancies,' conceded Mrs Thatcher. 'But are our opponents saying that you must stay in yesterday's practices and yesterday's mode of work and that you must necessarily pay more for that and therefore have a more expensive government? That is what our opponents say. Listen to them and we would still be in a hansom cab society with muskets. That is the way to poverty and bankruptcy.'[63]

There were also fears that the planned privatisation of electricity and water would lead to even more poverty and bankruptcy for Scots workers. In this case, however, the invisible hand of the Scottish Office went to work. Scotland's water suppliers were not privatised at all, while the North of Scotland Hydro-Electric Board (which became Scottish Hydro Electric) and South of Scotland Electricity Board (SSEB, which was renamed Scottish Power) were formed into two vertically integrated companies ahead of privatisation in June 1991. A separate publicly owned company, Scottish Nuclear, was also set up to operate Scotland's nuclear power stations and sell electricity to Scottish Power and Scottish Hydro Electric under contract.

Malcolm Rifkind made great play of that fact that this arrangement meant a lessening of competition within Scotland compared to the fuller privatisation of electricity in England. It was, he said, another example of devolution to the people. But to the intellectual architect of privatisation, John Redwood, it was simply baffling. 'We were always sensitive to the constitutional niceties of Scotland and that's why electricity and water weren't privatised,' he recalled. 'They've always gone for the big state, big monopoly, low economic-growth model, which never works, but that's what they wanted. We didn't interfere with that; we had enough to do trying to sort out England.'[64]

So why, if Scotland's economy was booming, unemployment was falling and its state-owned monopolies continued to escape the full rigours of private competition, did the impression linger that Thatcherism was damaging Scotland? Arguably, a lot of harm was done by the rhetoric of some senior ministers. Infamously, in a speech in Glasgow in November 1987, the

---

[62] Jenkins, *Accountable to None*, 37–38.
[63] Interview for *Scotland on Sunday*.
[64] Interview with John Redwood MP, 27/5/2008.

Chancellor Nigel Lawson identified what he called a 'culture of dependence' in Scotland. 'Despite the undoubted success so far, there is still a barrier along Scotland's road to prosperity,' he explained. 'That barrier is the pervasive presence of a hostile attitude to enterprise and wealth-creation, to the enterprise culture on which economic success in a free society depends.'[65]

The *Scottish Sun* summed this up the next day as 'Will ye stop your snivelling, Jock?' To Lawson, however, Scotland during the twentieth century had 'become the greatest redoubt of socialism and the socialist mind-set in the UK'. There were, he believed, at least three contributing factors: Scots seeking fame and fortune in the Empire had led to a 'brain drain'; England's relative wealth meant 'the Scots were inclined to argue that they deserved a better deal from the government in London'; 'And third, once the habit of electing Labour councillors became entrenched, so did the socialist mind-set.'[66] It was a mind-set Lawson summarised with the phrase 'dependency culture', a phrase that captured the attitude of several ministerial colleagues and, like the behaviour of Anglo-Scots backbenchers, was less than helpful to Rifkind's strategy as Scottish Secretary. The former steel and coal chief Sir Ian MacGregor, now settled in the Highlands, also contributed to the debate about where Scotland was going wrong. 'Government help is just like drugs,' he declared at an Adam Smith Insistute seminar in Glasgow, 'you become dependent on it.'[67] The Scots, he added, had become like drug addicts dependent upon state support.

Mrs Thatcher, on the other hand, refrained from indulging in such language and instead depicted Scotland's 'enterprising culture' in relentlessly positive terms. Nevertheless, there were frequent inferred slights. Her proclamation that the Channel Tunnel, which began construction in 1987, would be a market 'on your doorstep'[68] symbolised for many the government's 'south-east corner' mentality. Calls for fast rail links from Scotland to the Tunnel were ignored, while a new London airport at Stansted, the construction of the M25 motorway and the expensive regeneration of the Docklands all contributed to the impression that the government wanted to further develop what Mrs Thatcher called the 'crowded, high-priced South East' rather than more northerly regions. That the government had, at the same time, showered road building (such as the A9, A90 and the A96) and urban regeneration projects in Scotland with public money appeared not to matter.

---

[65] *Glasgow Herald* 24/11/1987. Lawson claimed credit for the phrase 'enterprise culture' but attributed 'dependency culture' to Mrs Thatcher. 'The model in this case was the United States – although that country had in turn derived it from the vigorous enterprise culture of Victorian England and Scotland, and developed it further.' (Lawson, *The View From No. 11*, 64)

[66] Lord Lawson to the author, 3/12/2008.

[67] *Daily Telegraph* 11/9/1987. The ASI seminar, 'The Renaissance of Scotland', also proposed widespread privatisation, an official Scottish residence for the Prime Minister and a separate Scottish passport.

[68] Speech opening Single Market Campaign, 18/4/1988, MTF.

The Prime Minister also could not resist hand bagging the trade unions, which in 1988 were still disproportionately strong in Scotland. When the SDA announced in the autumn of 1987 that 18 months of secret negotiations had persuaded the Ford Motor Company to build a £40 million components factory in Dundee employing up to 950 people, the news was greeted warmly. But when Ford pulled out of the project after unions failed to agree a single-union deal, Mrs Thatcher could not disguise her disdain: 'What I do not understand is that, in this modern age, some of the trade unions are more concerned with demarcation disputes, restrictive practices and sectional interests than in jobs for their fellow citizens.'[69] And it was not just trade unionists that were to blame. 'Even out of power, the ghost of Labour stalks the industrial landscape,' she informed the 1988 Scottish Tory conference, 'frightening away foreign investment and chilling the prospects of growth.'[70]

The SDA had been one component of 1970s corporatism that Mrs Thatcher had been willing to tolerate – thanks largely to George Younger – since coming to power in 1979. Always regarded with suspicion by Scottish true believers like Iain Sproat and Allan Stewart, it had survived by transforming itself into one of Europe's most market-orientated industrial agencies. By 1988, however, its days appeared to be numbered. Having drawn sharp criticism from the National Audit Office for its high-spending involvement in that year's Glasgow Garden Festival (visited by Mrs Thatcher) it was also felt to be increasingly biased towards the Strathclyde Region and Glasgow. Recent investment in the city, in fact, totalled £1 billion. There was a new shopping complex at St Enoch Square, a hotel near the Scottish Exhibition and Conference Centre, a shopping, leisure and entertainment development in Princes Square off Buchanan Street, a plan to convert Kelvin Hall into a Museum of Transport, and a scheme to build what later became the Glasgow Royal Concert Hall.

Bill Hughes, a Conservative-inclined businessman and chairman of the Scottish CBI, viewed this as unjustifiable urban bias. Dismayed by high unemployment in his native Falkirk, he had helped establish the Think Falkirk group to analyse what could be done to tackle it. Chaired by another Falkirk native, the STUC general secretary Campbell Christie, Think Falkirk reached the conclusion that the SDA was simply not interested in towns like Falkirk, while a myriad of local agencies concerned with business start-ups were not fit for purpose. In addition to that, believed Hughes, the government's centralised Training Agency (TA) was attempting to apply English solutions to Scottish problems.

So out of Falkirk sprang the idea to unify Scotland's training and industrial agencies into a single unit. Hughes explained his thinking to anyone who would listen, prompting the CBI's press officer Gerry O'Brien to declare as they drove along the A9: 'If you feel that strongly, Bill, then why don't you do

---

[69] *The Times* 31/3/1988.
[70] Speech to Scottish Conservative conference, 30/3/1988, MTF.

something about it?'[71] He did, and the story of what happened next became legend. Hughes and O'Brien produced a one-page draft to merge the TA and SDA under the tentative name, Enterprise Scotland. Although urged by Rifkind to send it to his civil servants, Hughes instead contacted Alf Young, a respected business journalist at the *Glasgow Herald*. The 'Hughes Plan' or 'Hughes Initiative', as it was dubbed, generated significant press coverage, much of it positive, and after Lord Goold, the Scottish Tory chairman and also a former chairman of CBI Scotland, agreed to raise it with the Prime Minister, Hughes found himself discussing it with her at Downing Street and later Chequers. As well as its potential economic and employment benefits, he sold it to Mrs Thatcher as something which would both 'significantly improve ballot box performance' and 'visibly deliver Thatcherism as the dynamo of Scottish economic recovery'.[72]

Perplexed at her continuing unpopularity in Scotland, the Prime Minister was probably willing to try anything. She once said of David Young, the businessman-turned-Trade and Industry Secretary, that others brought her problems while Young brought her only solutions. It therefore appeared to Mrs Thatcher that Hughes had presented her with a solution to Scotland's apparent resistance to Thatcherite enterprise. She made just one change. Instead of Enterprise Scotland the new agency was to be called Scottish Enterprise (the Highlands and Islands Development Board , meanwhile, was to remain distinct but become Highlands and Islands Enterprise). 'She had never been a fan of the SDA', recalled Hughes, 'so I knew it would have a degree of political acceptance. She was obviously enthusiastic.' He went on:

> That Saturday Rifkind and I went down to Chequers; Norman Fowler was there, as was Sir Hector Laing, he was one of the people she spoke to frequently; she obviously listened to him as he had created something called Scottish Business in the Community. So we spent a whole day discussing how Enterprise Scotland would work in practice and within two weeks the CBI in Scotland had its annual conference and there were just two speakers, myself and Mrs Thatcher – she didn't want anyone else to speak. At that she launched Scottish Enterprise.[73]

Indeed, the Prime Minister was almost gushing. 'You, Mr Chairman [Hughes], are leading by example,' she said. 'The proposals you have put forward for Scottish Enterprise have linked enterprise and training in a new and exciting way.' She continued:

> Your belief, and I share your view, is that if people can see for themselves the benefits that come to their local communities, then many more will come

---

[71] Brown & McCrone, eds, *Scottish Government Yearbook 1991*, 50.

[72] 'Enterprise Scotland Proposal', Cabinet Office files 26/8/1988.

[73] Interview with Bill Hughes, 27/5/2008.

forward to help than could do so nationally. Witness for example the excellent work done by Scottish Business in the Community. Like you, we believe that most is achieved when people are given responsibility and can see the results that flow from their efforts. Mr Chairman, you have identified a Scottish solution to respond to Scottish needs . . . We are working on your proposals urgently, with a view to a positive result.[74]

'Mrs Thatcher could take decisions; she didn't mess about,' recalled Hughes. 'She saw Scottish Enterprise as a solution.'[75] Indeed, as he later reflected,

[the] whole day [their initial meeting] was one of impatience with Scotland. She said, Why will you not come to me with solutions to your problems? To me Scotland is a problem. It's nothing but problems and you won't give me solutions to them. I'm not inhibiting you in any way. Why don't you come to me with ideas? . . . Why would my Scottish Ministers, why should my Scottish people not give me solutions? Take everything I believe in and apply it to Scotland and I'm happy. What she wasn't going to do was compromise her Thatcherism. If there was an interpretation of Thatcherism which would accommodate the Scottish dimension she would accept it straight away.[76]

Indeed, Rifkind later told Hughes that it was one of the swiftest idea-to-legislation transitions Parliament had ever considered (it received Royal Assent in 1990). Unusually for a Thatcherite initiative in Scotland, it also drew broad support. Although Labour instinctively opposed it the STUC, having proposed something similar in its otherwise left-wing manifesto, *Scotland – A Land Fit for People*, responded more favourably, largely because it involved responsibility for training being devolved to Scotland.

The STUC's pragmatism, however, went unrewarded when the legislation obliged a network of Local Enterprise Companies (LECs) to draw two-thirds of their members from the private sector. Campbell Christie's remark that Labour would have a ready-made machine with which to drive the Scottish economy on returning to office probably did not help, and the Scottish Office contrived to minimise public sector involvement in the new agency. 'Instead of having a vision on the A9,' remarked the former Labour councillor Laurence McGarry caustically, 'I sometimes wish . . . Bill Hughes had had a puncture.'[77]

Also incorporated in the Scottish Enterprise legislation was the winding up of Scotland's five New Town Development Corporations, like the SDA

[74] Speech to Scottish CBI, 8/9/1988, MTF.
[75] Interview with Bill Hughes.
[76] Kemp, *The Hollow Drum*, 189–90.
[77] Brown & McCrone, eds, *Scottish Government Yearbook 1991*, 50.

unlikely survivors of the Thatcher era. Enigmatically, Rifkind hailed the Enterprise and New Towns (Scotland) Bill as the most important piece of Scottish legislation since the government came to power in 1979. It was, he said, 'an idea whose time had come',[78] but for staff at the SDA it spelled possible redundancy and reports of demoralisation were widespread. 'Goodness me,' remarked Mrs Thatcher on hearing these complaints, 'we are going to do more about training, isn't that good?'[79]

A commitment from the government that everyone already employed by the TA (in Scotland) and the SDA should have their jobs guaranteed was probably politically necessary but, in Bill Hughes' opinion, 'not helpful'. 'What didn't work out was my vision that it [Scottish Enterprise] should last ten years and then be reviewed with a view to it being privatised,' reflected Hughes, 'It's not gone that way and has continued as a public-sector body.'[80] Indeed, it soon turned out to be as high spending a public-sector body as the SDA. Douglas Mason of the Adam Smith Institute despaired that Scottish Enterprise 'appears to be as firmly wedded as its predecessors to the notion that entrepreneurial spirit springs from a filing cabinet'.[81]

RURAL THATCHERISM

Scotland, particularly its farmers, had benefited enormously from European Community (EC) membership since 1973, via the Common Agricultural Policy (CAP) if not the Common Fisheries Policy (CFP), which involved difficult compromises. A negotiated concession, which gave 12-mile fisheries rights to the whole of Scotland's north and east coasts (as well as Shetland and Orkney), lasted until 1983, when it was extended to all EC member states. And despite being a minor economic concern, fishing in Scotland assumed disproportionate political importance as the 1980s wore on.

In terms of farming, the industry in Scotland began intensifying in the mid 1970s, while productivity increased, largely because of the CAP. Grants from Europe also had downsides. Increasing farm prices, production and advances in technology meant that the number of farm workers decreased dramatically, by about 50 per cent during the Thatcher era. By the mid 1980s, however, the CAP was becoming unsustainable through overproduction (with famous 'butter mountains' and 'wine lakes') and attack from environmentalists over its use of agrochemicals. Farm output started to decrease, hitting smaller, family-run farms in Scotland particularly hard. 'Scottish farmers have to compete in a world where trading conditions are tough and surpluses abound,' Mrs Thatcher told the 1988 Scottish Tory conference. 'In the European Community, we have had to put a limit on the budget in order to

---

[78] Interview with Bill Hughes.
[79] Interview for *Scotland on Sunday*.
[80] Interview with Bill Hughes.
[81] Massie, *et al.*, *Scotland and Free Enterprise*, 23.

reduce those surpluses and to bring supply more in line with demand . . . So Britain brought our European partners to face reality.'[82]

In response to these pressures, the EC turned its attention, and funding, towards supporting rural development, farm diversification and environmental concerns. This switch of emphasis undoubtedly benefited Scottish agriculture and, although few young people were able to begin careers in farming, the population of rural areas in Scotland actually increased in some areas as more Scots (and indeed the English) chose to live outside towns and cities, a trend that has continued ever since. The Scottish Agricultural Wages Board (SAWB), meanwhile, soldiered on untouched by Thatcherite forces. Comprising trade union representatives as well as ministerial nominees, in 2009 it still officiated over the wages of Scottish farm workers. The SAWB, much like the CAP and CFP, however, hardly embodied Thatcherism, which manifested itself more obviously in the debate over British forestry, much of which was in Scotland. A lot of Forestry Commission land was sold off as the usual debates raged about the relative merits of free enterprise and public access to Scotland's rugged terrain.

Although the environment did not become a mainstream political concern until Mrs Thatcher's groundbreaking speech to the Royal Society in September 1988 – with its emphasis on greenhouse gases, the hole in the ozone layer and acid rain[83] – throughout the 1980s there was a residual, albeit related, concern about the dumping of nuclear waste in Scotland. It began with the Mullwarchar Test Bores Inquiry in 1980, which overturned plans for nuclear dumping in the Galloway hills, and continued with local opposition to similar test drilling by Nirex (the UK body in charge of nuclear waste disposal) in Easter Ross, Buchan and Dounreay. Conspiracy theorists had a field day when in April 1985 Willie McRae, a prominent SNP-supporting lawyer and anti-nuclear campaigner, was found shot in his car at a lay-by on the A87. He died later in hospital, but the circumstances of his death – the gun with which he supposedly shot himself was found some distance from the car – together with its similarity to the death of another anti-nuclear campaigner called Hilda Murrell, led some to suspect that Nirex was disposing of more than just nuclear waste. To those on the Scottish left, meanwhile, nuclear dumping became another tangible example of the government's use of Scotland not just as a testing ground for unpopular policies, but also as a dumping ground for environmental waste.

As for nuclear weapons, Mrs Thatcher believed passionately in Britain's independent nuclear deterrent, and wasted no time on coming to office in opting to buy the American submarine-launched Trident system at a cost of £5 billion. These were to replace the old Polaris system based at Faslane near

---

[82] Speech to Scottish Conservative conference, 13/5/1988, MTF.

[83] Interestingly, the British Social Attitudes report of 1988 found that when asked if new jobs should be created, even if this might damage the countryside, almost twice as many Scots opted for new jobs than those living in the more prosperous south.

Helensburgh, and that naval base, together with the US base at Holy Loch, were the focus of frequent protests by the Scottish arm of the Campaign for Nuclear Disarmament, dormant since the Aldermaston marches of the 1960s. Membership rocketed and, supported by the Labour Party in Scotland and public opinion (relative to England), the protests increased after President Reagan announced his Strategic Defence Initiative (the so-called 'Star Wars') programme in 1983. The 1987 general election, however, with its emphasis on the nuclear-deterrent-related employment benefits for Scotland, largely neutralised opposition attacks in this respect.

A CLAIM OF RIGHT

'The Union with Scotland', as Mrs Thatcher observed in her memoirs, was 'inevitably dominated by England by reason of its greater population. The Scots, being an historic nation with a proud past, will inevitably resent some expression of this fact from time to time.'[84] This analysis of what was in 1988 a 281-year-old union, neatly sums up Mrs Thatcher's bewilderment at expressions of Scottish Nationalism during her premiership. To her, the Acts of Union were the best thing that ever happened to Scotland; attempts to reverse it were incomprehensible, while Nationalism – as in the 1970s – was a political bubble that would eventually burst.

Even more incomprehensible to the Prime Minister were persistent demands from some within her own party to honour her original 1975 pledge to establish a Scottish Assembly. For Tory devolutionists like Struan Stevenson (who warned the Tories could be reduced to a 'decimated rump acting solely as a conduit for Westminster legislation'), later an MEP, and the Edinburgh councillor Brian Meek (who believed 'devolution was inevitable' whether it took 'ten or fifteen years'[85]), it was a matter of principle which they presented to cynics in tactical terms: devolution would halt the Tory decline in Scotland by guaranteeing representation via proportional representation, high-spending regional councils could be abolished as a *quid pro quo*, fiscal autonomy could provide a pretext for the abolition of the troublesome Barnett Formula, while a related reduction in Scottish representation at Westminster could further erode Labour's chances of forming another government. For Scotland's other parties the devolution commitment ticked a variety of constitutional boxes. To the SNP it was a necessary concession on the road to independence; to the Liberals, 'home rule' was the natural extension of a long-held belief in federalism; for Labour, a commitment to 'self-government' was a mixture of expedience and principle.

Mrs Thatcher, however, lumped them all together as threats to the United Kingdom and dismissed calls from within the Scottish Conservative Party to

---

[84] Thatcher, *The Downing Street Years*, 624.
[85] Mitchell, *Conservatives and the Union*, 110.

look again at constitutional reform following the 1987 election. Indeed, shortly after polling day Lord Goold had called for 'a great debate' inside the party on the implications of that election. 'It was quite beyond him that the party might say anything other than that the government had done brilliantly and there was no need to change anything,' recalled the pro-devolution Tory activist and historian Michael Fry, 'only to carry on plugging away till Scotland realised the error of its ways.'[86]

Fry's response, along with Struan Stevenson and Brian Meek, was to establish the Conservative Constitutional Reform Forum (CCRF) as a vehicle to persuade Scottish Tories that devolution was not anathema. This split – although the party's devolutionists were never significant in strength – became public at the 1988 Scottish Tory conference in Perth. Malcolm Rifkind hinted at reopening the devolution debate in an enigmatic speech,[87] while the CCRF suggested the government reconsider devolution in a formal motion. But after a lively debate (the Scottish Young Conservatives held a 'Rock Against Devolution' disco and wore 'Devolution No; Thatcherism Yes' badges), delegates voted 300 to 11 against (one delegate produced stickers saying 'Expel the 11'). A spirited yet quixotic attempt to nudge Mrs Thatcher into considering constitutional reform had failed. 'We thought traditional Tory pragmatism would kick in at some point,' reflected Fry. 'Alick Buchanan-Smith, for example, was confident of this, and Rifkind's messages in code hinted how he thought of himself as the man for that moment. But we were all wrong.'[88]

'I am delighted that at this conference you resoundingly rejected the prospect of a second-class Scotland,' Mrs Thatcher declared in her conference speech shortly after the debate, 'cut off from the rest of the United Kingdom by tax barriers that would destroy her economy.' The opposition parties' proposals for devolution were, she added, 'utterly inadequate and superficial'. 'As long as I am Leader of this Party,' she proclaimed, 'we shall defend the Union and reject legislative devolution unequivocally.' It was almost the Declaration of Perth in reverse, 20 years after Ted Heath first committed the party to devolution. She continued:

> For in debate after debate we have endorsed a very different policy – a policy far bolder and more imaginative than that of our opponents. Not devolution to politicians and bureaucrats – but devolution to the Scottish people themselves. Devolution of housing, devolution of education, devolution of share-ownership and devolution of state-run industries to individuals . . . This policy of devolution to the people continues with our policy of Scottish privatisation.

[86] Michael Fry to the author, 24/12/2008.

[87] 'Malcolm also made some delphic remarks which were interpreted as suggesting that devolution was back on the agenda in Scotland,' wrote Mrs Thatcher in her memoirs. 'He was reverting to type.' (Thatcher, *The Downing Street Years*, 623)

[88] Michael Fry to the author.

Nationalisation took companies out of Scottish hands and into Whitehall; privatisation will hand them back to Scotland.[89]

This, of course, was not the kind of devolution many in Mrs Thatcher's own party and beyond had in mind. Constitutionally, hers was a take-it-or-leave-it unionism. Again and again the Prime Minister protested that Scotland already had huge levels of administrative devolution, to an extent that many Scots did not seem to realise. 'I get two things being said which are kind of in the opposite direction,' Mrs Thatcher mused during a 1988 interview. ' "Why do more of your Ministers not come up to Scotland?" But then I [say]: "Quite a number of my Ministers do not have any authority in Scotland". "Ah [they say], but we still want to see them".'[90]

Some of those close to Mrs Thatcher, however, believe she could have been more thoughtful when it came to legislative devolution. 'She had her Unionist instincts', recalled Andrew Turnbull, later Cabinet Secretary but in 1988 the Prime Minister's principal private secretary, 'but if she had really thought about the interests of the Conservative Party, she'd have reached the conclusion that devolution would have guaranteed some representation [for the party in Scotland], as it does now, whereas Labour would've reached a quite different conclusion that it was better off with first past the post. The two parties weren't pursuing policies which reflected their narrow party interests.' Instead, Turnbull added, 'I don't remember devolution ever being mentioned. They ran out of ideas [when it came to Scotland] really.'[91]

One idea surfaced in a pungent pamphlet called *Making Unionism Positive* written by the future Tory MP (and Scot) Liam Fox, the Conservative Research Department deputy director and historian Alistair B. Cooke, and the occasional Tory candidate Mark Mayall, for the Centre for Policy Studies. They advocated a strong rejection of legislative devolution (delivered by Mrs Thatcher in her 1988 Scottish conference speech) together with a 'fundamental re-examination' of existing levels of administrative devolution. Their ideal destination was 'the assimilation of Scotland, sensibly and pragmatically, within the overall framework of Conservative policies, making proper allowance within it for the distinctive characteristics of Scottish life'. Otherwise, there existed 'a real danger that Scotland will cease to regard itself as part of the "common stock" '.[92] This no doubt appealed to Mrs Thatcher's assimilationist instincts, and feedback from Number 10 was positive.[93]

---

[89] Speech to Scottish Conservative conference, 13/5/1988, MTF.

[90] Interview for *Scotland on Sunday*.

[91] Interview with Lord Turnbull, 3/6/2008.

[92] Fox *et al.*, *Making Unionism Positive*, 15.

[93] Private information. The Edinburgh district councillor Kenneth Ferguson went even further in calling for 'total Unionism', whereby the 'incompetent lot of officials in St Andrew's House' would be moved to London where they would 'slowly integrate it into United Kingdom ministries'. (Mitchell, *Conservatives and the Union*, 111)

'Wooing the Scots, impartially'

This analysis was also endorsed by the journalist T. E. Utley (fresh from offering advice on Mrs Thatcher's speech to General Assembly) in an article for *The Times* shortly after *Making Unionism Positive* was published. He swiftly dismissed the view that the mere act of U-turning on devolution would win the Conservatives more votes and seats. 'Probably the greatest single source of contempt for the Tories in Scotland is the widespread belief that their attitude to the place is entirely opportunistic,' he argued. 'This would be confirmed by a second *volte-face*.' He continued: 'Tories should realize that within every Scotsman, with his belief in thrift, personal endeavour, the mobile society and the virtues of moral inflexibility, there lurks a Thatcherite, and that the most hopeful course for the Tories is to appeal to these instincts rather than to corrupt them by offering Scotland a cosy refuge from the supposed rigours of the Prime Minister's economic policy.'[94]

Something which probably increased resentment of Mrs Thatcher's attitude towards that 'cosy refuge', however, was her willingness to 'devolve' power not only to privatised public utilities but also to what were often known as quangos (quasi-autonomous non-governmental organisations). The dearth of Tory councillors and MPs in Scotland meant that Scottish Office ministers,

---

[94] *The Times* 10/5/1988.

plucked from a shallow pool themselves, had to constantly fish around in a small pool of sympathetic businessmen to run such organisations, Mrs Thatcher having abandoned the convention whereby political opponents were appointed to health boards and the like. It could hardly be called democratic devolution, and turned whole swathes of Scottish life – from the Scottish Arts Council to subsidiary units of Scottish Enterprise – into a matter of management, and often not very good management. And given that many of these bodies were distinctly Scottish, it further fuelled the perception identified by David McCrone that Scotland itself was being attacked by the government.

It was also symptomatic of Mrs Thatcher's apparent inability to grasp Scottish Nationalist feeling of any kind, although she clearly could in an English context. She also had little understanding of the component nationalisms which co-existed within British patriotism, particularly what John P. Mackintosh called 'dual nationality', the sort on obvious display during the Falklands conflict. Paradoxically, however, Mrs Thatcher's Conservatives found themselves unable to tap into a sense of patriotism and national identity that was not British, despite notable success at doing just that between the wars and reaping the electoral benefits in Scotland. As the political academic Bill Miller observed, 'Thatcher redefined unionism in opposition to Scottish nationalism rather than recognising that unionism was an historic form of Scottish nationalism.'[95] Or, as James Mitchell put it, the 'fundamentalism of Thatcher's unionism was the mirror image of the fundamentalism of the SNP's nationalism'.[96]

Nigel Lawson identified nationalism as an essential component of what became known as Thatcherism, and indeed the Prime Minister seemed adept at playing a nationalist card within the context of moves toward closer European integration. 'No, no, no', she famously declared on Jacques Delors' tripartite strategy for a European superstate, but despite acknowledging that 'our ancestors—Celts, Saxons, Danes—came from the Continent' in her famous Bruges speech, Mrs Thatcher's inferred nationalism was English rather than Scottish. 'To try to suppress nationhood and concentrate power at the centre of a European conglomerate', she also said at Bruges, 'would be highly damaging and would jeopardise the objectives we seek to achieve.'[97] The feeling among some Scots, therefore, that Scottish nationhood was being suppressed within the British union probably did not even occur to her. And although the SNP's 'Independence in Europe' policy (launched at its 1988 conference) to an extent admitted that the Nationalists' big idea had been trimmed, it extended the concept of 'dual nationality' to Europe and thus provided a positive contrast to Mrs Thatcher's apparently negative approach. 'If those several movements were to succeed in their separatist ambitions,

---

[95] Kemp, *The Hollow Drum*, 190.
[96] Mitchell, *Conservatives and the Union*, 52.
[97] Speech to the College of Europe, 20/9/1988, MTF.

what would then be the position of the breakaway parts in relation to the Community?' Mrs Thatcher pondered the following year. 'I have no doubt about the answer. To fragment Europe would be to undermine its progress and destroy its strength.'[98]

By the late 1980s Unionism, much like Mrs Thatcher herself, had grown reactive and was increasingly perceived as negative. The former Scottish Tory chairman Michael Ancram remembered being shown to the door by the Prime Minister after one meeting with the memorable words: 'Michael, I am an English nationalist and never you forget it.'[99] But while she depended upon this nationalism for her success in England, Mrs Thatcher's unpopularity in Scotland was the flipside of that electoral support south of the border. While Harold Macmillan and Sir Alec Douglas-Home's brand of unionism was compatible with Anglo-British nationalism, its post-1979 incarnation was not.

'The enthusiasm which many working-class as well as middle-class English feel for Margaret Thatcher is related to their perception of their national identity,' wrote the academic Isobel Lindsay; 'she represents an assertive, maudlinly sentimental English nationalism – fulfilling a yearning for renewed imperial glory.' She continued: 'This dominant strand of English nationalism strikes few chords in Scottish hearts. Scottish national sentiment has developed in different directions. We are David rather than Goliath; we are the underdogs, with considerable sympathy for other underdogs; we are less xenophobic (if for no other reason than that so many of our friends and relatives live abroad); we have no delusions of potential "great power" status.' Therefore, concluded Lindsay, 'Thatcher's strand of English nationalism which has been accepted so warmly in the South, has produced attitudes ranging from the ambivalent to the antagonistic here.'[100]

In Scotland it was the antagonistic strain of that attitude which was about to assert itself on an unprecedented scale. Yes, Mrs Thatcher was used to cross-party lobbies opposing specific policies, but never before had so-called 'civic Scotland' contrived to oppose her government's very right to govern north of the border. There had long been talk of a cross-party body to challenge Thatcherism in Scotland, most notably in early 1984 when James Wilkie wrote about 'A Scottish Constitutional Convention: The door to the future' in *Radical Scotland*.[101]

So while devolution Bills came and went in the House of Commons (including a Scottish Assembly Bill introduced by Labour on 30 November 1987), the 'Claim of Right' published by the Campaign for a Scottish Assembly in July 1988 was all the more significant for having originated outside the Westminster village. Drafted in stirring prose by the retired

---

[98] Speech to Newspaper Press Fund, 3/2/1989, MTF.
[99] Naughtie, *The Rivals*, 21.
[100] McCrone & Brown, eds, *Scottish Government Yearbook 1988*, 40.
[101] *Radical Scotland* December/January 1984.

Scottish Office civil servant Jim Ross, it deliberately evoked the 1689 Claim of Right in its direct challenge to the Conservative mandate in Scotland, which it described as 'an illusion of Democracy'. 'In spite of which there is currently a Prime Minister dedicated to preventing the creation of a Scottish Assembly', the Claim continued, 'and equipped, within the terms of the English constitution, with overwhelming powers to frustrate opposition to her aims.'[102] *Radical Scotland* warned that if the Claim failed in its stated aim then 'the Thatcher project of dismantling Scottish institutions and Scottish distinctiveness would be allowed to march on unchecked'.[103]

Predictably, the government dismissed the Claim of Right as devolutionary 'mumbo jumbo'.[104] Labour's reaction, however, was less predictable. Initially Donald Dewar, the Shadow Scottish Secretary, gave only a cautious welcome to the proposal for a Scottish Constitutional Convention (SCC) based on the Claim. As a constitutionalist, he was uncomfortable with the growing clamour in his party to deploy the no-mandate argument, but was also under pressure from a new grouping called Scottish Labour Action (or the Scottish Liberation Army as some activists dubbed it), formed at the 1988 Scottish Labour conference. 'We took the view that in the absence of an assembly, which she'd promised in 1979 but not delivered,' explained the future First Minister Jack McConnell, one of the group's leading protagonists, 'that the gap was so significant between the party's power and representation that they had no mandate to govern. The divide in the Labour Party was between those who looked at that from a Scottish perspective and those who felt the retention of the Union was more important.'[105]

Also complicating the Labour response was Neil Kinnock's ill-disguised hostility to that Scottish perspective. When asked why he had not mentioned devolution in his speech to the 1988 Scottish Labour conference, Kinnock responded that there were lots of other things he had not mentioned, such as 'environmental conditions in the Himalayas'.[106] Nevertheless, in September Dewar became convinced of the need to participate and warned that 'Scots [we]re going to have to learn to live dangerously for a while'.[107]

What eventually pushed the Labour Party into unequivocal support for the SCC, however, was the bombshell of the Glasgow Govan by-election in November 1988. Won by the former Labour MP Jim Sillars with a swing of more than 20 per cent to the SNP in a supposedly safe Labour seat, it was a wake-up call to the main opposition party's prevaricating. Aggressively articulate, Sillars took up his seat in the Commons claiming that the people

---

[102] Dudley Edwards, ed., *A Claim of Right for Scotland*, 18.

[103] *Radical Scotland* August/September 1988.

[104] Brown & Parry, eds, *Scottish Government Yearbook 1990*, 25.

[105] Interview with Jack McConnell MSP, 25/6/2008.

[106] Marr, *The Battle for Scotland*, 185. Kinnock also told the *South Wales Echo*, 'Devolution reform will not provide a factory, a machine or jobs, or build a school, train a doctor or put a pound on pensions.' (*South Wales Echo* 1/11/1985)

[107] Brown & Parry, eds, *Scottish Government Yearbook 1990*, 25.

of Govan 'regarded her [Mrs Thatcher] and her policies as malicious, wicked and evil'.[108] He also suffered from no intellectual reticence when it came to the no-mandate argument warning that, if necessary, he would disrupt parliamentary proceedings to emphasise his party's case that the Prime Minister had no mandate to 'impose' her policies on Scotland. In short, Sillars' victory reduced the 'feeble 50' to the 'frightened 49', and gave added impetus to anti-Thatcher political sentiments.

Unsurprisingly, Malcolm Rifkind argued that Labour was simply reaping the reward of its 'flirtation with nationalist rhetoric', while Michael Forsyth described the 'log jam of Scottish politics'[109] as having been broken by the SNP's victory. Other Tory right-wingers went further. Allan Stewart reasoned that independence made more sense than devolution, and wondered if it was not time for Scots to make up their minds once and for all. Bill Walker even urged Mrs Thatcher to call a snap referendum on the question of 'Independence or the Union'.

In this context, it is often forgotten that the SCC was as anti-Scottish Nationalist in its political objectives as it was anti-Thatcherite in its rhetoric. The SNP, finding that independence would not be in the Convention's remit, withdrew after just one meeting describing it, not unreasonably, as a Unionist trap. So, as the historian Richard Finlay has written, 'Home rule climbed up the political agenda as much on account of its expedient value (as cohesive glue for the anti-Thatcher forces) as on its own merits.'[110] Indeed, it was at this point that the grand, STUC-led, anti-Thatcher issue coalitions began to fragment. Not only did the SNP refuse to join the SCC, but the party also fell out with shop stewards (predominantly Labour) at Ravenscraig, although not at the Dalzell Plate Mill[111] (where they were predominantly Nationalists). Now more confident as a political party, if not a movement, the SNP would also later pursue its own campaign of non-payment against the Poll Tax.

Despite the SNP's non-participation, the SCC could still claim to be broadly cross-party (Labour, Lib Dem, Greens) as well as including representatives from the Scottish churches, trades unions and other civic groups. The STUC general secretary Campbell Christie also played a prominent part, becoming the 'choirmaster of Scottish discontent'[112] having been deprived of a role in government policy-making. The SCC was, therefore, the apex of the argument that Scots rejected Thatcherism on account of a strong civic identity which needed a devolved assembly to best articulate its wishes. 'Her [Thatcher's] biggest impact in Scotland was the politicisation of the self-government movement,' reflected Alex Salmond. 'That sounds daft

---

[108] STV news rushes B7751, 14/11/1988.

[109] Brown & Parry, eds, *Scottish Government Yearbook 1990*, 27.

[110] Devine, ed., *Scotland and the Union*, 166.

[111] In 2009, the Dalzell Plate Mill was all that remained of the once thriving Lanarkshire iron and steel industry, employing several hundred people to fashion steel brought by train from Middlesbrough into plate steel of various shapes and sizes.

[112] Aitken, *The Bairns O' Adam*, 309.

but the movement over the past 100 years had been mainly cultural, to some extent in the 1970s it was economic, but not really political. She changed that.'[113] The SCC's emphasis on the notion of popular sovereignty was particularly significant – the belief that in Scotland sovereignty, and therefore government legitimacy, lay with the people and not Parliament. Thatcherism was therefore the antithesis of that national tradition.

But despite the consensus behind this newly politicised movement, the SCC had no real response to Thatcherism in Scotland beyond raising the prospect of a 'doomsday scenario II' at the next election. There was also a rather lazy notion that Mrs Thatcher would not be around forever, and that once she was out of the way her successor would quickly concede a referendum on constitutional reform. The SCC ignored tricky issues like the West Lothian Question, the future role of the Scottish Secretary and the number of Scottish MPs in the UK Parliament post-devolution, all debating points regularly deployed against Labour by the government and rarely answered. Therefore, quipped the Scottish Tory chief executive John Mac-Kay, the SCC was just 'the Labour Party Conference at prayer'.[114]

The SCC's two biggest problems, however – lack of public enthusiasm (polls showed little recognition of its existence or aims) and what would happen when Mrs Thatcher inevitably said 'no' to its demands – did not noticeably dent its self-confidence. When delegates gathered for the SCC's inaugural meeting on 30 March 1989, in the General Assembly hall where the Prime Minister had preached to the unconverted, they queued to sign a declaration based on the Claim of Right. The SCC was to be jointly chaired by Labour's Harry Ewing and the former Liberal leader Sir David Steel, but it was the Episcopalian cleric Canon Kenyon Wright who emerged as its public face.

Having prepared his speech as the Prime Minister was reported rejoicing at the birth of a grandchild by saying 'We are a grandmother', Wright played 'on that apparent delusion of grandeur' when he defiantly told the Convention: 'What if that other single voice we all know so well responds by saying, "We say No, We are the State." Well We say Yes and We are the People.'[115]

'WHAT DO YOU DO WHEN DEMOCRACY FAILS YOU?'

Although the composition of the SCC was predominantly political, industrial and clerical, the notion of 'civic Scotland' also relied heavily on support from leading voices in the cultural world. 'People forget now that it was the arts, theatre groups, writers and artists who kept Scotland's head up in the 1980s,'

[113] Interview with Alex Salmond.
[114] Brown & Parry, eds, *Scottish Government Yearbook 1990*, 30.
[115] Wright, *The People Say Yes*, 52.

said Campbell Christie. 'They wrote plays; wrote songs about how Scotland was being hammered by Thatcher. That was civic Scotland; then the Constitutional Convention gave it political leadership.'[116]

Indeed, one of the most intriguing developments of the 1980s was a revival in Scottish culture which had begun in anticipation of devolution in 1979, but continued in its absence. And instead of falling victim to Thatcherite cuts, as the literary academic Cairns Craig has observed, 'the 1980s proved to be one of the most productive and creative decades in Scotland this century – as though the energy that had failed to be harnessed by the politicians flowed into other channels'.[117]

Not only was there a stream of books on Scottish history but the literary revival of the 1970s continued apace; the rise of Scottish pop groups complemented a growing number of professional folk groups (the Corries' 'Flower of Scotland' was seen by some as an alternative Scottish 'national anthem'), while even the ability of Scottish football clubs to buy English players was considered an important factor in the development of national self-confidence. Some on the left, however, refused to go along with notions that Scots were any more culturally sophisticated than their southern neighbours. As Greg Michelson wrote acerbically in *Radical Scotland*, 'the reality of Scots culture: Tandoori, "Dallas", snooker, country and western, Princess Di, and holidays in Benidorm, all not much different from the rest of the U.K.'[118]

Patronage of Scots culture was overseen by the Scottish Arts Council, the northern arm of the Arts Council of Great Britain comprising 20 council members subject to the final approval of the Secretary of State for Scotland. Teddy Taylor once said his first act as Scottish Secretary would have been to abolish all arts subsidies (a popular refrain of the Adam Smith Insitute), but, instead, Scotland continued to receive a greater per capita allocation for arts funding than other areas of the UK. Funding announced in December 1986, for example, increased by 4.4 per cent to £14.1 million, with 45 per cent of it going to Scottish Opera, the Scottish National Orchestra, Scottish Ballet and the Scottish Chamber Orchestra.

But it was in Scotland's pop music, rather than its more traditional musical output, that anti-Thatcherism manifested itself most potently. The playful irony of early 1980s Scottish pop quickly gave way to more commercial sounds, big ideas, big anthems and a more ostentatiously Scottish sound. Pat Kane of the Glaswegian pop duo Hue and Cry said it was the 'raising of Scotland's voice', but many of the more successful acts were perhaps Thatcherite without realising it. They wanted to get on, get rich and had shrewd commercial sense in a competitive environment. They also oozed glamour and confidence in a hedonistic decade, but none sounded unequivocally Scottish until the Proclaimers.

---

[116] Interview with Campbell Christie, 6/6/2008.
[117] Dudley Edwards, ed., *A Claim of Right for Scotland*, viii.
[118] *Radical Scotland* June/July 1983.

Significantly, the twins from Auchermuchty refused to conform by compromising on their accents and appearance. Radical, political and Nationalist, their first album, *This is the Story*, addressed deindustrialisation, the value of language and Scotland's declining population. The 1987 number-one hit 'Letter From America' even likened the decline of Scottish manufacturing to the Highland Clearances, and included the famous refrain: 'Bathgate no more, Linwood no more, Methil no more, Irvine no more'.[119] The 'no-mandate' argument was also enshrined in song (on the Proclaimers' second album, *Sunshine on Leith*) when they sang, 'What do you do when democracy's all through. What do you do when minority means you?'[120]

Although bands like Deacon Blue were more moderate – they would often bemuse *Smash Hits* journalists by speaking about devolution during interviews – most, like the Proclaimers, were overtly Nationalist. The 'Artists for Independence' movement began in the late 1980s and the bands' London A&R men got jumpy, worried about offending audiences and declining sales. The high point was the 'Day For Scotland' summer festival of music held against the striking backdrop of Stirling Castle on 14 July 1990. More than 30,000 people listened to Runrig, Hue and Cry and Dick Gaughan, invited by the STUC in open defiance of Mrs Thatcher. Clive Lewis, that year's STUC president, even got up on stage wearing his son's leather jacket and started a chant of 'Ravenscraig, Ravenscraig'. 'Not many rock festivals', as the STUC's historian has observed, 'cheer for steelmills.'[121]

Scotland's writers, meanwhile, took a more cerebral approach to contemporary politics, although many of their novels' arguments against Thatcherism were essentially nostalgic. William McIlvanney's *The Big Man* (1985) dealt with the masculine working-class life of Scotland's west coast and the threat of deindustrialisation. McIlvanney was also politically active, and indeed his speech to the 1987 SNP conference is worth quoting at length for its lyrical exposition of the cultural case against Mrs Thatcher. '[W]e have never, in my lifetime, until now had a government whose basic principles were so utterly against the most essential traditions and aspirations of Scottish life,' he declared. 'We have never until now had a government so determined to unpick the very fabric of Scottish life and make it over into something quite different.' He went on:

Under this Government it is not only the quality of our individual lives that is threatened. It is our communal sense of our own identity. For this government is out to change it. The complex traditions and attitudes and ways of thought that have emerged from the Scottish people's long argument with their own experience – these things are not to be pushed aside. In favour of what? The

---

[119] 'Letter From America' (1987).
[120] 'What Do You Do?' (1988).
[121] Aitken, *The Bairns O' Adam*, 296.

abacus morality of monetarism? . . . For Margaret Thatcher is not just a perpetrator of bad policies. She is a cultural vandal. She takes the axe of her own simplicity to the complexities of Scottish life. She has no understanding of the hard-earned traditions she is destroying. And if we allow her to continue, she will remove from the word 'Scottish' any meaning other than the geographical.[122]

McIlvanney's contemporary James Kelman, however, was wary of over-emphasising Mrs Thatcher as an individual and ideology. 'The very notion of "Thatcherism",' he wrote in one typically strident essay, 'suggests what is now happening in this country began with her: and will therefore end with her.'[123] Kelman's 1984 novel, *The Busconductor Hines*, nevertheless addressed similar themes to McIlvanney in examining the purposelessness of a man doing a job soon to be rendered extinct by government policy beyond his control. Interviewed in 2008, the Scottish-born Tory MP Michael Gove identified Kelman and McIlvanney as having a particular vision of what constituted a good Scot: 'the traditional, west coast, industrialised working class'. 'When the person who was presiding over what happened, Margaret Thatcher,' Gove reasoned, 'wasn't someone who came across sympathetically to that constituency then you've got a problem.'[124]

Contemporary writers also employed a remarkable range of styles to capture what was happening in 1980s Scotland. Iain M. Banks's *Player of Games* used science fiction to depict a Thatcherite-like 'civilisation', while A. L. Kennedy's *So I am Glad* used magic realism to transform an unemployed down-and-out. But it was undoubtedly Irvine Welsh's *Trainspotting* that came to epitomise the Scottish literary response to Thatcherism in Scotland. Published in 1993, it boldly depicted Edinburgh as a post-Thatcherite dystopia, using drugs as a parody of the free market. Filmed to critical acclaim in 1996, *Trainspotting*'s author later surprised many by revealing himself as an unexpected convert to the New Realism. 'I'm a product of Thatcherism in many ways and I've benefited from everything I detested,' he said in 2006. 'I've had to come to terms with it.'[125]

It could be said that the view of working-class Scottish life depicted in words by Kelman and Welsh was also mirrored in the 'socialist realism' of the artists Ken Currie and Peter Howson, while Thatcherism also had a profound effect on both the style and content of Scottish theatre. The post-war assumption that most art forms, and particularly the theatre, would be subsidised was confronted by Mrs Thatcher, who often pointed to Andrew Lloyd Webber – whose musicals dominated London's West End throughout the 1980s – as a model of commercial theatrical success. At the other end of

---

[122] *Radical Scotland* December/January 1988.
[123] Kelman, *'And the Judges Said'*, 122.
[124] *Sunday Herald* 30/11/2008.
[125] *Sunday Telegraph* 15/07/2006.

this spectrum was John McGrath's 7:84 Company (named in reference to 7 per cent of the population owning 84 per cent of its wealth). Having produced the groundbreaking *The Cheviot, The Stag and the Black, Black Oil* in 1973, it continued to stage iconoclastic productions throughout the Thatcher decade. Ironically, a lot of events during Mrs Thatcher's premiership, and certainly her downfall in 1990, was the raw material worthy of dramatic theatre. Indeed, the Prime Minister's rather theatrical style (her memorable phrase 'The lady's not for turning' paraphrased the title of Christopher Fry's play, *The Lady's Not For Burning*) owed much to her speechwriter, the former playwright Sir Ronald Millar.

In terms of celluloid, however, Scottish cinema would not really achieve prominence until the 1990s. Although Bill Forsyth's films were not overtly political, *Gregory's Girl* (1980) captured something of the 1980s zeitgeist in its depiction of a Cumbernauld secondary school pupil enduring the horrors of being a teenage boy. *Local Hero* (1983), meanwhile, portrayed an alternative view of the North Sea oil boom by depicting the attempts of a US oil company to replace the fictitious seaside village of Ferness with a new refinery. Instead of resisting change, however, the villagers embrace the prospect of effortless enrichment through cash compensation.

Cutting across all these cultural forms was a determination to rid Scotland of historical and visual clichés, which some artists believed had held it back from embracing devolution in 1979. Mrs Thatcher, unfortunately, regularly played up to these tartan stereotypes during her Scottish visits. In 1988 she waxed lyrical about 'the benefits of living in a civilised city within five minutes of some of the finest scenery and fishing in the world – not to mention a handy golf course and a distillery or two'.[126] And when a journalist asked her about addressing Scottish sentiment in 1989, she retorted: 'We do address the sentiment. Look at the great Scottish Regiments, look at the great Scottish things. It is just there, the Scottish songs, the Scottish music, the Scottish scenery, the Scottish interests.' When the journalist added, 'But not a Scottish Assembly?' she responded: 'But how very prosaic can you get?'[127] To Mrs Thatcher, Scotland was indeed the land of bagpipes and tartan, an inoffensive view which nevertheless ensured that the increasing political divide between many Scots and Thatcherism was mirrored by an equally potent cultural divide.

THE POLL TAX

Beyond the loss of 11 Conservative MPs, the 1987 election result also demonstrated that the Poll Tax was not going to be a vote winner. Labour's manifesto had pledged its abolition, while the SNP proved 'effective in presenting the poll tax as something imposed on Scotland by the southern,

---

[126] Speech to Scottish Conservative conference, 13/5/1988, MTF.
[127] Interview for *Glasgow Herald*, 31/5/1989, MTF.

Thatcherite, English'.[128] The Poll Tax, however, was just one of many contributing factors to the Scottish result, and few Tory MPs – even those who lost their seats – thought it decisive. Even so, the momentum for its introduction in England and Wales increased in the months that followed. Kenneth Baker's original plan had been for a ten-year transition, with 'dual running' of the old and new systems.[129] This was later shortened to four years, and was truncated even further following the 1987 UK Conservative conference. There, Gerry Malone, a Scot who had lost his Aberdeen South seat that June, urged his English compatriots not to wait to ease the impact, but 'do it properly . . . do it as soon as we can'.

This impatient sentiment touched a nerve with the Prime Minister, who turned to Nick Ridley, the new Environment Secretary, on the platform and muttered: 'We shall have to look at this again, Nick.'[130] Ridley immediately gave a public pledge that the Cabinet would 'have another think'[131] about its timetable, and duly announced in November 1987 that the Poll Tax would begin in England and Wales in April 1990, exactly a year after its introduction in Scotland. Ironically, a Scot (Gerry Malone) had almost single-handedly brought forward its implementation in England and Wales by at least a few years.

The Poll Tax also began to acquire more ideological clothing. At a meeting of Tory backbenchers in July 1987 Mrs Thatcher had christened it the 'flagship of the Thatcher fleet',[132] although there were also indications that some Tory backbenchers were unhappy about sailing in it. One, the East Hampshire MP Michael Mates, even tabled an amendment to the English and Welsh legislation (the Local Government Finance Bill, introduced to the Commons on 16 December 1987) calling for a banded Poll Tax related to income tax thresholds. Debated on 18 April 1988, the government scraped home with a majority of just 25 votes. Addressing the Scottish Tory conference a month later, and just weeks after Scottish local authorities began preparations for collecting the new tax, the Prime Minister showed no signs of having second thoughts. 'It is absurd that out of almost four million local electors in Scotland, only one million pay full rates, and two million pay no rates at all,' she said. 'Yet all four million use local services and benefit from the rates paid by their neighbours. What's fair about that?'

Mrs Thatcher, of course, was interpreting fairness in a rather different way to her political opponents, although to be fair the inequities of the rating system were never adequately addressed by Labour. Her political reasoning was simple: if more people contributed to local government coffers, 'Hard left

---

[128] Butler et al., Failure in British Government, 106.

[129] It was widely accepted that the Poll Tax would take longer to introduce in England because of its higher population and greater number of local authorities.

[130] Ridley later claimed Mrs Thatcher said: 'Do you want another glass of water, Nick?' But, as he added in his memoirs, 'I don't think I was believed.' (Ridley, My Style of Government, 125)

[131] Young, One of Us, 537.

[132] Butler et al., Failure in British Government, 107.

councils will no longer be able to hide the cost of their socialist fads and anti-nuclear fancies by passing them on to business and the rate-paying minority. They will have to send the bill to everyone—and face the consequences at the next election.' And, the Prime Minister emphasised, the 'local level of community charge is not set by the Government. It is set by local councils'.[133]

The Community Charge was also to be collected by local councils, although a report commissioned by the government at the end of 1987 indicated that this would need significant additional staff and computing facilities in the period leading up to the introduction of the Poll Tax on 1 April 1989. Luckily for the government, in the months between the election and Poll Tax D-Day, the political spotlight was not so much on administrative problems but on how the Labour Party would respond. Internally, there was the problem of what to do about those pursuing an illegal campaign of non-registration and ultimately non-payment. And externally, there were two further problems: how to out-manoeuvre the SNP tactically and what to present as an alternative in policy terms.

The first issue came to a head at Labour's 1988 conference. Scottish Labour Action had already fought an unsuccessful internal battle to have non-payment adopted as party policy (the party's Scottish executive voted 17–13 against), while Neil Kinnock ended the UK conference by sacking two Scottish front benchers who had pledged publicly not to pay their Poll Tax. In November, seven Labour MPs nevertheless joined a 'Committee of 100' prominent non-payers unveiled at Glasgow's Winter Gardens.

Malcolm Rifkind, meanwhile, boasted to the Commons that 'more than 99 per cent' of adults in Scotland had registered despite a high-profile campaign not to, although he did not mention a developing phenomenon of voters disappearing from electoral registers in order to avoid payment by other means. The STUC's 'All Scotland Anti-Poll Tax Campaign' had recently depicted Rifkind in a poster campaign as a Gilbert & Sullivan-style governor-general with a paper hat and wooden sword. On 4 November 1988 the governor estimated that Poll Tax levels, based on 1987–88 council spending levels, would range from £313 per adult in Edinburgh to £84 in Orkney. It soon became clear, however, that the first year's Poll Tax was going to be around 16 per cent higher than Rifkind's estimates, if not even higher in certain areas. Ironically, the removal of rate capping as a *quid pro quo* had encouraged Scottish local authorities to spend about 13 per cent above government estimates.[134] So while the gap between the government grant and local budgets had actually been falling for the previous five years, in 1989–90 it was set to rise from 3.7 per cent to 6.5 per cent.

The Poll Tax, an abstract concept to most Scots voters since its creation in 1985, was fast becoming a reality. Opposition seemed to come from every

---

[133] Speech to Scottish Conservative conference, 13/5/1988, MTF.
[134] Mrs Thatcher 'agreed somewhat reluctantly' to the removal of rate capping, which Rifkind advocated on the basis of available time and legal advice. (Thatcher, *The Downing Street Years*, 655)

corner of Scottish society. The Anti-Poll Tax Campaign mobilised the youth of Scotland against the new tax – around 60,000 of whom were due to pay it for the first time – luring them through pop music to 'Rock Against the Poll Tax' at a special concert.[135] Meanwhile, Norman Shanks of the Church of Scotland and Canon Kenyon Wright, general secretary of the ecumenical Scottish Council of Churches and star of the SCC, helped deliver a 300,000-strong petition to Downing Street on 1 February 1989. At a rally in Edinburgh a month later Tommy Sheridan, the charismatic Scottish Militant leading the non-payment Strathclyde Anti-Poll Tax Federation, claimed attendance figures of 15,000 Scots and 5,000 sympathisers from England and Wales. A month later still, on 1 April 1989, the Poll Tax came into force in Scotland. Thatcherism's fate in Scotland was effectively sealed.

---

[135] From September 1988 unemployed school-leavers aged 16 and 17 had to take a place on a Youth Training Scheme or forego their benefit.

Chapter 9

'THE BEGINNING OF THE END OF THE THATCHER ERA' (1989–90)

When the Thatcher era draws to its close it will be re-evaluated with speed and disbelief. People will look back in amazement at the claims made on its behalf – an economic miracle, a social transformation, a political revolution, an industrial resurgence, the rebirth of Britain – and will very quickly begin to see the 1980s as a decade not of achievement but of missed opportunity.[1]

Gordon Brown, *Where There is Greed*

Kirsty Wark: Prime Minister, you have always said that you didn't enter politics in order to be popular, but why are you so unpopular in Scotland?

Margaret Thatcher: Well, I don't think I am necessarily the right person to answer that but I wouldn't entirely say it was true . . . What does please me is that Scotland is taking advantage of all the policies which is right, because I regard it as a very great honour to be Prime Minister of Scotland.

'The Margaret Thatcher Interview' (BBC Scotland) 9/3/1990

Margaret Thatcher was quintessentially English; unlike two previous Conservative Prime Ministers, Home and Macmillan, who were Scots and proud of it (even if they were English-educated and spoke with English accents). This clearly didn't go down well in Scotland. The Scots at that time were also inclined to mistake an English lack of interest in Scotland for a conscious desire to do Scotland down.[2]

Lord Lawson

The gap between England and what Thatcher – like nineteenth-century Conservatives – seemed to regard as 'the Celtic Fringe', between north and

---

[1] Brown, *Where There is Greed*, 1.
[2] Lord Lawson to the author, 3/12/2008.

south, between inner cities and suburbs, broadened and deepened. Socially and economically, and, partly as a consequence, also ethnically, Britain was a more divided nation in 1990 than it was in 1979.[3]

E. H. H. Green, *Thatcher*

Plainly there were large parts of the country into which neither the benefits of Thatcherism nor respect for its leader could be seen to reach. The extreme example was Scotland . . . Although it was probable that some of the leader's personal emanations – bossiness, smugness, righteousness and inextinguishably English gentility – made her peculiarly rebarbative to a nation with a powerful sense of its own identity, deeper attitudes were also important. Quite obviously, Scotland had to be excluded from any claim that Britain was unified around a Thatcherite consensus.[4]

Hugo Young, *One of Us*

FOR A NATION WHICH prided itself on possessing an international outlook, or internationalist mindset, it seems odd that Scotland appeared to take so little pride in the status of Margaret Thatcher abroad. In 1989 the Cold War came to an end, an event in which the Prime Minister played a significant part, while she continued to be feted on foreign walkabouts long after her domestic popularity began to fade. Mrs Thatcher's international instincts, however, were not always so sharp. Initially, she opposed German reunification, fearing the country would move away from NATO, and was heavily criticised for refusing to engage in sanctions against apartheid South Africa on the basis that the policy would make thousands of black workers unemployed.

The Scottish Secretary, Malcolm Rifkind, was even likened to the South African Prime Minister P. W. Botha. Not only had Rifkind worked for the University of Rhodesia,[5] but he had defended apartheid as a Foreign Office minister and, of course, governed Scotland with minority support. When the Commonwealth Games came to Edinburgh in the summer of 1986, 32 African, Asian and Caribbean countries boycotted proceedings because of Mrs Thatcher's maintenance of sporting links with South Africa. *Radical Scotland* said the immediate lesson of the Games row was 'that letting Scotland be tarred with the same brush of international odium as the British Government is no longer acceptable as a political arrangement'.[6]

True believers, meanwhile, continued to argue that Scotland was not being tarred with the same Thatcherite brush as the rest of the United Kingdom. 'Only now are Scotland's state-owned bus companies being privatised,[7] years

---

[3] Green, *Thatcher*, 196.

[4] Young, *One of Us*, 528.

[5] As an academic, however, Rifkind's politics had been anti-apartheid.

[6] *Radical Scotland* August/September 1986.

[7] The Transport (Scotland) Act, passed in 1989, finally privatised the companies comprising the Scottish Bus Group and fully deregulated the industry.

after their English counterparts,' wrote the self-styled 'father of the Poll Tax', Douglas Mason, in a polemic entitled *Scotland and Free Enterprise*. 'Associated British Ports passed into the private sector long ago. But only one of its constituent parts was in Scotland [actually two, Ayr and Troon]. Only now is legislation passing through Parliament that would allow Scotland's major ports to do the same – and then only because the Clyde Ports Authority took the initiative and sponsored its own private legislation.'[8]

Minority rule

He went on: 'Proposals to privatise the Forestry Commission have been consistently blocked by Scottish Office Ministers while there seems to have been no suggestion that water, in Scotland, should follow its English counterpart into the private sector. Even Scotland's Electricity Boards, which were prepared for privatisation in advance of those south of the border, find themselves last in the queue.'

To blame, continued Mason, were Labour-dominated local authorities as well as a 'curious unwillingness on the part of the Conservative Party to stand up for its beliefs and put its principles into practice'.[9] Members of the Downing Street Policy Unit may not have concurred with that, although they certainly believed Scotland needed more, rather than less, Thatcherism. Brian Griffiths, head of the Policy Unit, and John O'Sullivan, an adviser

---

[8] Massie, *et al.*, *Scotland and Free Enterprise*, 20. Forth Ports later took successful advantage of this legislation.

[9] Ibid., 21. A proposal by Mason to uproot the people of Hong Kong and move them to the west coast of Scotland as a solution to the problem of what to do with the colony post-1997 was widely ridiculed in June 1989.

responsible for Scotland, had visited Scotland on a fact-finding mission shortly after the 1987 general election and reported back to Mrs Thatcher. 'Our main theme was Scotland had been for political reasons excluded from Thatcherism,' remembered O'Sullivan. 'She liked it and said this was something we must start thinking about. But government is about short term-ism and at that point, from about 1988 onwards, she went through a very difficult period trying to battle against a lot of things: the Poll Tax, Nigel Lawson shadowing the Deutschmark, rising inflation, etc. She was preoccupied by that and it pushed other things out.'[10] Or, as Lord Lang put it, 'She was playing to a large audience and the fact that Scotland did things in different ways wasn't going to deflect her from that.'[11]

Indeed, by the end of 1989 the UK economy was entering recession, the old enemy of inflation was rising and interest rates reached the punitively high level of 15 per cent. Scottish home owners, many of whom had only recently been persuaded to become members of the property-owning democracy, began to feel the pinch. The issue of membership of the European Exchange Rate Mechanism (ERM), meanwhile, had become a running sore between Nigel Lawson (and the Foreign Secretary, Sir Geoffrey Howe) and the Prime Minister. The Chancellor had been pushing for the UK to join since 1985 in order to control rising inflation; Mrs Thatcher persistently disagreed and openly blamed Lawson for the problem after discovering that he had been shadowing the Deutschmark in preparation for membership. 'Nigel is a very good neighbour of mine,' she told the *Glasgow Herald* in May 1989, refusing to rule out ditching both him and Sir Geoffrey, 'and a very good Chancellor. Geoffrey is a very good Foreign Secretary.' But, she added, 'I'm not going any further.'[12]

Ultimately, Mrs Thatcher would lose both men, arguably two of what she had once called her 'six men strong and true',[13] over the ERM issue and the wider debate about Britain's place in Europe. Indeed, it was Europe rather than the Poll Tax which prompted a hitherto obscure Welsh Conservative backbencher, Sir Anthony Meyer, to challenge Mrs Thatcher for the leadership of the Conservative Party as 1989 drew to a close. She had undoubtedly grown more distant from the parliamentary party, many of whom increasingly viewed the Prime Minister as a liability and were minded to support Meyer. (There was even wild talk during 1989 and 1990 that Mrs Thatcher was losing her mental balance, when in fact it had more to do with overwork and growing old, celebrating her 64th birthday in October 1989). Ministers identified a bunker mentality, into which she increasingly retreated after Willie Whitelaw, always a stabilising force, withdrew from public life following a stroke in December 1987. In George Younger, the similarly emollient

---

[10] Interview with John O'Sullivan, 7/11/2008.
[11] Interview with Lord Lang, 11/11/2008.
[12] *Glasgow Herald* 31/5/1989.
[13] *The Downing Street Years* (BBC) 15/10/1993.

former Scottish Secretary, there was a possible successor to Whitelaw. But preoccupied with a new post at the Royal Bank of Scotland, Younger instead ran her campaign against Sir Anthony.

Mrs Thatcher easily beat her challenger, but few were under any illusions as to the significance of the 57 votes the Prime Minister had failed to secure (33 for Sir Anthony; 24 spoilt ballots). 'We are talking about the beginning of the end of the Thatcher Era,' declared Tristan Garel-Jones at a post-mortem meeting of the Prime Minister's campaign team. 'We have to try and ensure that that is managed in a way that enables her to go to the end of her Prime Ministership with dignity and honour.'[14] Others believed it was too late. Hubris – pride before a fall – had set in, and there was little anyone could do.

THATCHERISM REBUFFED

In his article 'Thatcherism in a Cold Climate', which appeared in the June/July 1989 issue of *Radical Scotland*, the Edinburgh University academic David McCrone argued that the apparent failure of the Prime Minister's ideology was not merely due to the particular socio-economic structure of Scotland. Rather it was that

> In Scotland, the attack on state institutions – the nationalised industries, the education system, local government, the public sector generally, even the church, institutions which carried much of Scotland's identity – was easily perceived as an attack on 'Scotland' itself. Essential to current Conservative appeal south of the border was an appeal to 'the nation' on whose behalf politicians and the state act. But Scots had a nation of their own, and the vision of recreating bourgeois England was out of kilter not only with Scottish material interests, but with this alternative sense of national identity.[15]

In other words Thatcherism lacked a Scottish strategy, one that made sense of separate development, separate institutions and separate ideological and cultural norms. And by May 1989 – Mrs Thatcher's tenth anniversary as Prime Minister[16] – it was becoming increasingly hard to contradict McCrone's analysis. To some extent the very length of Mrs Thatcher's premiership was beginning to erode her levels of support. New voters coming onto the electoral roll could scarcely remember the winter of discontent and were therefore more inclined to perceive the Prime Minister as dictatorial, rather than as the saviour of the British nation.

The impact of this in Scotland was further electoral decline. Following the

---

[14] Undated minute titled 'Post Mortem Meeting Notes', GYP.
[15] McCrone, *Understanding Scotland*, 172.
[16] Mrs Thatcher's portrait was painted by the Kelso-based artist Jane Robson to mark this anniversary.

June 1989 elections to the European Parliament, Scotland became a Tory-free zone, with the party sinking to just more than a fifth of the popular vote, polling fewer votes than the SNP and losing its remaining two MEPs.[17] One of them, James Provan, pinned the blame on Mrs Thatcher, whom he said was seen as a hectoring lady in London who had not achieved any popularity in Scotland, although the Poll Tax was a dominant feature of the campaign. It seemed that the Prime Minister's anti-European rhetoric, even if not matched by her actions, had failed to resonate in Scotland. Yet there was intriguing evidence that Mrs Thatcher herself was not the sole cause of falling Conservative support in Scotland. A *Scotsman* poll on 4 March 1989 found that while only 19 per cent of Scots expressed satisfaction with her government's performance, 8 per cent more said they approved of the job she was doing as Prime Minister. Nevertheless, following the European elections Labour moved into a poll lead and Mrs Thatcher's personal approval rating slumped sharply, never recovering.

Although the strategy of 'Thatcherism resurgent' had achieved nothing in polling or, more importantly, electoral terms since the 1987 election, the Prime Minister gamely continued to visit Scotland more than any other region of the United Kingdom from the middle of 1989 until her resignation at the end of 1990. She toured carefully selected factories, rallied activists, visited Glasgow's Garden Festival (and had lobbied for the city to be designated European City of Culture[18]), and even presided over the draw for the Scottish Cup semi-final in March 1990, although many sports journalists remember a feeling that the defeat of Will Carling, the England captain, was for many Scottish rugby fans a useful surrogate for sticking the proverbial boot into the Prime Minister.[19] She also addressed the Scottish Rugby Union two months later, an event at which Denis would have been more at home. It seemed, however, that Mrs Thatcher was damned if she did and damned if she did not: the more she visited the more Scots seemed to resent her 'interference' in Scottish affairs; and if she stayed away, the Prime Minister was accused of 'neglecting' Scotland.

'She wasn't keen on going to Scotland by then,' recalled Rae Stewart, a press officer at the Conservative Party's Scottish headquarters. 'She regarded it as pointless, a waste of time, travelling all that way to be amongst a resolutely hostile, ungrateful people. So all the events I was involved with were very tightly arranged so that she didn't have much to do with the public and they didn't have much to do with her. They were basically done behind closed doors.'[20] The feeling that Mrs Thatcher was personally remote, and

---

[17] The result was also bad UK-wide, the Conservatives winning 33.5 per cent of the vote to Labour's 38.7 per cent on a low turnout.

[18] 'When it came to our turn as the United Kingdom to have the City of Culture', Mrs Thatcher explained in April 1990, 'we did not, like the French, take the capital city, we chose Glasgow.' (*Scottish Daily Express* 23/4/1990)

[19] The author Sandy Jamieson fictionalised this encounter in his 1990 novel *Own Goal*, in which a character called Frank Hunter plots to assassinate the Prime Minister at Hampden Park on cup final day.

[20] Interview with Rae Stewart, 6/8/2008. Mrs Thatcher visited the Glasgow Garden Festival, for example, early in the morning and before it opened to the public.

her government guilty of ignoring Scotland, had been exacerbated by the suspension of the Scottish Affairs Select Committee in 1987 when three MPs refused to join. Michael Heseltine, a campaigning backbencher since his resignation over the Westland Affair in 1986, argued that 'because Scotland has its own machinery of Government it can get on with the job without much attention from south of the border'. This, he said, could 'be interpreted in Scotland as neglect'.[21]

Paradoxically, the Thatcher–Scotland dynamic developed to the point that the Prime Minister was simultaneously accused of neglecting Scotland, using it as a 'guinea pig' for English reforms (the Poll Tax, police powers, etc.), *and* imposing English reforms (school boards, opting out, legal reforms) on distinctively Scottish institutions. Councillor Jean McFadden, finance convener at Glasgow District Council, mixed a couple of these together when she declared: 'We have been used as a test-bed for legislation, and the impression you get is that she doesn't care a damn because she has nothing to lose here.'[22]

Also contributing to the problem was the lingering issue of unemployment. Although dole queues had begun to shrink in Scotland they did so more slowly than in England, so ten years after Mrs Thatcher promised to bring hope where there had been despair, the number of Scots out of work was still above 250,000, 70 per cent more than in May 1979. In the UK as a whole, the figure was generally 50 per cent higher. Nevertheless, noted the *Sunday Times*, many 'Scots have done well out of the Thatcherite revolution, but it has not been reflected in the polls, unlike in England'. 'In England that decried species, the Yuppies, proudly proclaim their Toryism,' the article continued, 'but in Scotland if they turn Tory they make sure nobody knows about it or, more likely, they continue voting as before.'[23]

From June 1989 to June 1990, therefore, approval ratings for the Conservatives hit an all-time low in Scotland, with eight out of ten Scots expressing dissatisfaction with the government's performance and the same proportion with Mrs Thatcher personally. The Scottish Business Group (SBG), however, remained staunch allies. Set up after the 1987 election and comprising figures like Bill Hughes of Grampian Holdings – soon to be appointed deputy chairman of the Scottish Conservative Party – Sir Hector Laing, Sir Ian MacGregor, Lord Weir and the merchant banker Angus Grossart,[24] it was chaired by James Gulliver, former head of the Argyll Group. The SBG claimed success in convincing Malcolm Rifkind to level the playing field on business rates after years of disparity between Scotland and

[21] *Glasgow Herald* 22/4/1988.
[22] *Radical Scotland* August/September 1990.
[23] *Sunday Times* 30/4/1989.
[24] According to a Labour Party survey, 13 Scottish companies gave a total of £173,250 to the Conservative Party through the SBG in 1988, including General Accident in Perth, Scottish & Newcastle, Christian Salvesen, the Scottish National Trust, John Menzies, Weir Group, Macfarlane Group, Highland Distillers and Murray Group.

England, while its members were also heavily involved with the Focus in Scotland dinner, the Conservative Party's major annual fundraiser.[25]

Malcolm Rifkind, meanwhile, tried to soften the political tone at the 1989 Scottish Conservative conference by promising that he would be 'listening' throughout the coming parliamentary session. The implication was that after two years of controversial legislation there was to be a period of consolidation as the party reverted to more traditional One Nation Conservatism. The election of the moderate Glaswegian lawyer Ross Harper as president of the Scottish Conservative and Unionist Association (SCUA), the party's voluntary wing, appeared to reinforce this change of direction. The choice of Michael Forsyth to succeed Lord Goold as Scottish Tory chairman, however, did not. A rare example of Mrs Thatcher being proactive in terms of her party's position in Scotland, the appointment of Forsyth also directly undermined Rifkind's authority as Scottish Secretary.

The Prime Minister may have referred to Rifkind as her 'splendid Secretary of State'[26] during her 1989 Scottish conference speech, but relations had long since broken down between the two. Regarded as completely saturated on the ideological scale of wet and dry by many of Mrs Thatcher's acolytes, the Prime Minister had come to agree. 'No one could doubt his intellect or his grasp of ideas,' she said of Rifkind in her memoirs: 'Unfortunately he was as sensitive and highly strung as he was eloquent. His judgement was erratic and his behaviour unpredictable. Nor did he implement the radical Thatcherite approach he publicly espoused; for espouse it he certainly did. After the 1987 election Malcolm made speeches up and down Scotland attacking dependency and extolling enterprise. But as political pressures mounted he changed his tune.'

Indeed, by March 1990, 'Malcolm Rifkind . . . fell back with a vengeance on the old counter-productive tactic of proving his Scottish virility', observed Mrs Thatcher in her memoirs, 'by posturing as Scotland's defender against Thatcherism.' So while the Prime Minister approved of the recent Scottish Homes and Scottish Enterprise initiatives, although neither had emanated from Rifkind, she had become 'convinced, however, that it was only by having someone who shared my commitment to fundamental change in Scotland spearheading the Party's efforts there that real progress would be made'. She continued:

I did not want to move Malcolm Rifkind who, for better or worse, had established himself as a major political force. But the Chairman of the Scottish Conservative Party, Sir James [now Lord] Goold, for whose loyalty and dependability I always had the highest regard, had told me that he wished

---

[25] The Scottish artist Anne Mackintosh was commissioned to paint the Prime Minister's portrait for the 1990 Focus in Scotland dinner. It was later gifted to Mrs Thatcher and still hangs in her drawing room.

[26] Speech to Scottish Conservative conference, 12/5/1989, MTF.

to stand down when I had found a suitable successor. Both he and I believed that that successor was now available in the form of Michael Forsyth.[27]

Mrs Thatcher pitched Forsyth's name to Malcolm Rifkind in January 1989 but found it lobbed back at her. After mulling it over, the Scottish Secretary returned with the alternative suggestion of Ross Harper, the SCUA president, arguing that Forsyth could not be spared from his ministerial duties.[28] Appointed under-secretary for education and health in 1987, Mrs Thatcher regarded Forsyth as the 'real powerhouse for Thatcherism at the Scottish Office'. 'So in July I overrode Malcolm Rifkind's objections', she recalled in her memoirs, 'and appointed Michael Chairman and Bill Hughes his Deputy.'[29]

A radical break with the tradition that the Scottish Secretary was Scotland's representative in the Cabinet, the 34-year-old Forsyth would be the other side of the dialectic: Mrs Thatcher's man in Scotland. He was also a complete contrast to Rifkind. A true believer, a radical iconoclast who was eager to break with the corporatist traditions of Scottish Unionism, Forsyth's aim was to mount a social revolution in Scotland. Tories of his persuasion believed Scots voted Labour not because they were ideologically predisposed, or because of any particular feeling of nationality, but because most lived and worked in the public sector and therefore voted for the party of the state.

Forsyth was also utterly devoted to Mrs Thatcher, unlike the increasingly circumspect Scottish Secretary, and would openly admit as much to anyone who would listen.[30] Forsyth's loyalty was repaid by almost doting attention from the Prime Minister, but then their political instincts were at one and Mrs Thatcher knew there would be no backsliding over devolution with her 'young Lochinvar'[31] in place.

Indeed, Forsyth was certainly faithful in his love of Thatcherism and dauntless in going to war against its critics. Assessing the first (for he was certain it was only the first) decade of Scotland under Thatcherism for the *Sunday Express*, Forsyth claimed that ten years 'of the Thatcher revolution have brought massive and sweeping improvements to Scotland'. 'With Thatcherism,' he enthused, 'harmony has replaced strife, and efficient order has taken over from shambling chaos.' He nevertheless acknowledged that the Prime Minister was not universally popular. 'Even some Scottish Tory

---

[27] Thatcher, *The Downing Street Years*, 620–22.

[28] Goold pushed for Forsyth to succeed him although Downing Street advisers had suggested the former Scottish Tory MP Gerry Malone (then editor of *Sunday Times Scotland*) as a compromise candidate.

[29] Thatcher, 620–21.

[30] The Scottish Office civil servant Peter Mackay remembered Forsyth bowing, as if in prayer, before a formal portrait of Mrs Thatcher at the Department of Education, 'and he wasn't joking'. (Interview with Peter Mackay, 11/4/2002)

[31] Clements *et al.*, *Restless Nation*, 91. This nickname is attributed and refers to the dashing knight in Sir Walter Scott's poem *Marmion*.

MPs occasionally question her judgment,' Forsyth continued, 'believing that, if they push her hard enough, she will somehow bend to them. They are misguided. Mrs Thatcher, quite rightly, will not change her style. She knows it has served Scotland well.'[32]

Forsyth's style, meanwhile, was now a direct threat to Rifkind. Not only did he have responsibility for health and education at the Scottish Office, but Forsyth now controlled party organisation in Scotland and, most importantly of all, had a direct line to the Prime Minister. Unsurprisingly, Rifkind resented this enormously. Indeed, the presence of Forsyth was almost as unacceptable to Rifkind as that of the economist Sir Alan Walters to Nigel Lawson.[33] This Rifkind–Forsyth schism inevitably spilled over into the Scottish media, which already had the new chairman's card marked. The *Glasgow Herald* dubbed Forsyth 'Thatcher in drag',[34] while Kelvin Mackenzie, editor of the UK *Sun*, informed his Scottish editor, Jack Irvine, that following Forsyth's appointment as chairman it was now acceptable to 'put the boot in'[35] to Malcolm Rifkind as Scottish Secretary.

EDUCATIONAL THATCHERISM

The pace of change at the Scottish Office also caused tension, with Forsyth pursuing a more overtly Thatcherite policy agenda. 'It is he who has pressed ahead with competitive tendering in the health service where his predecessors backed away,' observed the *Sunday Times*. 'It is also he who has ensured the agenda for the education debate is of the government's choosing and not of the education unions.'[36]

Indeed, education was to become the key battleground of Thatcherism in decline, despite the Scottish Office's desire to keep things on an even keel following the divisive teachers' strike of 1984–86. And although Scottish teachers had emerged from that dispute in better shape than their English colleagues, the fact that the government had been forced to cede some ground in the settlement simply stiffened Forsyth's resolve when it came to reducing teacher and local authority power. The passage of the School Boards (Scotland) and Self-Governing Schools (Scotland) Acts were, therefore, fraught with difficulties. As with subsequent reforms to Scotland's health service and legal system, the latter Bill was essentially a tartan version of English legislation, in this case the Education Secretary Kenneth Baker's Education Act of 1988, although much less ambitious in scope. Dubbed 'Gerbil' – Baker's Great Education Reform Bill, as it was known before Royal Assent – it established a

---

[32] *Sunday Express* c1/1990.

[33] Nigel Lawson resigned as Chancellor in October 1989 largely as a result of Sir Alan's conflicting advice to the Prime Minister.

[34] *Glasgow Herald* 10/7/1989.

[35] Kemp, *The Hollow Drum*, 193.

[36] *Sunday Times* 30/4/1989.

National Curriculum, City Technology Academies, testing at ages 7, 11 and 14 with published results, and powers for head teachers to take control of their own budgets and establish grant-maintained schools. Only one aspect encompassed Scotland as well as England and Wales. Academic tenure, jealously guarded by certain university staff for obvious reasons, was to end.

Much of the Baker prescription, centralising the curriculum and decentralising budgets, was also pursued by Forsyth via the two aforementioned Bills but, if anything, failed to take root in Scotland to an even greater extent than in England. Both were publicly controversial – the Forum on Scottish Education was established with the stated aim of safeguarding Scottish schools from Thatcherite interference – and politically divisive, even within the Scottish Conservative Party (Rifkind was not convinced). By his own admission, Forsyth was a young man in a hurry. 'I felt that Scotland was in the grip of an old-fashioned socialist consensus that was destroying our competitive advantage in terms of education and other areas,' he recalled in 2005, 'and that we had to try and use our period in office to create choice and opportunity for people who couldn't afford to buy it on the market.'[37]

To that end Forsyth proposed a system of national testing (*a la* Baker) that would enable parents in Scotland to assess the performance of local schools. He was also keen to emulate Baker's City Technology Academies (only 15 of which were eventually set up), but despite an offer of £2 million from the hotelier Lord Forte to establish one at Allan Glen's School in Glasgow (which closed in 1989), Strathclyde Regional Council refused to co-operate because the school would be selective. Instead, the School Boards (Scotland) Bill of 1988 marked the opening salvo in Forsyth's educational crusade. Its aim, as with many Thatcherite reforms, was to further erode the power of local government, and specifically its education department fiefdoms, by giving parents a direct say over how their children's school would be run.

Opponents depicted the boards as 'alien' to the Scottish educational tradition, although this conveniently ignored the fact that regional school boards had existed in Scotland until 1918, and a provision in the Local Government (Scotland) Act of 1973 had allowed for elections to school councils, although these had little power. Boards consisted of elected parents and staff members, and other members (such as local businessmen) co-opted by the elected members. Mrs Thatcher hailed this as 'devolving more influence to the parent and widening his choice',[38] but in reality that influence was limited to routine monitoring of a school's performance. The consultation process, contrary to the perception that Mrs Thatcher was unwilling to compromise, was largely responsible for this weakness of power. Instead of school budgets being devolved to each board, as in England, the cash instead went to the head teacher, while the extent of exempt categories of expenditure (such as school milk, transport and special needs) was enhanced in Scotland beyond that in England.

---

[37] Interview with Lord Forsyth, 7/12/2005.
[38] Speech to National Press Fund, 3/2/1989, MTF.

The first school board elections took place in 1989–90 and, at least in terms of take-up, were a success. By the end of 1990, 96 per cent of secondary schools in Scotland and 80 per cent of primaries had established boards. 'But if you see, the parents in Scotland went to vote for the School Boards,' Mrs Thatcher triumphantly told the *Scottish Daily Express* in April 1990, 'so our policy is right.'[39]

If the Prime Minister had applied the same criteria to the natural extension of the School Boards Bill, the Self-Governing Schools (Scotland) Bill, then she could not have reached the same conclusion. The notion that individual schools should be able to 'opt out' of local authority control altogether first surfaced in April 1988 when correspondence between the private secretaries of Mrs Thatcher and Rifkind was leaked to the *Glasgow Herald*. This revealed that the Scottish Tory backbencher Allan Stewart was to introduce an amendment to the School Boards Bill to this end, the intention being to drop the amendment once Rifkind had been bounced into line on school boards and promised to legislate for opting out.

While Rifkind supported school boards only reluctantly, when it came to opting out he was unconvinced. What forced his hand was pressure to intervene when certain local authorities, most notably Strathclyde Regional Council, moved to close a particular school. The *cause célèbre* in this context was Paisley Grammar School. Not a grammar school in the English sense and no longer selective, it was targeted for closure despite being a magnet school with high standards. Andrew Neil, an old boy and editor of the *Sunday Times*, pressured Rifkind to step in, but although the Scottish Secretary exuded sympathy he pleaded limited powers of intervention. Neil then threatened to go over his head direct to the Prime Minister – even though relations were strained following publication of excerpts from the controversial book *Spycatcher* – as 'I think she knows she's presided over the death of quite enough grammar schools'.

Neil launched a campaign to 'save' Paisley Grammar School in the Scottish edition of the *Sunday Times* as he made contact with Brian Griffiths, head of the Downing Street Policy Unit. A Welsh grammar-school boy, Griffiths dismissed Rifkind as being in 'the pocket of the Scottish Office'[40] and promised to raise it with the Prime Minister as long as Neil got Paisley's rector to petition Downing Street. 'I was moved by the appeals I received from the staff and parents,' recalled Mrs Thatcher in her memoirs. 'I also saw this as a test case. We must show that we were not prepared to see the Scottish left-wing establishment lord it over people it was our duty to protect.'[41]

Outraged by Rifkind's indifference, the Prime Minister instructed him to issue a new regulation giving the Scottish Office powers to save schools where 80 per cent of parents disagreed with a local authority's closure plans. The

[39] *Scottish Daily Express* 23/4/1990.
[40] Neil, *Full Disclosure*, 240.
[41] Thatcher, *The Downing Street Years*, 620.

School Boards Bill provided a convenient means of doing so, and Paisley was saved. The Cabinet minister Peter Walker later told Neil that Mrs Thatcher had beckoned Rifkind over to her at a Cabinet dinner and said sternly: 'You must always remember, Malcolm, that it's your job to save good schools, not preside over their closure.'[42] There was an obvious irony in that she had presided over the closure of several grammar schools as Education Secretary in 1970–74, a record for which Neil reckoned she was trying to do penance. To Neil, the battle for Paisley Grammar School not only symbolised the Thatcherite struggle against the left, but also the Scottish Office's irretrievable wetness.

'I also had to take a very firm line on the issue of whether Scottish schools should be allowed to opt out of local authority control,' Mrs Thatcher recalled in her memoirs, 'like their English counterparts.' Her argument was that once school boards had been established there was no reason to prevent them seeking grant-maintained status. 'Yet Malcolm resisted this,' she noted sniffily, claiming 'that there was not sufficient demand for opting out in Scotland'. 'However, from my postbag and Brian Griffiths's enquiries I knew otherwise,' continued Mrs Thatcher. 'I insisted and had my way. In 1989 legislation was accordingly introduced to bring the opportunity of grant-maintained schools to Scotland.'[43]

To Mrs Thatcher, all forms of autonomy – except legislative devolution – were good and pure. 'Parents, if they choose, will be able to vote for self-government,' she explained in February 1989. '[But] the money to run the school will still come from the public purse.' Local authorities, she said, 'want to keep the power to themselves. And some of them want to do it with the aid of yet another layer of government. That is not our way. This Government believes in devolution to the individual citizen – a devolution which is now being achieved within the United Kingdom.'[44]

Public opinion in Scotland, however, was split, and a poll in December 1988 revealed that 49 per cent of Scots opposed opting out (31 per cent were in favour) while only half of Conservative voters supported it. Not for the first time Mrs Thatcher's insensitivity to Scottish sentiment fatally undermined a well-intentioned proposal. The Educational Institute of Scotland described the reforms as constituting 'Anglicisation',[45] while the Scottish Tory back-benchers Alick Buchanan-Smith and Sir Hector Monro opposed the Bill outright, arguing that school boards should be allowed to bed down before any further changes were made. When Forsyth made up numbers in the Commons by drafting in right-wing English allies to get it through, the opposition presented itself as defending a historic education system from 'alien' interference that not even every Scottish Tory MP supported.

[42] Neil, *Full Disclosure*, 241.
[43] Thatcher, *The Downing Street Years*, 621.
[44] Speech to National Press Fund.
[45] *Times Educational Supplement Scotland* 14/10/1988.

Not only were relations between Rifkind and the Prime Minister strained by the battle over opting out, but the Scottish Secretary fell out spectacularly with his under-secretary Michael Forsyth. 'We didn't disagree as to end results; it was a question of pace and manner and tone,' Rifkind reflected in 2005. 'I had no problem with opting out as an objective but in England they had had school councils for years, and therefore a degree of autonomy, while in Scotland we didn't even have school boards. But Michael persuaded the Prime Minister that there was this huge demand in Scotland.'[46]

Rifkind's claim that there was not sufficient demand for opting out appeared to be vindicated when only two Scottish schools exercised their new legislative right once the Self-Governing Schools (Scotland) Bill became law.[47] The whole affair, meanwhile, increased the impression that not only was Mrs Thatcher seeking to impose English solutions upon Scottish problems, but that she was hostile to Scotland's entire educational establishment. To the Prime Minister, however, the reforms met 'the fundamental dignity and freedom of the individual and the Scots should be the first to take advantage of it'. 'They do not have to say: "She was right",' she told an interviewer in April 1990, 'they do not have to actually bring themselves to say that at all, they just have to say: "Look, do not let this go, it is too valuable for the future of our children".'[48] But Scots did let it go, almost as soon as the Scottish Parliament was established in 1999. Scotland's sole opted-out school was brought back under local authority control, while a 2006 Act abolished school boards and replaced them with a two-tier system of Parent Forums and Parent Councils.

By the late 1980s more Scottish school leavers than ever before were going on to study at university: 24 per cent in 1990 compared with 15 per cent across Britain as a whole. Scotland was home to eight of the UK's 45 universities and 16 per cent of the country's undergraduates. There were also negatives. The percentage of working-class university students in Scotland fell from 26 per cent in 1980 to 18 per cent ten years later, while one survey showed that nearly a third of graduates had to leave Scotland in order to find work, a figure even higher in the science and technology sector despite the success of Silicon Glen. Indeed, at a time when the UK graduate market was increasing, the Scottish share actually declined from 9.4 to 7 per cent. And it was not just students – whose grants were being eroded in favour of loans – who felt the heat. Sir William Kerr Fraser, who became principal of Glasgow University on retiring as permanent under-secretary at the Scottish Office in 1988, regularly encountered hostility from ministers suspicious of the way they believed universities shielded inefficiencies behind a commitment to research.

---

[46] Interview with Sir Malcolm Rifkind MP, 17/11/2005.

[47] These were St Mary's Episcopal Primary School in Dunblane and Dornoch Academy, although the latter only did so to avoid closure and opted back in soon afterwards. In England and Wales fewer than 1,000 primary and secondary schools out of 24,000 chose to opt out, often through fear of closure.

[48] *Scottish Daily Express* 23/4/1990.

'Our intellectual institutions, on which our civilisation depends, have never before had to live in such a hostile climate,' wrote the Rector of Dundee University, Paul Henderson Scott, in April 1989. 'We are now faced with the most anti-intellectual, the most philistine government in our history.'[49]

The University Grants Committee – renamed the University Funding Committee (UFC) in 1988 – continued to allocate funds in Scotland based not only upon the quality of teaching but also of research. Aberdeen University consistently lost out, as did Glasgow, and some academics raised the prospect of a separate Scottish funding council. 'I know that some people felt that maybe they would do better if the Scottish universities were in a group of their own,' Mrs Thatcher said in May 1989. 'We did set up a little group to enquire, but only two universities wanted to be in a separate Scottish group and six wanted to stay within the whole university family.'[50] Her only concession, therefore, was to sanction a Scottish Committee within the UFC, which largely consisted of businessmen rather than academics. And although Scottish universities followed government instructions to seek private funding in addition to government grants, their finances simply could not cope with the sheer increase in student numbers, which rose by 25 per cent between 1979 and 1989.

Scotland's academic institutions remained under Whitehall control via the Department of Education, and it struck no one as a good idea that power should be devolved to Michael Forsyth at the Scottish Office. Many Scottish academics also loathed Mrs Thatcher with a passion that verged on hysteria. The journalist Harry Reid remembers Professor Nigel Grant, a respected educationalist at Glasgow University, booing and hissing at the Prime Minister as she addressed the National Press Fund in Glasgow in early 1989. 'Even at an event known for boorish behaviour,' he recalled, 'it was an extraordinary display, but he genuinely detested her.'[51] Extreme reactions such as Grant's, however, were not a specifically Scottish phenomenon, as evidenced by the refusal of Oxford University to grant the Prime Minister an honorary degree in 1985. Nevertheless, in Mrs Thatcher's memoirs her university reforms earn a rare note of contrition (broadcasting was another), conceding that her critics 'had a stronger case than I would have liked'.[52]

NURSE THATCHER

Until the end of her premiership Mrs Thatcher had approached the health service with caution. She realised outright privatisation was politically impossible, but in appointing the true believer John Moore (often spoken of as a future Tory leader) to the Department of Health and Social Security in 1987,

[49] Seawright, *An Important Matter of Principle*, 92.
[50] Interview for *Glasgow Herald*, 31/5/1989, MTF.
[51] Interview with Harry Reid, 31/7/2008.
[52] Thatcher, *The Downing Street Years*, 599.

together with Forsyth as under-secretary for health at the Scottish Office, indicated that in the NHS, as in education and the legal system, the Prime Minister was becoming increasingly impatient for reform.

Although there were howls of anguish about waiting times initiatives making extensive use of Scotland's relatively small private hospital provision, the main controversy in Scotland prior to 1987 had been the contracting out of ancillary services such as cleaning and catering. There were huge protests and rallies in Glasgow, Aberdeen and Edinburgh, even though the number of private contracts remained small, with most tenders being awarded 'in-house' by Scottish health boards. Forsyth met with some success in changing this. From 1987 to 1989 he managed to increase the number of new domestic services contacts from 3 to 60, and new catering contracts from 44 to 47. By March 1991, 68 per cent of domestic contracts and 67 per cent of catering contracts in Scotland had been put out to tender. Meanwhile, economies were made by abolishing free dental check-ups in January 1989, and free eye tests in April, both cuts later reversed by the devolved Scottish Executive.

The UK white paper *Working for Patients*, however, further extended what Labour attacked as 'privatisation by stealth'. Published in January 1989, it introduced the concept of an 'internal market' in which the providers and purchasers of health services were separated. New supposedly autonomous NHS 'trusts' were also to be established across the UK, providing negotiated services to commissioning health boards. The market concept was also to apply to general practice, with GPs enabled to control their own budgets and purchase services from the new trusts. The central argument came down to efficiency. Advocates of the internal market claimed the reforms would make the NHS more streamlined and responsive to patients; opponents claimed it simply added another layer of bureaucracy which ran counter to the Scottish tradition of co-operation rather than competition in healthcare.

The most controversial proposal, however, was that which would allow individual hospitals and GPs – much like schools – to opt out of state control. Fought tooth and nail by Labour, doctors, hospitals and patient groups, the overall package of reform had mixed results across the UK. Despite reluctance from health boards, the trust system eventually bedded down and standards began to improve. Staffing the trusts, however, was a different matter. The new trusts required hundreds of lay appointees, and as all local authority representation on regional and district health boards had ended, this strained Conservative patronage considerably, particularly in Scotland. GP fund-holding, meanwhile, never really took off as it did in England, although it was genuinely popular among GPs in some Scottish regions like Grampian.

The opting out provision must have been the biggest disappointment for Mrs Thatcher and Forsyth. Only two Scottish hospitals held ballots on freeing themselves from state control – South Ayrshire hospital and the Aberdeen Royal Infirmary – and in both the vast majority of consultants voted against. Labour's Shadow Health Secretary, Robin Cook, pledged that any hospitals which did opt out would be compelled to opt back in when his party returned to government. 'Under our reforms, no hospital will be privatised,' Mrs Thatcher told the 1989 Scottish Tory conference a little defensively. 'And those major hospitals which choose – I repeat, choose – to become self-governing, will stay within the Health Service. And they will be run, not by some distant committee, but by those closest to the patient, who can make decisions quickly.'[53]

The NHS in Scotland, however, was now being run by its first chief executive, Don Cruikshank, recruited from the private sector to report directly to the Secretary of State for Scotland. To Mrs Thatcher it almost seemed as if the principle of the reform mattered more than uptake. 'Why should all the purse strings be held tightly by the Scottish Office or by London, why?' she asked a journalist rhetorically.

We are saying to people – I got this from Scotland, this is Adam Smith – our policy enables you to create the wealth of nations. The more you create, the smaller proportion we have to take in government. This whole idea [is] that you use your talents and abilities, they are your own, they are not state-given, and freedom is God-given, it is not state-given; it is not for us to take it away except insofar as we need – and this has worked to the benefit of Scotland.

The refrain was certainly sincere but was beginning to sound a little tired. 'The idea came from Scotland and one day,' reflected Mrs Thatcher, 'I hope very much that they will acknowledge that this is what they believe in.'[54]

'CAN'T PAY, WON'T PAY'

The Scots, meanwhile, showed no signs of believing in the Poll Tax, the idea for which also came, in part, from Scotland. The new method of collecting local taxation began on 1 April 1989 and, at least initially, projections for those refusing to pay appeared to have been exaggerated. By July, there were reports that 78 per cent of adults in the Strathclyde Region had paid up, a figure the regional treasurer described as 'higher than expected'.[55]

As the months rolled on, however, the SNP and Anti-Poll Tax Federation got the number of defaulters up to 900,000 of the 3.8 million Scots eligible to pay. In early September, Grampian Region said its non-payment level was 15 per cent; in Lothian it was 17 per cent; and unofficial estimates reckoned it to be around 20 per cent in Strathclyde. By December, council treasurers were describing collection as a 'nightmare'. Summary warrants were distributed to thousands of those refusing to pay. 'Since the Scots had made a practice over the years of complaining bitterly about every initiative the

[53] Speech to Scottish Conservative conference, 12/5/1989, MTF.
[54] *Scottish Daily Express* 23/4/1990.
[55] *Independent* 26/7/1989.

Government had ever taken,' Nigel Lawson wrote of the non-payment figures, 'this occasioned little surprise, let alone alarm.'[56]

The government did, however, respond by exempting those with degenerative illnesses from payment and promising help for anyone facing an increase of more than £3 a week in their Poll Tax demands. This created confusion as well as compromising the rationale behind the reform. Interviewed by Grampian TV in September 1989, Mrs Thatcher not unreasonably denied the Community Charge was a flat-rate tax at all. 'So some people are paying nothing,' she said. 'Other people are paying the small proportion. Other people a bigger proportion . . . It is not flat-rate. It is rebated according to your ability to pay.' Nevertheless – for those not eligible to receive rebates – the fact that the Poll Tax placed the same liability on the Duke of Buccleuch, Scotland's richest landowner, as on his unemployed tenant in Wanlockhead, was a contrast persistently highlighted.

Mrs Thatcher was more likely to be moved by the image of a widowed pensioner living in Morningside, with no children at home, paying thousands of pounds in rates while her neighbours, with several wage earners in the same household, paying minimal rates together with their council-subsidised rent. The old rates system, the Prime Minister said in the same interview with Grampian TV, had been 'bitterly unfair'. On a separate but related matter, she also admitted to being worried about declining Tory support north of the border. 'We must win more seats in Scotland in order to win the next election,' Mrs Thatcher declared. 'I don't think really that we have had enough credit for everything we've done in Scotland and the prosperity that Scotland is enjoying . . . It's difficult to understand why the message isn't getting through.'[57]

The Poll Tax message was further complicated that autumn as the government unveiled a transitional relief scheme 'of mind-boggling complexity'[58] for England, and a related package to be introduced retrospectively for Scotland. By mid October, meanwhile, the Convention of Scottish Local Authorities estimated that 600,000 Scots, 15 per cent of those eligible to pay, had not paid anything towards their Community Charge bills. In December the first Poll Tax-related legal actions, in Grampian and Fife Regions, began. Scottish Militant's non-payment campaign, neatly summed up in the slogan 'can't pay, won't pay', appeared to be yielding results.

Thereafter, in interview after interview, Mrs Thatcher was asked about the Poll Tax. Did she really consider it to be fair? And why had it been introduced in Scotland a year ahead of England and Wales? On the latter point the Prime Minister's well-rehearsed response was to indulge in a laborious recap of the 1985 rates revaluation. It was obvious, however, that she felt badly advised. 'Both the English and the Scottish Party demanded

---

[56] Lawson, *The View From No 11*, 582.
[57] Interview with Grampian TV, 7/9/1989, MTF.
[58] Butler, *Failure in British Government*, 143.

fundamental changes in the rates,' noted Mrs Thatcher in her memoirs. 'It was the Scottish Party which insisted upon the early introduction of the community charge in Scotland.'[59]

The Prime Minister's other standard defence was to point out that Scots contributed less to local government coffers relative to their English brethren. Again, this was true. 'The community charge will meet in England only about 25 per cent of local council expenditure,' she explained to an audience of Young Conservatives in February 1990. She went on: 'Some 50 per cent is paid by the taxpayer and the other 25 per cent is paid by business. So, the community charge meets about a quarter. It is less in Scotland [20 per cent]. It is less in Wales, because we English who are marvellous people are really very generous to Scotland and very generous to Wales. Someone has to speak up for we English, we're the most underestimated people in the United Kingdom.'[60]

It had frequently been said that Mrs Thatcher was an English nationalist. 'I am proud of being English,' she told one journalist. 'I expect the Scots to be proud of being Scots.'[61] The Prime Minister even got quite ratty during an interview with the *Scottish Daily Express* on the issue of nationality and the Poll Tax. 'My answer to you on the community charge is that if you wish to take it on a Scots versus English basis,' she said, then

My answer to our Scots friends is: 'Right! Let us all do the same thing about community charge if that is what you prefer – the whole of the same thing! We will all pay the same proportion!'

Interviewer: But Prime Minister, what you are saying is that the English are subsidising the Scottish handsomely?

Thatcher: Yes. We are the United Kingdom. Yes. It is always known.[62]

Arguably the most damaging incident in terms of how Scots viewed the Poll Tax occurred in John Major's first, and only, Budget of March 1990. There was immediate uproar, led by a typically effective Donald Dewar, when the Chancellor doubled the savings limit for Poll Tax rebates in England and Wales from £8,000 to £16,000. In the rush to devise the concession, however, the Treasury had forgotten about backdating the rebate to 20,000 residents north of the border. With the Community Charge not yet operational south of the border, it looked like an unashamed sop to southern protests while those of Scots were ignored. According to Major's memoirs, Rifkind threatened resignation if the Treasury did not cough up £4 million.

---

[59] Thatcher, *The Downing Street Years*, 653.
[60] Speech to Young Conservative conference, 10/2/1990, MTF.
[61] Interview with Grampian TV.
[62] Interview for *Scottish Daily Express* 23/4/1990.

Mrs Thatcher, meanwhile, protested that Rifkind had failed to voice any reservations about the Budget's additional relief measures when they had been discussed at Cabinet. 'They were not discussed,' recalled Rifkind. 'The Treasury had excluded the Scottish Office and other Departments from any foreknowledge that this would be in the Budget on the grounds of Budget Secrecy.' He continued:

> The first we (and everyone else apart from the PM) knew of them was at the Cabinet on the morning of the Budget when Major summarised his whole Budget including these proposals. The Cabinet were informed not consulted. I was present and was pleased that the proposals would apply to Scotland as well as England. I did not appreciate that they would not be backdated for the first year of the poll tax in Scotland. This only became clear as a result of Dewar's interruption during the Budget speech.

This is when things got really messy. Bernard Ingham began leaking details of negotiations between the Scottish Secretary, Major and the Prime Minister to the lobby, even boasting that Rifkind had been 'carpeted' by Mrs Thatcher during one meeting and that nothing could be done to backdate the rebate in Scotland. (Rifkind knew about this because the *Scotsman* always named Ingham as the source of lobby briefings.) 'Against that background I saw Margaret the following morning and made clear I could not continue as her SofS with authority and credibility unless we agreed a compromise that contradicted Ingham's statement,' remembered Rifkind. 'She accepted this . . . I then foolishly made some rather triumphalist remarks in an interview with the *Mail on Sunday* shortly afterwards, which really narked her.'[63]

Nark her they did. 'Having damaged the reception of John's skilfully conceived budget,' Mrs Thatcher recalled in her memoirs, 'Malcolm then went on to revel publicly in Scotland in his 'victory' . . . He also told the press that I had fallen into line with his better judgement. This childish behaviour did the Conservative cause in Scotland great harm and prompted letters of protest from outraged Scottish Tories.'[64] But to other Scots it reinforced their suspicion that Scotland was not on the Prime Minister's radar. In the first year of the Poll Tax there had been minimal Scottish compromises, yet when voters in England and Wales complained they were lavished with transitional relief, capping and further exemptions. Crudely speaking, it looked very much as if the government was treating its 'testing ground' as an afterthought.

Then, on 31 March 1990, the Community Charge put the UK, or rather London, on news bulletins throughout the world. Anti-Poll Tax marches had been organised for both London and Edinburgh, but it was that in London

---

[63] Sir Malcolm Rifkind MP to the author, 10/1/2009, and interview with Sir Malcolm Rifkind, 2/4/2008.
[64] Thatcher, *The Downing Street Years*, 622.

which 'turned from a good-natured demonstration into a full-scale and bloody riot'.[65] The march in Edinburgh, by contrast, passed off without a riot shield in sight. It was at this moment that commentators began to speak of the Poll Tax precipitating the Prime Minister's resignation. 'The force of people power will force Mrs Thatcher to stand down', said the Militant non-payment campaigner Tommy Sheridan, 'and then the whole house of cards will fall.'[66]

That house of cards was certainly becoming more precarious. And as the Poll Tax had come to be associated with Mrs Thatcher personally, 'the failure to reform it was seen as a condemnation of her personally'.[67] It also became the pledge by which the Prime Minister's personal resolve was to be judged. 'She did latterly play up to her Iron Lady image; she loved it,' recalled Lord Lang. 'In reality she thought because it had paid off to be tough in certain respects she should be tough on everything else, that's why she learned nothing from the mistakes of the Poll Tax in Scotland when it came into force in England.'[68]

Indeed, therein lay an obvious retort to the 'guinea pig' argument: why, having 'tested' the Poll Tax unsuccessfully in Scotland, was it then applied to England and Wales? 'Despite the obvious signs that the Scottish guinea pig was suffering,' observed Sir Ian Gilmour, 'the poll tax was then extended to England and Wales. Nearly all official advice was against it. Yet apart from [Peter] Walker and Lawson, the cabinet was supine and the overwhelming majority of the parliamentary party innocently obedient.'[69] The guinea pig charge obviously rankled with Mrs Thatcher. '[I]f, as the Scots subsequently claimed, they were guinea pigs for a great experiment in local government finance', she reflected in her memoirs, 'they were the most vociferous and influential guinea pigs which the world has ever seen.'[70]

The Poll Tax seemed to embody everything those 'influential guinea pigs' apparently did not like about the Mrs Thatcher: inflexibility, not caring for the poor and using Scotland as a test bed for unpopular policies. All this was rolled up into a ball called the Poll Tax and thrown at 4 million Scots, less than a quarter of whom were better off as a result. Indeed, to Sir Ian

---

[65] Butler, *Failure in British Government*, 151. 'As the anti-Poll Tax protestors took to the streets to proclaim the supposed injustice of introducing the community charge twelve months earlier in Scotland than in England', noted Douglas Mason wryly, 'it apparently never occurred to them that significant sections of "Thatcherite" policy were yet, years later, still to be applied in Scotland.' (Massie, *et. al., Scotland and Free Enterprise*, 20)

[66] *Glasgow Herald* 3/4/1990.

[67] Butler, *Failure in British Government*, 155.

[68] Interview with Lord Lang.

[69] Gilmour, *Dancing With Dogma*, 268.

[70] Thatcher, *The Downing Street Years*, 653. Malcolm Rifkind was sensibly cautious about fuelling the guinea pig charge. When David Hunt, the English local government minister, proposed visiting Scotland in August 1989 to see how the Poll Tax was being administered ahead of its introduction in England, Rifkind said no on the basis that 'It would be seen as proof of the argument that Scotland has been used as a guinea pig for the Community Charge'. (SOE6/1/1460)

Gilmour, 'the imposition of the poll tax confirmed the Scottish conviction that the British Conservative government regarded Scotland not as a proud nation but as a small and tiresome province which needed bringing up to scratch by a sharp course of Thatcherism'.[71]

That may have been true, but there were no indications that the government lost even more Scottish support as a result. In the regional council elections of May 1990, the Conservative share of the vote actually increased by nearly 3 per cent compared with the previous poll in 1986. Even in Westminster terms the Poll Tax does not seem to have dented Conservative Party support. Again, its share of the vote actually increased between the 1987 and 1992 general elections.

Nor were overspending councils punished at the polls, one of the central arguments for the Poll Tax.[72] It also failed in other respects. Although another stated aim, truly accountable local government, was laudable, accountability actually diminished as the government was forced to increase the central grant in order to reduce inequities. And far from being 'simpler' than the rates, collection costs soared, while initial predictions that the Poll Tax would prove a vote-winner turned out to be hideously misplaced. So instead of becoming 'one of the most far-reaching and beneficial reforms ever made in the working of local government',[73] as Mrs Thatcher put it in her memoirs, the reform entered the history books as one of the most detested and regressive taxes ever introduced in the UK. The Prime Minister would have done well to consult the Enlightenment wisdom of Adam Smith, who said that the 'subjects of every state ought to contribute to the support of the government, as nearly as possible, in proportion to their respective abilities'.[74]

Devolutionists often argued that Scotland would have been protected from some of the policies pursued by Mrs Thatcher's governments had there existed a Scottish Assembly. The Poll Tax gave them a perfect example. Opponents, however, proved less able to articulate alternatives to the Community Charge. One poll demonstrated that Labour's proposal for a 'Roof Tax' – which differed from the rates only in assessing payment on the basis of a property's capital worth rather than its notional rental value – was actually less popular than the Poll Tax. Michael Forsyth's imaginative onslaught against it also marked a rare campaigning success for the Scottish Conservative Party. 'To Everyone Who Liked Paying Rates,' read a Tory leaflet distributed during the 1990 regional council elections. 'Relax. Labour's Roof Tax Will Bring Them Back With A Vengeance.' 'It's a tax to penalise self help,' Mrs Thatcher declared at the 1990 Scottish Tory conference, 'a tax to penalise effort and a tax to penalise improvement: that's socialist taxation

---

[71] Gilmour, *Dancing With Dogma*, 271.

[72] 'In the second year of the operation of the community charge in Scotland,' Mrs Thatcher wrote in 1993, 'there was evidence that the benefits of increased accountability had begun to restrain local authority spending. So the indications were mixed.' (Thatcher, *The Downing Street Years*, 655)

[73] Ibid., 993.

[74] Smith, *The Wealth of Nations*, 451.

for you.'[75] As a result, Labour's plan to launch a similar campaign in England and Wales was quietly dropped. Curiously, no one accused the opposition of 'testing' the Roof Tax in Scotland.

It is, however, important to remember that the Poll Tax was rejected everywhere in the UK. But while England and Wales revolted against it as an unfair tax, in Scotland it was much more than that. 'When Poll Tax bills appeared on Scottish doormats, it brought the democratic deficit – and the urgency of the constitutional question – plopping into every home,' observed the broadcaster Allan Little. 'The Poll Tax revolt in England and Wales was visceral and at times violent, but it didn't call into question the right of the Westminster government to govern.'[76] So the Poll Tax effectively sealed the fate of Thatcherism in Scotland, with opposition to it becoming inseparable from a new sense of Scottish identity.

THE FORSYTH SAGA

Michael Forsyth, meanwhile, was busy nudging the Scottish Conservative Party into the Thatcher era. Although even Ross Harper initially hailed Forsyth's appointment as 'imaginative',[77] feelings quickly turned sour, not least because Harper was pushing for the SCUA to raise its profile and develop a distinctive style for Scottish Conservatism. 'I believe that if the SCUA can be shown to be producing challenging policies and not be afraid to examine some of the fringes of Government policy,' he argued, 'then our vote-winning potential (and that's what it is all about) would increase. Such talk could of course send shivers up the spine of Central Office.'[78] In organisational terms, however, the Scottish party simply was not capable of shaping either policy or – with the exception of the Roof Tax – a successful counter-attack in the face of Labour's opposition and rhetoric. It struck many as lamentable that the state of the party appeared to be no better nearly three years after the 1987 election debacle.

Naturally, this sorry set of affairs prompted extensive soul searching within the party's Chester Street headquarters. One report by Andrew Thomson, Mrs Thatcher's former agent in Finchley, painted a highly critical picture of bumbling, apathetic fools running Scottish Central Office. 'We have failed the Party,' he concluded, 'we have failed our people and we have failed our nation.' He went on:

> 1979 is a significant year because it brought Margaret Thatcher to power. She has transformed the United Kingdom and Scotland has benefited. It is also significant within the Party because it gives all those opposed to Margaret

[75] Speech to Scottish Conservative conference, 12/5/1990, MTF.

[76] *Thatcher and the Scots* (BBC Scotland) 1/1/2009.

[77] Harper, letter to SCUA Executive, 31/8/1989, Acc 12514 (2), SCUAP.

[78] Acc 12514 (2), SCUAP , 'Draft thoughts to office bearers of SCUA due to take office 12th May'.

Thatcher's philosophy the opportunity to blame all Scotland's ailments, both in the Party and in the wider social field on Margaret Thatcher. Ergo, 'That woman and the poll tax' have become an excuse for poor candidates, laziness and apathy.[79]

While it was obvious where Thomson's loyalties lay, a report by the former Tory MP Michael Hirst was more realistic. 'Canvassers uniformly reported that the Prime Minister is still perceived to be disinterested [sic] in Scotland,' he informed members of the SCUA's Executive Committee. 'The Opposition parties have succeeded in whipping up the "hate factor" as fiercely as ever before, and disaffection is marked among public sector employees.'[80]

Another internal memo, written by the future Scottish Conservative leader David McLetchie, also touched upon a much wider problem for the party north of the border. 'I believe that the perception of the Conservatives as an English-based and English-run party is the biggest single factor in our current standing in Scotland,' he argued. 'In my experience, all Scots are nationalists with a small "n" at heart and we have ignored this at our peril. There is a far wider constituency of support for Conservative policies in Scotland than is currently reflected in Conservative votes.'[81]

Such erudite thoughts quickly became academic as the oldest political party in Scotland descended into internal squabbles, bitter recriminations, accusations, counter-accusations, and even childish name-calling reminiscent of the Labour Party circa 1981. Often depicted as a straightforward fight between 'wets' and 'dries' for the soul of the Scottish Conservative Party, to the journalist Alan Cochrane the titanic struggle for pre-eminence between Rifkind and Forsyth was in fact 'a classic class war'. In other words it was a battle between state-educated boys like Forsyth (Arbroath High School), Bill Walker (Logie Junior Secondary School, Dundee) and Allan Stewart (Bell Baxter High School, Cupar), and public-school-educated party grandees like Rifkind (George Watson's), George Younger (Winchester) and Michael Ancram (Ampleforth). 'The clash of cultures, as much as the clash of ideology,' wrote Cochrane in the *Mail on Sunday*, 'has riven the Tories asunder in Scotland. Forsyth's abrasiveness [has] led to disarray among the party's professional staff, more used to the gentlemanly approach of his forerunners.'[82]

Indeed, Forsyth's style of chairmanship did not go down at all well with the party's old guard, and particularly with the SCUA. And although there was an ideological element to their hostility – the Scottish Tory Reform Group

---

[79] Ibid., 'The Scottish Conservative Party Organisation: The Future', 4/7/1989.
[80] Ibid., 'Report on the 1989 Euro-Election Campaign'.
[81] Ibid., 'SCUA – 1989 and beyond: Observations of David McLetchie'. When polled by *Scotsman/ ICM* in August 1990, 56 per cent of Conservative respondents said they perceived their party as mainly English and having little relevance to Scotland.
[82] *Mail on Sunday* 9/9/1990.

(STRG) was particularly outspoken – it was largely cultural, or to put it more crudely, based on snobbery. 'The party organisation was stuffed with musty, amateurish old retainers who toodled around the place eating cake and were much happier discussing recipes than politics,' recalled Rae Stewart, a press officer who left just before Lord Goold retired as chairman. 'Then suddenly Forsyth brings in a bunch of young, impatient people who were into modern campaigning techniques. The old guard just found them too brash, too rude, too aggressively political.'[83]

The brash young men now occupying desks at Chester Street included Simon Turner, later Forsyth's Stirling agent (and previously agent for John Redwood and Norman Tebbit) and the new director of organisation; Iain Kerr, director of youth operations; and Russell Walters, formerly of the Adam Smith Institute and now chief of staff. Brian Monteith, later a Tory MSP, also acted as an adviser via his public relations company Leith Communications, while a mysterious American called Grover Norquist (responsible for George Bush's heavily criticised negative campaigning in the 1988 Presidential election) produced, at Forsyth's behest, a critical report on the party's organisation. And although certainly not brash, Douglas Young was appointed director of organisation. Regarded with suspicion by right-wingers as not 'one of us', Young later resigned, as did Turner and Walters. Meanwhile, in a calculated snub the party's chief executive, John MacKay was moved to the party's Glasgow office, an impotent outpost since the 1960s ('Perhaps I wasn't as tactful as I should have been,' Forsyth later conceded). Many of the new recruits were on high salaries, which together with the money spent on a new glossy magazine, *Scottish Conservative*, was not exactly in keeping with the New Right's Friedmanite penny-pinching.[84]

Although most in the party had been willing to give Forsyth and his new team the benefit of the doubt, many of the bright young things soon revealed themselves to be inexperienced, naïve and in some cases offensive ('I'd certainly made mistakes as chairman in terms of appointments,'[85] Forsyth later admitted). As a result anonymous letters began appearing in the letterboxes of constituency chairmen across Scotland. 'Appointed by the Prime Minister, he [Forsyth] was seen by many of us as the last chance for the Party in Scotland,' read one onslaught from 'A Chairman'. 'But we do not need the extremist riff-raff that Forsyth has brought into Chester Street . . . concerns now appear to be not those of the many former Tory voters we all meet on the doorsteps, but the concerns of an extreme and unpleasant minority of far-right troublemakers whose involvement bring nothing but shame on the Party.'[86]

---

[83] Interview with Rae Stewart.

[84] In the first issue of *Scottish Conservative*, Sir Nicholas Fairbairn described the Scottish press as 'little Scotlanders . . . yearning to return to those far-off days when Scotland was an independent oatmeal republic with a squabbling parliament presiding over abject poverty'. (Smith, *Paper Lions*, 40)

[85] Interview with Lord Forsyth, 8/9/2008.

[86] Letter to constituency chairmen, 11/1989, Acc 12514 (3), SCUAP.

However, while constituency chairmen concentrated their fire on far-right troublemakers in Central Office, Forsyth's followers were apparently preparing to topple Malcolm Rifkind (his ally Ross Harper, by accident rather than design, had already resigned as SCUA president[87]). The resulting war of words often descended into petty squabbling rather than internal ideological debate. Arthur Bell, chairman of the STRG, spoke of 'blue trots' rampaging through Central Office while Allan Stewart called Bell 'a pig-ignorant pipsqueak' (although that, he reflected later, was unfair to pigs). Forsyth even declared on BBC Radio Scotland that 'it was well known that Bell was the stupidest man in the Scottish Conservative Party'.[88] And when the Law Reform (Miscellaneous Provisions) (Scotland) Bill was introduced to the House of Lords in December 1989, the bickering factions found an unlikely focus.

LEGAL THATCHERISM

The Bill had its roots in the elevation of James Mackay, the former Lord Advocate, from the Scottish bench to head the English legal system as Lord Chancellor in October 1987. This creatively bold move took many in the legal establishment by surprise. 'It was as if', wrote the journalist Simon Jenkins, 'a foreigner had been appointed a cabinet minister.'[89] The appointment of this foreigner, however, was carefully calculated. With his independent-minded austere brand of Wee Free Presbyterianism, Lord Mackay of Clashfern – as he became – would not be afraid of shaking up English legal traditions as his predecessors Lord Hailsham (a rare devolutionist in Mrs Thatcher's Cabinets) and Sir Michael Havers (father of Nigel, the popular actor) were perceived to have been.

Mackay did not disappoint. He threw himself into reforming the English courts and legal system, encouraged by the Treasury and backed up by an increasingly radical Prime Minister. Much like Gerry Malone imploring England to follow Scotland's lead on the Poll Tax, this was the Thatcher–Scotland dynamic in reverse: a Scot was administering Thatcherism to a reluctant English institution. He was not the only one. Between October 1987 and January 1988 there were five Scots in Mrs Thatcher's Cabinet – Mackay, Willie Whitelaw (Leader of the Lords), John MacGregor (agriculture), George Younger (defence) and Malcolm Rifkind – three of whom commanded UK-wide briefs or roles.

Lord Mackay's brief, however, primarily covered England and Wales. In

---

[87] On the morning of Mrs Thatcher's July 1989 visit to Scotland, the *Sun* ran a front-page story falsely accusing Harper of having been involved with a prostitute. He later won a libel action against the newspaper, but the incident wrecked Mrs Thatcher's first appearance in Scotland under Forsyth's chairmanship.

[88] Kemp, *The Hollow Drum*, 204.

[89] Jenkins, *Accountable to None*, 194.

January 1989 he published three green papers, the main thrust of which was an end to the monopoly of barristers by allowing solicitors to plead in court and become High Court judges. The reforms, which also included a regulatory Legal Affairs Commission appointed by the government and dominated by non-lawyers, were greeted with howls of anguish from their target. Initially, Mrs Thatcher backed her Lord Chancellor, as she did when he was suspended as an elder of the Free Presbyterian Church of Scotland for attending the funeral masses of two close Roman Catholic friends. Asked for her opinion of this theological dispute, the Prime Minister took cover beneath some florid imagery. When the Lord Chancellor is 'no longer with us', she told the *Glasgow Herald*, 'there will be a massive guard of honour by the whole heavenly host in the next world! There really will, because he has been such a marvellous example.'[90] (Michael Forsyth was more forthright when it came to Scottish clerics. In March 1990 he attacked the Church of Scotland for its leftward drift – despite surveys showing that 34 per cent of Kirk members still voted Tory – a bias that led to the resignation of the Conservative Bob Kernohan as editor of the Kirk's magazine, *Life & Work*).

The Law Reform (Miscellaneous Provisions) (Scotland) Bill, meanwhile, essentially adhered to the central aim of the English legislation by proposing an end to the monopoly of Scottish solicitors in the provision of conveyancing and executry services. The monopoly of the Faculty of Advocates when it came to appearing in the Court of Session and High Court of the Justiciary was also to be eroded with the introduction of solicitor-advocates. The Bill, therefore, meant that of Scotland's troika of distinct institutions – legal, educational and religious – none would remain untouched by the Thatcher revolution. As in England, the proposals provoked predictable hyperbole from the Law Society of Scotland, judges (Lord McCluskey said 'We have gone a-whoring after strange gods'[91]), and opposition peers (Lord Grimond warned it would tamper 'with one of the expressions of Scottish nation-hood'[92]). Paradoxically, however, the thoroughly Thatcherite proposals also drew fire from otherwise true-believing Scottish Tory backbenchers. By the beginning of the 1990s it could be said that Thatcherism in Scotland had become a confused ideology, an uneasy balancing act between ideological purity, political personalities and a desire to play the Scottish card.

Led by the flamboyant former Solicitor-General Sir Nicholas Fairbairn, the rebel Scottish backbenchers (Bill Walker and Allan Stewart) threatened to vote against the government in the Bill's standing committee on the grounds that not enough time had been allocated for its consideration (Fairbairn refused to succumb to what he called the 'thumbscrews of exhaustion'[93]). Their actions, however, had less to do with ideological purity than a desire to

---

[90] Interview for *Glasgow Herald*.
[91] Rodger, 'The future of the legal profession in Scotland', *Juridical Review* 1 (1991), 2.
[92] Brown & McCrone, eds, *Scottish Government Yearbook 1991*, 13.
[93] Ibid., 14.

damage fatally Malcolm Rifkind. In the end, the Scottish Secretary was compelled to respond to the Law Society's persistent lobbying by agreeing not to immediately enact the provision which could award rights of audience to other professions.[94] He still claimed, however, to have ended the solicitors' monopoly, something the rebels preferred to call 'minimal non-effective competition'.[95] In England, too, the reforms were watered down. The Legal Affairs Commission was dropped and the training for non-barristers to plead in court made so tough that few bothered.

Although Forsyth had nothing directly to do with the rebellion, on the other hand he did nothing to discourage it. His supporters were also thought to have been behind lobby briefings to the effect that Rifkind was not up to the job of Scottish Secretary (deliberately timed during difficulties over Ravenscraig and Poll Tax rebates), and that Mrs Thatcher was actively considering his replacement with Forsyth. At the Scottish Conservative conference in May 1990 – held in Aberdeen rather than Perth for security reasons – matters reached a comic opera finale when Bill Walker emerged as Forsyth's self-appointed stalking horse. He called publicly for Rifkind's replacement with Forsyth, arguing that the recent regional council elections had proved once and for all that he had to go, an analysis he also despatched to the Prime Minister by letter. Rifkind, always quick off the mark with a response, brought down the house when he opened his keynote speech by looking at his watch and saying, 'Well, it's 12 o'clock and I'm still here.'[96] 'I didn't know Scotland was a West African republic,' remarked one senior Tory wryly, 'because that's where flight-lieutenants normally lead coup attempts.'[97]

Forsyth sensibly rejected the speculation in his chairman's speech at the same conference, saying he had 'quite enough on my plate at present'. He also launched a spirited defence of hard-line Thatcherism. 'Radical policies do pay dividends,' he argued. 'Being weak-kneed will neither achieve our objectives nor win us support. Where we show we shall not waiver we reap the dividends.'[98] Nevertheless, it was at this conference that the counter-revolution finally got under way, ostensibly led by Arthur Bell, chairman of the STRG. The counter-revolutionaries were convinced that details of recent events had been deliberately withheld from the Prime Minister and sought out the former Scottish Secretary George Younger, now preparing for an easier life as chairman-designate of the Royal Bank of Scotland, to tell Mrs Thatcher what had really been happening. Rifkind, too, appeared to have been emboldened by the attempted conference coup. When, just days after

---

[94] These provisions were only finally 'commenced' in March 2007 ahead of further, more fundamental, reforms to the Scottish legal market.
[95] Brown & McCrone, eds, 14.
[96] *Scotsman* 13/5/1990.
[97] Kemp, *The Hollow Drum*, 203. Bill Walker's nickname was 'Biggles'.
[98] *Glasgow Herald* 13/5/1990.

the Aberdeen gathering, the newly privatised British Steel decided finally to close the Ravenscraig steelworks, Rifkind stated publicly that he 'deplored'[99] the decision. This simply confirmed the suspicions of right-wing Tory MPs like Nick Ridley that the Scottish Office was the last bastion of the begging-bowl, subsidy-addicted corporatist culture of the Butskellite years. Ridley's Department of Trade and Industry even briefed the lobby to the effect that the Scottish Secretary had gone too far with his 'interventionist Labour-speak'.[100]

By way of response, Arthur Bell called publicly for the Scottish Conservative chairman to be sacked. Together with the resignations of three right-wing appointees from Scottish Central Office, this intervention weakened fatally the position of Forsyth (who dismissed the infighting as 'midsummer madness generated by the summer heat'[101]) who had hitherto felt able to endure criticism safe in the knowledge that he had the Prime Minister's full backing. It is possible, however, that Mrs Thatcher failed to grasp just how serious the situation in the Scottish party had become. 'She never accepted that . . . it was a dreadful business,' recalled Lord Lang, who was then a minister at the Scottish Office. 'I had to go to a lunch in Number 10 near the end. She came in and made an absolute beeline to me and said, "What's all this nonsense about Scotland?", as if it was just a storm in a teacup.'[102] Forsyth was further isolated when, in July 1990, he was almost alone in issuing a statement supporting Nick Ridley, who had been forced to resign from the Cabinet following an anti-German outburst in the *Spectator*.

The storm was still raging when, in August 1990, meetings between Mrs Thatcher and Rikfind, George Younger and the former Deputy Prime Minister Willie Whitelaw, convinced a reluctant Prime Minister that Forsyth (who 'was becoming depressed at the . . . unrelenting campaign pursued against him and his supporters') had to go. Her all-important postbag, bulging with letters both pro- and anti-Forsyth, also told her the game was up. 'It had been a brave attempt to bring the Scottish Tory Party into the latter half of the twentieth century and offer leadership and vision to people who had become all too used to losing or – even worse – winning on their opponents' terms,' recalled Mrs Thatcher bitterly. 'His [resignation] was taken as a sign that the attempt to extend Thatcherism to Scotland had come to an end. This combination of the Left and the traditional establishment of the Party to rebuff Thatcherism in Scotland was a prelude to the formation of the same alliance to oust me as leader of the Conservative Party a few weeks later – although I did not know it at the time.'[103]

---

[99] Brown & McCrone, eds, 22.

[100] Ibid., 23.

[101] *Scotsman* 6/8/1990.

[102] Interview with Lord Lang.

[103] Thatcher, *The Downing Street Years*, 623. James Gulliver, chairman of the Scottish Conservative Business Group, was reckoned by some observers to have been a decisive voice in Forsyth's removal on the basis that the internal row was having a negative impact on donations.

Although the link between the two events owed more to paranoia than political reality, the Forsyth saga undoubtedly weakened the Prime Minister's already precarious position within the party. If her attempt to impose the Thatcher revolution from above had failed in Scotland, some believed, then perhaps it was time for her to go. Mrs Thatcher, however, had no such intention, and appeared to further snub Rifkind when she promised to 'make a point of continuing to seek your advice and thoughts on future policy'[104] in her published reply to Forsyth's letter of resignation. And that, as Andrew Marr has written, 'was the beginning and the end of Scotto-Thatcherism in the Conservative Party'.[105]

The response from most in the Scottish party, not just those who had been agitating for Forsyth's removal, was relief. Senior ministers, however, were generally more gloomy. 'We shall be lucky to hold on to five seats at the next election,' one told the *Sunday Times* anonymously. 'This has solved nothing.'[106]

It had, at least, put an end to the public infighting while Mrs Thatcher neatly avoided losing Forsyth altogether by simultaneously promoting him to Minister of State at the Scottish Office, a face-saving compromise suggested by the ever-ingenious Rifkind. 'Once I knew he was ceasing to be Chairman I was relaxed about him staying in the Scottish Office,' recalled Sir Malcolm. 'I had no desire to humiliate him and he was a good Minister. We were short enough of talent as it was.'[107] Lord Sanderson of Bowden, close to Mrs Thatcher through his chairmanship of the National Union of Conservative and Unionist Associations Executive Committee (1981–86), succeeded Forsyth and promptly sacked all but one of his predecessor's appointments (although talk of him ordering the locks to be replaced at Chester Street was a newspaper fabrication).

Bill Hughes later judged that Forsyth had been guilty of immaturity, impatience and poor judgement during his tenure as chairman. But if that were true of him what did it reveal about Mrs Thatcher's judgement in appointing Forsyth in the first place? When asked if, in retrospect, mistakes had been made, she responded: 'None whatsoever, none whatsoever, he is a bonny fighter and so am I.' 'He has this tremendous political feel,' she added. 'Scottish to his bone-marrow and young and vital.'[108] Although only 36 when he became chairman, Forsyth did not feel 'young and vital' after more than a year in the job. 'It was a terrible time for me,' he reflected in 2008. 'I hated it.' He explained:

I think it was a mistake; I didn't want to do it. It was never going to work really because it put Malcolm Rifkind in a difficult position and it put me in a difficult

[104] Margaret Thatcher to Michael Forsyth, 7/9/1990, MTF.
[105] Marr, *The Battle for Scotland*, 171.
[106] *Sunday Times* 9/9/1990.
[107] Sir Malcolm Rifkind to the author, 30/10/2008.
[108] Interview for *Scotland on Sunday*, 13/9/1990, MTF.

position as his junior minister. I was 36 and saw things in black and white so I'm sure there were faults on both sides. I was very driven by our political agenda so I was probably not the best person to appoint as party chairman because schmoozing skills were not my thing. But what I was good at was campaigning, identifying weaknesses in my opponents and presenting policies in a way that attracted attention – that caused jealousies and resentments.

When eventually, in July 1990, Forsyth went to see the Prime Minister it was to persuade her to let him quit as chairman. He was aware there was a plot to move him to the Department of Energy (DoE) as Minister of State, something Forsyth resisted, seeing logistical, not to mention political, dis-advantages in moving to a UK ministry when he was trying to defend a marginal seat. Mrs Thatcher agreed, but deferred a decision on the chair-manship until September. By then, Forsyth had resolved to quit not just the chairmanship but the government itself:

> I felt I was getting nowhere. I took a copy of the *Daily Record* – which was reporting that I was to be sacked, the result of briefing from someone senior – with me [to the meeting]. She said: 'I want you to stay; you have my support'. I threw it [the *Daily Record*] across to her and said 'this is where we are Margaret'. She threw it back at me and said 'but it isn't true, I want to promote you to Minister of State'.

She now meant as Minister of State at the Scottish Office, Forsyth having made it clear he would not accept the same post at the DoE. 'She wouldn't take no for an answer so I agreed,' recalled Forsyth, who then shared the Prime Minister's car en route to the House of Commons in a public show of support. 'One of the reasons I gave for going was that I could see a cabal forming for her to go,' he explained. 'I felt I had become a liability to her; I felt I was damaging her. In a game of chess the most important thing is to protect your king but I'd become a stone in her shoe.' Nigel Lawson had recently resigned as Chancellor while Mrs Thatcher's final, ultimately destructive, row with Sir Geoffrey Howe was also looming. 'If she had wanted me to run Scotland she should have appointed me Secretary of State. What she did [making him chairman] wasn't good for me or for Malcolm. But in the end I did what she said because she was the boss.'[109]

MAGGIE! MAGGIE! MAGGIE!

As well as the Poll Tax and her party's continuing woes north of the border, the question that surfaced most frequently during Prime Ministerial inter-views in 1989/90 was that of Mrs Thatcher's personal unpopularity in

---

[109] Interview with Lord Forsyth.

Scotland. This provoked a range of responses from contrite puzzlement to barely concealed irritation. Both were on display during a celebrated encounter with the then little-known broadcaster Kirsty Wark. 'You have always said that you didn't enter politics in order to be popular,' began Wark, 'but why are you so unpopular in Scotland?' Mrs Thatcher's response was polite, but also cool. 'Well, I don't think I am necessarily the right person to answer that but I wouldn't entirely say it was true,' she said. 'What does please me is that Scotland is taking advantage of all the policies which is right, because I regard it as a very great honour to be Prime Minister of Scotland.'

Although constitutionally correct, Mrs Thatcher's assertion that she was 'Prime Minister of Scotland', together with frequent allusions to 'we in Scotland',[110] ensured that Wark versus Thatcher – broadcast on BBC Scotland in March 1990 – became one of the definitive expressions of an apparently imperious Prime Minister's disconnection from her Scottish subjects. Although a talented television performer, Mrs Thatcher's appearances had grown strained since Brian Walden grilled her over Nigel Lawson's interview the year before. With Wark pursuing a similarly aggressive line of questioning, Mrs Thatcher frequently appeared taken aback and unsure of how to respond.

The sexual dynamic was also important. Even in 1990 a woman aggressively interviewing another woman was not a common sight, and certainly not an experience the Prime Minister was used to. It is commonly believed that Mrs Thatcher's policies harmed women despite her achievements in a man's world, although reality, as ever, was more complicated. Benefits stagnated, which generally harmed women, although in Scotland an increasing trend towards part-time work resulted in the number of unemployed females actually decreasing from 1979 to 1987. The expansion of Silicon Glen and Edinburgh's financial services sector increased employment opportunities for women, although jobs in the former were generally low-paid assembly work. Changes in housing were also liberating. Higher employment levels allowed more to gain tenancies or ownership in their own right, while the Matrimonial Homes (Family Protection) (Scotland) Act 1981 conferred occupancy rights to the matrimonial home irrespective of ownership.

In narrowly defined feminist terms, however, Mrs Thatcher did little and nor did she seek to, prouder of being the first scientist to become Prime Minister rather than the first woman. Was there an element of misogyny in the Scots' reaction to what one journalist called 'a bustling Englishwoman with a comically false upper-class accent'[111]? It is hard to escape the

---

[110] 'The Margaret Thatcher Interview' (BBC Scotland) 9/3/1990, MTF. 'I said that I had often heard her say "You in Scotland", when she was north of the Border,' recalled Sir Malcolm Rifkind by way of an explanation for the curious phraseology. 'It made it sound as if she was visiting a foreign country. Try not to use that phrase, I suggested. She took the point and was in full agreement. She went in to record the interview and Michael Forsyth and I watched on the monitor. To our disbelief we heard her saying "We in Scotland" not once, but several times. Not what I had had in mind!' (Sir Malcolm Rifkind to the author, 6/12/2008)

[111] *Guardian* 23/4/1990.

conclusion that there was. 'Scots, even socialists, expect women to keep their place,' was George Younger's judgement in 1993. 'Everyone who ever canvassed during her time experienced the coarse and uncivilised abuse about "that bloody woman".'[112] Both Willie Whitelaw and Malcolm Rifkind were also fond of quoting Lord Home, who apparently remarked: 'Mrs Thatcher was a woman, an English woman, and a bossy English woman.' One of these, it was implied, might have been acceptable but not all three.

Mrs Thatcher, by and large, concurred. 'I sometimes think that the decisions that you have to take in my job as Prime Minister, if a man took them they would be – goodness me – great leadership, courageous, just what we expect of a leader,' she told Kirsty Wark in March 1990. 'Somehow they don't always expect that of a woman, but nevertheless women have to take them.'[113] The Thatcher–Scotland dichotomy, therefore, cooled even further. 'At the Scottish end of the relationship,' observed Ian Aitken in the *Guardian*, 'it is probably fair to say that it ranges all the way from irritated incomprehension to something not far short of paranoid hatred. Even quite Conservative-minded Scots find that the Iron Lady personifies all the characteristics they most dislike in the English.' Aitken's list of what it was that rankled with the Scots included 'a suffocating self-righteousness, coupled with a patronising air of regret that Scots seem congenitally unable to recognise what is good for them'.[114] The result was a collective Caledonian flinch each time the Prime Minister appeared in Scotland. Indeed, at endless rallies opposition to the government was stated in an intensely personal way. 'Maggie! Maggie! Maggie!' anti-Poll Tax demonstrators would chant, 'Out! Out! Out!'[115]

The Prime Minister often made things worse by alluding again and again to out-moded Scottish stereotypes. When the generally sympathetic journalist Geoffrey Parkhouse asked Mrs Thatcher about the 'sentiment' of being Scottish she listed Scottish regiments, names and scenery, the sort of Victoriana she regularly resorted to when under pressure. 'All that is true,' said Kirsty Wark in her televised confrontation with Mrs Thatcher, 'but don't you understand that people find that rather patronising?'

> Well, if it did, I'm very sorry. I come from a county in the Midlands – Lincolnshire, I'm a Lincolnshire girl – wherever I go in the world people come up and say "You're Lincolnshire, so am I". We feel a fellow feeling, just because we come from that part. I'm really rather proud of things that went on in Lincolnshire, so I know what it's like to feel pride and I just assumed that other people from other regions, other countries, other nationalities would feel the same pride. And if they did, well, I do hope they won't take it that way.[116]

---

[112] *Scotland on Sunday* 17/10/1993.
[113] 'The Margaret Thatcher Interview'.
[114] *Guardian* 23/4/1990.
[115] The author's childhood memories.
[116] 'The Margaret Thatcher Interview'.

And as if to demonstrate the Prime Minister's lack of feel when it came to grasping Scottish national sentiment, her last speech to the Scottish Tory conference trampled over all the usual tartan territory. 'Denis has his Scottish favourites too,' she joked after praising Scotland's thriving cities. 'Turnberry, Carnoustie and Gleneagles. Not to mention Glenfiddich, Glenmorangie, and Glenlivet! And at the end of a difficult day, I am inclined to share his enthusiasm, for the latter at least.' There then followed the usual name-checks for David Hume and Adam Smith, condemnation of Labour's devolution plans and an uncharacteristically aggressive assault on the SNP, a party which usually did not warrant more than a passing reference in her Scottish speeches. As with devolution, Mrs Thatcher sought to contrast her interpretation of independence with that of the SNP:

I don't mean the SNP's kind of independence. That would impoverish and isolate the Scottish nation. It would mean not just the end of the United Kingdom, but the end of Scotland as we know it . . . I want the sort of independence which enriches the lives of the people. The independence that comes from owning your own home, from owning a little bit of Scotland. The independence that comes from having a stake in the company for which you work, and in other companies too. The independence that comes from being able to build up savings to hand on to your children. In short, the independence that comes from running your own life – and not being told how to run it by the Socialist state.

'And never forget,' concluded Mrs Thatcher melodramatically, 'the SNP are a Socialist Party – the Socialist Nationalist Party.'[117] All this was music to Alex Salmond's ears, for he understood that even if most Scots did not actively desire independence, nor did they want the Prime Minister attacking a legitimate expression of Scottish national identity. 'My own view is that people in Scotland, whatever their view on devolution,' said Graeme Carter, Rifkind's special adviser in the late 1980s, 'believed that Mrs T. by not giving way on constitutional reform was depriving them of something they believed they wanted, not that they necessarily desperately wanted.'[118] As a result, Mrs Thatcher unwittingly increased support for some sort of home rule. 'Think of it – Mrs Thatcher as the midwife of Scottish Home Rule,' wrote David McCrone in 1989. 'Perhaps someone should tell her?'[119]

By mid 1990, however, Mrs Thatcher's personal unpopularity was by no means limited to Scotland. There was a feeling across the UK that she had gone on too long, and indeed she had resisted advice from both political colleagues and her husband to call it a day on reaching her tenth anniversary

---

[117] Speech to Scottish Conservative conference, 12/5/1990, MTF.
[118] Graeme Carter to the author, 27/8/2008.
[119] *Radical Scotland*, June/July 1989.

as premier. Her last Scottish speech demonstrated her belief that resignation would jeopardise all her achievements to date. Not only did she interpret the recent regional council elections as the beginning of a Tory recovery in Scotland (the Tory share of the vote increased from 16.9 to 19.6 per cent), but repeated her determination to go on and on with her reforming agenda. 'And we shall continue those policies,' she declared. 'They revived our country's fortunes – and we shall take them further. There's a lot more to do – a woman's work is never done. Radical policies have helped us to win three General Elections. And they will win us a fourth. Four on the trot – that's the target.'[120] Two years after her fourth election victory, Mrs Thatcher reasoned in 1993, she would have stood aside for a carefully groomed successor although, as she conceded (paraphrasing Burns), 'the best laid plans gang aft agley'.[121]

The vision of Mrs Thatcher leading the Conservative Party into a fourth general election campaign in 1991 or 1992 filled many of her senior colleagues with dread. But for many opposition Scottish politicians it was almost desirable. The reaction in Scotland to a fourth Thatcher government (especially if the number of Scottish Tory MPs declined further), the argument went, would either lead inevitably to some form of devolution or to a massive upsurge in pressure for full independence. So another electoral endorsement for Mrs Thatcher's brand of unionism would, in an ultimate piece of political irony, become a vote to end the three-century old union between England and Scotland. With that analysis in mind, the term 'doomsday scenario' seemed strangely apt.

TWILIGHT THATCHERISM

'As Socialism goes down all over Europe, so it will be in Britain,' declared Mrs Thatcher in her final Scottish Conservative conference speech. 'And tomorrow, as today, will be ours.'[122] But while the 1990s would certainly belong to Thatcherites – whether Conservative or New Labour – it would not belong to Mrs Thatcher personally.

Indeed, the final year or so of Mrs Thatcher's premiership produced an odd mix of policies and initiatives which lacked coherence or the populist touch present at the peak of her powers. Perhaps her swansong in terms of employment policy was the abolition in April 1989 of the National Dock Labour Scheme (NDLS), a relic of post-war industrial relations which guaranteed work for dockers even when there was none. Norman Fowler, then Employment Secretary, told MPs the scheme had become an anachronism which stood in the way of a modern and efficient ports industry. Lord Sanderson, Fowler's ministerial counterpart at the Scottish Office, remembers travelling to Aberdeen to announce the news to the city's dockers.

---

[120] Speech to Scottish Conservative conference.
[121] *The Downing Street Years* (BBC) 29/10/1993.
[122] Speech to Scottish Conservative conference.

'They weren't very happy,'[123] he recalled. The dockers came out on strike in July but by then it was too late. Remarkably, even the Labour Party barely mustered opposition to the move. It seemed that even the party responsible for setting up the NDLS had come to accept Thatcherite logic.

There were other, more minor, Thatcherite flourishes as the decade drew to a close. Despite a vigorous campaign by George Younger and the Labour MP George Foulkes to prevent Thatcherism in the sky, CBI Scotland's policy of 'Open Skies' was finally taken up by the government and as a result ended Prestwick's jealously guarded status as Scotland's sole transatlantic gateway. Proposals for the UK to switch to European Time (sometimes called 'double summer time') also provoked a mini-Scottish Lobby, and gave rise to further accusations that ministers did not care about Scotland. Labour pointed out that Scottish farmers would have to start work in darkness, while the government argued that fewer children would be killed returning from school in the evening. The idea was quietly shelved in June. The creation of a Child Support Agency, meanwhile, was Mrs Thatcher's response to growing numbers of children born out of wedlock. The flagship Environmental Protection Bill perhaps represented the most positive legacy of twilight Thatcherism. Although a UK Bill, it included tartan edges through its proposal to merge the Scottish parts of the Nature Conservancy Council (NCC) with the Countryside Commission in Scotland to create a new agency called Scottish Natural Heritage. The decentralist Labour Party paradoxically attacked the Bill as weakening the effectiveness of the UK NCC, while Rifkind counter-attacked on the basis that the opposition were resisting further administrative devolution to Scotland.

The Scottish Constitutional Convention, meanwhile, was preparing to release its final report with a recommendation for the creation of a Scottish Parliament. The frequent claim that the Convention represented Scottish public opinion, however, was dismissed curtly by Mrs Thatcher. 'It is not a cross-section,' she declared when interviewed by *Scotland on Sunday* in September 1990. 'What you have got in the Scottish Convention is self-selected people who already hold a particular view – that is very far from being a cross-section. We had a long dialogue in the House of Commons, we had a referendum, the results you know.'[124] As far as the Prime Minister was concerned, the devolution issue had been settled once and for all in 1979.

Broadcasting, on the other hand, was ripe for further reform. Indeed, Mrs Thatcher had warned broadcasters after the 1987 election that their industry was 'the last bastion of restrictive practices'.[125] The Broadcasting Act of 1990 meant that ITV franchises – what Mrs Thatcher called 'little local monopolies' who thought they had a 'divine right'[126] to broadcast – were no longer automatically renewed but instead handed to the highest bidder. The auction

[123] Interview with Lord Sanderson, 29/8/2008.
[124] Interview for *Scotland on Sunday*.
[125] Campbell, *The Iron Lady*, 567.
[126] Interview for *Glasgow Herald*.

took place some months after Mrs Thatcher left office and was, as many predicted, a fiasco. Some existing companies like STV had their franchises renewed for a mere £2,000, while Grampian paid £250,000 and others millions. Although this aspect of the reforms was criticised for lowering broadcasting standards and penalising otherwise successful franchise-holders, it also changed the face of Scottish television in arguably more positive ways. New licensing arrangements gave the green light to more cable and satellite channels, while the BBC and ITV were obliged to buy 25 per cent of their programmes from independent producers, a requirement which helped companies like Wark Clements (co-founded by Mrs Thatcher's March 1990 interrogator, Kirsty, that same year) become a major, not to mention commercially successful, force in UK broadcasting.

The 1990 Broadcasting Act also committed £8 million to Gaelic broadcasting, a result of heavy lobbying by Malcolm Rifkind, dispensed to Scotland's public, commercial and independent broadcasters via the Gaelic Television Fund. This rounded off a positive, if modest, Thatcherite legacy in terms of Scotland's native tongue. *An Comunn Gaidhealach*, or the Royal National Mod, had received direct Scottish Office support since 1979–80, while *Comunn na Gaidhlig*, the Gaelic development body, was established in 1984 and received similar central government funding. A scheme of specific grants for Gaelic education had also begun in 1986, although even this did little to stem its continuing decline as a spoken language.

It also did little to stem the continuing electoral decline of the Scottish Conservatives, never particularly strong in any case in Gaelic-speaking areas. And although the ousting of Forsyth as chairman had momentarily cleared the air in the party, his departure had done little to remedy more profound problems. 'It is undoubtedly the case, particularly here in Scotland, that the perceived aggressive, hectoring attitude of the Prime Minister is doing us enormous damage,' wrote the SCUA vice-president Adrian Shinwell[127] to the SCUA president Sir Michael Hirst on 6 November 1990. 'It matters not whether she is right or wrong, it is her presidential style, her tone and her manner which are creating the concern.' He went on:

> If we are to pretend that the Prime Minister is other than an electoral liability in Scotland, then we are failing to recognise the deep-rooted concern that is expressed all around us . . . Given her enormous energy, ability and commitment to the country in the past, it would be a tragedy if the Prime Minister were to be brought down by her own Party and yet I fear that this will happen if she does not see the writing on the wall and step down with her reputation intact.

'The fight is no longer for the minds of the Scottish people but for their hearts,' concluded Shinwell. 'Without them, we shall lose and we shall have

---

[127] Shinwell's political provenance was not exactly true blue. His great uncle was the legendary Red Clydesider Manny Shinwell.

failed our Party and our country.'[128] Shinwell's letter was unknowingly prescient. Just days later, Sir Geoffrey Howe's carefully calculated resignation speech precipitated a seismic series of events which resulted in Mrs Thatcher being brought down, as Shinwell had predicted, by her own party.

The leadership battle which followed was not exactly a model of political campaigning. The former Scottish Secretary George Younger chaired it rather half-heartedly, while the third-generation Scot Alan Clark was alarmed to discover the future laird of Islay, Peter Morrison, dozing in his office, so complacent was he about the result. The flamboyant Michael Heseltine, Mrs Thatcher's only challenger for the leadership, was not exactly Scotland-friendly. But he had Celtic origins (born in Swansea), considerable panache, interventionist enthusiasm for urban regeneration and regional policy and, above all, hatred for the disastrous Poll Tax.[129]

It was not to be, either for Heseltine or Thatcher. When the Prime Minister won the first ballot but without a sufficient margin to avoid another, she was reduced to consulting Cabinet colleagues as to whether she should carry on. Rifkind ('probably my sharpest personal critic in the Cabinet') told her bluntly that she should not, but promised not to campaign against her if she chose otherwise. 'Silently,' recorded Mrs Thatcher in her memoirs, 'I thanked God for small mercies.'[130] Others brought similar messages. It was, as she later recalled, 'treachery with a smile on its face'.[131] Peter Lane, chairman of Conservative Party's National Union executive, also took soundings at constituency level. He found that 70 per cent of associations in England wanted Mrs Thatcher to stay; in Scotland, by contrast, most constituency chairmen were loyal, but party workers wanted her to go.

That evening, as the Prime Minister prepared her speech for a Labour-initiated no-confidence debate due the following day, several true believers came to Downing Street to convince her to fight on. Representatives of the No Turning Back group, including the St Andreans Michael Forsyth and Michael Fallon, implored Mrs Thatcher to fight the second ballot, but 'Their arguments were demolished, rather bravely, by John Gummer who was there helping with the speech.'[132] When Forsyth turned up again at 6.30 a.m. the following morning – according to some reports in tears – Charles Powell, Mrs Thatcher's trusted foreign affairs private secretary, refused him access.

Mrs Thatcher chaired her final Cabinet two-and-a-half hours later, a meeting brought forward to allow ministers to attend the memorial service for Lady Home (ironically, the leadership system which defeated Thatcher had

---

[128] Adrian Shinwell to Micky Hirst, 6/11/1990, Acc 12514 (4), SCUAP.

[129] 'I fear your request is unrealistic,' he replied when asked by the author what his pitch to Scotland would have been. 'I do not want to invent attitudes in answer to questions nearly twenty years out of date! Getting rid of the poll tax was the obvious first task.' (Lord Heseltine to the author, 2/6/2008)

[130] Thatcher, *The Downing Street Years*, 852.

[131] *The Downing Street Years* (BBC) 29/10/1993.

[132] Campbell, *The Iron Lady*, 739.

been devised by her husband Lord Home). A statement was issued to the effect that Mrs Thatcher would not contest the second ballot and would resign as Prime Minister as soon as her successor as Conservative leader was elected. She almost broke down twice while reading her resignation statement to the Cabinet. Lord Mackay of Clashfern, always a favourite of the Prime Minister, then read a statement of appreciation on behalf of the Cabinet.

Mrs Thatcher delivered a virtuoso performance in that afternoon's no-confidence debate. 'The Prime Minister is aware that I detest every single one of her domestic policies,' spat the SNP MP and future deputy leader Jim Sillars in one exchange, 'and I have never hidden that fact.' The outgoing Prime Minister, however, gave as good as she got. 'I think that the Hon. Gentleman knows that I have the same contempt for his socialist policies as the people of east[ern] Europe, who have experienced them, have for theirs.'[133]

And at Mrs Thatcher's final Prime Minister's Questions on 27 November (she resigned formally the following day), one exchange neatly captured the 11-year-old Thatcher–Scotland dynamic. 'When the Prime Minister recalls the day when she quoted St. Francis of Assisi on the steps of Downing Street,' asked the Labour MP for Edinburgh East, Gavin Strang, 'will she contemplate the increase in family poverty that resulted from her repeated refusal to increase child benefit?' He continued:

Will she recall the increased hardship that resulted from the 1988 social security changes? Will she think about the homeless, whose numbers have doubled since she came to power? Is she aware that Opposition Members represent communities some of which have still not recovered from the unprecedented rates of unemployment that she inflicted on them in the early 1980s? Those are some of the reasons why she will go down in history as the Prime Minister who rewarded the rich and punished the poor.

Having handled every other question with panache that afternoon, Strang's onslaught – the last Commons question to Mrs Thatcher as Prime Minister – presented no problem for the Iron Lady. 'Perhaps the Hon. Gentleman will also recall that Scotland is enjoying greater prosperity than it has ever known under any previous Government;' she responded, 'that there are now 2 million more jobs than there were when I took over; and that, remembering the situation when I took office in 1979, there is much more peace in the coal industry now than there was then . . . He should also recall that we have had the lowest number of strikes this year in the whole post-war period.'[134] Fittingly, the most recent Employment Act had reached the statute book just four weeks before, outlawing the closed shop and enabling employers to dismiss the instigators of 'wildcat' strikes.

---

[133] Hansard 181 c445–53.
[134] Ibid., c741.

In Scotland it was almost as if a palpable sense of relief greeted the news of the Prime Minister's resignation. A sense that she had gone; she had dispensed unwanted medicine, indeed awful and often painful medicine, but nurse Thatcher had finally gone. 'Thatcherism is dead', rejoiced Arthur Bell, 'long live Conservatism.'[135] Leaving Downing Street for the last time on 28 November, Mrs Thatcher said 'we're very happy that we leave the United Kingdom in a very, very much better state than when we came here eleven and a half years ago'.[136]

The *Scotsman* judged Mrs Thatcher's legacy to be a 'revolution past its sell-by date' and reiterated all the familiar explanations for its rejection in Scotland. There, the editorial asserted, 'sovereignty resides in the people' and she had failed to appreciate the Scots' 'traditional sense of community and their ancient links with Europe'. That she tried to 'hijack' Adam Smith just made things worse. 'Private affluence and public squalour [sic] flourished as nationalised industries were sold into the private sector,' it continued. 'It would be hypocritical of us to say anything other than that we think it right that Mrs Thatcher has resigned.' The *Glasgow Herald* judged that 'Thatcher's bellicosity, her determination to confront, her homespun verities, are not as relevant now as they were in the eighties when the enemies were so largely within'.[137] More bluntly, the *Daily Record* hailed her departure with an editorial headlined: 'Jobless at last.'[138]

Representatives of civic society in Scotland also condemned Mrs Thatcher's record in Scotland as uniformly bad. Bill Speirs, the deputy general secretary of the STUC, said the 'lives blighted by unemployment and poverty throughout the Thatcher years will rejoice at her going, particularly in such an ignominious and humiliating fashion'. Alex Salmond, elected leader of the SNP a few months earlier, said he was over the moon. 'Thatcher has done enormous damage to Scotland over the past 11 years', he said, 'and we are delighted to be rid of her.' Much like Mrs Thatcher, Salmond was fond of deploying the royal 'we'. Two days after the Prime Minister's resignation, *Towards Scotland's Parliament* was published by the Scottish Constitutional Convention, depicting devolution as a device to strengthen Scotland's place in the Union.

In local government there was also an unmistakable air of 'rejoice, rejoice'. 'Thatcherism has produced not only an economic system which I find totally unacceptable,' said one council leader, 'but attitudes within the whole of our society that I find totally unacceptable.' The Labour leader of Dundee District Council, Mary Ward, meanwhile, described Mrs Thatcher's departure as good news for Dundee but added that the city was 'still awaiting the departure of Thatcherism'. 'The industrial map of Scotland', she added,

---

[135] *Sunday Times* 25/11/1990.
[136] Remarks departing Downing Street, 28/11/1990, MTF.
[137] *Glasgow Herald* 23/11/1990.
[138] *Daily Record* 23/11/1990.

'remains pitted with the bomb sites of Tory party policy.' Even Lord James Douglas-Hamilton, a minister at the Scottish Office, had no choice but to acknowledge that Mrs Thatcher had not always endeared herself to Scotland. But, he added, 'I think in the years to come Scots will appreciate her great strengths.'

'One often reads that she does not care about Scotland,' reflected Malcolm Rifkind in the *Scotsman*. 'It couldn't be more untrue. She is as concerned about Scotland's welfare and prosperity as about that of England and the United Kingdom as a whole.' True, he conceded, 'there may be occasions when she has not understood our sensitivities or preoccupations, but the same can be said about Neil Kinnock.' Above all, Rifkind concluded, 'she shares one characteristic of supreme importance to most Scots. She believes in advancement on merit alone and has little time and no sympathy for snobbery, privilege or prejudice.'[139]

The truth was that for many Scots the contrary often appeared to be true. But although Mrs Thatcher was gone and the song, as Irving Berlin once wrote, was ended, the Thatcherite melody was to linger on – even in Scotland.

---

[139] *Scotsman* 23/11/1990.

Chapter 10

THATCHER AND SONS (1990–2009)

Most of the claims for advances made under her administration are bogus. True, unemployment figures have been dropping, but only from the astronomical heights to which she pushed them in the early 1980s. The corner shop philosophy of putting a nest egg aside, paying your bills, living within your means, etc., has ended up with an uncontrolled spending spree of overdrafts, crippling mortgages and credit card debt run riot.[1]

Donald Stewart, *A Scot at Westminster*

There was, and is, no dividing line between a government's social and economic policies, with the former shaped and, in her case, crushed by the consequences of the latter. The society we have today, with generations who have never experienced the world of work, with all the attendant social ills that has created, is a direct consequence of the brutal market economy she sponsored with so much relish.

Jim Sillars, *Herald* 22/8/2008

IT MUST HAVE BEEN tempting for Scottish Conservatives to believe that the resignation of Mrs Thatcher in November 1990 had solved, in one brutal stroke, most of their political problems in Scotland. Activists reported relief that less than a week ahead of two by-elections in Paisley[2] the inevitable doorstep resistance to Thatcherism had been removed and they would no longer have to make excuses for 'that woman'. A System Three poll conducted after Michael Heseltine's challenge, but before the Prime Minister's resignation, appeared to boost the Scottish Tories, nudging them ahead of the SNP.

'We had to accept that, although irrational, a real dislike of Mrs Thatcher existed in Scotland,' said the future Scottish Tory MEP Struan Stevenson, while Arthur Bell, the former Scottish Tory Reform Group chairman and

---

[1] Stewart, *A Scot at Westminster*, 90.
[2] In the event, the Conservative vote in both by-elections held up well.

arch Thatcher critic, speculated the party would 'perhaps be less subject to personalised campaigns which I perceived as racist and sexist against Mrs Thatcher'. The Scottish Conservatives, he added, could now 'tackle those problems within Scotland without being sidetracked into debating the personality of the Prime Minister'.

Relief, however, was not the reaction of every Conservative in Scotland. 'I think there will be some members of the party who will find it difficult to conceive of life after Thatcher', Struan Stevenson conceded, 'and may decide no longer to serve the party in whatever position they currently find themselves.' Indeed, the party's Chester Street headquarters was reportedly inundated by phone calls from activists, many accompanied by threats of resignation. The vice-chairman of the Scottish Young Conservatives, Adrian Goulbourn, even claimed that 'revulsion'[3] rather than relief typified the true reaction of the Scottish Conservative Party.

In the leadership campaign that followed, hopes grew among pro-devolution campaigners that whoever succeeded Mrs Thatcher might engage more constructively with the Scottish Constitutional Convention (SCC), the initial recommendations from which appeared just days after the Iron Lady left Downing Street. Soon, however, each of the three candidates – John Major, Douglas Hurd and Michael Heseltine – ruled out any U-turn on devolution (all three also pledged abolition of the Poll Tax). The 'Thatcher veto' may have been removed, but it had swiftly been replaced by three more.

The *Glasgow Herald* backed Douglas Hurd, who boasted Scottish roots and had opposed Mrs Thatcher's U-turn on devolution in 1976. The initial favourite, Michael Heseltine, had no Scottish lineage but had written glowingly of the Scottish Development Agency in his book, *Where There's A Will*, and seemed likely to be more sensitive to the Scottish dimension. John Major, on the other hand, was presented as Thatcherism with a human face. Supported by, among others, the Scottish Office minister Ian Lang, the grey man from Brixton won.

On the face of it, John Major removed most of the problems associated with his predecessor in Scotland: he was male, from humble origins, possessed a curiously classless accent, and appeared to be more sensitive. He also moved swiftly to remove key Thatcherite shibboleths from the agenda. Notice was given that the Poll Tax was to be scrapped ('its unpopularity . . . was central to the argument for devolution,' observed Major in his memoirs, 'The Poll Tax cast a long shadow.'[4]) while the new Prime Minister promised to 'listen and learn' during his first visit to Edinburgh.

Changes at the Scottish Office, meanwhile, were also calculated not to offend. The new Secretary of State, Ian Lang, was a middle-class professional who was Thatcherite by instinct if not in tone ('his persuasive qualities were

---

[3] *Glasgow Herald* 23/11/1990.
[4] Major, *The Autobiography*, 171.

exactly what we needed', thought Major, 'to address the Scots' perception of the Tories as uncaring and extreme'[5]), while contrary to expectation a shell-shocked Michael Forsyth was kept in place as Minister of State and joined by another St Andrean, Allan Stewart, who rejoined the government – paradoxically as his heroine left – with responsibility for the Community Charge and what was left of Scottish industry. The St Andrews 'school' of economics, not to mention the No Turning Back group, appeared to be in the ascendant at St Andrew's House.

Some on the left of the Scottish party feared this Forsyth–Stewart axis would reopen old wounds, yet to heal after the Forsyth saga the previous year, but Mrs Thatcher's protégé had already started to mature politically while Stewart, never a rhetorical extremist, kept his head down and prepared to unpick a system of local government finance he had strongly supported for the past five years. Major, meanwhile, got off to a good start with the voting public, although in Scotland his election did not immediately transform Conservative fortunes. The first System Three poll of 1991 saw the party recover by just three points to reach 21 per cent. To the Scottish Tory peer Lord Fraser, however, the change of political atmosphere was palpable. 'I remember John Major visiting one of those woollen mill shops on Princes Street just after he became Prime Minister,' he recalled, 'and people were outside applauding; if she'd been there people would've been throwing eggs.'[6]

Major, at least, was prepared to try and halt his party's seemingly inexorable decline north of the border. Interestingly, neither Major nor Lang ('her departure enabled us to restore our position in Scotland'[7]) considered the Thatcher legacy a handicap in doing so. In UK terms, however, Mrs Thatcher had other ideas. 'I shan't be pulling the levers there,' she told the press after Major's election, 'but I shall be a very good back-seat driver.'[8] Although a comment without intended malice it nevertheless gave the impression that Major would not be his own man. But even had Mrs Thatcher remained silent, her shadow would still have loomed large, not just over Major but also his Labour successors. It fell not just in Whitehall and Downing Street but at St Andrew's House and Bute House in Edinburgh. The perception grew that Major would be a 'son of Thatcher'. Inescapably he was, as were all of the mainstream politicians who followed her: John Major, Tony Blair, David Cameron and Gordon Brown at a UK level; Ian Lang, Michael Forsyth, Alex Salmond and his Labour predecessors as First Minister in Scotland. All, whether they admitted it or not, were

---

[5] Ibid., 417. Madsen Pirie of the Adam Smith Institute later told Ian Lang about Mrs Thatcher's reaction to his appointment. 'Apparently she had a glass of whisky in hand and exclaimed: "I was told I couldn't do that",' Lang recalled. 'That was quite revealing because she'd toyed with moving Malcolm Rifkind, but was told she couldn't because he was liked and we needed continuity.' (Interview with Lord Lang, 11/11/2008)

[6] Interview with Lord Fraser, 9/6/2008.

[7] Interview with Lord Lang.

[8] *Independent* 27/11/1990.

influenced by Mrs Thatcher and, as Gerry Hassan has written, 'their politics shaped, defined and framed by her and her achievements'.[9]

'TREADING ON EGGSHELLS'

Major indicated on his first visit to Scotland in January 1991 that he was willing to 'listen' to Scottish grievances on the constitution and other matters, although his open mind clearly did not extend to the SCC, something the Prime Minister dismissed as 'a fraud, a joke, a Labour Party front which has decided nothing'.[10] It seems, however, that Major and Lang had already decided that the constitutional status quo was a Pandora's Box best left unopened, as it had been by Mrs Thatcher during the previous decade.

On a second visit to Scotland in March, Major went even further, declaring that he was not prepared to take on board demands for a Scottish Assembly with tax-raising powers. There were calls from some on the left of the Scottish party to capitalise on the post-Thatcherite mood and actually endorse devolution, perhaps scrapping the regional tier of Scottish local government as a *quid pro quo*, but this was never likely to be entertained by Major. The new Scottish Secretary, meanwhile, remained convinced that 'there were more people against devolution at that time than there were Conservatives'.[11]

It was this rationale that guided Conservative thinking both in the run up to, and after the 1992 general election. Until then Thatcherism consolidated itself in Scotland, albeit with mixed results. In terms of health and education – the focus of twilight Thatcherism steered by Michael Forsyth in the late 1980s – there was a palpable lack of success. By August 1991 only six of Scotland's 53 hospital units had, or were about to, make applications to become self-governing, while only eight out of 1,096 Scottish general practices had opted to take control of their own budgets. Similarly, no Technology Academies were established, academic testing was boycotted across Scotland, and few schools opted out of state control despite Forsyth-inspired ballots. Major, therefore, resisted advice to promote grant-maintained schools more strongly in Scotland, explaining that he 'trusted the judgement of Scottish ministers that this would be seen as imposing English solutions on Scotland'. 'In this,' he added in his memoirs, 'as in many other areas with Scotland, I felt we were treading on eggshells.'[12]

More positive was the continued growth of the Scottish economy, although the political benefits of this were mitigated by the final demise of Ravenscraig in April 1992,[13] by which point unemployment in Lanarkshire remained high

---

[9] www.opendemocracy.net 26/8/2008.
[10] *Radical Scotland* February/March 1991.
[11] Interview with Lord Lang.
[12] Major, *The Autobiography*, 422–23.
[13] Ironically, the closure of Ravenscraig later gave Scotland a head start in reducing carbon emissions.

at 14.4 per cent. In the rest of Scotland, however, the number of people out of work had been falling steadily since the late 1980s. Indeed, for a period Scottish unemployment levels were actually below the UK average. While England and Wales entered recession by the usual growth measurements, Scotland did not. 'In addition, the Scottish economy was now more diversi-fied,' wrote the historian Tom Devine. 'The old and risky dependence on one or two exporting giants had been reduced and instead the industrial structure now resembled more closely that of the UK as a whole.'[14]

One aspect of the Scottish economy, however, did not resemble that of the UK. Following more than a decade of Thatcherism, with its emphasis on innovation and enterprise, Scotland's business start-up rate was still lamen-table. Scottish Enterprise devoted a lot of time and money to its Business Birth Rate Strategy, but the figures barely budged. A well-received report, *Scotland's Business Birth Rate* (1993), surveyed companies established in the UK since 1978 which were still operating independently by 1990. While in the south-east of England there were 4,801 such companies per million of the population, in the West Midlands the comparative figure was 2,818 and in Scotland just 1,807. Not only were entrepreneurs in Scotland perceived to make less of a contribution to society than in England and Wales, but the report identified a greater belief that government investment, rather than private enterprise, was more likely to create jobs. Scottish Enterprise, however, failed to meet its own target of 10 per cent growth for business start-ups, and the rate actually fell between 1993 and 1999.

Once-mighty Scottish industries, meanwhile, continued to disappear from the political agenda and therefore the public consciousness. The announce-ment of further pit closures was clumsily handled and, by 1991, the National Union of Mineworkers had fewer than 2,000 members in Scotland.[15] Ex-pectations of victory in any future confrontation between organised labour and the state were now but a pipe dream. Even so, public attitudes in Scotland seemed curiously immovable. In 1992, 42 per cent of Scots believed public services and industry should be state-owned, compared with 34 per cent in the Midlands and southern England.

'It was the success of the changing Scottish economy, not its failure, that did the Conservatives most harm,' Major reflected in his memoirs.'Margaret Thatcher's economic medicine served Scotland well, and I carried it forward in the 1990s. Such changes are always painful. There were job losses in the shipyards on the Clyde, in the coalfields and, most symbolic of all, in the decline and closure of the steel plant at Ravenscraig. All were hurtful. And each one was presented as the result of an 'uncaring' English government.' Furthermore, argued Major, the fact that Scotland's economy had been

---

[14] Devine, *The Scottish Nation*, 597–98.
[15] The National Coal Board was privatised in 1994. In 1997 a buyout at Monktonhall failed, leaving just Longannet among Scotland's deep mines. Longannet itself closed in 2002, although in 2009 open-cast mining produced more coal than in 1980.

transformed from one of 'continual decline, palliated only by a drip-feed of subsidy' to a 'renewed sense of self-confidence', merely 'led more Scots to believe that Scotland could go it alone'.[16]

The Poll Tax, meanwhile, was doomed but seemed to take a horribly long time to die. By the end of September 1991, it was estimated that in Scotland 12 per cent of the tax for 1989/90 was still unpaid, plus 23 per cent of the tax for 1990/91 and 77 per cent of that for 1991/92. Scottish public opinion seemed more favourable towards joint UK–US efforts to evict Iraq from Kuwait (shades of the Falklands), although the proposed abolition of the Gordon Highlanders and the Royal Scots as part of post-Cold War defence cuts initiated a Scottish Tory backbencher-supported campaign to save them. Meanwhile, Scotland's universities – still under Whitehall control – were appeased with proposals to 'devolve' university finance by creating a Scottish Higher Education Funding Council. Major also proved adept at playing the Scottish card. In May 1991 he chose Glasgow Cathedral as the venue for a service of national thanksgiving to mark the successful conclusion of the Gulf War.[17]

Major's reward was Scottish approval ratings of around 40 per cent in the early months of 1991 (Mrs Thatcher had struggled to get 20 per cent), while two *Glasgow Herald* polls conducted in September 1989 and June 1991 showed a demonstrable 'Thatcher factor' affecting Scottish perceptions of the Tory government. While 77 per cent of those polled in 1989 believed Mrs Thatcher treated Scots as second-class citizens, in 1991 a more palatable 41 per cent believed the same of Major.[18] Scottish Election Study surveys in 1987 and 1992 also indicated that Major was regarded as more egalitarian, moderate and substantially more caring, whereas Mrs Thatcher had always been regarded as strong, but at the same time 'extreme' and uncaring.

So there was evidence that Major's approach to Scotland – more presentational than political – was receiving modest credit from the Scottish public.[19] Whether these relatively favourable impressions, however, translated into additional support for the Conservatives in Scotland was another matter. And as a general election was due by the middle of 1992, it was not long before 'Majorism' was put to the test. In Scotland, it became inevitable that the national question would dominate the campaign. A MORI poll the year before showed that a majority of Scots, and even 60 per cent of Tory voters, favoured some kind of devolved Scottish Assembly. And given that many observers expected a repeat of the 1987 'doomsday scenario' leading to the loss of more, if not all, Scottish Tory MPs, Ian Lang convinced Major to campaign on the Union almost to the expense of everything else.

---

[16] Major, *The Autobiography*, 416.
[17] This event was marred by a very Scottish row over which denomination would give the sermon.
[18] *Glasgow Herald* 20/9/1989 & 19/6/1991.
[19] The author asked Sir John in 2008 if it was fair to say he had taken a different approach to Scotland than his predecessor. 'I took a *completely* different approach,' he replied quickly and firmly.

Major, curiously, became positively evangelical in a way Mrs Thatcher had never quite managed. The Prime Minister 'could see tears streaming' down activists' faces during an election rally in Edinburgh on 26 March 1992, and another at Wembley on 5 April 'contained the almost apocalyptic warning': 'If I could summon up all the authority of this office, I would put it into a single warning: the United Kingdom is in danger. Wake up, my fellow countrymen. Wake up now before it is too late.'[20]

Although Scots did not exactly 'wake up' to Major's call, on polling day it appeared that a certain number of Tory abstainers had been frightened back to voting Conservative as a result of his impassioned cry. Not only did the government gain two MPs to reach a total of 11,[21] but the party modestly increased its share of the vote to 25.6 per cent with an equally modest swing of 2.5 per cent. Expectations had been so low, however, that the result looked like a triumph. It was also a blow for the opposition parties, representing no major advance for Labour, the Liberal Democrats or the SNP. Jim Sillars, the Nationalists' deputy leader, famously dismissed his fellow countrymen as '90-minute patriots', while the writer Owen Dudley Edwards observed that a 'nationalism basing itself on anti-Thatcherism will have the greatest of difficulty in immunising itself from the infection of counter-Thatcherism'.[22] The deliberations of the SCC appeared to have made little electoral impact.

It has often been remarked that Mrs Thatcher's unpopularity destroyed the Scottish Conservative Party but in fact, overall, her impact was curiously neutral. In the October 1974 general election, held just months before she became leader, the Scottish Tories polled 24.7 per cent; at the 1992 election, which took place more than a year after her resignation, the party polled slightly more at 25.6 per cent. Mrs Thatcher herself left the Commons at that election, making a memorable appearance in Allan Stewart's Eastwood constituency the day after announcing her intention to do so. 'Thatcherism will live,' she wrote in the American magazine *Newsweek* following the election result. 'It will live long after Thatcher has died.'[23] Indeed, as if to prove his Thatcherite credentials, Major even authorised one privatisation Mrs Thatcher had expressly forbidden: British Railways.

But, as the writer William McIlvanney said of the Scottish result, 'one swallow doesn't make a summer and one more seat is not a recovery'.[24] Despite unexpected victory in the country at large, Major's majority

---

[20] Major, *The Autobiography*, 424.

[21] Although there were ten Scottish Tory MPs at the point of Mrs Thatcher's resignation in 1990, this had been reduced to nine when the party lost the Kincardine and Deeside by-election to the Liberal Democrats in 1991. The by-election had been caused by the death of Alick Buchanan-Smith.

[22] Dudley Edwards, ed., *A Claim of Right*, 182–83.

[23] Fowler, *A Political Suicide*, 97.

[24] *Scotsman* 11/4/1992. Iain McLean at Nuffield College calculated that the Tory vote had been artificially boosted by Poll Tax avoidance, having removed two per cent of Scottish voters from the electoral roll.

uncomfortably resembled Callaghan's in the late 1970s, while in terms of policy, personalities and overall direction, his administration began to unravel almost immediately. Having promised to 'take stock' of Scottish governance in the run up to the election, Major also had to try and square devolutionary aspirations with an acceptable Unionist compromise.

When *Scotland in the Union – A Partnership for Good* finally appeared in the spring of 1993, the press and political reaction was mixed but predominantly cynical. The Scottish Grand Committee (SGC) was to be beefed up and allowed to question Scottish Office ministers, the Scottish Affairs Select Committee (SASC, mothballed under Mrs Thatcher's final administration) was to be revived, training development and control of the Scottish Arts Council were to be 'devolved' to the Scottish Office from the Department of Employment and National Heritage Department respectively, while civil servants dealing with North Sea oil regulation were to be 'dispersed' from London to Aberdeen.

Although the more cosmetic changes involving the SGC and SASC could just as easily have been endorsed by Mrs Thatcher, it seems unlikely that she would have been happy transferring yet more functions to an already over-burdened Scottish Office. But in 'presentational terms', as the academic James Mitchell has observed, 'it marked a shift away from the period of Mrs Thatcher's approach'.[25] Not only were Lang and Major tinkering at the edges of administrative devolution but they were shouting about it, something the Iron Lady would never have done.

There was also tinkering with Barnett, of which Mrs Thatcher would surely have approved. Following more than a decade of Treasury attacks on the Scottish Block Grant and Barnett Formula, the latter had finally been recalibrated in 1992 to take account of population change in Scotland. Per capita spending still remained disproportionately high north of the border, but paradoxically this was now presented to voters as a justifiable benefit of the United Kingdom membership. Meanwhile a steady trickle of new responsibilities for the Scottish Office (such as control of universities) was the manifestation of clever Whitehall slight of hand. While it looked good politically, the new functions absorbed more of the Scottish Block as extra money rarely accompanied their 'devolution' to St Andrew's House.

In 1995 Lang boasted that every aspect of his white paper had been implemented, but by then it was already too late. Major had continued to make an effort north of the border in other respects, choosing Edinburgh to host the December 1992 European summit and restating his commitment to the European Exchange Rate Mechanism (ERM) during a speech in Glasgow. The UK economy, however, was already going into recession and sterling dropped out of the ERM a few days after the Prime Minister's speech.

---

[25] Mitchell, 'Conservatives and the changing meaning of Union', *Regional and Federal Studies 6 1* (1996), 40.

Furthermore, there was a growing revolt over the Maastricht Treaty with Teddy, now Sir Teddy, Taylor to the fore. Thatcherites and Euro rebels had merged into a single group of rebels of dubious parentage, as Major later implied in a media slip-up. But despite fears Scotland would suffer competitively within the Single European Market when it was inaugurated in 1992, a Brussels-sponsored doomsday did not arrive and money from the European Regional Development Programme and the European Social Fund, not to forget cash via the Common Agricultural and Fisheries Policies, continued to fund infrastructure and agriculture in one of the newly styled European Union's peripheral regions.

On 1 April 1993, four years to the day since the introduction of the Poll Tax in Scotland, Major replaced the Community Charge with the Council Tax. It had cost £1.5 billion to set up and then destroy, while the rebates scheme was estimated to have consumed a massive £20 billion. Douglas Mason, playing up to his 'father of the Poll Tax' nomenclature, condemned the new tax as akin to 'killing off a child when it is one year old – simply because it cannot fully walk or talk'.[26] In terms of other Thatcherite reforms, meanwhile, there were further indications that Scots remained unreconstructed. In 1994, for example, a referendum organised by Strathclyde Regional Council resulted in overwhelming opposition to the prospect of Scottish Water being sold to the highest bidder.

There was, however, a degree of détente with Scotland's trade unions unthinkable during the Thatcher era. The STUC general secretary Campbell Christie accepted an invitation to address the Conservative Party's Scottish Council in 1994 and two years later Lord Lindsay, under-secretary for agriculture at the Scottish Office, became the first Conservative minister in 99 years to address the STUC's annual congress. Scotland's monolithic regional local authorities were also finally abolished (a move Mrs Thatcher would surely have supported) in a long-awaited reorganisation, although in the first elections to 32 new unitary authorities in April 1995 the Conservatives failed to win control of a single council. A month later the party lost Perth and Kinross, one of Scotland's most prosperous constituencies, in a by-election caused by the death of Sir Nicholas Fairbairn, formerly Mrs Thatcher's much-liked but tragically short-lived Solicitor-General for Scotland.

In June 1995, at his wits end after months of party in-fighting over Europe, John Major challenged his critics to 'put up or shut up' and resigned as Conservative leader. Ian Lang ran his successful re-election campaign and was rewarded with promotion to the Department of Trade and Industry. 'By looking at issues on their merits, John Major is actually taking the radical agenda further than his predecessor did,' Lang had claimed in a 1994 lecture. 'At the same time, he is far more in the mainstream of tradition than his critics.'[27] Major's predecessor did not agree, often implying in public that he

---

[26] Butler, *Failure in British Government*, 177.
[27] 'Doing the Right Thing', 1994 Swinton Lecture, PUB 183/18, CPA.

had squandered her legacy. The journalist Simon Jenkins said Mrs Thatcher had 'become the Arthur Scargill of the right, peddling myths of the party's ideological history'.[28]

'THE BEAST OF THATCHERISM'

Although it was said that Baroness Thatcher (she was elevated to the Lords in 1992) despaired of Major's leadership and tacitly supported the Euro rebels, the former Prime Minister struck many as a lonely figure. 'Five years on, there is no monument to Baroness Thatcher,' wrote the journalist Andrew Marr. 'The woman who was once a political iconoclast, a radical force of world class, is reduced to the level of an exiled Stuart, restlessly travelling and remembering past glories.'[29]

Thatcher had remembered many of those past glories in the first volume of her memoirs, *The Downing Street Years*, published in 1993. Unlike most prime ministerial memoirists, she devoted several pages to her legacy in Scotland – which she judged to be 'lopsided' – and analysed the constitutional debate more frankly than she had been able to as Prime Minister. 'As a nation, they [the Scots] have an undoubted right to national self-determination,' she wrote, 'thus far they have exercised that right by joining and remaining in the Union.' She went on:

> Should they determine on independence no English party or politician would stand in their way, however much we might regret their departure. What the Scots (nor indeed the English) cannot do, however, is to insist upon their own terms for remaining in the Union, regardless of the views of the others. If the rest of the United Kingdom does not favour devolved government, then the Scottish nation may seek to persuade the rest of us of its virtues; it may even succeed in doing so; but it cannot claim devolution as a right of nationhood inside the Union.[30]

Baroness Thatcher also wrote glowingly of Michael Forsyth, who she said was the 'real powerhouse for Thatcherism at the Scottish Office'.[31] She was referring to the late 1980s but Forsyth, via the Home Office and Department for Employment, remained close to Thatcher and, following the leadership contest in July 1995, returned to his old department as John Major's second Secretary of State for Scotland.

---

[28] *The Times* 13/1/1996.

[29] *Independent* 23/11/1995.

[30] 'It is understandable that when I come out with these kind of hard truths many Scots should resent it,' Mrs Thatcher added. 'But it has nothing whatever to do with my being English. A lot of Englishmen resent it too.' (Thatcher, *The Downing Street Years*, 624)

[31] Ibid., 620–21.

The Scottish media was predictably hostile, referring to Forsyth as 'the demon king' and even likening him to the horror film character Freddie Krueger. 'He'd changed,' remembered Lord Lang, 'but perceptions of him hadn't. He was still portrayed as the beast of Thatcherism.'[32]

Major, on the other hand, while recognising that Forsyth was 'a robust supporter for Thatcherite economic medicine', believed he had mellowed sufficiently to be a success: 'Like Enoch Powell, he was a thinking man's populist. Privately quite liberal, and by conviction something of a libertarian, he possessed a sharp-toothed feel for the saleable parts of his Thatcherite inheritance, particularly those saleable in Scotland. But he suffered from the fact that he always looked as if he was plotting, even when he was not.'[33] Major's judgement, however, was perceptive, and Forsyth not only managed to endear himself to the Scottish press, but even to former enemies as it became clear he had returned to the fold a more experienced, astute and moderate politician. 'The old Thatcherite hardliner', observed Arthur Bell, 'had given way to a more emollient, more easy-going politician who promised to respond to the mood in Scotland.'[34]

So there was no substantial attempt by Forsyth to revive Thatcherism during his two years as the last pre-devolution Scottish Secretary. Still a true believer, he had nevertheless tempered his Thatcherite convictions with a heavy dose of political reality and instead embarked upon a spirited attempt to salvage what he could of Conservative support in Scotland. There were some notable successes. His campaign against the so-called 'Tartan Tax' (christened by Lang but brought to life by Forsyth) cleverly highlighted the prospect of a devolved parliament setting higher taxes and putting Scots consumers and businesses at a competitive disadvantage. And there were also some failures. An attempt to continue Forsyth's desired 'revolution' in Scottish education by increasing choice through a voucher scheme stalled in the face of local authority opposition.

The real hallmark of Forsyth's two years as Scottish Secretary, however, was his rhetoric. No longer afraid of arising nationalistic refrains, he attacked the paucity of Scottish history taught in schools, beefed up the SGC (again), revived the Scottish Economic Conference, waxed lyrical about the Highlands and Islands, and famously repatriated the Stone of Destiny to Scotland. Widely interpreted at the time as a cynical attempt to steal SNP votes, it was in fact damage limitation in anticipation of the 700th anniversary of the Stone's removal by Edward I and the imminent release of government papers relating to its theft in 1950. Whatever Forsyth's calculation, the gesture did not meet with Thatcherite approval. It led to, he remembered, 'the biggest row I ever had with her'.[35]

---

[32] Interview with Lord Lang.
[33] Major, *The Autobiography*, 425.
[34] *Scotsman* 4/7/1996.
[35] Interview with Lord Forsyth, 22/4/2008.

With 'Scottishness' increasingly being hijacked by Scotland's three main opposition parties, Forsyth did not really have any choice but to pursue this tack. 'It is our birthright to be Scottish,' he told the 1996 Scottish Conservative conference. 'It is our good fortune to be British. It is our duty to be Unionists.'[36] But this did not preclude populist pops at that other Union based in Brussels. Smarting from a beef ban which kept prime cuts of Aberdeen Angus from continental dinner tables, Forsyth marked Europe Day on 9 May 1996 by refusing to allow the EU flag to fly from Scottish government buildings. Even so, Forsyth faced the prospect of being challenged by a candidate from the anti-European Referendum Party. 'I am obviously regarded as a dangerous federalist', joked Forsyth after a campaigning visit from Baroness Thatcher, 'and I would be very surprised if Margaret who has come and campaigned for me, and has offered to do so again, would want to see any resource she provided being used for that kind of purpose.'[37]

But even the campaigning skills of Forsyth's former patron could not save him in Stirling when polling day came in 1997. A second doomsday scenario, postponed in 1992, removed every single Conservative MP from the Scottish political map, a wipe-out most commentators, and later academics, did not hesitate to attribute to the potent legacy of Thatcherism even seven years after the election of John Major.

'No! No!'

BLATCHERISM IN SCOTLAND

'There is nothing at all new about New Labour,' wrote the Scottish Socialist Tommy Sheridan shortly after the election. 'It is old Toryism in a New Suit,

---

[36] *The Times* 10/5/1996.
[37] *Scotsman* 4/7/1996.

Thatcherism with a grinning face. Tony Blair is in essence a political used-car salesman, who has taken the battered old wreck of Thatcherism, painted over the rust, and changed the mileage on the clock.'[38] Although polemical, Sheridan – who had risen to prominence through his Militant opposition to the Poll Tax – captured the fact that at its core New Labour was, in the words of the sociologist Zygmunt Bauman, 'Thatcherism consolidated'.[39] A stated aim of Mrs Thatcher's had been to rid Britain of socialism. The rebranding of Labour as New Labour acknowledged that she had succeeded. Blair had no problem with this interpretation. As Lord Turnbull, Mrs Thatcher's former private secretary, pointed out, 'Blair was canny enough to realise that Mrs Thatcher had done much of the dirty work for him.'[40]

And like Thatcherism, Blairism – or 'Blatcherism' as it was dubbed by the journalist Simon Jenkins – had no distinctively Scottish creed. Beyond, that is, an unequivocal commitment to a devolved Scottish Parliament. Although in truth Blair (unlike, initially, his Chancellor Gordon Brown) was no more enthusiastic about constitutional reform than his two predecessors, he recognised the political necessity of seeing through what John Smith had called the 'settled will' of the Scottish people.[41] Otherwise Blair, the son of working-class Glaswegian parents, at once embraced the central tenets of Thatcherism – free markets, deregulation, privatisation and strong authoritative government – while also appearing to reject them. 'In short,' observed the academic E. H. H. Green, 'New Labour not only used the institutions and structures of the market, but also adopted its vocabulary of consumers.'[42] Not only that, as Simon Jenkins argues convincingly in his book *Thatcher & Sons*, but Blair pushed Thatcherite notions of choice and private management in public services to an unnecessarily complicated extreme.

This 'Alice in Wonderland politics', as Gerry Hassan has called it, was perhaps even more pronounced in Scotland where the Scottish Labour Party was about to gain the added advantage of an institutional manifestation of its anti-Thatcherism. Devolution referendum day was set for 11 September 1997, and led to Baroness Thatcher's first intervention in Scottish politics since her resignation as Prime Minister. Although containing little that was new, her article in the *Scotsman* two days before polling delighted the Yes-Yes campaign and apparently dismayed the Tory-backed No-No camp, 'which has been privately advising her not to intervene in the debate, fearing that she will alienate more people than she convinces'.[43] 'If you still need a reason to vote

---

[38] Sheridan & McCoombes, *Imagine*, 114.

[39] www.opendemocracy.net.

[40] Interview with Lord Turnbull, 3/6/2008.

[41] 'You can't have Scotland doing something different from the rest of Britain', Blair told Paddy Ashdown when the Scottish Executive began departing from his policy agenda. 'I am beginning to see the defects in all this devolution stuff.' (Ashdown, *Diaries*, II, 446)

[42] Green, *Thatcher*, 190.

[43] *Scotsman* 9/9/1997.

Yes,' noted the *Daily Record*, referring both to Thatcher and her article, 'here's one.'[44]

Although unlikely to have been written by Thatcher personally (at this stage Robin Harris usually drafted her newspaper articles) the piece – headlined 'Don't wreck the heritage we all share' – included a lot of her familiar anti-devolution arguments from the 1980s: Labour would use it to increase the 'Tartan Tax'; the Scottish Secretary would lose his influence in the Cabinet; no new jobs would be created as a result; the 'monstrosity' of the West Lothian Question, and so on. 'Creating a new set of politicians, with new powers and spending more money', Thatcher wrote, 'is essentially what all the airy talk about devolution is about.'

There was also the familiar Thatcherite invocation of past Scottish glories: 'Scottish engineers, scientists, doctors, economists, philosophers, business-men, soldiers, explorers and statesmen have helped make Britain what it is. And the spread of British civilisation, by trade, by conquest, by settlement, by education and by example has provided Scots with opportunities that would otherwise have been unthinkable.' Baroness Thatcher concluded: 'I do not believe that most Scots want to end the Union. But separation is the destination towards which the present devolution proposals lead . . . Scottish voters can do no greater service to their country than to reject them.'[45]

The majority of Scottish voters, of course, did not take her advice. 'If you want shorthand for Thatcherism in Scotland,' said the journalist Keith Aitken, 'then it was the difference in the vote for devolution between 1979 and 1997.'[46] Indeed, both the main referendum question and a second relating to tax-raising powers were overwhelmingly endorsed by the Scottish electorate. Devolution was unstoppable, and no longer could Thatcherites point to the equivocal 1979 referendum result as proof that the vast majority of Scots were not serious about constitutional reform. In their Fabian pamphlet *New Scotland, New Britain*, Gordon Brown and Douglas Alexander even linked devolution directly with Thatcher's legacy. 'The old settlement between Scotland and the rest of Britain . . . could not endure,' they argued, because of her 'lack of commitment to social justice'.[47]

Meanwhile, the Scottish Conservative and Unionist Party (the old Scottish Conservative and Unionist Association, or SCUA, was wound up shortly after the election) sought to regroup and adapt to new political and institutional realities. Perhaps as a result, the journalist Alan Cochrane detected 'a growing temptation to try to pretend that . . . the Thatcher years, from 1979–90 . . . were like some form of interregnum, a horrible period when normal life was suspended and an alien force ruled the land'.[48]

---

[44] *Daily Record* 10/9/1997.

[45] *Scotsman* 9/9/1997.

[46] Interview with Keith Aitken, 29/10/2008. Similarly, the SNP leader Alex Salmond hailed 'Mrs Poll Tax' as 'the living memorial as to why the Scots want their own Parliament'. (*Independent* 11/9/1997)

[47] Brown & Alexander, *New Scotland, New Britain*, 6–7.

[48] *Scotsman* 7/4/1998.

By the late 1990s much of the Scottish mythology about that 'alien force' was already firmly in place. In Channel 4's 1998 documentary, *A Parcel of Rogues*, for example, Jimmy Reid reminisced about what a proud, enterprising nation Scotland had been, bursting with vibrant heavy engineering and shipbuilding firms, before Mrs Thatcher laid waste to its industrial heartland. And when Members of the Scottish Parliament began debating in the Church of Scotland's General Assembly building on the Mound in July 1999 – 11 years after Mrs Thatcher's 'Sermon on the Mound' – Scottish politicians found a new platform for expressions of this mythology.

A cursory glance at the Scottish Parliament's Official Report shows that barely a week went by without some reference to Thatcher or Thatcherism, cautiously positive Tory voices drowned out by a chorus of hostile opposition references. The SNP MSP Kenny MacAskill regularly spoke in Orwellian terms of a 'Thatcherite boot stamping all over Scotland', while Labour MSPs constantly reminded the Scottish Conservatives of their treachery. 'When Scotland was isolated by the Tories, when the Tories did not listen to us and Mrs Thatcher did not respond to issues in Scotland, what did members of the Executive parties do?' asked Margaret Curran during a debate in March 2007. 'We reframed the constitutional settlement and we campaigned for devolution. Where were the Tories and the SNP then? They were nowhere to be seen. We delivered devolution.'[49] Ironically, Labour's Jack McConnell had shown no qualms about inviting one of those Tories, Michael Forsyth (now Lord Forsyth), to Bute House shortly after he became First Minister.

Nationalists also could not resist getting stuck in. Shona Robison chastised the Scottish Conservative leader David McLetchie for the cardinal sin of trying 'to extol the virtues of what Thatcher achieved for Scotland'. 'Rather than Stalinist devotion,' she added, 'Mr McLetchie still has Thatcherite devotion in spades.'[50] Tory philosophy, argued the SNP's Mike Russell, 'is not defined in terms of communal solidarity; it is about the cult of the individual, as Margaret Thatcher indicated in this very hall'. 'It is not a belief in democratic processes,' he added. 'The Conservative party opposed the democratic process in Scotland and would not take part in [the] debate that led to this Parliament.'[51] When Donald Dewar, Scotland's first First Minister, died in 2000, he was christened the 'father of the nation'. But, as the historian Richard Finlay has argued, 'that honour should instead go to Margaret Thatcher – no doubt made of iron'.[52]

In legislative terms, the governing Labour–Liberal Democrat coalition also sought to dismantle certain aspects of the Thatcher legacy in Scotland. An early Act of the Scottish Parliament returned St Mary's Episcopal Primary

---

[49] Official Report c33439, 22/3/2007.
[50] Ibid., c8431, 19/5/2004.
[51] Ibid., c15803, 28/11/2002.
[52] Devine, ed., *Scotland and the Union*, 157.

School in Dunblane, which had opted out of the state sector under the Self-Governing Schools (Scotland) Act, to local authority control, although in terms of healthcare the private sector infiltrated the Scottish Health Service to an extent unthinkable just ten years before, not only in terms of provision but also construction. New hospitals were built at Hairmyles, Law and Edinburgh (a new Royal Infirmary) via the Private Finance Initiative.

Even Scottish Tories were prepared to overturn aspects of their own legacy. Scottish Enterprise, still a public body with a seemingly endless budget, came to be regarded by many right-wingers in much the same way as the Scottish Development Agency in the late 1970s and 1980s. Some, including the party's future deputy leader Murdo Fraser, even called for its total abolition. The UK Conservatives, meanwhile, led by William Hague, attempted to win over Scotland. In the 2001 general election the party was rewarded with just one MP north of the border and Hague's successor, the Edinburgh-born quiet man Iain Duncan Smith (IDS), attempted to consolidate this modest progress by publicly apologising for the 'imposition' of the Poll Tax in Scotland, thereby shoring up the very mythology his party had previously refuted.

On succeeding IDS as Tory leader following the general election of 2005, the youthful David Cameron (who also had, in his own words, 'Scottish blood coursing through his veins') went even further in his attempt to 'detoxify' the Tory brand in Scotland. 'A series of blunders were committed in the 1980s and 1990s of which the imposition of the poll tax was the most egregious,' he said in a much-reported 2006 Glasgow speech. 'We all know why it happened – the rates evaluation and the rest of it. But the decision to treat Scotland as a laboratory for experimentation in new methods of local government finance was clumsy and unjust. The decision to oppose devolution for so long was another bad idea. We fought on against the idea of a Scottish parliament long after it became clear it was the settled will of the people.'

It was an explicit rebuke of Thatcher's Scottish legacy which not only bought into Scottish political mythology but, together with Cameron's declaration that 'there is such a thing as society' at a UK level, deliberately sought to distance his 'modern' vision of Conservatism from that of the Iron Lady. With elections due in Scotland the following May, Cameron's strategy was obvious, as was that of Labour's leader-in-waiting Gordon Brown, who had recently reasserted his Britishness to the Scottish Labour Party and, like Cameron, pledged his commitment to the United Kingdom. Cameron's speech drew predictable ire from the SNP leader Alex Salmond. 'Margaret Thatcher used to "handbag" Scotland and now Cameron is trying to softsoap us – neither will work,' he said. 'Mr Cameron will find out next May at the polls that Scots have long memories and no amount of re-branding can disguise the fact that he is an anti-Scottish Tory.'[53]

[53] *Guardian* 15/9/2006.

At the 2005 election which preceded Cameron's election as leader, Baroness Thatcher made perhaps her final contribution to Scottish politics. While staying at Lord Forsyth's home near Stirling, Thatcher met veterans from several Scottish regiments at Aberfoyle in the Trossachs. A few months before, the Defence Secretary Geoff Hoon had indicated that Scotland's distinctive regiments would be subsumed within a new Royal Regiment of Scotland. 'Recent events have shown that evil is always with us and that we must be forever vigilant,' she said in a letter to the Tory candidate in Stirling. 'This is a time for strengthening our defences, not weakening them. The campaign to stop Labour's disastrous decision is a vital one. Save the Argylls and all the Scottish regiments!'[54] Such statements were, by 2005, rare. In March 2002, following several small strokes, Baroness Thatcher had announced an end to her career in public life.

Some aspects of her Scottish legacy appeared to decline with her. In 1998, long-standing concerns about Silicon Glen were fulfilled when the Lite-On plant in Lanarkshire was mothballed. Job losses were also announced at Compaq in Irvine, Viasystems in the Borders, National Semiconductor at Greenock and Motorola in East Kilbride. Edinburgh's financial services sector and, to a lesser extent, the north-east of Scotland's North Sea oil industry, however, continued to thrive.

TARTAN TORYISM

Ironically, the victory of the SNP in the 2007 Scottish Parliamentary elections at least vindicated Thatcher in one important respect. Although in the 1970s she had regarded Scottish Nationalism as essentially transient and protest-based, in the 1980s – and again in her *Scotsman* article on the eve of the devolution referendum – Thatcher warned that 'those who have set the agenda for change . . . are hell-bent on separation and will not be appeased'.[55]

Indeed, not only did Salmond evoke Harold Macmillan's post-imperial refrain by speaking of a 'wind of change' that had blown across Scotland, but the new First Minister was indeed committed to, if not 'hell-bent', on Scottish independence. And as his newly named Scottish Government unveiled its policies for minority government ('One characteristic we share with Thatcher,' Salmond quipped, 'is that we're a minority in Scotland') it seemed clear that the SNP was also keen to roll back key aspects of Thatcherism north of the border.

The Health Secretary, Nicola Sturgeon, rejected further private sector intrusion in the Scottish NHS, and announced plans to restrict Right to Buy in property hotspots, while Salmond relaxed central government control of Scotland's local authorities. Yet in other respects the SNP administration also

---

[54] *Scotland on Sunday* 17/4/2005.
[55] *Scotsman* 9/9/1997.

belied the fact that 21st-century Nationalism was a broad ideological church that embraced fully elements of the Thatcherite legacy it claimed to reject unequivocally. Not only did the First Minister promise 'light-touch' regulation for financial services in an independent Scotland, but he boosted small businesses by cutting rates, wooed big business in general and advocated 'small government' through abolishing or merging quangos. He also extolled the virtues of his Council Tax Abolition (Scotland) Bill (reminiscent of Thatcher's Abolition of Domestic Rates (Scotland) Bill) as a tax cut for 70 per cent of Scots by moving to a Local Income Tax. Plans were also unveiled to 'lease', or in other words privatise, 25 per cent of the Forestry Commission estate. Twenty years earlier the SNP would have attacked such a move as unacceptable.

Speaking a year after becoming First Minister, Salmond presented these apparent contradictions as political pragmatism. 'Yes, we're undoing some of the problems,' he said, adding: 'Thatcherism had consequences. Everyone liked Right to Buy until you ran out of houses, so what we've done is pragmatic.' He went on: 'In terms of how the SNP see a competitive advantage we might view that in a different way, we might do it by lowering corporation tax, not removing half our industry. But nobody owes us a living; we've got to be competitive. We're very happy to embrace that but if the idea is that you have to break up the social fabric in the country then no.'[56]

But to Salmond's erstwhile colleague Isobel Lindsay (who defected to Labour before the Scottish Parliament was established), far from demonstrating pragmatism the modern Nationalist movement was in fact indulging in political expediency. 'Salmond has bought into the Thatcherite economic orthodoxy to an extent,' she said. 'There has been a bit of a tendency with the current SNP leadership to be very strongly social democratic while in economic terms moving away from anything one could consider socially democratic.' Basically, added Lindsay, Salmond is 'trying to have his cake and eat it'.[57] Or as one Labour MSP later commented: 'The SNP wants Irish levels of taxation and Scandinavian levels of public services, but there is a contradiction there and they can't quite make up their minds.'[58]

In an interview during the summer of 2008 the normally unflappable Salmond slipped up in a way which not only highlighted the tensions inherent in SNP policy, but also in Thatcher's continuing potency when it came to Scottish politics. Explaining why Scotland 'didn't take to Lady Thatcher' Salmond appeared to imply sympathy for Thatcherism. 'We didn't mind the economic side so much,' he told the Tory blogger Iain Dale. 'But we didn't like the social side at all.'[59]

---

[56] Interview with Alex Salmond MSP, 24/6/2008.

[57] Interview with Isobel Lindsay, 2/9/2008.

[58] *Edinburgh Evening News* 28/8/2008.

[59] *Total Politics* September 2008. 'The SNP has a strong social conscience, which is very Scottish in itself,' Salmond also said. 'One of the reasons Scotland didn't take to Lady Thatcher was because of that.'

Scenting political blood, Labour politicians swooped in for the proverbial kill. Iain Gray, the Scottish Labour Party's new leader, even called on Salmond to make a public apology. 'Any Scot old enough remembers that Thatcher's economics had at their core the belief that mass unemployment was not just a price worth paying but necessary in a modern economy,' he stormed in a press release. 'Far from 'not minding' these economics, Scotland's communities were devastated by them . . . We should never allow Thatcher's economics to ravage Scotland again.'[60] Salmond was even attacked by his former deputy, Jim Sillars, who called his comments 'revisionist nonsense'. 'Alex Salmond is, of course, entitled to express his own opinion about Thatcher's economic policies,' he wrote to the *Herald*, 'although it will come as a surprise to those of us who were engaged with him in campaigning against them to discover that – years later – he, unlike us, was only pretending.'[61]

A defensive Salmond telephoned the BBC radio programme *Good Morning Scotland* the following day in an attempt to salvage the situation. 'I was commenting on why Scots, in particular, were so deeply resentful of Thatcher', he explained, 'and I think here her social message . . . cut against a very Scottish grain of social conscience. That doesn't mean that the nation liked her economic policies, just that we liked her lack of concern for social consequences even less.'[62]

That the comments provoked such a storm probably said more about the Scottish media ('unreconstructed wankers', in the memorable words of Tony Blair) than any lingering hostility to Thatcherite economics, but was none-theless telling. A few months later, David Cameron suffered a similar fate at the hands of the Scottish Labour spin machine. Referring to James Callaghan during his 2008 Conservative Party conference speech, Cameron declared: 'thank God we swapped him for Margaret Thatcher'.

'Mrs Thatcher devastated people's lives across Scotland,' stormed the Labour MP Jim Sheridan in response. 'Mr Cameron is totally out of touch with these comments. We must also remember that Alex Salmond says he endorses her economic policies.'[63] The irony was palpable. For Labour, whose former leader Tony Blair had invited Baroness Thatcher to tea at Downing Street, to attack either Cameron or Salmond in these terms was almost laughably hypocritical.

Equally ironic was the tacit expectation emanating from SNP headquarters that Scotland's folk memory of Thatcherism would hasten independence should Cameron replace Brown as Prime Minister. For not only had Con-servative MSPs played a crucial role in passing the SNP's first budget, but a Thatcher-era ban on forming coalitions with Tories in local government had

[60] Scottish Labour press release, 21/8/2008.
[61] *Herald* 22/8/2008.
[62] *Good Morning Scotland* (BBC Radio Scotland) 22/8/2008.
[63] Scottish Labour press release, 1/10/2008.

been overturned by the SNP in late 2007. 'That was a bigger sea-change than many people realised at the time,' admitted one Nationalist. 'The Tories were no longer the bogeymen, we could do deals with them.'[64]

In an orgy of anti-Thatcher rhetoric, three of Scotland's mainstream political parties (only the Scottish Liberal Democrats remained aloof) had sought to tar each other with sympathy for Thatcherism. Meanwhile, during by-elections in Glasgow East and Glenrothes, SNP activists distributed leaflets (having demonised her in the infamous 'She's got Scotland's oil' campaign in the 1980s) reminding voters that Gordon Brown had also invited Baroness Thatcher to Downing Street for refreshments. The new Prime Minister's appreciation of his predecessor had seemingly blossomed since he had praised Thatcher as a 'conviction politician'[65] in September 2007. Downing Street sources also revealed that one of Brown's 'biggest and earliest political memories'[66] had been an invitation to visit the then Prime Minister in her Commons office in 1983 to discuss a speech he had made. 'His youthful aversion to Thatcherism was intense and tribal,' wrote Simon Jenkins of the Brown–Thatcher dynamic. 'His conversion to it over the course of the 1990s was at first tactical, then institutional.'[67]

The two Prime Ministers made for a fascinating psychological comparison. Indeed, Brown's childhood was not unlike that of Thatcher's. Alderman Roberts, much like the Kirk minister John Brown, did not believe in frippery, vanity or waste. Roberts was a pillar of the local community, as was Brown's father in Kirkcaldy. He was the single biggest influence on her, just as Brown's father was on him. Politically, they also had much in common. Brown made much of prudence, just as Thatcher had with sound money, while he lacked a hinterland and disliked the showbiz aspect of modern politics, not unlike the Iron Lady. A major difference, of course, would have been devolution, but then that was old news; a battle which no longer defined the wider political war.

So while Blair's Thatcherite inheritance had been purely policy orientated, Brown's was more instinctive, and in fact crystallised nearly 20 years before he reached the top of the greasy pole. Although his 1982 book (co-written with Robin Cook) *Scotland: The Real Divide* had rejected monetarism in favour of Clement Attlee's post-war consensus, his second, *Where There is Greed. . . Margaret Thatcher and the Betrayal of Britain's Future*, conceded that 'Only by combining public with private intervention, not to suppress the market or dictate to it for reasons of dogma, but to ensure that its forces serve public objectives, can we succeed.'[68]

Essentially, Brown meant using Thatcherite economics towards socially

---

[64] *Edinburgh Evening News* 28/8/2008.

[65] *Independent* 5/9/2007.

[66] BBC News Online 13/9/2007.

[67] Jenkins, *Thatcher & Sons*, 270.

[68] Brown, *Where There is Greed*, 3.

just ends, an argument which later became the basis of the 'Third Way'; so much for Thatcherism being an alien ideology. In 1994 Brown admitted to the columnist Hugo Young that 'Thatcher's main achievement was to identify what was wrong with what had gone before. It was more negative than positive – [but] justifiably critical . . . there was a lot wrong.'[69] If proof were needed that the 1980s had spawned a new business called Thatcher and Sons, then Scots needed look no further than the pro-devolution son of the manse who was now their Prime Minister.

---

[69] Trewin, ed., *The Hugo Young Papers*, 419.

Chapter 11

'WE'RE ALL THATCHERITE NOW'

Margaret Thatcher made a terrific effort to understand Scotland and she did go that extra mile to win the hearts of the Scottish people . . . She would have been less than human if she had not felt somewhat disillusioned by the Scots although she loved Scotland as a country. The truth is her character as a powerful English woman made her an easy target for her political enemies in Scotland whatever she did . . . Margaret was not blameless herself in her actions in Scotland, but she did far more good than harm.

George Younger, *Scotland on Sunday* 17/10/1993

The Thatcher years may have been deeply unpopular in Scotland, as much for its 'me, now' tone as for any of the policies it implemented. But some of the benefits – and it may be heresy to remind people of them – such as council house sales, the breaking of trade-union power and the virtues of an enterprise economy, are now set in concrete in this country.

Alan Cochrane, *Scotsman* 7/4/1998

SPEAKING IN 2002, THE former Labour Cabinet minister Peter Mandelson declared that, in purely economic terms, 'we are all Thatcherite now'.[1] The somewhat glib phrase captured the sense that however opposed many voters and politicians remained to Mrs Thatcher and Thatcherism, they were at the same time operating within her heavily revised rules of the political game. The term, however, was not new. 'In other words, like it or not, we are all Thatcherites now,' wrote the *Glasgow Herald*'s business editor Ronald Dundas in 1987, 'even good socialists, practising sound housekeeping, clipping the wings of the unions, battling against inflation, and privatising recently profitable industries in state hands. You may not like it, but you cannot deny it.'[2]

While many Scots undoubtedly did not like it, they certainly continued to deny it. The political commentator Gerry Hassan identified this as the first

---

[1] BBC News Online 10/6/2002.
[2] Stewart, ed., *Apostles Not Apologists*, 5.

cardinal rule of Scottish politics post-Thatcher, 'that is namely to vilify, degrade and denounce Thatcher and Thatcherism with every word in your vocabulary, while being influenced, shaped and following in her footsteps'.[3] Before looking at this phenomenon in greater depth it is worth beginning with Mrs Thatcher's own analysis of her Scottish legacy. 'As late as 1979 only a third of Scots owned their own home,' she wrote in 1993. 'By the time I had left office this had risen to over half – thanks in part to the "Right to Buy" scheme.' But, she acknowledged, 'however valuable socially those initiatives were, they had little political impact.' She continued:

> The 1992 election showed that the fall in Tory support had been halted; it had yet to be reversed. Some part of this unpopularity must be attributed to the national question on which the Tories are seen as an English party and on which I myself was apparently seen as a quintessentially English figure. About the second point I could – and I can – do nothing. I am what I am and I have no intention of wearing tartan camouflage. Nor do I think that most Scots would like me, or any English politician, the better for doing so.

'The Tory Party is not, of course, an English party but a Unionist one,' concluded Mrs Thatcher. 'If it sometimes seems English to some Scots that is because the Union is inevitably dominated by England by reason of its greater population. The Scots, being an historic nation with a proud past, will inevitably resent some expressions of this fact from time to time.'

Mrs Thatcher's analysis, therefore, emphasised the 'national question' above everything else, although it seems to the author that the Scottish economy during the Thatcher era was at least as important, and indeed she went on to declare:

> After a decade of Thatcherism, Scotland had been economically transformed for the better.
>
> People moved in large numbers from the older declining industries such as steel and shipbuilding to new industries with a future such as electronics and finance. Almost all the economic statistics – productivity, inward investment, self-employment – showed a marked improvement. As a result, Scottish living standards reached an all-time high, rising by 30 per cent from 1981 to 1989, outperforming most of the English regions.[4]

All that was true, but let us begin with the national question. It is important to remember that Margaret Thatcher became Prime Minister, at least in part, because of the Callaghan government's failure to answer this question in the

---

[3] www.opendemocracy.net 26/8/2008.
[4] Thatcher, *The Downing Street Years*, 623–4.

form of a Scottish Assembly. Indeed, Michael Foot's words in the no-confidence debate which followed the referendum defeat are worth quoting: 'I hope that every section of the House, whatever its preliminary views on the matter, will be prepared to discuss these issues afresh, otherwise there will be a deep gulf and breach, which will grow in years to come, between Scotland and the rest of the United Kingdom.'[5] Following the devolution referendum and May general election, however, Mrs Thatcher felt her 'preliminary views' on devolution had been vindicated. Not only that, but those views did not alter materially in the 11 years that followed.

So, arguably, a 'deep gulf and breach' did develop between Scotland and the rest of the United Kingdom, although not solely because of the events of 1979. Scottish and English voting patterns had been diverging since the early 1970s, most notably in the general election of October 1974, although in fact there was minimal enthusiasm for a Scottish Assembly even by 1979. With time, however, opposition to Thatcher and Thatcherism became inextricably linked for many with a desire for devolution. 'The case for an Assembly', declared an editorial in *Radical Scotland* in 1985, 'is also the case against Thatcher.'[6]

Yet the regularly expressed belief that an Assembly would have protected Scotland from Thatcherite reforms is simplistic. True, in certain domestic areas there would have been differences. As Gordon Brown wrote in 1989, 'With a Scottish Assembly there would have been no Poll Tax, no opt-out schools or opt-out hospitals, and no buses or electricity privatisation.'[7] That is true (except, arguably, for the last in his list), but on the other hand there *would* have been monetarism, industrial decline, trade union reform, the Falklands War and, later, economic revival. 'Devolution was not the correct response to privatisation, Trident, taxation, etc.,' observed the Scottish Tory MSP David McLetchie in 2008, 'but Labour got sucked into it. The only coherent response was either full independence or a Labour government.'[8]

Politically, however, the devolutionary response was more expedient. In truth, demands for devolution were predominantly a political concern in the 1980s rather than a genuine grassroots desire. The Campaign for a Scottish Assembly was a fringe concern for much of that decade, and the no-mandate argument a red herring. As Labour's Robin Cook admitted, he did not 'give a bugger if Thatcher has a mandate or not – I will simply do whatever I can to stop her'.[9] And even after 1987, the devolutionary campaign was largely a preoccupation of the self-styled civic Scotland, as symbolised by the Scottish Constitutional Convention. Yet a feeling did grow that Mrs Thatcher's governments, as the academic James Mitchell has argued, lacked 'legitimacy' in Scotland, whatever

---

[5] Hansard 965 c579.
[6] *Radical Scotland* August/September 1985.
[7] Brown, *Where There is Greed*, 182.
[8] Constitutional Futures seminar, 21/11/2008, University of Edinburgh.
[9] *Radical Scotland* June/July 1984.

the constitutional, legal and political bases of their UK-wide mandate. Thus devolution became a panacea for all Scotland's ills. '[I]t is the convenient answer to every grievance, real or imagined,' wrote the Scottish Tory MP Allan Stewart in 1987. 'There can be few social or economic problems for which devolution has not been put forward as the solution.'[10] It was also a largely negative, not to mention reactionary, argument. To Richard Finlay, 'little was said about the potential positive benefits of home rule; rather it was mainly about stopping unpopular policies'.[11]

Was Mrs Thatcher's response the correct one? For her, yes; for the Conservative Party, arguably not. Given that she had U-turned on the previous Conservative commitment in 1976, such a move would have lacked political credibility. As T. E. Utley argued in 1988: 'Probably the greatest single source of contempt for the Tories in Scotland is the widespread belief that their attitude to the place is entirely opportunistic. This would be confirmed by a second *volte-face*.'[12] The Anglo-Irish Agreement, however, demonstrated that Mrs Thatcher was capable of compromising her unionism with such a *volte-face* (as did her signing of the Single European Act), while devolution in Scotland could have fulfilled certain, albeit opportunistic, short-term political objectives. In retrospect, it is impossible to conclude that Mrs Thatcher did not question her stance, in 1976 or thereafter. As Lord Griffiths, the former head of the Downing Street Policy Unit, conceded, 'I suspect we could have been much more sensitive to local needs and aspirations than we were.'[13]

On devolution, however, the lady was not for turning, but while opinion polls indicated increasing public support for a Scottish Assembly or Parliament as the decade progressed, a view of Mrs Thatcher 'as the midwife of Scottish Home Rule'[14] is also simplistic. Had Labour won the general elections of 1979, 1983 (in coalition with the Alliance), 1987 or, indeed, 1992, some sort of Scottish Assembly would have been established. It is therefore truer to say that opposition to Mrs Thatcher shaped the *sort* of devolution eventually implemented in 1998/99. As Alex Salmond has argued, her predominant influence was to politicise an already extant self-government movement, not instigate it. So by 1988, as Michael Gove has observed, 'you could only be a good Scot if you were pro-Parliament and anti-Thatcher; the three became one'.[15] The three also became one at Holyrood in Edinburgh. There, the Scottish Parliament – elected by proportional representation and guided by consensus and coalitions – is an undeniable manifestation of that anti-Thatcher influence.

That manifestation, however, is also paradoxical. By the time devolution was enacted in 1998 there was a Labour government at Westminster, the so-called 'democratic deficit' had been swept away in a Labour landslide,

---

[10] Stewart, ed., *Apostles Not Apologists*, 7.
[11] Murdoch, ed., *The Scottish Nation*, 150.
[12] *The Times* 10/5/1988.
[13] Interview with Lord Griffiths, 1/12/2008.
[14] *Radical Scotland*, June/July 1989.
[15] Interview with Michael Gove MP, 28/7/2008.

and – more to the point – Scotland no longer resembled the communitarian, collectivist nation devolutionists claimed would be embodied by the new Scottish Parliament. As the academics Lindsay Paterson, Frank Bechhofer and David McCrone pointed out in their statistical study *Living in Scotland*, Mrs Thatcher's governments presided over a very real and substantial growth in individual opportunity in Scotland, producing a tension in the 1990s within a 'newly educated, newly individualised populace articulating the inherited values of community'. Furthermore, the communitarian (and therefore anti-Thatcherite) rhetoric that pervaded the campaign for Scottish self-government also persisted well into the twenty-first century, even though it could not 'coherently'[16] do so. By 1999, in other words, Scottish society embraced a devolved Parliament which purported to embody ideas of community it had largely abandoned.

Crucial to this societal change was the transformation of the Scottish economy. Initially, of course, this was traumatic, and disproportionately so in Scotland, although it is ludicrous to imply that Mrs Thatcher's planned reforms were formulated with Scotland specifically in mind. In retrospect, to have persevered with policies designed to reform the trade unions, tackle high inflation, reformulate regional policy and phase out incomes policy in the midst of a recession did require political courage. And Scotland – not to forget the rest of the UK – did ultimately benefit from the resulting 'shake out'. Inflation and interest rates came down and, with periodic fluctuations, remained low for much of last quarter of a century. Meanwhile the government concentrated on the magic trio of North Sea oil, Silicon Glen and financial services to ease Scotland's transition from old industries to new. And while economic commentators remain divided on the precise impact of each, in the short term they did generate employment for increasing numbers of Scots while ensuring that total employment figures were not significantly eroded.

And despite frequent rhetoric to the contrary, as the historian Tom Devine has pointed out, 'the Conservative governments did not disengage entirely from either the promotion of economic regeneration or the provision of a safety net for those who were the victims of structural economic change'.[17] Regional aid (which had arguably failed in its original form) continued, albeit in a more selective way; spending on social security was not cut significantly; and Mrs Thatcher championed inward investment as enthusiastically as the Scottish Development Agency. Scotland's preferential spending levels were also retained, no matter how much Downing Street distrusted the figures, and Mrs Thatcher accepted most Scottish Office advice, no matter how interventionist, when it came to industrial shibboleths like Ravenscraig. (Far from 'closing Ravenscraig' as the popular mythology dictates, she actually kept the plant open long beyond British Steel's preferred closure date. It finally shut down in 1992, two years into John Major's premiership and four years after privatisation.)

---

[16] Paterson, *et al.*, *Living in Scotland*, 153–54.

[17] Devine, *The Scottish Nation*, 598.

In that context, it can hardly be asserted that Mrs Thatcher somehow hated, or at the very least 'did not care', about Scotland. In fact she was usually pragmatic, if not overly cautious, when it came to Scotland, and accepted willingly the need to appeal to the Scottish dimension, even if her attempts at doing so were not particularly effective. It is truer to say that she 'hated' socialism and the socialist culture she saw in Scottish trade unions, Scottish local government and Scottish housing schemes. But then in this respect, Scotland was no different in her eyes from parts of England or, indeed, the nations of Eastern Europe. Her policies were therefore geared towards 'liberating' Scots and Britons (and, in a sense, Eastern Europeans) from what she saw as the disease of socialism. So whatever the outcome of those policies, their application to Scotland was well intentioned rather than hostile.

Nevertheless, the Conservatives – and particularly Mrs Thatcher – 'were blamed for administering the [economic] medicine that, in retrospect, all agreed was necessary'.[18] As Scotland's economy improved, therefore, opponents began to modify their critique. As one *Glasgow Herald* editorial put it: 'What is at issue is not the necessity of industrial change but the way in which it is being managed, with inadequate regard to the social consequences or to the particular needs of Scotland.'[19] But a lot of Scots, as Keith Aitken has written, seemed 'preoccupied with the melancholy imagery of industrial decline as a totem of national injustice'.[20] The Proclaimers' refrain ('Linwood no more, Bathgate no more') undoubtedly echoed the mood of the time, but it was, as the economist Professor Sir Donald Mackay has written, 'a lament to an industrial structure which was past its "sell by date"'.[21] Scotland's traditional industries were at a serious disadvantage against low-cost producers in developing countries, but then it was easier to sing of things being 'no more' than welcoming new jobs in electronics, North Sea oil and financial services. That was simply harsh economic reality, not bloody-mindedness on the part of Mrs Thatcher. 'Over two decades on,' reflected Baroness Thatcher in 2009, 'only a handful of die-hards would argue that Scottish industry could have carried on as it was in the 1970s.'[22]

Sir Donald Mackay identified 1988 as the turning point in the Scottish economy, a year which marked a clean break not only with the recession-dominated period of 1979–88, but also – at least in terms of employment – with a much longer period dating back to the Macmillan era. From 1988 to 1994 Scotland progressed to being second among the UK regions in terms of GDP per capita and average income, while self-employment in Scotland grew at four times the UK rate (an indication of individual enterprise often perceived as lacking among Scots), and levels of unemployment between

---

[18] Devine, ed., *Scotland and the Union*, 168.

[19] *Glasgow Herald* 24/11/1987.

[20] Aitken, *The Bairns O' Adam*, 1.

[21] Mackay, *More or Less Competitive?*, 22. Mackay had been a prominent supporter of Scottish devolution in the late 1970s.

[22] Interview with Baroness Thatcher, 20/1/2009.

Scotland and the UK barely differed. Even employment in overseas-owned plants proved much more stable than that in indigenous plants, while far from struggling to compete within a single European market, Scotland emerged with a competitive advantage in a number of sectors. 'It might be said that regulation and nationalisation removed much of the commercial heart of Scotland,' concluded Sir Donald, 'which has been returned by deregulation and privatisation.'[23]

In some cases, for example British Airways, British Telecom and British Gas, and later Stagecoach, FirstGroup and Forth Ports, privatisations were an unqualified success in Scotland, leading to better services and better value for money than was available from state providers. The resulting takeover of many Scottish firms by foreign companies and domestic competitors was not necessarily a bad thing. Indeed, even the left-leaning economist Brian Ashcroft argued that it 'frequently served to invigorate what were often sleepy and moribund concerns'.[24]

Later, of course, things did not look quite so rosy as Scottish Power faced a hostile takeover by the German utility giant E.on,[25] and giants of Silicon Glen began to crumble, although much of the resulting unemployment was quickly absorbed by other areas of the Scottish economy. Even in 2007 *Living in Scotland* found predominantly good things emanating from the 1980s in terms of Scottish employment, education and opportunity. Compared with 1979, more Scots than ever before were in work, enjoying less dangerous conditions (working in a coal mine was considered unthinkable by 1999), more professional occupations and better pay – average incomes rose in real terms by more than a fifth between 1979 and 1997 – while by 1999 nearly 20 per cent of Scottish employees enjoyed some sort of flexible working pattern. It is true, however, that a lot of the new jobs created in the 1980s, particularly in Silicon Glen, were low-paid, although increased educational attainment did reduce inequality. Mrs Thatcher presided over a massive expansion of those staying at secondary school and going on to higher education – indeed, it was proportionately greater in Scotland than in England and Wales – patterns that continued after she left office. 'For all the longevity of Scotland's self-belief as a land of open opportunity,' the authors of *Living in Scotland* concluded, 'never before in its history has it had so many lads and lassies o' pairts.'[26]

The quality of life enjoyed by those lads and lassies o' pairts was also higher in 2007 than it was possible to conceive of 50, or even 30 years, before. The shift in housing tenure was particularly striking. In 1982 fewer than 40 per cent of Scottish households were owner-occupied; by 2005 that figure had risen to nearly 70 per cent. Although there had been a similar pattern of

[23] Mackay, *More or Less Competitive?*, 31.
[24] Ashcroft, *Scotland's Economic Problem*, 27.
[25] E.on's bid failed and in 2006 Scottish Power became instead a subsidiary of the Spanish energy company Iberdrola. Its headquarters remained in Glasgow.
[26] Paterson, *et al.*, *Living in Scotland*, 150.

change across much of Europe, it had been particularly dramatic in Scotland, where the level of ownership had increased by almost a third since the early 1980s. Despite a sluggish start, Scots came to embrace not only Right to Buy, but Mrs Thatcher's borrowed vision of a 'property-owning democracy'. True, there were drawbacks in the case of depleted supply of social housing, but the social change engendered by increased home ownership, not to mention the massive transfer of wealth this involved, cannot and should not be under-estimated. Of course, promoting property ownership and compelling local authorities to sell off housing stock at a massive discount do not necessarily go hand in hand. But together with modest changes to public sector educational provision, a major achievement of Mrs Thatcher's first term was a major attitudinal shift that few in Scotland subsequently sought to reverse.

It seems clear in retrospect, however, that while 1988 may have marked a turning point in the Scottish economy, it also signified a point of no return for Mrs Thatcher or the Scottish Conservatives. Economic recovery simply came too late for either to reap the political rewards, as they did in much of England. The general election of 1987 had halved Tory representation in Scotland, while the early implementation of the Poll Tax convinced a majority of Scots that the government's intentions were irretrievably hostile. And as social mobility increased in terms of occupation and living standards, Scotland's growing professional and middle classes – always disproportionately rooted in the public sector – identified more and more with Labour and self-government rather than the governing party which had allowed them to make the transition in the first place. 'The middle class saw themselves as the guardians of the welfare state; any threat to their hegemony was interpreted as a threat to Scotland itself,' observed the academic Lindsay Paterson. 'Thus Thatcher did not have to be deliberately anti-Scottish for her policies to be received as such.'[27]

Judging Mrs Thatcher by her own stated aim of eroding this state hegemony, however, she arguably failed. As John Campbell has written, 'she actually failed to curb public spending significantly, [and] failed to prune or privatise the welfare state'. Indeed, Scotland's public sector continued to grow throughout the 1980s, 1990s and in the early twenty-first century, to the extent that in 2009 every major Scottish party accepted that it needed to be reduced, although most apparently shared Mrs Thatcher's inability to actually achieve it. And despite innumerable reforms to the welfare state during the same period, parts of Glasgow still had a higher proportion of Incapacity Benefit and Jobseeker's Allowance claimants than any other city or region in the UK. Although the size of Scotland's worst areas of deprivation actually diminished during the Thatcher era, the condition of those within them worsened.

As a result, the gap between the richest and poorest Scots continued to widen, although it is important to note that this pattern was not significantly reversed by 12 years of Labour government from 1997 to 2009. In 1977, for example, the difference in GDP between the richest (Grampian) and poorest

---

[27] Paterson, *The Autonomy of Modern Scotland*, 169.

(Strathclyde) regions of Scotland was 18 per cent. By 1995 it was 62 per cent, although the poorest region had by then become the Highlands and Islands. A cultural revolution appeared to contribute to a greater tolerance of very high and very low incomes. But, as John Campbell has also observed, 'Ultimately the balance sheet demands a judgement as to whether the economic benefits of that cultural revolution outweighed the social cost.'[28] Considering, however, that Labour ultimately embraced, and arguably took further, the argument that the welfare state had to be controlled if not cut down to size, the balance inevitably tips in Mrs Thatcher's favour. Even then, to depict her as having cut the safety net of the post-war consensus is an exaggeration. Although her language in this respect, as Simon Jenkins has written, 'could seem heartless and ruthless',[29] Mrs Thatcher did not tamper significantly with the 'five giants' of the welfare state and never seriously eroded the social security budget.

Thirty years after she became Prime Minister, however, there exists a reluctance to concede that any aspect of Scotland's economic transformation had anything to do with Mrs Thatcher. As the SNP MSP, Kenny MacAskill, put it in 2006, 'Anything that Scotland got from Thatcher was more by accident than design'.[30] But to argue, as many do, that the social, cultural and economic revolution of the 1980s 'would have happened anyway' again misses the point. Some sort of welfare state would have been created immediately after the Second World War even had Churchill won the election, but that does not take anything away from the significant achievements of Clement Attlee's 1945–50 government. As Simon Jenkins has argued, 'no serious historian could deny that Thatcher's coming to power in 1979 "saved Britain" in a realistic sense. It began a transformation in its political economy and, for the overwhelming majority of Britons, it was a change for the better.'[31] Mrs Thatcher's flair and seemingly limitless energy guided that transformation in a way neither James Callaghan nor Michael Foot could have. And given the impact of that transformation in the political economy on Scotland's society and culture, this legacy cannot be underestimated.

WHITHER THATCHERISM?

What, then, of Thatcherism beyond the economy and devolution? It seems clear that the period between the 1983 and 1987 general elections marked the point at which the Thatcher–Scotland relationship turned sour. In 1983, despite unprecedented levels of unemployment and industrial decline, the Conservative Party's share of the vote and number of seats barely altered compared with that in 1979. Four years later, however, the government lost

[28] Campbell, *The Iron Lady*, 800–01.
[29] Jenkins, *Thatcher & Sons*, 151.
[30] BBC News Online 18/11/2006.
[31] *Guardian* 18/7/2008.

4.4 per cent of its vote share and all but ten of its Scottish MPs. (It is important to note, however, that in England the Conservatives' share of the vote also declined at each election – general, local and European – and that Mrs Thatcher never achieved anything approaching a popular majority.)

So in 1983 and not yet viscerally hated, a government with a properly presented radical agenda could have consolidated Conservative support and convinced greater numbers of Scots that aspects of Thatcherism could be beneficial. To an extent, this proved the case with the privatisation agenda, but the potential benefits of that were quickly militated by the continuing rise of unemployment in Scotland and lengthy strikes by miners and teachers, the last of which fuelled increasing middle-class disillusion with the government, particularly north of the border. Add into the mix the 1985 rates revaluation and subsequent Community Charge legislation, and the 1987 election result does not look at all surprising.

There has been, however, a tendency to exaggerate Mrs Thatcher's impact on the electoral prowess of the Scottish Conservative Party. The 1987 'doomsday scenario' was certainly the nadir, but overall Mrs Thatcher actually increased support for the Conservatives in Scotland at the 1979 election, support which held up remarkably well four years later despite a crowded party political scene. And although in 1987 the government sank to just over 24 per cent of the vote in Scotland, it is had not been much above that in October 1974 (when the share of the vote fell by 8.2 per cent on February 1974), several months before Mrs Thatcher became Conservative leader. In fact, when the 1974 result is compared with that in 1992 (long after she ceased being leader), Mrs Thatcher's impact on the Scottish Conservative Party was surprisingly neutral. Local government elections (not to forget those to the European Parliament), however, were a different matter.

Mrs Thatcher may have succeeded in bringing the 'runaway train' of local government under control – although the supposedly spendthrift nature of Scottish local government was always overstated by the government – but as the historian David Stewart has written, 'in doing so she had irreparably damaged the Scottish Conservatives' electoral credentials'.[32] Few governments, however, had ever enjoyed genuinely cordial relations with local government, particularly in Scotland, and it could be said that by constraining local authority spending Mrs Thatcher had simply been continuing Labour's policy under James Callaghan in the late 1970s. Even so, by utilising, as Arthur Midwinter has observed, 'creative accounting, increased charges, efficiency savings, and tax increases',[33] Scottish councils were able to escape the worst of the Thatcherite axe. Realising this, an outcry over the rates revaluation presented the government with a convenient excuse to launch a renewed assault on local government finance via the Community Charge, an assault which had disastrous consequences and effectively sealed

---

[32] Stewart, 'Challenging the consensus', 241.
[33] Midwinter, *Public Finance in the Thatcher Era*, 22.

Mrs Thatcher's fate in Scottish terms. But no matter how misguided the Poll Tax was, the popular image of it having been 'tested' on Scotland a year ahead of England and Wales is perhaps the most grotesque caricature of all. Labour politicians like Dennis Canavan continued to claim 'that the Thatcher government was using the Scottish people as guinea pigs'[34] but that did not make it true. A badly thought out and unfair tax? Certainly. A tax maliciously 'tested' on Scotland? Certainly not. As noted in the text, there was in fact a much stronger argument for Scotland having been used as a test bed for a host of earlier reforms like rate capping.

Not everything in Mrs Thatcher's local government legacy, however, was negative. The free-market policy of Compulsory Competitive Tendering (CCT) forced councils to examine the real cost of providing local services for the first time in decades, and tighten their work practices even when contracts ended up remaining in-house. Again there was eventual cross-party support despite bitter opposition at the time. The policy of 'Best Value' as introduced by Labour in 1997 could be described as CCT by another name, while the SNP's pursuit of a Local Income Tax meant the complete removal of the power of local authorities to raise (or vary) a proportion of their own revenue, a right even Mrs Thatcher never seriously disputed. Indeed, few of the controls introduced in the early 1980s were reversed by subsequent devolved Scottish Executives so, ironically, devolution clipped Scottish local government wings more than was anticipated. The SNP Government elected in May 2007 appeared to reverse this trend by ending ring-fencing, but even then its 'historic concordat' placed as many obligations on councils as it removed.

The attempt at 'Thatcherism resurgent' in 1987–88, meanwhile, appears in retrospect to have been ill-advised. Legislation enabling Scottish schools and hospitals to 'opt out' from state control were too far ahead of their time and obvious targets for opposition abuse, although both were subsequently revived in different forms by the governments of Tony Blair. The Scottish Labour Party, however, made a virtue out of not extending Blair's city academies and foundation hospitals to Scotland, as if to demonstrate that it would not be imposing 'English solutions' on 'Scottish problems' now that the Scottish Parliament was up and running. Blair, interestingly, was not amused.

Another example of Thatcherism resurgent was the replacement of the Scottish Development Agency and the Highlands and Islands Development Board with Scottish Enterprise and Highlands and Islands Enterprise respectively. These ended up becoming 'no more successful than the old ones they replaced in generating recovery in the declining parts of the Scottish economy'.[35] Bloated and inefficient by the time of the 2007 Scottish Parliamentary elections, both the Scottish Conservatives and SNP advocated either abolishing Scottish Enterprise or significantly altering its remit. Indeed, the SNP Government subsequently announced its intention to scrap Local

---

[34] *Thatcher and the Scots* (BBC Scotland) 1/1/2009.
[35] Devine, ed., *The Transformation of Scotland*, 231.

Enterprise Companies, considered by Mrs Thatcher to have been integral to the success of Scottish Enterprise.

The appointment of Michael Forsyth as chairman of the Scottish Tory Party in 1989 also demonstrated Mrs Thatcher's faltering political touch. 'Give me six men strong and true,' she once said, 'and we'll get through.'[36] Despite the presence of Forsyth, however, the Prime Minister had never really been able to identify six men strong and true in Scotland. George Younger was certainly strong but never a true believer, while Malcolm Rifkind was only strong and true for about a year after the 1987 general election. Other Scottish acolytes were bit players, lacking influence on the wider political stage. The result was diminishing support for Mrs Thatcher even within the Scottish arm of her own party.

At the same time, perhaps unwittingly, that party allowed its political opponents to portray their actions as 'anti-Scottish', despite the creation of agencies ostentatiously called Scottish Enterprise and Scottish Homes. Again, it was a case of too little, too late. So, as the journalist Peter Jones observed the week Mrs Thatcher resigned as Prime Minister, 'Thatcherism came to Scotland a decade too late, when its time was past, and its memory in Scotland will be a bitter one.'[37] But what more could they have done to make that memory a happier one? 'We should have tried to introduce some particularly Scottish element into privatisation,' thought the Conservative activist Bob Kernohan, 'like a privately run Scottish Steel Corporation.'[38] Indeed, defending Scottish nationhood in this way had been part of the Conservative stock in trade for decades, exploited by leaders like Stanley Baldwin, Winston Churchill and even Edward Heath. Instead, Mrs Thatcher saw Scotland as 'nothing but problems'.[39] Not only that, but problems without solutions. Only in 1995 did Michael Forsyth seek to effectively combine Thatcherite nationalism/populism with a free-market approach, by which point it was too late. When the author asked Lord Forsyth if there was anything which, with the benefit of hindsight, his party might have approached differently he replied, in a slightly exasperated way, 'What more could we have done?'[40] Revealingly it is a difficult question to answer.

At least, however, Mrs Thatcher's governments had ideas, no matter how unpopular. Although the former Scottish Labour leader Wendy Alexander's assertion that the last time 'the Labour movement in Scotland made a real intellectual contribution to the UK Labour Party'[41] had been in 1906 was not entirely fair, most Labour thinking during the Thatcher era operated stubbornly within the old rules of the game. Mrs Thatcher changed those rules, but it took the People's Party a remarkably long time to catch up.

---

[36] *The Downing Street Years* (BBC) 8/10/1993.

[37] *Scotsman* 23/11/1990.

[38] Interview with Bob Kernohan, 6/6/2008.

[39] Kemp, *The Hollow Drum*, 189.

[40] Interview with Lord Forsyth, 22/4/2008.

[41] *Daily Telegraph* 30/9/2002.

Intellectually, Gordon Brown helped ensure they eventually did, while Labour thinkers often ended up reaching the same conclusions as the game's former mistress.

Is it also necessary to deal with the right-wing critique that the reason Scotland did not like Thatcherism was that they were not properly experiencing it, an argument to which Mrs Thatcher's alludes in her memoirs. In that vein, the view that Teddy Taylor, as Scottish Secretary, 'might have been able to build up a working-class Toryism that could have undermined the nationalist case being made by the middle class'[42] does not stack up. Urban Tory decline meant Taylor could not hold on to his own constituency never mind revive the party nationally, and importantly – beyond Europe and, perhaps, law and order – he did not differ in any substantial way from those of George Younger's ilk politically. While the skilled working-class vote courted by Taylor was responsive to Thatcherism in England, it remained unreconstructed in Scotland. Moreover, the central thrust of Mrs Thatcher's revolution would have required trimming in order to appease an increasingly resentful Scottish middle class. 'Thatcher's supreme blunder was not to exploit the class nature of this resentment,' judged the academic Lindsay Paterson, 'to fail to mobilise a countervailing sectional interest that would be just as Scottish but on her side ideologically.'[43] But when the fundamental 'sectional interest' was private versus public it is difficult, frankly, to see how she could have achieved this, even assuming she had wanted to.

'It is precisely because Scots have endured the rigours of Thatcherism, but have shown a growing distaste for it,' observed the academic Paul Carmichael in 1992, 'that Scotland's treatment and hence its experience are perceived as having been different. An adverse reaction to the medicine, in contrast to many recipients in the south, should not be confused with a failure of the doctor to administer the dose in the first place.'[44] This is a crucial point in the light of subsequent Thatcherite mythology. 'There was no privatisation in Scotland before 1987,' claimed the historian Michael Fry. 'There were no working-class people with shares in their pockets with the value of those shares rising and feeling richer all of a sudden. Popular Thatcherism had not come to Scotland so there was nothing to offset the pain.'[45] While it is true that bus services in Scotland were not privatised before the 1987 election, as they were in England, Fry's analysis conveniently avoids the sale of British Telecom in 1984, British Gas in 1986 and British Airways in February 1987. All three applied UK-wide and therefore benefited Scottish workers in each utility.[46]

So 'Thatcherism did happen in Scotland,' as Andrew Marr wrote in *The*

---

[42] Paterson, *The Autonomy of Modern Scotland*, 170.

[43] Ibid.

[44] Carmichael, 'Is Scotland different? Local government policy under Mrs Thatcher', *Local Government Policy Making 18 5* (May 1992), 31.

[45] Fry, *Thatcher and the Scots* (BBC Scotland).

[46] Indeed, the author's father was one of them, receiving a tranche of shares from BT when it was privatised in 1984.

Battle for Scotland. 'George Younger and Malcolm Rifkind, displaying skill, good humour and loyalty, were the men who made it happen.' Even Younger's subtle modifications – for instance over the sale of Ferranti – amounted to little more than sensitive public relations. 'The changes they initiated through Scottish legislation,' added Marr, 'combined with the UK-wide trade-union reforms, public-spending restraint, income-tax cuts and the curbing of local authorities, added up to a substantial shift in the mood and structure of Scottish public life.'[47] So Scotland did not escape the worst of Thatcherism, nor did it escape the best. A rise in unemployment was felt across the country, as was the fall in inflation. Furthermore, many regional differences had historical origins, while a lot of the industrial decline identified with Mrs Thatcher was well under way – not least in coal, manufacturing and shipbuilding – before she became Prime Minister. Similarly, even judged in these terms Scotland was not the worst affected part of the UK. Unemployment in the West Midlands was much worse, yet there was no specific reaction against Thatcher in that region.

So did the United Kingdom weaken, as the broadcaster Allan Little claimed in his BBC programme, *Thatcher and the Scots*, as a result of this tension between reforming Thatcherism and civic Scotland? Perhaps it did, which is ironic considering Mrs Thatcher's sincerely held unionism. While in England there was opposition to Thatcherism, it rarely manifested itself in a nationalist form. In Wales, by contrast, there was a similar reaction to that in Scotland without similar institutional manifestations. In the summer of 2008, for example, there was a furious row over a giant steel artwork of Mrs Thatcher which was displayed in the windows of the National Assembly for Wales. A Plaid Cymru Assembly Member also claimed the Assembly's Plaid–Labour coalition was dedicated to pursuing policies which were the 'antithesis of Thatcherism'.[48] In Northern Ireland, meanwhile, Mrs Thatcher managed to offend both the Nationalist community (largely over hunger strikes in the early 1980s) and its Unionists (following the Anglo-Irish Agreement in 1985). Unlike in Scotland and Wales, however, voters in the province never had the option of voting for or against her, which put talk of a Scottish 'democratic deficit' in some perspective.

In truth, the no-mandate argument never quite stacked up. As the academic Richard Rose observed of the 1964 election, in which Labour lost in England but won in the UK as a whole, 'The Tories did not issue demands for the creation of a devolved English Assembly to meet in Winchester, on the grounds that Labour was unrepresentative of England. Losers as well as winners accepted that the power of government belonged to the party winning the most seats in Britain overall.'[49] As the losers (in UK terms) in 1979, 1983 and 1987, many in the Labour Party chose to reject this consensus

---

[47] Marr, *The Battle for Scotland*, 172.
[48] *Western Mail* 28/12/2007.
[49] Kavanagh and Selsdon, eds, *The Thatcher Effect*, 259.

on expedient political grounds. Furthermore, the no-mandate argument was a specific creation of 1980s devolutionism. It was rarely articulated in the 1970s, and even in the 1980s it did not represent mainstream Labour opinion. To argue that the government lacked 'legitimacy' in Scotland made more sense, but lacked the political potency of the no-mandate rallying cry.

All of this leads inescapably to the conclusion that there were distinct Scottish factors working against Thatcherism, although these were more institutional (Scots law, Scottish education, the Kirk) than innate differences of character (more caring, more egalitarian, less commercially minded) as identified by civic Scotland. ('I think that, to an extent, the references to Scottish communitarian or caring traditions was more of an afterthought,' thought the writer Neal Ascherson, 'to legitimise hating Thatcher for a number of other reasons.'[50]) Regular opinion polling did indeed show opposition to most central aspects of Thatcherite reform, but then even UK-wide surveys in the late 1980s demonstrated a similar failure to identify with Thatcherite principles in terms of the private sector and greater choice. This led the academic Ivor Crewe to conclude that 'there has been no Thatcherite transformation of attitudes or behaviour among the British public',[51] an assertion which surely misses the point. While Mrs Thatcher may not have changed attitudes as assessed by opinion polls and social attitude surveys, she demonstrably did change behaviour – however sub-consciously manifested – as measured by political language, home-ownership statistics, the consumer boom and individual pursuit of wider choice. 'History certainly relates events, statistics record economic performance, letters and documents are preserved for posterity to tell us what happened,' Nick Ridley noted perceptively in his memoirs. 'But the impact of individuals on the course of history can never be accurately assessed by historians, try though they may.'[52]

This historian would obviously beg to differ on Ridley's final point, but his central assertion rings true. It is always much easier for people, particularly when questioned in surveys, to deny the influence of a negatively perceived ideology than admit to having embraced its core aspects. Unemployment was a case in point. Poll after poll suggested that public concern over unemployment remained high throughout the 1980s, particularly in Scotland, and that most people believed a government's duty was to create jobs whatever the cost. Yet, as Hugo Young observed, 'How to stop worrying and live with unemployment was one of the principal lessons Thatcherism administered to the country, and it achieved a permanent social shift in the process.'[53] 'Repetition of the thought helped to establish a new social norm, if

---

[50] Neal Ascherson to the author, 27/6/2008.

[51] Kavanagh and Selsdon, eds, *The Thatcher Effect*, 241. Polling suggested that following 11 years of Thatcherism 78 per cent of Scots felt there should be no more privatisation and 85 per cent believed subsidising employment was justifiable. (Midwinter, *Local Government in Scotland*, 4)

[52] Ridley, *My Style of Government*, 266.

[53] Young, *One of Us*, 534.

not universal approval for it,' he added. 'It was now fashionable to be rich not poor, to consume rather than to "care".'[54] There are few signs that Scotland resisted this fashion. As the authors of *Living in Scotland* again concluded, Scottish society in 2004 was no longer viewed as an old-fashioned collective, but 'rather as a web of individual opportunity and choice'.[55] Even in the 1980s, despite the frequent incantations of civic Scotland, there was little evidence that Scots were any more immune than the English to both. To Richard Finlay, 'the idea of civil society was an aspiration. It was how the Scots would like their society to be rather than how their society really was.'[56]

'THAT BLOODY WOMAN'

'The interesting question is would the policies associated with Thatcherism have been much more acceptable had they been expounded with a Scottish accent,' said the financial journalist Bill Jamieson, 'by a Scot with a more persuasive, sympathetic, embracing way of getting people on board. Saying, 'Look, we've got to bite the bullet and do it, we don't want to be stuck being dependent forever".'[57]

The election result in Scotland in 1983, and the reaction to George Younger as Secretary of State for Scotland, perhaps demonstrates that a gentler exposition of Thatcherite arguments did, and could have continued to, render them more acceptable, something confirmed by the reaction to Michael Forsyth from the other extreme. Further proof comes from the fact that a whole generation of Labour and SNP politicians, most notably Jack McConnell and Alex Salmond, were able to speak the language of Thatcherism without fear of becoming political pariahs.

So there was something in 'that woman's' voice, something unpalatable in her style and manner, which meant Scotland was never going to warm either to her personally or her political message. The debate became highly personalised, to the point that in the Scotland of the 1980s everything considered to be bad was bundled up in one harsh-sounding word, 'Thatcher', while everything deemed to be good was similarly bundled up in another word, 'devolution'. This had unintended consequences. Hating Mrs Thatcher (who apparently hated Scotland) became a convenient excuse for not, or indeed a convenient distraction from, addressing some of the issues she legitimately raised in relation to the role of the state and the status of the individual. 'In diverting attention to treatment of symptoms (be they council housing or North Sea oil), Scotland has historically avoided confrontation with the underlying conflicts causing its political, economic and cultural problems,' observed Sara Krusenstjerna in 1989. 'As a result, it now finds

---

[54] Ibid., 537.

[55] Paterson, *Living in Scotland*, 9.

[56] Murdoch, ed., *The Scottish Nation*, 153.

[57] Interview with Bill Jamieson, 18/11/2008.

itself caving in beneath a centuries-old accumulation of unresolved internal and external pressures.'[58]

Few of those pressures were genuinely resolved by the idea of a distinctive Scottish political identity, one that opposed Thatcherism on the basis of altruistic notions of community and public service, and explicity neglecting its emphasis on individualism and 'greed'. As the literary academic Cairns Craig observed when the Claim of Right was published in 1988, 'Too often, in Scotland, a particular way of seeing our culture, of representing ourselves, has come to dominate our perceptions because it has gone unchallenged – worse, unexamined.'[59] An understandably attractive notion of Scottish civic society – to which Mrs Thatcher was not necessarily hostile – became, as Richard Finlay has observed, 'a convenient way of masking the fact that numerous elements within Scottish society were in decline and losing social and political relevance'.[60]

So to claim, as the writer William McIlvanney did in 1987, that Mrs Thatcher wanted to destroy distinctively Scottish institutions is to miss the point. 'She cannot see an institution', quipped Julian Critchley, 'without hitting it with her handbag.'[61] In that sense, Scotland's Kirk and systems of education and law were not singled out for attack any more than their English counterparts. Across the UK, and in virtually every area of public life, Mrs Thatcher wanted institutions and individuals to re-examine themselves, and even where this re-examination was resisted she arguably left her mark. Where once Scottish universities, local authorities, businesses and council tenants looked to the state for solutions, within the space of a decade they – at least in part – also looked to markets and the private sector. 'She forced the political debate in Britain onto the ground of who can best run a market economy in Britain,' observed Nick Ridley in his memoirs, 'it is no longer about whether we have a market economy or a socialist one.'[62]

Even so, Mrs Thatcher was also pragmatic, refusing to significantly extend free-market principles into the NHS or state education. 'She was not some dogmatic, driven harridan, who was determined to impose a free-market system on Britain,' remarked Lord Forsyth, still, in 2009, a self-confessed 'Thatcher groupie'. He went on:

> She had a map and a compass; the map led to a more open society but the compass led her in different directions. She was pragmatic and that's why we didn't do lots of things in health and education that we should have. She was not always ideological. For instance, she was absolutely adamant about retaining Mortgage Interest Tax Relief because it did encourage people to buy houses, but Nigel Lawson and I argued against it. I now think she was right

[58] Brown & McCrone, eds, *Scottish Government Yearbook 1989*, 170.
[59] Dudley Edwards, ed., *A Claim of Right for Scotland*.
[60] Devine, ed., *Scotland and the Union*, 167.
[61] *The Times* 21/6/1982.
[62] Ridley, *My Style of Government*, 255.

about that, it was simply a matter of political judgement. She just had this instinct for how far she could go.

Her main legacy, added Forsyth, not only in Scotland but in the rest of the UK, was 'having changed the way people think'.[63] Take, for example, the words of the SNP MSP Alex Neil, a Nationalist but also a respected political economist. 'The fact of life is that we're living in a world where relatively speaking there's free trade,' he said, 'it's an open economy; it's a global society and I don't think it'd be possible to, even if you wanted to, to turn the clock back, quite frankly. And I don't think most people want to, to be blunt. The reality of life is that you can't go back to those old days.'[64]

Nevertheless, Mrs Thatcher is simply too convenient a political stick with which to beat up Conservative opponents for most Scottish parties and politicians to willingly lay it down. That the nature of this opposition is often hypocritical seems not to matter. An SNP First Minister was attacked by Labour for claiming Scots 'did not mind' the economic aspect of Thatcherism just months after a Labour Prime Minister entertained Baroness Thatcher to tea at Downing Street. The rump of the Scottish Conservative Party, meanwhile, was dismissed by every other party as an irrelevant hangover from the Thatcher era as the minority SNP government relied upon support from Tory MSPs to pass its budget, a financial package which essentially propagated Thatcherite economic ortho-doxy. Mantras of small government, value for money, enterprise, property ownership and low taxation also pervaded government documents and opposi-tion manifestos, yet few thought of this as in any way inconsistent.

So when the author interviewed people for this book praise for Mrs Thatcher or Thatcherism was predictably scarce; an indication of the likely reaction when she joins the legions of departed world leaders. The former STUC general secretary Campbell Christie said he could not think of anything which in retrospect was good, even blaming Mrs Thatcher for the spread of hospital-acquired infections (because of contracting out in the 1980s). The Scottish First Minister, Alex Salmond, could only bring himself to praise her leadership during the Falklands War ('There's no serious doubt that the test of mettle came out in her favour') although he did concede that 'she was a substantial figure who shifted the axis of politics',[65] while his predecessor Jack McConnell argued that although 'some of the objectives were admirable, the way in which they were applied in Scotland was a disaster'.[66] Only the former anti-Poll Tax protestor and Socialist MSP Tommy Sheridan was unequivocal: 'I couldn't endorse any semblance of what she stood for. I even refuse to give it a special status; what was Thatcherism other than capitalism stripped naked?'[67]

---

[63] Interview with Lord Forsyth.
[64] Interview with Alex Neil MSP, 22/4/2008.
[65] Interview with Alex Salmond MSP, 24/6/2008.
[66] Interview with Jack McConnell MSP, 25/6/2008.
[67] Interview with Tommy Sheridan, 22/6/2008.

Former ministers, not surprisingly, were more balanced. 'I think the fault was as much on the Scots' side as on hers,' said Lord Lang. 'She was giving them credit for characteristics that didn't exist.'[68] As for the characteristics that did exist, added Lang, Mrs Thatcher could certainly understand them; it was just that she could not empathise with them. And nor, indeed, could most Scots empathise with Mrs Thatcher, despite her best efforts to make them see something of themselves in her and her aspirations.

Some lyrics from the pen of Johnny Mercer seem apt:

When an irresistible force such as you
Meets an old immovable object like me
You can bet just as sure as you live
Something's gotta give, something's gotta give, something's gotta give.

Mrs Thatcher's was certainly an irresistible force, while Scotland's over-dependence on the state must have appeared to her as an immoveable object. So something did have to give, although it did on both sides. The Conservatives, if not Mrs Thatcher, were compelled to concede an irrefutable Scottish dimension by belatedly endorsing devolution, while Scotland was forced to let go, however painfully, of its old economic refrain.

And, importantly, it was an economic refrain which echoed around the world. Scotland was swept up in global events harnessed by Mrs Thatcher, and yes, it undoubtedly suffered, often disproportionately so. But to see what happened in the 1980s through the highly personalised prism of 'Thatcher hates Scotland' was absurd then, and is even more absurd decades after the event. To boil it all down to Mrs Thatcher mispronouncing 'Falkirk', as Dennis Canavan did in *Thatcher and the Scots*, does Thatcherism, not to mention Scotland and its Labour movement, a disservice.

So why, then, did Mrs Thatcher not get along with her Scottish subjects nor they with her? In reality there was not, nor could there have been, a single defining reason. The effect was both composite and cumulative. The composite comprised her femininity (with a touch of misogyny on the receiving end), aggression, general style and Englishness – few of which she could have done much about – and had rather less to do with policy than has been claimed. The cumulative effect came via rising unemployment and economic woe, which crucially lasted much longer in Scotland than in much of England. This was amplified by Scotland's disproportionately public-sector-based middle classes, who resented constant attacks from the government, both perceived and real. This anger grew over time, accumulating 'civic' clothing and was set in stone by the Poll Tax. The overall effect was then reinforced by opposition spin, media repetition and the seemingly insurmountable force of Scottish mythology.

---

[68] Interview with Lord Lang, 11/11/2008.

There are, however, hints that the historical judgement of Thatcherism and Scotland may be undergoing some revisionism. In 2005 the widely-respected historian Tom Devine declared that in 'terms of popular culture I don't think the Thatcher years have been considered fairly', adding that the 'negative effects may have been exaggerated and some of the other effects have been marginalised'. Although Devine still believed that Mrs Thatcher could have handled economic change more sensitively, he had shed his earlier belief that Scotland had been governed 'by an alien force'. 'What happened in the 1980s was not the end of the Scottish economy,' he said. 'It was a process of transition and transformation. We came through it and we are now undeniably more affluent, though there are huge pockets of disadvantage.' Furthermore, Devine argued that the anger Mrs Thatcher generated in Scotland actually had a beneficial effect on Scottish cultural and political life. 'It is almost as if Thatcher gave a relatively somnolent political democracy a kick in the backside.'[69]

As Simon Jenkins asserted in his book, *Thatcher & Sons*, 'The test of any revolution is, did it work and did it last?'[70] Looking at Scotland in 2009, even with an SNP administration, it seems clear that key elements of the Thatcher revolution did work and also endure. Even in a recession Scots no longer have to worry seriously about balance-of-payments deficits, or indeed pay and incomes policies, while rippling strikes are more or less a thing of the past. Thirty years ago the British state still controlled wages, ran factories, collected rents, installed telephones and supplied electricity and gas in Scotland. Now, as Allan Little has written, 'all of these things are done – if they're done at all – by the free market'.[71]

Attitudes have also changed. The consumer is now king and Scots can choose freely a new telephone or utility supplier in order to get a cheaper deal. Frequent holidays are accompanied by high spending, while almost every employment sector – even Scotland's ever-growing public sector – is witness to thrusting careerists and freelancers, the latter unthinkable on any scale in the 1979. More to the point, as the Labour-leaning economic commentator Alf Young observed of the later Thatcher period: 'People were better off. I think that's the most obvious physical manifestation of the change; out of that long period of despair and decline, people found there were other ways to make a living . . . people ha[d] begun to see the uplands on the other side of th[e] deep depression.'[72]

Yet still a corrosive, unthinking anti-Thatcherism persists. Ironically, having succeeded in breaking up one consensus, that of the post-war era, Mrs Thatcher inadvertently gave rise to another. In short, the Scots may never learn to love Mrs Thatcher, but they really ought to get over her.

---

[69] *Sunday Times* 27/2/2005
[70] Jenkins, *Thatcher & Sons*, 1.
[71] *Sunday Times* 28/12/2008.
[72] Young, *Thatcher and the Scots* (BBC Scotland).

Margaret Thatcher's speech to the General Assembly of the Church of Scotland, 21 May 1988

MODERATOR: I AM GREATLY honoured to have been invited to attend the opening of this 1988 General Assembly of the Church of Scotland; and I am deeply grateful that you have now asked me to address you.

I am very much aware of the historical continuity extending over four centuries, during which the position of the Church of Scotland has been recognised in constitutional law and confirmed by successive Sovereigns. It sprang from the independence of mind and rigour of thought that have always been such powerful characteristics of the Scottish people, as I have occasion to know. *[Muted laughter]* It has remained close to its roots and has inspired a commitment to service from all people.

I am therefore very sensible of the important influence which the Church of Scotland exercises in the life of the whole nation, both at the spiritual level and through the extensive caring services which are provided by your Church's department of social responsibility. And I am conscious also of the value of the continuing links which the Church of Scotland maintains with other Churches.

Perhaps it would be best, Moderator, if I began by speaking personally as a Christian, as well as a politician, about the way I see things. Reading recently, I came across the starkly simple phrase: 'Christianity is about spiritual redemption, not social reform.'

Sometimes the debate on these matters has become too polarised and given the impression that the two are quite separate. But most Christians would regard it as their personal Christian duty to help their fellow men and women. They would regard the lives of children as a precious trust. These duties come not from any secular legislation passed by Parliament, but from being a Christian.

But there are a number of people who are not Christians who would also accept those responsibilities. What then are the distinctive marks of

Christianity? They stem not from the social but from the spiritual side of our lives, and personally, I would identify three beliefs in particular:

First, that from the beginning man has been endowed by God with the fundamental right to choose between good and evil. And second, that we were made in God's own image and, therefore, we are expected to use all our own power of thought and judgement in exercising that choice; and further, that if we open our hearts to God, He has promised to work within us. And third, that Our Lord Jesus Christ, the Son of God, when faced with His terrible choice and lonely vigil *chose* to lay down His life that our sins may be forgiven. I remember very well a sermon on an Armistice Sunday when our Preacher said, 'No one took away the life of Jesus, He chose to lay it down'.

I think back to many discussions in my early life when we all agreed that if you try to take the fruits of Christianity without its roots, the fruits will wither. And they will not come again unless you nurture the roots.

But we must not profess the Christian faith and go to Church simply because we want social reforms and benefits or a better standard of behaviour; but because we accept the sanctity of life, the responsibility that comes with freedom and the supreme sacrifice of Christ expressed so well in the hymn: 'When I survey the wondrous Cross, On which the Prince of glory died, My richest gain I count but loss, And pour contempt on all my pride.'

May I also say a few words about my personal belief in the relevance of Christianity to public policy – to the things that are Caesar's?

The Old Testament lays down in Exodus the Ten Commandments as given to Moses, the injunction in Leviticus to love our neighbour as ourselves and generally the importance of observing a strict code of law. The New Testament is a record of the Incarnation, the teachings of Christ and the establishment of the Kingdom of God. Again we have the emphasis on loving our neighbour as ourselves and to 'Do-as-you-would-be-done-by'.

I believe that by taking together these key elements from the Old and New Testaments, we gain: a view of the universe, a proper attitude to work, and principles to shape economic and social life.

We are told we must work and use our talents to create wealth. 'If a man will not work he shall not eat' wrote St. Paul to the Thessalonians. Indeed, abundance rather than poverty has a legitimacy which derives from the very nature of Creation.

Nevertheless, the Tenth Commandment –Thou shalt not covet – recognises that making money and owning things could become selfish activities. But it is not the creation of wealth that is wrong but love of money for its own sake. The spiritual dimension comes in deciding what one does with the wealth. How could we respond to the many calls for help, or invest for the future, or support the wonderful artists and craftsmen whose work also glorifies God, unless we had first worked hard and used our talents to create the necessary wealth? And remember the woman with the alabaster jar of ointment.

I confess that I always had difficulty with interpreting the Biblical precept to love our neighbours 'as ourselves' until I read some of the words of C. S. Lewis. He pointed out that we don't exactly love *ourselves* when we fall below the standards and beliefs we have accepted. Indeed we might even hate ourselves for some unworthy deed.

None of this, of course, tells us exactly what kind of political and social institutions we should have. On this point, Christians will very often genuinely disagree, though it is a mark of Christian manners that they will do so with courtesy and mutual respect. *[Applause]* What is certain, however, is that any set of social and economic arrangements which is not founded on the acceptance of individual responsibility will do nothing but harm.

We are all responsible for our own actions. We can't blame society if we disobey the law. We simply can't delegate the exercise of mercy and generosity to others. The politicians and other secular powers should strive by their measures to bring out the good in people and to fight down the bad: but they can't create the one or abolish the other. They can only see that the laws encourage the best instincts and convictions of the people, instincts and convictions which I'm convinced are far more deeply rooted than is often supposed.

Nowhere is this more evident than the basic ties of the family which are at the heart of our society and are the very nursery of civic virtue. And it is on the family that we in government build our own policies for welfare, education and care.

You recall that Timothy was warned by St Paul that anyone who neglects to provide for his own house (meaning his own family) has disowned the faith and is 'worse than an infidel'.

We must recognise that modern society is infinitely more complex than that of Biblical times and of course new occasions teach new duties. In our generation, the only way we can ensure that no-one is left without sustenance, help or opportunity, is to have laws to provide for health and education, pensions for the elderly, succour for the sick and disabled.

But intervention by the State must never become so great that it effectively removes personal responsibility. The same applies to taxation; for while you and I would work extremely hard whatever the circumstances, there are undoubtedly some who would not unless the incentive was there. And we need their efforts too.

Moderator, recently there have been great debates about religious education. I believe strongly that politicians must see that religious education has a proper place in the school curriculum. *[Applause]*

In Scotland, as in England, there is an historic connection expressed in our laws between Church and State. The two connections are of a somewhat different kind, but the arrangements in both countries are designed to give symbolic expression to the same crucial truth: that the Christian religion – which, of course, embodies many of the great spiritual and moral truths of Judaism – is a fundamental part of our national heritage. And I believe it is the wish of the overwhelming majority of people that this heritage should be preserved and fostered. *[Applause]* For centuries it has been our very life blood. And indeed we are a nation whose ideals are founded on the Bible.

Also, it is quite impossible to understand our history or literature without grasping this fact, and that's the strong practical case for ensuring that children at school are given adequate instruction in the part which the Judaic-Christian tradition has played in moulding our laws, manners and institutions. How can you make sense of Shakespeare and Sir Walter Scott, or of the constitutional conflicts of the seventeenth century in both Scotland and England, without some such fundamental knowledge?

But I go further than this. The truths of the Judaic-Christian tradition are infinitely precious, not only, as I believe, because they are true, but also because they provide the moral impulse which alone can lead to that peace, in the true meaning of the word, for which we all long.

To assert absolute moral values is not to claim perfection for ourselves. No true Christian could do that. What is more, one of the great principles of our Judaic-Christian inheritance is tolerance. People with other faiths and cultures have always been welcomed in our land, assured of equality under the law, of proper respect and of open friendship. There's absolutely nothing incompatible between this and our desire to maintain the essence of our own identity. There is no place for racial or religious intolerance in our creed.

When Abraham Lincoln spoke in his famous Gettysburg speech of 1863 of 'government of the people, by the people, and for the people', he gave the world a neat definition of democracy which has since been widely and enthusiastically adopted. But what he enunciated as a form of government was not in itself especially Christian, for nowhere in the Bible is the word democracy mentioned. Ideally, when Christians meet, as Christians, to take counsel together their purpose is not (or should not be) to ascertain what is the mind of the majority but what is the mind of the Holy Spirit – something which may be quite different. *[Applause]*

Nevertheless I am an enthusiast for democracy. And I take that position, not because I believe majority opinion is inevitably right or true – indeed no majority can take away God-given human rights – but because I believe it most effectively safeguards the value of the individual, and, more than any other system, restrains the abuse of power by the few. And that *is* a Christian concept.

But there is little hope for democracy if the hearts of men and women in democratic societies cannot be touched by a call to something greater than themselves. Political structures, state institutions, collective ideals – these are not enough.

We Parliamentarians can legislate for the rule of law. You, the Church, can teach the life of faith.

But when all is said and done, the politician's role is a humble one. I always think that the whole debate about the Church and the State has never yielded anything comparable in insight to that beautiful hymn 'I Vow to Thee my Country'. It begins with a triumphant assertion of what might be described as secular patriotism, a noble thing indeed in a country like ours: 'I vow to thee my country all earthly things above; entire, whole and perfect the service of my love'.

It goes on to speak of 'another country I heard of long ago' whose King can't be seen and whose armies can't be counted, but 'soul by soul and silently her shining bounds increase'. Not group by group, or party by party, or even church by church – but soul by soul – and each one counts.

That, members of the Assembly, is the country which you chiefly serve. You fight your cause under the banner of an historic Church. Your success matters greatly – as much to the temporal as to the spiritual welfare of the nation. I leave you with that earnest hope that may we all come nearer to that other country whose 'ways are ways of gentleness and all her paths are peace.' *[Enthusiastic applause]*

Margaret Thatcher: Complete Public Statements 1945–1990. Database and Compilation © OUP 1999.

Appendix 2

Percentage share of Conservative vote in Scotland 1974–97

Election	Share of the vote	Number of seats
February 1974	32.9%	21
October 1974	24.7%	16
1979	31.4%	22
1983	28.4%	21
1987	24.0%	10
1992	25.6%	11
1997	17.5%	0

District and Regional Council elections 1980–90

Year	Share of the vote	Number of seats
1980 (district)	24.1%	229
1982 (regional)	25.1%	119
1984 (district)	21.4%	189
1986 (regional)	16.9%	65
1988 (district)	19.4%	162
1990 (regional)	19.6%	52

Source: *Scottish Government Yearbook 1989* (district) & *Scottish Government Yearbook 1991* (regional).

European Parliament elections 1979–89

Year	Share of the vote	Number of seats
1979	33.7%	5
1984	25.7%	2
1989	20.9%	0

Source: *Scottish Government Yearbook 1990*.

Appendix 3

Mrs Thatcher and Scotland:

A CHRONOLOGY

11 February 1975
Margaret Thatcher elected Conservative leader on second ballot.

21 February 1975
Mrs Thatcher visits Scotland for the first time as Conservative leader.

17 May 1975
Mrs Thatcher reiterates devolution pledge at annual Scottish Conservative conference.

8 July 1975
The Scottish Development Agency (SDA) is established.

22 November 1975
A government white paper, *Our Changing Democracy*, proposes a legislative assembly for Scotland and an executive assembly for Wales.

16 March 1976
Harold Wilson resigns as Prime Minister. James Callaghan succeeds him on 5 April.

4 October 1976
The Right Approach is published.

28 November 1976
The Scotland and Wales Bill is published.

1 December 1976
The Shadow Cabinet agrees to oppose the government's Scotland and Wales Bill. Alick-Buchanan Smith, the Shadow Scottish Secretary, and his deputy

Malcolm Rifkind, resign more than a week later. Teddy Taylor succeeds Buchanan-Smith after Betty Harvie Anderson declines promotion to the Tory front bench.

13 December 1976
Mrs Thatcher leads for the opposition at the second reading of the Scotland and Wales Bill.

1977
The Adam Smith Institute think tank is founded.

22 February 1977
The government is defeated on a guillotine motion on the Scotland and Wales Bill by 312 votes to 283.

April 1977
An internal Scottish Conservative Party committee chaired by Russell Fairgrieve reports to Mrs Thatcher. It recommends stronger ties with Conservative Central Office in London.

8 October 1977
The Right Approach to the Economy is published.

25 January 1978
George Cunningham's amendment to the Scotland Bill, stipulating that 40 per cent of the Scottish electorate has to endorse devolution in a referendum, is carried.

22 February 1978
A new, standalone Scotland Bill is given a third reading by 297 votes to 257.

May 1978
Onward to Victory: A Statement of the Conservative Approach for Scotland is published.

The Conservatives win 136 seats and 30.3 per cent of the vote in Scotland's second regional council elections.

26 October 1978
Labour holds Berwick and East Lothian with 47.7 per cent of the vote, to the Conservatives' 40.2 per cent.

3 January 1979
The 'winter of discontent' begins.

13 February 1979
Lord Home urges Scots to vote 'no' for a better devolution Bill at the behest of Mrs Thatcher.

1 March 1979
40 per cent of the Scottish electorate fails to support a Scottish Assembly. Mrs Thatcher says it has been 'a good day for the United Kingdom'.

28 March 1979
The government is defeated on a motion of no confidence by 311 to 310 votes. The SNP votes with the Conservatives.

3 May 1979
Mrs Thatcher becomes Prime Minister after winning the general election with an overall majority of 44. In Scotland the Conservatives gain 31.4 per cent of the vote and 22 seats. Teddy Taylor loses his Cathcart constituency and George Younger becomes Scottish Secretary.

12 May 1979
Mrs Thatcher addresses the Scottish Conservative conference in Perth, her first public speech as Prime Minister.

June 1979
The Select Committee on Scottish Affairs is revived. The Labour MP Donald Dewar becomes chairman.

7 June 1979
In the first direct elections to the European Parliament the Scottish Conservatives win 33.7 per cent of the vote and five seats, beating both Labour and the SNP.

12 June 1979
Sir Geoffrey Howe unveils his first budget, cutting direct taxation but almost doubling VAT.

20 June 1979
The repeal of the Scotland Act is passed by 311 votes to 206.

11 July 1979
Mrs Thatcher visits the Scottish Office in Edinburgh as part of her Whitehall tour.

26 July 1979
Review of regional policy concludes. Most parts of Scotland downgraded to Intermediate Status, although dispersal of civil service posts to Glasgow and East Kilbride goes ahead.

August 1979
Mrs Thatcher holidays on Islay with Lord Margadale.

2 January 1980
Steel strike begins (and ends on 3 April).

14 January 1980
The Tenants' Rights Etc (Scotland) Bill is introduced, including the 'Right to Buy' for council house tenants.

1 March 1980
The Campaign for a Scottish Assembly (CSA) is formed.

14 May 1980
STUC marches take place in Glasgow and Edinburgh in protest at Jim Prior's Employment Bill.

29 July 1980
Clydebank designated Scotland's first Enterprise Zone following the closure of the Singer sewing-machine plant.

10 February 1981
National Coal Board announces pit closures, including several in Scotland. The plans are abandoned eight days later.

11 February 1981
Peugeot-Citroen announces the closure of the Linwood car plant. The pulp mill at Corpach, the engineering company Carron, and the British Leyland commercial vehicle plant at Bathgate also close during 1981.

March 1981
The Education (Scotland) Bill is introduced, with provisions for the Assisted Places Scheme and the Parents' Charter.

10 March 1981
Sir Geoffrey Howe's Budget defies Keynesian convention by increasing taxes and further cutting public spending at the height of a recession.

26 March 1981
Social Democratic Party (SDP) is formed, followed by an Alliance with the Liberals on 16 June.

May 1981
Total registered unemployment in Scotland reaches 288,200.

28 May 1981
The SNP's annual conference votes to support civil disobedience against the Conservative government. Jim Sillars, a leading exponent of what becomes known as 'The Scottish Resistance', is elected vice-chairman for policy.

11 June 1981
The Local Government (Miscellaneous Provisions) (Scotland) Act is passed.

21 July 1981
George Younger moves orders to cut the Rate Support Grant to Lothian Regional Council by £47 million, Dundee District Council by £2 million and Stirling District Council by £1 million.

15 January 1982
The Monopolies and Mergers Commission's report on two attempted take-overs of the Royal Bank of Scotland is published, advising against both.

15 February 1982
The Scottish Grand Committee meets in Edinburgh for the first time.

25 March 1982
The SDP wins Glasgow Hillhead from the Conservatives at a by-election, depriving the governing party of its last Glaswegian stronghold.

2 April 1982
Argentinian forces seize the Falkland Islands.

May 1982
Total recorded unemployment in Scotland reaches 324,709. Conservatives sustain further losses in regional council elections.

14 May 1982
Mrs Thatcher gives a barnstorming speech to the Scottish Conservative conference as a British Task Force heads for the South Atlantic.

30 July 1982
The Local Government and Planning (Scotland) Act is passed.

November 1982
The Energy Secretary Nigel Lawson authorises the first share issue for Britoil, formerly the Glasgow-based British National Oil Corporation.

20 December 1982
The Ravenscraig steelworks is given a three-year reprieve by the government.

9 May 1983
The British Shipbuilders Act is passed, privatising Scotland's shipyards.

14 May 1983
Mrs Thatcher launches the Conservative general election campaign at the Scottish Tory conference in Perth.

9 June 1983
The Conservatives win the UK general election with a majority of 144. The government retains 21 seats in Scotland.

September 1983
The Scottish Office issues a circular asking health boards to explore 'contracting out' of hospital services like cleaning and catering.

January 1984
The Adam Smith Institute publishes its Omega Report on Scottish Policy.

12 March 1984
The miners' strike begins.

May 1984
The Conservatives suffer further losses at the district council elections, losing control of Edinburgh and Eastwood councils.

14 June 1984
The Conservatives lose three of their five Scottish MEPs in elections to the European Parliament and slump to 25.7 per cent of the vote.

16 June 1984
The Treasury gives notice that it intends to cut the baseline Scottish Office budget.

20 November 1984
British Telecom is privatised.

December 1984
A year-long strike by Scottish teachers begins.

12 February 1985
New Scottish rateable values announced, leading to an outcry from the Scottish Conservative Party.

3 March 1985
The National Union of Mineworkers votes to end the miners' strike.

31 March 1985
Meeting of ministers held at Chequers to discuss replacing the rates with a 'poll tax'.

9 April 1985
Adam Smith Institute publishes *Revising the Rating System* by Douglas Mason, a Glenrothes councillor, advocating a poll tax, possibly starting first in Scotland.

9–11 May 1985
The Scottish Tory conference convinces George Younger and Willie White-law to push for a poll tax first in Scotland. Press reports suggest the government is sympathetic.

7 August 1985
The government announces a further reprieve of Ravenscraig but the closure of the Gartcosh finishing mill.

Autumn 1985
Brian Unwin, the Deputy Cabinet Secretary, chairs a review of the Barnett Formula following further disputes between the Scottish Office and the Treasury over the Scottish Block.

November 1985
A group of right-wing Tory MPs, including Michael Forsyth and Allan Stewart, publish *No Turning Back: a new agenda from a group of Conservative MPs*.

15 November 1985
The Anglo-Irish Agreement is signed at Hillsborough Castle in Dublin, giving the Irish Republic a consultative role in the running of Northern Ireland.

2 December 1985
The Single European Act is agreed at Luxembourg European Council.

9 January 1986
Michael Heseltine walks out of the Cabinet over the Westland Affair. George Younger replaces him as Defence Secretary and Malcolm Rifkind becomes Secretary of State for Scotland.

28 January 1986
Paying for Local Government published, proposing a Community Charge in place of the rates.

April 1986
The STUC publishes *Scotland – A Strategy for the Future*.

May 1986
The Conservatives sink to their lowest ever share of the vote and tally of councillors in the regional council elections.

July 1986
Unemployment peaks in Scotland at 358,988 as the price of oil slumps.

July–August 1986
Commonwealth Games held in Edinburgh. Several countries boycott the event because of the UK's refusal to engage in sanctions against South Africa.

27 October 1986
The 'Big Bang' takes place in the City of London.

26 November 1986
The Abolition of Domestic Rates Etc. (Scotland) Bill is introduced.

26 February 1987
Malcolm Rifkind announces that the Poll Tax will start in Scotland on 1 April 1989.

Spring 1987
The STUC publishes *Scotland: A Land Fit for People*.

15 May 1987
The Scottish Poll Tax legislation gets Royal Assent. Mrs Thatcher again launches the general election campaign at Scottish Tory conference in Perth.

11 June 1987
The Conservatives win a third term at the UK general election with a majority of 101 but return just ten MPs in Scotland. Michael Forsyth joins the Scottish Office.

2 September 1987
Mrs Thatcher visits Scotland for the first time since the election and rules out any concessions on devolution. The Scottish Tory Party is reorganised.

23 September 1987
Mrs Thatcher tells *Woman's Own* that 'there is no such thing as society'.

6 October 1987
The UK Conservative conference revolts against dual running and votes for the immediate replacement of rates in England and Wales with the Poll Tax. The speech of the defeated Aberdeen South MP Gerry Malone is instrumental.

19 October 1987
'Black Monday' – Dow Jones falls by 23 per cent.

23 November 1987
During a speech in Glasgow the Chancellor Nigel Lawson identifies what he calls a 'culture of dependence' in Scotland.

3 December 1987
Kenneth Clarke announces that the British Steel Corporation is to be privatised, but includes caveats for the Ravenscraig steelworks.

January 1988
Health boards in Scotland are instructed to introduce Compulsory Competitive Tendering.

10 January 1988
Lord Whitelaw leaves the government following a mild stroke in December 1987.

24 February 1988
The government relinquishes its 'golden share' in Britoil, enabling BP to take it over.

15 March 1988
Highest rate of income tax reduced to 40 per cent and basic rate cut to 25 per cent in Budget.

29 March 1988
Rifkind publishes *New Life for Urban Scotland*. Scottish Homes, a new national housing agency, is also established.

1 April 1988
Sir William Kerr Fraser retires as permanent under-secretary at the Scottish Office. Mrs Thatcher tries to find a replacement from outside the Scottish Office, but eventually settles for Russell Hillhouse.

11 April 1988
The Social Security Act comes into force.

May 1988
District council elections see further losses for the Scottish Conservatives.

13 May 1988
Mrs Thatcher delivers her first Scottish Conservative conference speech since the election, declaring that 'Scottish values are Tory values – and vice versa'. An attempt to bounce her into compromising over devolution fails.

14 May 1988
Mrs Thatcher attends the Scottish Cup Final at Hampden in Glasgow.

17 May 1988
Interest rates are cut to 7.5 per cent, the lowest level of Mrs Thatcher's premiership.

21 May 1988
Mrs Thatcher delivers her 'Sermon on the Mound' to the General Assembly of the Church of Scotland.

13 July 1988
The Campaign for a Scottish Assembly publishes 'A Claim of Right for Scotland'.

8 September 1988
Mrs Thatcher launches 'Scottish Enterprise' at the Scottish CBI conference following a proposal from its chairman, Bill Hughes.

20 September 1988
Mrs Thatcher delivers her 'Bruges speech' at the College of Europe.

10 November 1988
Jim Sillars wins Glasgow Govan for the SNP at a by-election.

15 November 1988
The School Boards (Scotland) Act is passed.

31 January 1989
The UK white paper *Working for Patients* is published, proposing an internal market for the NHS and giving hospitals the option of opting out from state control.

30 March 1989
First meeting of the Scottish Constitutional Convention.

1 April 1989
The Poll Tax is introduced in Scotland a year ahead of England.

4 May 1989
Mrs Thatcher celebrates ten years as Prime Minister.

15 June 1989
Conservatives win no Scottish MEPS in elections to the European Parliament and gain only 20.9 per cent of the vote.

6 July 1989
Michael Forsyth succeeds Lord Goold as chairman of the Scottish Conservative Party.

21 July 1989
The Transport (Scotland) Act privatises the Scottish Bus Group and fully deregulates the industry.

27 July 1989
Scotland's electricity companies are privatised.

1 August 1989
Compulsory Competitive Tendering begins in Scottish local government.

15 September 1989
Figures show that 15 per cent of Scots are not paying their Poll Tax.

26 October 1989
Nigel Lawson resigns as Chancellor. He is succeeded by John Major.

16 November 1989
The Self-Governing Schools (Scotland) Act is passed, allowing individual schools to opt out from state control.

28 November 1989
Sir Anthony Meyer stands against Mrs Thatcher for the Conservative leadership. She is re-elected on 5 December with 314 votes to 33 and 24 spoilt ballot papers.

19 December 1989
The Law Reform (Miscellaneous Provisions) (Scotland) Bill is introduced to the House of Lords, proposing an end to the monopoly of solicitors in conveyancing.

6 March 1990
Demonstrations against Poll Tax take place across Britain.

9 March 1990
Mrs Thatcher is interviewed on BBC Scotland by Kirsty Wark.

30 March 1990
A Trafalgar Square anti-Poll Tax demonstration turns into a riot. The tax is introduced in England and Wales the following day.

29 April 1990
Mrs Thatcher sets up a Cabinet committee to review the Poll Tax.

May 1990
Supporters of Michael Forsyth attempt to oust Malcolm Rifkind as Scottish Secretary at the Scottish Conservative conference in Aberdeen.

16 May 1990
The newly privatised British Steel Corporation announces its intention to close the Ravenscraig steelworks.

14 July 1990
The 'Day for Scotland' rock festival held by Artists for Independence group.

26 July 1990
Scottish Enterprise and Highlands and Islands Enterprise created to replace the Scottish Development Agency and Highlands and Islands Development Board. Scotland's five New Town Development Corporations are also wound up.

7 September 1990
Michael Forsyth resigns as chairman of the Scottish Conservative Party and is succeeded by Lord Sanderson.

5 October 1990
The UK joins the Exchange Rate Mechanism.

1 November 1990
The Environmental Protection Act creates a new body called Scottish Natural Heritage.

The Broadcasting Act ends the automatic renewal of ITV franchises and establishes a Gaelic Television Fund.

Sir Geoffrey Howe resigns as Leader of the House. His resignation speech on 13 November is bitterly critical of the Prime Minister. Michael Heseltine declares his candidacy for the Conservative leadership the following day.

20 November 1990
Mrs Thatcher wins the first ballot in the leadership election but announces two days later that she will not contest the second ballot.

28 November 1990
Margaret Thatcher resigns as Prime Minister following the election of John Major as Conservative leader.

30 November 1990
The Scottish Constitutional Convention publishes its blueprint for a Scottish Parliament.

Appendix 4

Employment rates, Scotland and the UK 1960–2000

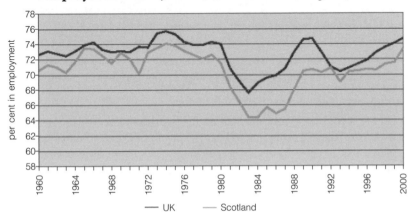

Source: *Scottish Economic Statistics 2001*

Changes in Scottish housing tenure 1979–90 (thousands)

	Owner-occupied	Public rented	Housing associations	Private rented	Public authority sales to tenants
1979	699	1,073	–	210	1
1980	721	1,074	–	202	6
1981	718	1,027	36	191	11
1982	747	1,016	38	182	14
1983	781	1,001	41	174	18
1984	816	987	45	167	17
1985	850	974	47	161	15
1986	884	962	50	154	18
1987	922	943	54	147	19
1988	972	914	59	139	32
1989	1,033	877	62	133	39
1990	1,088	845	65	126	33

Source: *Scottish Economic Statistics 2001*

Average weekly earnings of employees – Scotland and Great Britain 1975–2000

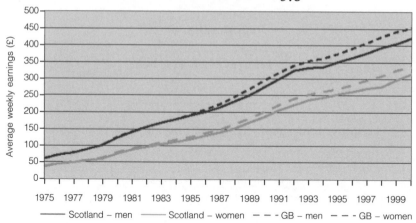

Source: New Earnings Survey, National Statistics

BIBLIOGRAPHY

ARCHIVES

Cabinet Office files (Whitehall)
Conservative Party Archive (CPA, University of Oxford)
Margaret Thatcher Foundation (MTF, www.margaretthatcher.org)
Margaret Thatcher Papers (Churchill College, University of Cambridge)
National Union of Mineworkers (NUM, Scottish Area, National Library of Scotland)
Scottish Conservative and Unionist Association Papers (SCUAP, National Library of Scotland)
Scottish Office files (NAS, National Archives of Scotland)
Scottish Trades Union Congress Archive (STUC, Glasgow Caledonian University)
Treasury files (Whitehall)
Tweedsmuir Papers (Priscilla Buchan, Baroness Tweedsmuir) (National Library of Scotland)
Younger, 4th Viscount (George K. H. Younger) (GYP, Private Collection)

PUBLISHED SOURCES

Aitken, Keith, *The Bairns O' Adam: The Story of the STUC* (Edinburgh 1997)
Ascherson, Neal, *Stone Voices: The Search for Scotland* (London 2002)
Ashcroft, Brian, *Scotland's Economic Problem: Too Few Entrepreneurs, Too Little Enterprise?* (Glasgow 1996)
Ashcroft, Brian, Love, James and Malloy, Eleanor, *New Firm Formation in the UK Counties with Special Reference to Scotland* (Glasgow 1990)
Ashdown, Paddy, *The Ashdown Diaries: Volume Two 1997–1999* (London 2001)
Braddon, Russell, *Roy Thomson of Fleet Street* (London 1965)
British Social Attitudes: Report 1986 (Aldershot 1988)
British Social Attitudes: Report 1988 (Aldershot 1990)
Brown, Alice and McCrone, David, eds, *The Scottish Government Yearbook 1989 & 1991* (Edinburgh 1989, 1991)

Brown, Alice, McCrone, David and Paterson, Lindsay, *Politics and Society in Scotland* (Basingstoke 1996)

Brown, Alice and Parry, Richard, eds, *The Scottish Government Yearbook 1990* (Edinburgh 1990)

Brown, Gordon, *Where There is Greed . . . Margaret Thatcher and the Betrayal of Britain's Future* (Edinburgh 1989)

Brown, Gordon and Alexander, Douglas, *New Scotland, New Britain* (London 1999)

Butler, David, Adonis, Andrew and Travers, Tony, *Failure in British Government: The Politics of the Poll Tax* (London 1994)

Butler, David and Kavanagh, Dennis, *The British General Election of 1979* (London 1980)

Campbell, John, *Margaret Thatcher Volume One: The Grocer's Daughter* (London 2000)
— *Margaret Thatcher Volume Two: The Iron Lady* (London 2003)

Carmichael, Paul, 'Is Scotland different? Local government policy under Mrs Thatcher', *Local Government Policy-Making 18 5* (May 1992)

Catterall, Peter, ed., *Reforming the Constitution: Debates in Twentieth-Century Britain* (London 2000)

Clements, Alan, Farquharson, Kenny and Wark, Kirsty, *Restless Nation* (Edinburgh 1996)

Cmnd 8472, *The Hongkong and Shanghai Banking Corporation; Standard Chartered Bank Limited; The Royal Bank of Scotland Group Limited: A Report on the Proposed Mergers* (London 1982)

Cmnd 9714, *Paying for Local Government* (London 1986)

A Conservative Manifesto For Scotland (Edinburgh 1986)

Cosgrave, Patrick, *Thatcher: The First Term* (London 1985)

Coutts, Ben, *Bothy to Big Ben: An Autobiography* (Aberdeen 1988)

Craig, Carol, *The Scots' Crisis of Confidence* (Edinburgh 2003)

Crick, Michael, *Scargill and the Miners* (London 1985)

Crickhowell, Nicholas, *Westminster, Wales & Water* (Cardiff 1999)

Dale, Iain, ed., *Margaret Thatcher – A Tribute in Words and Pictures* (London 2005)

Dalton, Hugh, *High Tide and After: Memoirs 1945–1960* (London 1962)

Dalyell, Tam, *Devolution: The End of Britain?* (London 1977)

Darlow, Michael, *Independents Struggle* (London 2004)

Devine, Tom, *Scotland in the 20th Century* (Edinburgh 1996)
— *The Scottish Nation 1700–2000* (London 1999)

Devine, T. M., ed., *Scotland and the Union 1707–2007* (Edinburgh 2008)

Devine, T. M., Lee, Clive H. and Peden, George C., eds, *The Transformation of Scotland: The Economy Since 1700* (Edinburgh 2005)

Dickson, A. D. R., 'The peculiarities of the Scottish: national culture and political action', *The Political Quarterly 59 3* (July–September 1988)

Donnachie, Ian, ed., *Forward! Labour Politics in Scotland 1888–1988* (Edinburgh 1989)

Donoughue, Bernard, *Downing Street Diary Volume 2: With James Callaghan in No. 10* (London 2008)
— *Prime Minister: The Conduct of Policy under Harold Wilson & James Callaghan* (London 1987)

Drucker, H. M. and Drucker, N. L., eds, *The Scottish Government Yearbook 1982* (Edinburgh 1981)

Dudley Edwards, Owen, ed., *A Claim of Right for Scotland* (Edinburgh 1989)

Finlay, Richard, *Modern Scotland 1914–2000* (London 2004)

FitzGerald, Garret, *All in a Life: An Autobiography* (Dublin 1991)

Forsyth, Michael, *The Case for a Poll Tax* (London 1985)

Fowler, Norman, *A Political Suicide: The Conservatives' Voyage into the Wilderness* (London 2008)

Fox, Liam, Mayall, Mark and Cooke, Alistair B., *Making Unionism Positive: Proposals for a Tory Agenda for Scotland* (London 1988)

Galbraith, John Kenneth, *The Affluent Society* (London 1999)

Galbraith, Russell, *Inside Outside: The Biography of Tam Dalyell – The Man They Can't Gag* (Edinburgh 2000)

Gilmour, Ian, *Dancing With Dogma: Britain Under Thatcherism* (London 1992)

Government Social Research, Research Findings No. 235/2006 (Edinburgh 2006)

Green, E. H. H., *Thatcher* (London 2006)

Hamilton, Sir William, ed., *The Collected Works of Dugald Stewart*, Volume X (Edinburgh 1858)

Harvie, Christopher, *Travelling Scot: Essays on the History, Politics and Future of the Scots* (Argyll 1999)

Heath, Edward, *The Course of My Life* (London 1998)

Henderson Scott, Paul, *A Twentieth-Century Life* (Argyll 2002)

Jenkins, Simon, *Accountable to None: The Tory Nationalization of Britain* (London 1996)

— *Thatcher & Sons: A Revolution in Three Acts* (London 2006)

Junor, John, *Listening for a Midnight Tram* (London 1990)

Kavanagh, Dennis and Selsdon, Anthony, eds, *The Thatcher Effect: A Decade of Change* (London 1989)

Keating, Michael and Boyle, Robin, *Re-making Urban Scotland: Strategies for Local Economic Development* (Edinburgh 1986)

Kelman, James, *'And the Judges Said . . .' Essays* (Edinburgh 2008)

Kemp, Arnold, *The Hollow Drum: Scotland Since the War* (Edinburgh 1993)

Lawson, Nigel, *The View from No. 11: Memoirs of a Tory Radical* (London 1992)

Lynch, Peter, *SNP: The History of the Scottish National Party* (Cardiff 2002)

Macinnes, John, 'The Broadcasting Media in Scotland', *Scottish Affairs 2* (1993)

MacGregor, Ian, *The Enemies Within: The Story of the Miners' Strike 1984–5* (London 1986)

Mackay, Professor Sir Donald, *More or Less Competitive? A Case Study of the Scottish Economy* (Edinburgh 1997)

Major, John, *The Autobiography* (London 1999)

Marr, Andrew, *The Battle for Scotland* (London 1992)

— *A History of Modern Britain* (London 2008)

Marx, Karl, *The Eighteenth Brumaire of Louis Napoleon* (London 2005)

Massie, Allan, *The Thistle and the Rose: Six Centuries of Love and Hate Between the Scots and the English* (London 2005)

Massie, Allan, Marwick, Ewan and Mason, Douglas C., *Scotland and Free Enterprise* (London 1991)

Maude, Angus, ed., *The Right Approach to the Economy* (London 1977)

McCrone, David, *Understanding Scotland: The Sociology of a Stateless Nation* (Edinburgh 1991)

McCrone, David, ed., *The Scottish Government Yearbook 1983, 1984* & *1986* (Edinburgh 1982, 1983, 1986)

McCrone, David and Brown, Alice, eds, *The Scottish Government Yearbook 1988* (Edinburgh 1988)

Midwinter, Arthur, *Local Government in Scotland: Reform or Decline?* (London 1995)

— *Public Finance in the Thatcher Era* (Glasgow 1992)

Midwinter, Arthur, Keating, Michael and Mitchell, James, *Politics and Public Policy in Scotland* (London 1991)

Miller, Bill, *Testing the Power of a Media Consensus: A Comparison of Scots and English Treatment of the Falklands Campaign* (Glasgow 1983)

Mitchell, James, *Conservatives and the Union: A Study of Conservative Party Attitudes to Scotland* (Edinburgh 1990)

— 'Conservatives and the changing meaning of Union', *Regional and Federal Studies* 6 1 (1996)

Moore, Charles and Heffer, Simon, eds, *A Tory Seer: The Selected Journalism of T. E. Utley* (London 1989)

Morgan, Kenneth O., *Callaghan: A Life* (Oxford 1997)

Murdoch, Alexander, ed., *The Scottish Nation, Identity and History: Essays in Honour of William Ferguson* (Edinburgh 2007)

Nairn, Tom, *After Britain: New Labour and the Return of Scotland* (London 2000)

Naughtie, James, *The Rivals: The Intimate Story of a Political Marriage* (London 2001)

Neil, Andrew, *Full Disclosure* (London 1996)

Omega Report: Scottish Policy (London 1983)

Paterson, Lindsay, *The Autonomy of Modern Scotland* (Edinburgh 1994)

Paterson, Lindsay, Bechhofer, Frank and McCrone, David, *Living in Scotland: Social and Economic Change since 1980* (Edinburgh 2004)

Pearce, Edward, *The Lost Leaders* (London 1997)

Raban, Jonathan, *God, Man and Mrs Thatcher* (London 1989)

Reid, Harry, *Deadline: The Story of the Scottish Press* (Edinburgh 2006)

— *Outside Verdict: An Old Kirk in a New Scotland* (Edinburgh 2002)

Ridley, Nicholas, *My Style of Government: The Thatcher Years* (London 1991)

The Right Approach (London 1976)

The Right Approach to the Economy (London 1972)

Rodger, Alan, 'The future of the legal profession in Scotland', *Juridical Review* 1 (1991)

Roy, Kenneth, *Conversations in a Small Country: Scottish Interviews* (Ayr 1989)

Scotland, James, *The History of Scottish Education Volume 2* (London 1969)

Seawright, David, *An Important Matter of Principle: The Decline of the Scottish Conservative and Unionist Party* (Aldershot 1999)

Sheridan, Tommy and McCoombes, Alan, *Imagine: A Socialist Vision for the 21st Century* (Edinburgh 2000)

Sillars, Jim, *Scotland: The Case for Optimism* (Edinburgh 1986)

Skidelsky, Robert, ed., *Thatcherism* (Oxford 1989)

Smith, Adam, *An Inquiry into the Nature and Causes of the Wealth of Nations* (London 2008)

Smith, Maurice, *Paper Lions: The Scottish Press and National Identity* (Edinburgh 1994)

Stewart, David, 'Challenging the consensus: Scotland under Margaret Thatcher, 1979–1990' (unpublished PhD thesis University of Glasgow 2004)

Stewart, Donald, *A Scot at Westminster* (Sydney 1994)

Stewart, Susie, ed., *Apostles Not Apologists, The Eastwood View* (Paisley 1987)

STUC 89th Annual Report STUC (Glasgow 1986)

Taylor, Edward M., *Teddy Boy Blue* (Glasgow 2008)

Taylor, Teddy, Younger, George and Fletcher, Alex, *Onward to Victory: A Statement of the Conservative Approach for Scotland* (Edinburgh 1978)

Thatcher, Margaret, *The Downing Street Years* (London 1993)

— *The Path to Power* (London 1995)

Thorpe, D. R., *Alec Douglas-Home* (London 1996)

Trevor-Roper, Hugh, *The Invention of Scotland: Myth and History* (London 2008)

Trewin, Ion, ed., *The Hugo Young Papers: Thirty Years of British Politics – Off the Record* (London 2008)

Walker, Peter, *Staying Power* (London 1991)

Warner, Gerald, *The Scottish Tory Party: A History* (London 1988)

Watkins, Alan, *A Conservative Coup: The Fall of Margaret Thatcher* (London 1991)

Wolmar, Christian, *Fire & Steam: A New History of the Railways in Britain* (London 2007)

Wright, Canon Kenyon, *The People Say Yes: The Making of Scotland's Parliament* (Argyll 1997)

Young, Hugo, *One of Us: A Biography of Margaret Thatcher* (London 1989, 1991)

BROADCAST SOURCES

Britain Today (BBC 1969)

Thatcher and the Scots (BBC Scotland 2008)

Thatcher: The Downing Street Years (BBC 1993)

Truth, Lies, Scotland and Oil (BBC Scotland 2008)

The Thatcher Factor (Channel 4 1989)

Spitting Image (ITV 1987)

STV VT archive (STV)

Weekend World: The Tories' Tartan Gamble (LWT 1988)

ELECTRONIC SOURCES

Collins, Chris, ed., *Margaret Thatcher: Complete Public Statements 1945–1990 on CD-ROM* (Oxford 1999)

INDEX